LEARN, TEACH...

SUCCEED...

With **REA's GACE Early Childhood Education**
test prep, you'll be in a class all your own.

WE'D LIKE TO HEAR FROM YOU!
Visit **www.rea.com** to send us your comments
or email us at **info@rea.com**

GACE® EARLY CHILDHOOD EDUCATION (001, 002)

GEORGIA ASSESSMENTS FOR THE CERTIFICATION OF EDUCATORS®

 TestWare® Edition

Judith F. Robbins, Ph.D.
Julie G. Maudlin, Ed.D.
Susan T. Franks, Ed.D.

Research & Education Association

Visit our Educator Support Center: www.rea.com/teacher
Updates to the test and this book: www.rea.com/GACE/EarlyChild.htm

Planet Friendly Publishing
✔ Made in the United States
✔ Printed on Recycled Paper
Text: 10%   Cover: 10%
Learn more: www.greenedition.org

At REA we're committed to producing books in an Earth-friendly manner and to helping our customers make greener choices.

Manufacturing books in the United States ensures compliance with strict environmental laws and eliminates the need for international freight shipping, a major contributor to global air pollution.

And printing on recycled paper helps minimize our consumption of trees, water and fossil fuels. This book was printed on paper made with **10% post-consumer waste**. According to Environmental Defense's Paper Calculator, by using this innovative paper instead of conventional papers, we achieved the following environmental benefits:

Courier Corporation, the manufacturer of this book, owns the Green Edition Trademark.

**Trees Saved: 6 • Air Emissions Eliminated: 1157 pounds
Water Saved: 1037 gallons • Solid Waste Eliminated: 341 pounds**

For more information on our environmental practices, please visit us online at **www.rea.com/green**

Research & Education Association
61 Ethel Road West
Piscataway, New Jersey 08854
E-mail: info@rea.com

Georgia GACE® Early Childhood Education (001, 002) with TestWare

Printed in the United States of America

Library of Congress Control Number 2010927872

ISBN-13: 978-0-7386-0814-3
ISBN-10: 0-7386-0814-9

For all references in this book, Georgia Assessments for the Certification of Educators® and GACE® are trademarks, in the U.S. and/or other countries, of the Georgia Professional Standards Commission and Pearson Education, Inc., or its affiliates.

Windows® is a registered trademark of Microsoft Corporation. All other trademarks and product names cited in this publication are the property of their respective owners.

The competencies presented in this book were created and implemented by the Georgia Professional Standards Commission and Pearson Education, Inc., or its affiliate(s).

REA® and TestWare® are registered trademarks of Research & Education Association, Inc.

H11-0101

About Research & Education Association

Founded in 1959, Research & Education Association is dedicated to publishing the finest and most effective educational materials—including software, study guides, and test preps—for students in middle school, high school, college, graduate school, and beyond.

REA's Test Preparation series includes books and software for all academic levels in almost all disciplines. Research & Education Association publishes test preps for students who have not yet entered high school, as well as for high school students preparing to enter college. Students from countries around the world seeking to attend college in the United States will find the assistance they need in REA's publications. For college students seeking advanced degrees, REA publishes test preps for many major graduate school admission examinations in a wide variety of disciplines, including engineering, law, and medicine. Students at every level, in every field, with every ambition can find what they are looking for among REA's publications.

REA's practice tests are always based upon the most recently administered exams and include every type of question that you can expect on the actual exams.

REA's publications and educational materials are highly regarded and continually receive an unprecedented amount of praise from professionals, instructors, librarians, parents, and students. Our authors are as diverse as the fields represented in the books we publish. They are well-known in their respective disciplines and serve on the faculties of prestigious high schools, colleges, and universities throughout the United States and Canada.

Today, REA's wide-ranging catalog is a leading resource for teachers, students, and professionals.

We invite you to visit us at *www.rea.com* to find out how REA is making the world smarter.

Acknowledgments

We would like to thank Larry Kling, Vice President, Editorial, for his editorial direction; Pam Weston, Vice President, Publishing, for setting the quality standards for production integrity and managing the publication to completion; John Cording, Vice President, Technology, for coordinating the design, development, and testing of REA's TestWare® ; Diane Goldschmidt, Senior Editor, and Alice Leonard, Senior Editor, for pre-flight editorial review; Kathleen Casey, Senior Editor, for project management; Heena Patel, Technology Project Manager, for software testing; Christine Saul, Senior Graphic Artist, for cover design; and Rachel DiMatteo, Graphic Artist, for post-production file mapping.

We also gratefully acknowledge Alice Leonard, Senior Editor; and Renee Kusch of Creative Kids for copyediting; Caragraphics, for typesetting; the Editors of REA for proofreading, and Terry Casey for indexing the manuscript.

About the Authors

Judith F. Robbins, Ph.D., serves as the chair of the Early Childhood Education B.S. Ed. program in the Department of Teaching and Learning, College of Education at Georgia Southern University in Statesboro, Georgia. She earned her Ph.D. from Florida State University in Language and Literacy Education and has taught at Georgia Southern since 1991. Dr. Robbins is an associate professor of Early Childhood Education and teaches courses in the language arts, including the reading, writing and children's literature methods courses at both the graduate and undergraduate levels. She also supervises student teachers and interns in a number of field-based courses, and works with area schools in a variety of capacities. She is actively involved in a number of organizations, including the Eastern Educational Research Association, an affiliate of the American Educational Research Association, where she serves as chair of Professional Development, Division 9. Dr. Robbins frequently presents at national and international conferences.

Julie Garlen Maudlin, Ed.D., is an assistant professor of Early Childhood Education at Georgia Southern University, in Statesboro, Georgia, where she teaches courses in P–12 Curriculum, Instruction and Assessment. Dr. Maudlin is a former elementary school teacher and instructional coach, and is certified as a K–5 educator by the Georgia Professional Standards Commission. She lives in Southeast Georgia with her husband, Chris, and their three children.

Susan T. Franks, Ed.D., is an associate professor of Early Childhood Education and serves as the chair of the Early Childhood Education M.Ed. program in the Department of Teaching and Learning, College of Education at Georgia Southern University in Statesboro, Georgia. She earned her Ed.D. from Virginia Polytechnic Institute and State University in Elementary Education with an emphasis in Curriculum and Instruction. Dr. Franks teaches courses in the language arts, including reading and children's literature methods courses at the graduate and undergraduate levels. She also supervises student teachers and interns in a number of field-based courses and works with classroom teachers in an ongoing program of consultant work. She is actively involved in a number of organizations including the Eastern Educational Research Association, an affiliate of the American Educational Research Association, where she serves as chair of Human Development, Division 3. Dr. Franks frequently presents at national and international conferences.

Contents

Chapter 1: Introduction   1

About This Book and TestWare® 1
About the GACE Early Childhood Education Assessment 2
How to Use This Book and TestWare® 7
Studying for the GACE Early Childhood Education Assessment 8
Format of the GACE Early Childhood Education Assessment 9
The Day of the Test 11
During the Test 13
After the Test 14

Chapter 2: Reading and English Language Arts   15

Objective 0001 16
Objective 0002 21
Objective 0003 25
Objective 0004 29
Objective 0005 35
Objective 0006 41
Objective 0007 47
Objective 0008 52

Chapter 3: Social Studies   59

Objective 0009 60
Objective 0010 95
Objective 0011 105
Objective 0012 114

Chapter 4: Mathematics   119

Objective 0013 120
Objective 0014 128
Objective 0015 138
Objective 0016 141
Objective 0017 146

Chapter 4: Science   161

Objective 0018 162
Objective 0019 169
Objective 0020 174
Objective 0021 178

Chapter 6: Health, Physical Education and the Arts   189

Objective 0022 190
Objective 0023 200
Objective 0024 210

Practice Test 1   245

Answer Sheet 247
Practice Test 248
Answer Key 284
Progress and Competency Chart..290
Detailed Explanations of Answers 294

Practice Test 2   325

Answer Sheet 327
Practice Test 328
Answer Key 364
Progress and Competency Chart..370
Detailed Explanations of Answers 374

Index   401

Installing REA's TestWare®   408

Introduction

About This Book and TestWare®

REA's *GACE Early Childhood Education (001, 002)* assessment is a comprehensive guide designed to assist you in preparing to take this GACE assessment. To help you to succeed in this important step toward your teaching career in Georgia schools, this test prep features:

- An accurate and complete overview of the GACE Early Childhood Education (001, 002) assessment

- The information you need to know about the exam

- A targeted review of each subarea

- Tips and strategies for successfully completing standardized tests

- Diagnostic tools to identify areas of strength and weakness

- Two full-length, true-to-format practice tests based on the most recently administered GACE Early Childhood Education (001, 002) assessment

- Detailed explanations for each answer on the practice tests. These allow you to identify correct answers and understand not only why they are correct but also why the other answer choices are incorrect.

When creating this test prep, the authors and editors considered the most recent test administrations and professional standards. They also researched information from the Georgia Department of Education, professional journals, textbooks, and educators. The result is the best GACE test preparation materials based on the latest information available.

About Test Selection

The GACE assessments are offered during morning and afternoon test sessions. Each test session is four hours in length. The morning session has a reporting time of 7:45 A.M. and ends at approximately 12:30 P.M. The afternoon session has a reporting time of 1:00 P.M. and ends at approximately 5:45 P.M. You may select tests for a single test session or for both the morning and afternoon test sessions.

The number of tests you may register to take in one test session is determined by the assessment(s) for which you are registering. Each assessment consists of one or more tests. Because you are registering for an assessment that includes multiple tests, you may take one or two Early Childhood Education tests in the same test session.

About the GACE Early Childhood Education Assessment

The purpose of the GACE Early Childhood Education test is to assess the knowledge and skills of prospective Georgia Early Childhood teachers in the areas of Reading and English Language Arts, Social Studies, Mathematics, Science, Health, Physical Education and the Arts. The GACE Early Childhood Education assessment actually contains two tests:

- Test I—Test Code 001:

    Reading and English Language Arts: (approximately 40 selected-response questions and one constructed-response question)

    Social Studies: (approximately 20 selected-response questions and one constructed-response question)

- Test II—Test Code 002:

    Mathematics: (approximately 25 selected-response questions and one constructed-response question)

    Science: (approximately 20 selected-response questions and one constructed-response question)

    Health, Physical Education, and the Arts: (approximately15 selected-response questions and no constructed-response question)

What Does the Test Cover?

The table on pages 4–5 lists the objectives used as the basis for the GACE Early Childhood Education assessment and the approximate number of questions in both Tests I and II. A thorough review of all the specific skills tested on the exams is the focus of this book.

How Is the GACE Early Childhood Education Test Scored?

Test Score

Your total raw score is converted to a scaled score. A scaled score is a combination of the number of scorable questions you answered correctly on the selected-response section of the test and the scores you received on any constructed-response assignments and then converted to a scale from 100 to 300. The score of 220 is the passing score for any GACE test. The passing score for each test is established by the Georgia Professional Standards Commission and is based on the professional judgments and recommendations of Georgia educators. "Pass" or "Did Not Pass" status is based on your total score for each test. If you met the passing score, your total test scaled score is not reported in order to preclude the use of GACE scores for purposes other than Georgia educator certification (e.g., employment, college admission screening).

Passing the two parts of the GACE Early Childhood Education Assessment.

The passing scaled score for each part is 220. There is no composite or combining both tests. Each must be passed individually.

Test Framework

Test I (Test Code 001)			
Basic Skills	**Objectives**	**Skill Tested**	**Approximate Number of Questions**
Reading and English Language Arts Chapter 2	0001	Understand the concepts of print and phonological awareness.	40 Selected-Response 1 Constructed-Response Assignment
	0002	Understand word identification strategies, including phonics	
	0003	Understand the development of vocabulary knowledge and skills across the curriculum	
	0004	Understand reading fluency and comprehension across the curriculum	
	0005	Understand comprehension strategies for literary and informational texts across the curriculum	
	0006	Understand skills and strategies involved in writing for various purposes across the curriculum	
	0007	Understand the conventions of standard English grammar, usage, and mechanics	
	0008	Understand skills and strategies involved in speaking, listening, and viewing across the curriculum	
Social Studies Chapter 3	0009	Understand important events, concepts, and methods of inquiry related to Georgia, U.S., and world history	20 Selected-Response 1 Constructed-Response Assignments
	0010	Understand major concepts, principles, and methods of inquiry related to geography	
	0011	Understand major concepts, principles, and methods of inquiry related to U.S. government and civics.	
	0012	Understand major concepts, principles, and methods of inquiry related to economics	

		Test II (Test Code 002)	
Basic Skills	**Objectives**	**Skill Tested**	**Approximate Number of Questions**
Mathematics Chapter 4	0013	Understand processes and approaches for exploring mathematics and solving problems	25 Selected-Response

1 Constructed-Response Assignment |
	0014	Understand concepts and skills related to numbers and mathematical operations	
	0015	Understand principles and skills of measurement and the concepts and properties of geometry	
	0016	Understand concepts and skills related to algebra	
	0017	Understand concepts and skills related to data analysis	
Science Chapter 5	0018	Understand the characteristics and processes of science	20 Selected-Response

1 Constructed-Response Assignment |
	0019	Understand concepts and principles of earth science	
	0020	Understand concepts and principles of physical science	
	0021	Understand concepts and principles of life science	
Health, Physical Education, and the Arts Chapter 6	0022	Understand basic principles and practices related to health and safety	15 Selected-Response
	0023	Understand basic physical education principles, practices, and activities	
	0024	Understand basic elements, concepts, and techniques associated with the arts	

When Will I Receive My Score Report and What Will It Look Like?

Reporting of Scores

Your scores are reported directly to the Georgia Professional Standards Commission and are automatically added to your certification application file. Your scores are also reported to the Georgia institution of higher education or other agency that you indicated when you registered. The score report is for your information only and you are not to submit it with your application for certification. Of course, as with any important document, you should keep a copy for your permanent records.

Unofficial test scores are posted on the Internet at 5:00 P.M. Eastern Time on the score report dates listed on *http://www.gace.nesinc.com/GA4_testdates.asp*.

For each test date, the unofficial scores are kept on the Internet for approximately two weeks. For security reasons, you may only view these scores once during the posting period.

Can I Retake the Test?

If you wish to retake a test, you may do so at any subsequent test administration. Please consult the GACE Website at **www.gace.nesinc.com** for information about test registration. The GACE website also includes information regarding test retakes and score reports.

Who Administers the Test?

The Georgia Professional Standards Commission (PSC) has contracted with Evaluation Systems to assist in the development and administration of the Georgia Assessments for the Certification of Educators (GACE). The GACE tests are aligned with state and national standards for educator preparation and with state standards for the pre-kindergarten through twelfth grade student curriculum (Georgia Performance Standards).

For additional information you can contact:

GACE Program
Evaluation Systems
Pearson
P.O. Box 660
Amherst, MA 01004-9002
(800) 523-7064 or (413) 256-2894
Fax: (413) 256-7082 (Registration forms may not be transmitted by fax.)

For operator assistance, call 9:00 A.M. to 5:00 P.M., Eastern Time, Monday through Friday, excluding holidays.

The Automated Information System is available 24 hours daily.

When Should I Take the Test?

Georgia law requires that teachers demonstrate mastery of basic skills, professional knowledge, and the content area in which they are specializing. To receive information on upcoming administrations of the GACE Early Childhood Education assessment, consult the GACE website at *www.gace.nesinc.com*.

Do I Pay a Registration Fee?

To take the GACE, you must pay a registration fee. For the latest information about the fees, log on to http://www.gace.nesinc.com/GA4_testfees.asp

How to Use This Book and TestWare®

When Should I Start Studying?

It is never too early to start studying for the GACE Early Childhood Education assessment. The earlier you begin, the more time you will have to sharpen your skills. Do not procrastinate! Cramming is not an effective way to study because it does not allow you the time you need to think about the content, review the subareas, and take the practice tests.

What Should I Study First?

We strongly recommend that you begin your preparation with the TestWare® tests. The software provides the added benefits of instant, accurate scoring and enforced time conditions.

What Do the Review Sections Cover?

The targeted review in this book is designed to help you sharpen the skills you need to succeed on the GACE Early Childhood Education assessment, as well as provide strategies for answering the questions.

Each teaching area included in the GACE Early Childhood Education assessment is examined in a separate chapter. The skills required for all areas are extensively discussed to optimize your understanding of what the examination covers.

Your schooling has taught you most of the information you need to answer the questions on the test. The education classes you took should have provided you with the know-how to make important decisions about situations you will face as a teacher. The review sections in this book are designed to help you fit the information you have acquired into the objectives specified on the GACE. Going over your class notes and textbooks together with the reviews provided here will give you an excellent springboard for passing the examination.

Studying for the GACE Early Childhood Education Assessment

Choose the time and place for studying that works best for you. Some people set aside a certain number of hours every morning to study, while others prefer to study at night before going to sleep. Other people study off and on during the day—for instance, while waiting for a bus or during a lunch break. Only you can determine when and where your study time will be most effective. Be consistent and use your time efficiently. Work out a study routine and stick to it.

When you take the practice tests, simulate the conditions of the actual exam as closely as possible. Turn off your television and radio, and sit down at a table in a quiet room, free from distraction. After completing a practice test, score it and thoroughly review the explanations to the questions you answered incorrectly; however, do not review too much in one study session. Concentrate on one problem area at a time by reviewing the question and explanation, and then study the related review chapters in this test prep until you are confident that you have mastered the material.

Keep track of your practice test scores so you can gauge your progress and discover general weaknesses in particular sections. Give extra attention to the reviews that cover your areas of difficulty, so you can build your skills in those areas. Many have found the use of study or note cards very helpful for this review.

How Can I Use My Study Time Efficiently?

The following study schedule allows for thorough preparation for the GACE Early Childhood Education assessment. The course of study presented here is for seven weeks, but you can condense or expand the timeline to suit your personal schedule. It is vital that you adhere to a structured plan and set aside ample time each day to study. The more time you devote to studying, the more prepared and confident you will be on the day of the test.

Study Schedule

Week 1	After reading this chapter to understand the format and content of the GACE, take the first practice test on CD. It covers all of the subjects for the 001 and 002 tests. The scores will indicate your strengths and weaknesses. Make sure you simulate real exam conditions when you take the tests. Afterward, score the practice test and review the answer explanations, especially for questions you answered incorrectly.
Week 2	Review the explanations for the questions you missed on the practice test, and read through the appropriate chapter sections. Useful study techniques include highlighting key terms and information, taking notes as you review each section, and putting new terms and information on note cards to help retain the information.
Weeks 3 and 4	Reread all your note cards and refresh your understanding of the competencies and skills tested on the exam. Study the review chapters in this book, especially those that cover the areas in which you feel weak. Review your college textbooks and read over notes you took in your college classes. This is also the time to consider any other supplementary materials that your counselor or the Georgia Department of Education suggests. You can visit the department's website at http://www.gace.nesinc.com. Make additional notes as you study each chapter.
Week 5	Condense your notes and findings. A structured list of important facts and concepts, based on your note cards and the GACE Early Childhood Education competencies, will help you thoroughly review for the test. Study our review chapters and focus on any areas that are confusing or you feel you need improvement.
Week 6	Have someone quiz you using the note cards you created. Take the second full-length practice test on CD, adhering to the time limits and simulated test day conditions.
Week 7	Using all your study materials, review areas of weakness revealed by your score on the second set of practice tests. Study the detailed answer explanations for the questions you answered incorrectly. Then retake sections of the practice tests to give you extra practice before exam day.

Format of the GACE Early Childhood Education Assessment

What Types of Questions Are on the Test?

- The Reading and English Language Arts subarea has approximately 40 selected-response (multiple-choice) questions and one constructed-response question.

- The Social Studies subarea has approximately 20 selected-response questions and one constructed-response questions.

- The Mathematics subarea has approximately 25 selected-response questions and one constructed-response question.

- The Science subarea has approximately 20 selected-response questions and one constructed-response question.

- The Health, Physical Education, and the Arts subarea has approximately 15 selected-response questions and no constructed-response question.

Can I Take the Test Online?

As of this writing, computer-based testing is not available for the GACE Early Childhood Education test. To verify this, go to *http://www.gace.nesinc.com/GA4_cbtoverview.asp*. Exams on the computer have the advantage of providing you with a notice of pass or fail immediately after completing the exam, which can be scheduled at a time that is convenient for you.

Test-Taking Tips

Although you may not be familiar with tests like the GACE, this book will acquaint you with this type of exam and help alleviate your test-taking anxieties. By following the seven suggestions listed here, you can become more relaxed about taking the GACE, as well as other tests.

Tip 1. Become comfortable with the format of the GACE. When you are practicing, stay calm and pace yourself. After simulating the test only once, you will boost your chances of doing well, and you will be able to sit down for the actual GACE with much more confidence.

Tip 2. Read all the possible answers. Just because you think you have found the correct response, do not automatically assume that it is the best answer. Read through each choice to be sure that you are not making a mistake by jumping to conclusions.

Tip 3. Use the process of elimination. Go through each answer to a question and eliminate as many of the answer choices as possible. If you can eliminate two answer choices, you have given yourself a better chance of getting the item correct, because only two choices are left from which to make your guess. Do not leave an answer blank. It is better to guess than not to answer a question on the GACE test because there is no additional penalty for wrong answers.

Tip 4. Place a question mark in your answer booklet next to the answers you guessed, and then recheck them later if you have time.

Tip 5. Work quickly and steadily. You will have four hours to complete the test, so the amount of time you spend will depend upon whether you take both 001 and 002 tests in one test session. Taking the practice tests in this book or on the CD will help you learn to budget your precious time.

Tip 6. Learn the directions and format of the test. This will not only save time but also will help you avoid anxiety (and the mistakes caused by being anxious).

Tip 7. When taking the multiple-choice portion of the test, be sure that the answer oval you fill in corresponds to the number of the question in the test booklet. The multiple-choice test is graded by machine, and marking one wrong answer can throw off your answer key and your score. Be extremely careful.

The Day of the Test

Before the Test

On the morning of the test, be sure to dress comfortably so you are not distracted by being too hot or too cold while taking the test. Plan to arrive at the test center early. This will allow you to collect your thoughts and relax before the test and will also spare you the anguish that comes with being late. You should check your GACE Registration Bulletin to find out what time to arrive at the center.

What to Bring

Before you leave for the test center, make sure that you have your admission ticket. Your admission ticket lists your test selection, test site, test date, and reporting time. See the Test Selection at www.gace.nesinc.com/GA4_testselection.asp.

You must also bring personal identification that includes one piece of current, government issued identification, in the name in which you registered, bearing your photograph and signature and one additional piece of identification (with or without a photograph). If the name on your identification differs from the name in which you are registered, you must bring official verification of the change (e.g., marriage certificate, court order).

If for any reason you do not have proper identification or your admission ticket, you will need to report immediately and directly to the Information Table at the test site. You may be required to complete additional paperwork, which may reduce your available testing time.

You must bring several sharpened No. 2 pencils with erasers, because none will be provided at the test center. If you like, you can wear a watch to the test center. However, you cannot wear one that makes noise, because it might disturb the other test takers. Dictionaries, textbooks, notebooks, calculators, cell phones, beepers, PDAs, scratch paper, listening and recording devices, briefcases, or packages are not permitted. Drinking, smoking, and eating during the test are prohibited. You may not bring any visitors, including relatives, children, and friends.

You may bring a water bottle into the testing room, as long as it is clear without a label but with a tight lid. During testing, you will have to store your bottle under your seat.

Security Measures

As part of the identity verification process, your thumbprint will be taken at the test site. Thumbprints will be used only for the purpose of identity verification. If you do not provide a thumbprint, you will not be allowed to take the test. No refund or credit of any kind will be given. This thumbprint does not take the place of the complete fingerprint set requirement for Georgia teacher certification.

Enhanced security measures, including additional security screenings, may be required by test site facilities. If an additional screening is conducted, only screened persons will be admitted to the test site. If you do not proceed through the security screening, you will not be allowed to test and you will not receive a refund or credit of any kind.

Late Arrival Policy

If you are late for a test session, you may not be admitted. If you are permitted to enter, you will not be given any additional time for the test session. You will be required to sign a statement acknowledging this.

If you arrive late and are not admitted, you will be considered absent and will not receive a refund or credit of any kind. You will need to register and pay again to test at a future administration.

Absentee Policy

If you are absent, you will not receive a refund or credit of any kind. You will need to register and pay again to test at a future administration.

A day or so before your scheduled test, be sure and check the GACE website for any changes to the test site rules at *http://www.gace.nesinc.com/GA4_siterules.asp*.

During the Test

The GACE Early Childhood Education assessment is given in one sitting, with no breaks. However, during testing, you may take restroom breaks. Any time that you take for restroom breaks is considered part of the available testing time. Procedures will be followed to maintain test security. Once you enter the test center, follow all the rules and instructions given by the test supervisor. If you do not, you risk being dismissed from the test and having your score canceled.

When all the materials have been distributed, the test instructor will give you directions for completing the informational portion of your answer sheet. Fill out the sheet carefully, because the information you provide will be printed on your score report.

Once the test begins, mark only one answer per question, completely erase unwanted answers and marks, and fill in answers darkly and neatly.

After the Test

When you finish your test, hand in your materials and you will be dismissed. Then, go home and relax—you deserve it!

Reading and English Language Arts

This chapter provides a review of the Reading and English Language Arts portion of the GACE Early Childhood Education Assessment. It is designed to assess objectives related to concepts of print and phonological awareness, word identification strategies, vocabulary knowledge and skills across the curriculum as well as reading fluency and comprehension across the curriculum. It is comprised of 40 selected-response (multiple-choice questions) and 1 constructed-response assignment.

Remember, the more you know about the skills tested, the better you will perform on the test. The objectives on which you will be tested are contained in the following list:

- 0001 Understand concepts of print and phonological awareness.

- 0002 Understand word identification strategies, including phonics.

- 0003 Understand the development of vocabulary knowledge and skills across the curriculum

- 0004 Understand reading fluency and comprehension across the curriculum.

- 0005 Understand comprehension strategies for literary and informational texts across the curriculum

- 0006 Understand skills and strategies involved in writing for various purposes across the curriculum

- 0007 Understand the conventions of standard English grammar, usage, and mechanics.

- 0008 Understand skills and strategies involved in speaking, listening, and viewing across the curriculum.

Let's examine the content of the reading and language arts objectives more closely.

Objective 0001: Understand concepts of print and phonological awareness.

For example:

- recognizing developmental stages in learning to read and write

- demonstrating knowledge of characteristics and purposes of printed information and developmentally appropriate strategies for promoting students' familiarity with concepts of print

- demonstrating knowledge of phonological awareness

- demonstrating knowledge of phonemic awareness

- analyzing the significance of phonological and phonemic awareness in reading acquisition

- recognizing developmentally appropriate strategies for promoting students' phonological and phonemic awareness

The first objective deals with concepts related to emerging literacy. This includes the stages of reading and writing development, concepts of print, phonological and phonemic awareness and effective strategies teaching phonological and phonemic awareness.

Language learning is a very complex process involving a system for creating meaning through socially shared conventions. Children come to school with a basic mastery of their native oral language. In school, they learn how to apply that knowledge of oral language as they learn more formal concepts of written language.

Language is organized using four systems that together make oral and written communication possible. The four systems are: the phonological or sound system, the syntactic or structural system, the semantic or meaning system and pragmatic or social and cultural use system of language. No one system is more important than the others but the phonological system is a critical part of early literacy.

Reading and Writing Development

Children's reading and writing develop gradually and naturally as they interact within a language-rich environment. Children's understanding of the relationship between speech and print is a vital first step in learning to read. Without learning the relationship between speech and print, the beginner will never make sense of reading or achieve independence in it.

Children's writing develops through stages from scribbling to conventional writing. The stages are 1) **emergent writing**, 2) **beginning writing** and 3) **fluent writing**. The **emergent writing** stage begins with the first marks they make on a page and they move from scribbles to the use of single letters to represent an idea. They begin making a distinction between drawing and writing, showing an interest in writing.

As children begin to learn about letter-sound relationships they move into the beginning writing stage. In the beginning writing stage children begin to write using sentences, they begin to use multiple letters to represent words through invented or temporary spelling. Their early attempts at writing sentences may lack spaces between words. They move from capitalizing random words and the use of punctuation only at the end of sentences to more conventional use of capitalization and punctuation within sentences. In the fluent writing stage children's writing appears more conventional. They use the writing process to write including one or more paragraphs and apply knowledge of spelling patterns and rules of mechanics and usage as well as more advanced vocabulary to write text in various genres (Tompkins, 2007).

Similarly, reading develops through a series of developmental stages. As in writing development children move through three stages: 1) **emergent reading**, 2) **beginning reading** and 3) **fluent reading**. They begin by "pretend reading" with no real connection to what is on the page to picture reading whereby they make up a story in their own words based on the illustrations in the story. They may also retell a story from memory. They are demonstrating awareness that print is used for communication in this stage as they "read" print in the environment.

As children begin to develop the basic concepts of print they move into the beginning reading stage. They begin making one-to-one correspondence between spoken words with the printed text and are able to recognize a few words as sight words and begin decoding words. As children are exposed to more formal reading instruction they begin to build on this knowledge of basic sight words and predictable text patterns to navigate text. They use word identification tactics such as picture, semantic and syntactic clues when they encounter a word not known by sight. With further instruction these word identification skills are applied strategically as they read more complex texts in the final, fluent reading stage. Knowledge of these developmental stages is critical for making instructional decisions as we facilitate children's writing and reading development.

Knowledge of Print

Concepts of print refer to the knowledge of how print looks and how it works. Emergent readers recognize that print is organized in predictable ways. The words are read from left-to-right and top-to-bottom. The letters are grouped together to form words, and the words are grouped to form sentences that represent ideas.

Concepts of print can be divided into two categories: print awareness and technical aspects of print. Children who demonstrate print awareness understand that the words carry the message and that the function of print is dependent on the context. They understand that what can be said orally can be written then later read. Print awareness is the basis for all future literacy learning.

Technical aspects of print address directionality, organization of books, and terminology related to books. Students should understand that we read from left to right, swing back, and continue from the top of the page to the bottom. We turn the pages from left to right, and the book has a "beginning," "middle," and "end." Students should be able to identify the cover of the book and the title page, and they should hold the book right side up. They should be able to find the first and last page of the book, and they should identify the top and bottom of the page. Students should distinguish between letters and words, and they should be able to point to the punctuation at the end of sentences.

As children interact in a language-rich environment they begin to learn that print carries meaning and that reading and writing are used for many different purposes. These purposes are demonstrated as children learn to read and write through natural experiences involving oral and written language. Teachers can involve children in many authentic learning activities including language-experience activities that allow children to share and discuss experiences as the teacher models written language. Language experiences that revolve around speaking and listening, visual expression, singing, movement and rhythmic activities build on children's natural language abilities. This connection between oral and written language is a vital first step in learning to read and write.

Dramatic play centers also allow children to use language naturally as they role-play a variety of roles. Shared reading experiences such as the reading aloud of big books allow children to participate in real reading, exposing them to the basic concepts of print. Centers that allow children to reread favorite stories give students practice in authentic "reading" as they retell stories from illustrations or memory. Other activities such as drawing and writing in journals, writing messages to other classmates, recording information on charts allow students to use language for a variety of purposes as they communicate naturally.

Phonological and Phonemic Awareness

Phonological awareness is based on the phonological or sound system of language. Phonological awareness is defined as a student's awareness of the phonological structure of a spoken word. The focus of phonological awareness includes identifying and manipulating larger parts of spoken language, such as words, syllables, onsets and rimes as well as the individual phonemes that make up the word. Phonological awareness relates only to speech sounds, not to written symbols that represent sounds. Phonological awareness instruction includes activities at the syllable level such as onsets and rimes and phoneme manipulation.

Phonemic awareness is a subcategory of phonological awareness. It is the ability to notice, think about, and work with the individual sounds in spoken language. An example of how beginning readers show they are phonemically aware is by combining or blending the separate sounds of a word to say the word ("/d/ /o/ /g/ - *dog*."). Phonemic awareness tasks used for assessment and instructional purposes include: rhyming, phoneme identification, phoneme blending, phoneme substitution, phoneme addition, phoneme deletion, and phoneme segmentation. Phonemic awareness is not phonics. Phonemic awareness is an auditory skill that enables students to identify and orally manipulate the sounds of language.

Other parts of phonological awareness are auditory syllabication and parts of syllables called onsets and rimes. An onset is the initial consonant sound of a syllable (the onset of *bat* is *b-*; of *swim* is *sw-*). The rime is the part of a syllable that contains the vowel and all that follows it (the rime of *bat* is *-at*; of *swim* is *-im*). Onset and rime substitution tasks are often referred to as "word family" activities.

The ability to segment and blend phonemes is critical for the development of decoding skills, reading fluency, and spelling. Understanding the relationship between speech and print is a vital first step in learning to read and spell.

Teaching Phonological and Phonemic Awareness

Children develop phonemic awareness by singing songs, chanting rhymes, and listening to parents and teachers read books read aloud. Teachers also teach lessons to help students understand that their speech is composed of sounds. Big books are valuable tools for interactive reading, which assists children in developing phonemic awareness.

Phonemic and phonological awareness can be that directly through a variety of strategies. For example:

1. Teach the child to isolate sounds in a word. To follow a pattern from the simplest to the most difficult, begin with initial and final sounds first, then add medial phonemes. For example: "What is the first sound in *bat*?" (The first sound is /b/), "What is the last sound in *bat*?" (The last sound is /t/), "What sound do you hear in the middle of *bat*?" (The medial sound is /a/)

2. Teach blending by guiding children to identify the word created when the following sounds are blended: /c/, /a/, /t/.

3. Teach word segmentation by saying a word then guiding children to identify the sounds that they hear. For example, "What sounds do you hear in the word *dog*?" (The sounds are /d/ /o/ /g/)

4. Teach minimal pairs, which are sets of words that differ in only one phoneme like *pail* and *bail*, to guide students to notice the difference. Teachers should pronounce both words and ask students if the words are the same or different. Begin with words with the same initial consonant sounds like *cat* and *mat*, then later expand to include more complex pairs like b*i*t, b*ee*t.

5. Guide children to blend onsets and rimes. For example: "What word can you make when you blend the sounds *b* and *oat*, or *c* and *oat*?"

6. Guide children to identify a word like *tape* and then remove the onset and ask the child: "What word is left when we remove the first sound?"

Objective 0002: **Understand word identification strategies, including phonics.**

For example:

- recognizing how beginning writers and readers learn to apply knowledge of the relationship between letters and letter combinations of written words and the sounds of spoken words

- demonstrating knowledge of phonics skills and their application to decoding unfamiliar words

- applying knowledge of structural analysis as a word identification strategy

- demonstrating knowledge of the use of spelling patterns and syllabication as techniques for decoding unfamiliar words

- applying knowledge of developmentally appropriate instruction and curriculum materials for promoting students' decoding skills and word identification strategies

The second objective deals with word identification strategies, including phonics, structural analysis, spelling patterns and syllabication. Children use their knowledge of phonics and the structure of words in their own reading and writing.

Phonics

Phonics builds on phonemic awareness. Using the rules of phonics we teach children to associate symbols—a specific written letter or letter combinations—to represent each speech sound. There are several components including consonants, consonant blends, consonant digraphs, vowels, vowel digraphs, vowel diphthongs, and r-controlled vowels.

Consonants are all sounds represented by letters of alphabet except *a, e, i, o, u*. There are twenty-one single consonant letters in our language.

Consonant digraphs are two or more consonants combined to produce a new sound. Examples include *ch, sh, th* as in the words *ch*air, *sh*oe or *th*e. The digraphs, in this case consonant digraphs, are two-letter combinations that represent a single speech sound.

Consonant blends are two or more consonants appearing together in words whose individual sounds are blended together. Examples include *bl, cr, sk, str* such as in the words *bl*ue, *cr*ack, *sk*ate or *str*ong. These are called blends because the consonants are sounded—neither the *b* or *l* in *blue* loses its identity—but they are blended.

Vowels are all sounds represented by *a, e, i, o, u*, and sometimes *y* or *w*. Vowels have either the long or short sound. The long vowel sound is a speech sound similar to the letter name of the vowel as in the word *be*. Short vowels are also sounds represented by vowel letter as in the word *bat*.

Vowel diphthongs are sounds that consist of a blend of two separate vowel sounds. Examples are *oi, oy, au, aw, ou, ow* such as in the words *oi*l, b*oy*, t*au*ght, s*aw*, pr*ou*d and h*ow*. Vowel digraphs are two vowels that are adjacent to one another and only form one sound. The first vowel is usually a long sound and the 2nd is usually silent. Examples include *oa, ee, ea, ai, ay* as in the words b*oa*t, b*ee*t, *ea*t, r*ai*n and s*ay*.

Some consonants affect vowels. For example, the letter *a* has a different sound when followed by an *l* such as in the word *shallow*. The most important example of consonant influenced vowels are r-controlled vowels such as in the words *fir, far, for*, etc.

Structural analysis is closely related to phonics. It involves the use of known word parts to identify unknown words. This includes the use of affixes, inflectional endings such as -s, -ed, -ing, -ly, contractions and compound words.

Affixes and **root words** are a common word identification strategy. Affixes may be either **prefixes** that come before the root word, or **suffixes** that are at the end of a word. By pulling the word apart one can identify parts of the words that may help with identifying the word as a whole. Common prefixes include *un-* (not), *re-* (do again), *pre-* (before). Common suffixes include *-ist* (one who does), *-ment* (quality or act), *-able* (capable of). Added to root words prefixes and suffixes carry meaning. **Inflectional endings** such as *-s, -ed, -ing, -ly*, are suffixes that change the tense or degree of a word but not its meaning.

Contractions and compound words are also taught as part of structural analysis. **Contractions** are formed when two or more words are shortened into one word. An apostrophe is used to indicate one or more missing letters. The word meaning does not change but the word is spelled differently. For example, the words *do not* are combined into the contraction *don't* or the words *we will* are combined into the contraction *we'll* (Fox, 2010).

CHAPTER 2

Compound words are two or more root words that are combined into For example, *butter* and *fly* are combined to form the new word *butterfly* important word identification strategy because it uses known words to attack unknown or unrecognized words.

• **Spelling patterns and syllabication** are useful as techniques for decoding unfamiliar words. The following are common vowel patterns and spelling patterns:

Long vowel sounds:

- CV—consonant, vowel such as in the word *me*
- Cve— consonant, vowel, silent e as in the word *bike*
- CVVC—consonant, vowel, vowel, consonant as in the word *meet*

Short vowel sounds:

- VC—vowel, consonant such as in the word *at*
- CVC—consonant, vowel, consonant, as in the word *pot*.

R-controlled sounds:

- Vr—vowel followed by r as in the word *art*
- CVr—consonant, vowel followed by r as in the word *car*

Digraph/dipthong variations:

- VV—vowel digraph as in *look* or vowel diphthong as in *soil*

There are the three primary syllabication patterns that signal how to break down a word into syllabic units. They are:

VCCV: When there are two consonants between two vowels the word is usually divided between the consonants. There is one exception to this rule: Do not split consonant digraphs –*sh, -th, -ng* (as in *fa-ther, sing-er*)

VCV #1: When one consonant is between two vowels the word is usually divided before the consonant. For example *apart* would be divided into *a-part*

VCV #2: If using the VCV pattern #1 doesn't result in familiar word, divide the word after the consonant. For example: *salad* (if divided after the vowel would be sā lad) (Vacca, et al, 2009, pp. 210–211)

Teaching Word Identification

Teaching decoding and word identification strategies is a process that varies based on the developmental needs of students. The stages of spelling development provide a guide for the teaching of phonics and structural analysis. All instruction should be done in the context of authentic, hands-on opportunities for manipulating word concepts and applying critical thinking skills (Bear, Invernizzi, Templeton & Johnston, 2007).

For very young children, who are at the emergent stage of reading and writing, word study should include vocabulary and concept development, phonological awareness activities and alphabet recognition activities. The focus is on the sounds that make up spoken words using pictures and texts read aloud. This can be achieved through activities such as concept sorts with picture sorting, phonological awareness activities such as phoneme isolation (e.g., the first sound in the word mat is /m/), phoneme identity (e.g., matching words with the same beginning sounds or the same ending sounds), phoneme categorization (e.g., identifying a word that begins with a different sound than the others in a group of words—such as *bat*, *ball*, *cow*.

Rhyming games, blending activities where children are given separate sounds then they blend the sounds to identify a word (e.g., /m/ /a/ /t/, says mat), or segmenting activities where they are asked to identify the individual sounds in a word (e.g., the sounds in bat are /b/ /a/ /t/), activities such as clapping the syllables in spoken words and identifying onset and rimes in one-syllable words are also valuable phonemic and phonological awareness activities. Alphabet games that involve students in letter recognition are also valuable activities for children at the emergent stage of development (Bear, at al, 2007).

At the beginning writing and reading stage, instruction shifts to a focus on sound-symbol relationships. In the early grades students learn beginning and ending consonants, digraphs, blends and word families (Appropriate for the letter name-alphabetic stage of spelling development—addressed in objective 0006). They progress to reading one-syllable words, some vowel patterns including long vowels and r-controlled vowels (Appropriate for the within word stage of spelling development—addressed in objective

0006). Instruction focuses on manipulating words through word sorts using word tiles or flip books.

As students progress to the fluent stage of reading and writing development, they are ready for lessons in structural analysis—including prefixes, suffixes and root words—as well as long vowel patterns in multisyllabic words and words with inflected endings (Appropriate for the syllables and affixes stage of spelling development—addressed in objective 0006). As students mature in the upper elementary grades and above they begin learning alternative consonant and vowel sounds as well as learning Greek and Latin prefixes, suffixes, and roots (Appropriate for the derivational relations stage of spelling development—addressed in objective 0006).

Objective 0003: Understand the development of vocabulary knowledge and skills across the curriculum.

For example:

- recognizing criteria for selecting appropriate words to increase students' vocabulary knowledge

- demonstrating knowledge of developmentally appropriate strategies for promoting and reinforcing students' oral and written vocabulary knowledge

- applying knowledge of how context is used to determine the meaning of unfamiliar words

- recognizing ways to help students identify and use references such as dictionaries and thesauri for various purposes

The third objective deals with the development of vocabulary knowledge. Vocabulary knowledge is grounded in the semantic, or meaning, system of language. This includes development in both oral and written vocabularies. The more words children can recognize immediately the more likely they are to comprehend more quickly and easily. Also, the more deeply a concept is developed, the more fluent a child can make meaning through varied language use.

When choosing words it is important to select those that students will read or hear most often and that are useful to them. This includes sight words such as *the, of* or *is*, since they are not easily decoded through word identification strategies such as phonics.

Another important consideration is selecting words that tend to be confusing and key words in content area learning. All are important sources for vocabulary instruction. Overall, the following are types of words that are taught as part of vocabulary instruction.

Antonyms are words that are opposite in meaning. For example, *day* is the opposite of *night* or *wet* is the opposite of *dry*. There are also different shades of meaning. For example, *hot* is the opposite of *cold* but there are a continuum of words that express varying degrees of meaning. For example, *cold, frigid, chilly* or *cool* are all opposite of *hot* but some are more extreme than others. Antonyms provide variety in expressing meaning.

Synonyms are words that have the same or nearly the same meaning. As with antonyms there are varying shades of meaning. For example, synonyms for *hot* are *scorching sizzling* or *sultry.* All have similar meanings but provide variety in written text.

Multiple-meaning words are, as the phrase suggests, words that have more than one meaning. As students progress through the elementary grades they begin to enrich their vocabularies as they learn the various meaning of words. For example, there are multiple meanings for the word *bat.* It could mean 1) what you use to hit a baseball, 2) a nocturnal flying creature or 3) to swing at something (as in my cat bats at the ball of yarn). Similarly, there are as many as 12 different meanings for the word bank. Knowledge of the multiple meanings of words provide enhanced comprehension in reading and listening and provide variety for writing and speaking.

Homonyms are another category of words that are important for vocabulary development. Homonyms are words that have similar sounds or spellings. Words can be either homophones, homographs or homographic homophones.

Homophones are words that sound the same but are spelled differently. Each conveys a separate meaning. For example, *two, to* and *too* are all pronounced the same but have different meanings. Other common homophones are *their; there* and *they're; our and hour; bare,* and *bear.*

Homographs are words that are spelled the same but are pronounced differently. Again, each conveys a different meaning. For example, *tear* meaning to rip something (as in "don't tear it") or droplets from the eye (as in "dry your tears"). Though these two words are spelled the same, the pronunciation varies. Therefore, context becomes vital to determining the meaning of the word.

Homographic homophones are words that are spelled the same and pronounced the same but have different meanings. For example, *ball* could be a spherical object that is thrown, a dance (as in "Cinderella went to the ball"), or a good time (as in "we had a ball"). Again, because they are spelled the same and pronounced the same, context becomes vital to determining meaning.

Idioms are words that have a figurative rather than literal meaning. For example, don't "let the cat out of the bag" or don't "spill the beans" both mean don't tell the secret. Other examples of idioms include "an arm and a leg," meaning something is very expensive, "up for grabs" meaning something is available and whoever is first or best will get it or "hold your horses," meaning you need to slow down or be patient.

Vocabulary Instruction

Vocabulary knowledge deals with both concept development and word knowledge as labels for concepts. Vocabulary should be taught in the context of their own reading, writing, speaking and listening activities. When planning vocabulary instruction it is important to consider the levels of word knowledge. Beck, McKeown and Kucan (2002) identify a continuum of word knowledge from no knowledge, to incidental knowledge or partial knowledge, to full knowledge.

Vocabulary should be taught indirectly though activities such as read-aloud, conversations, discussions, and independent reading. Direct instruction involves students in learning words that they do not commonly come into contact with in their everyday, incidental experiences. These include words in the content areas such as science, social studies and mathematics as well as words students come into contact with in their basal or other reading materials. Word study involves students in meaningful study of word meanings that moves beyond the superficial "word and definition." Students are given the chance to act upon their knowledge as they participate in activities such as word posters, word maps, dramatizations, word sorts, word chains or semantic feature analysis (Tompkins, 2009).

Classifying or categorizing words helps students to study words in relation to other words. This involves them in more critical thinking skills as they work through the relationships between words, leading to deeper, richer vocabulary knowledge. This is especially true in vocabulary that is specific to the content areas across the curriculum.

Context Clues

Context clues are those clues taken from words, phrases, sentences surrounding the unknown word used as recognition aids. These include picture clues that use accompanying pictures as clues for unknown words, semantic clues that are clues derived from meanings of surrounding words and syntactic clues that are clues derived from grammar knowledge (i.e., certain words appear in certain positions in sentences).

Illustrations in books can often help children determine the meaning of unfamiliar words. This is a good first step for teaching about context clues. This is not a good strategy in the upper grades though since the texts will have fewer and fewer illustrations. Semantic clues require a child to think about the meanings of words and what is already known about the topic being read. For example, when reading a story about bats, good teachers begin by activating background knowledge about bats. This helps to develop an expectation that the selection may contain words such as *swoop, wings, mammal*, or *nocturnal* that are associated with bats. This prereading discussion helps children gain a sense of what vocabulary might be reasonable in a sentence. Finally, syntactic clues, relate to word order based on grammar rules. For example, in the sentence, "Bats can _____ at night" the order of the words in the sentence gives clues that the missing word must be a verb. Based on their knowledge of verbs they can determine that the missing word would indicate an action.

Dictionaries and thesauri can be useful for a range of information related to vocabulary.

Dictionaries include important information such as definitions, pronunciation guides, grammatical information, possible synonyms, etc. They usually have an introduction that gives information on how to use the dictionary including an explanation of the marks, abbreviations and symbols used. Dictionaries are arranged in alphabetical order and include guide words, the first and last words on a page, to aide in locating a word.

Thesauri are used to find synonyms and antonyms and, like dictionaries, are arranged in alphabetical order. They are useful for finding a variety of words in order to express meaning more effectively in order to avoid repeating the same words monotonously.

Objective 0004: **Understanding reading fluency and comprehension across the curriculum.**

For example:

- demonstrating knowledge of the concepts of rate, accuracy, expression, and phrasing in reading fluency and recognizing factors that affect fluency

- analyzing the relationship between reading fluency and comprehension

- recognizing the effects of various factors on reading comprehension

- distinguishing among literal, inferential, and evaluative comprehension

- identifying strategies for promoting students' literal, inferential, and evaluative comprehension

- applying knowledge of strategies that facilitate comprehension before, during, and after reading

The fourth objective deals with reading fluency and comprehension across the curriculum. Fluency is the ability to read text with **accuracy**, **appropriate rate**, and good **expression** or prosody. Fluent readers read smoothly, maintaining a natural rhythm that resembles speaking. The fluent reader is focused on the meaning of the text rather than on decoding unfamiliar words, resulting in improved comprehension.

Accuracy in word identification is vital. Readers need to be able to accurately identify words, both through effective decoding skills and immediate word recognition, in order to focus attention on making meaning. Skill in accuracy directly impacts reading rate.

Reading rate refers to the speed with which the student reads a given text. Since students with faster reading rates read more than those with slower reading rates in the same amount of time, therefore they read less and are often unmotivated to read.

Another element that indicates that a student is reading fluently is expression, or prosody. Prosodic features affect expression and include stress, intonation, and phrasing. Prosodic reading reflects understanding of the meaning through appropriate phrasing and intonation, and reflects understanding of text features such as punctuation and headings.

Relationship between Fluency and Comprehension

There is a direct correlation between reading fluency and comprehension. Poor readers are characterized by slowly plodding through a passage as they struggle to decode many unknown words. By the time they finish reading the passage, it is a struggle to remember what was read. Comprehension is compromised for students who read with insufficient fluency because they are more focused on decoding than on the meaning of the text. Students for whom reading is a struggle have fewer experiences with text and get less meaningful practice which, in turn, limits the development of comprehension skills and slows vocabulary growth.

Teachers help readers to chunk ideas into phrases in a sentence in order to read more fluently. This is done through activities such as read-aloud or choral reading.

Factors that Influence Fluency and Comprehension

Factors that influence fluency and comprehension include prior knowledge, context, vocabulary knowledge, and attention to graphic cues. A sound comprehensive language arts program addresses all of these factors through assessment and instruction. Attention to these elements is necessary for students' literacy growth.

Prior Knowledge

Comprehension demands prior knowledge because written language contains semantic interruptions where knowledge is taken for granted. Subsequently, understanding is based on making sound inferences, asking questions, or using research and reference tools.

Disruptions in comprehension impact fluency. For example, the student reads, "Larry kept jumping in front of Moe to reach the jar on the shelf until Moe told him to knock it off." In this sentence Larry is continually jumping in front of Moe. Moe tells Larry to "knock it off" or stop the action. The intent of the text is compromised if the student's background knowledge lacks an understanding of the idiom "knock it off."

Three ways to increase background knowledge include: questioning to build on what students already know about a topic, providing more in-depth information about the topic, to add to prior knowledge, and providing real or vicarious experiences, to scaffold knowledge about the topic. Teachers have a wealth of resources to aid this process efficiently through technology.

Context

Language arts instruction spans genres and content areas. Comprehension strategies for literature differ from strategies for mathematics. Story structure for folk tales does not match story structure of other genres. For many students the transference of skills from story reading to non-fiction text is difficult, therefore students should have guided experience using strategies for understanding different kinds of text.

Vocabulary Knowledge

A major determinant of reading comprehension is vocabulary knowledge. If the student sounds out a word and fails to recognize its meaning, the ability to understand the text is lost. In order for the reader to understand what is written, the words must reside it their meaning vocabulary. According to the National Reading Panel (2000), vocabulary instruction is a major component of a comprehensive reading program.

Attention to Graphic Cues

Graphic cues include spacing, text size or font, bolding, highlighting, and underlining of text, and punctuation. The cues are used primarily to show emphasis or importance. Graphic cues can be introduced to students at a young age through shared reading. Shared writing using technology is also effective for using graphic cues to aid comprehension.

Levels of Comprehension

Comprehension skills include the ability to identify supporting details and facts, the main idea or essential message, the author's purpose, fact and opinion, point of view, inference and conclusion. To help students develop these skills teachers can consistently emphasize meaning in the classroom and should focus on three levels of comprehension: 1) literal, 2) interpretive and 3) evaluative.

Literal Level of Comprehension

The most basic, or lowest, level of comprehension is **literal**. This level of comprehension involves *reading the lines*, or reading and understanding exactly what is on the page. Students may give back facts or details directly from the passages as they read. For example, a teacher works with students as they make their own play dough and use the recipe to practice authentic reading (Davis, 2004). The teacher might question the students on the literal level as they mix their ingredients. For example:

Factual Question: How much salt do you add to the mixture?

Sequence Question: What is the first step in making the play dough?

Contrast Question: Do you add more or less salt than you did flour?

All of the information needed to answers the questions is literally stated in the text (in this case, a recipe).

Interpretive Level of Comprehension

The second level of comprehension is the **interpretive** level, which requires students to *read between the lines*. At this level of comprehension, the student must explain figurative language, define terms and answer interpretive and inferential questions. Inferential questions require the students to infer, or figure out, the answers. Asking students to identify the author's purpose, the main idea or essential message, the point of view and the conclusion are examples of inferential questions. Inferential questions may require students to draw conclusion, generalize, derive meaning from the language, speculate anticipate, predict and summarize. All such questions are from the interpretive level.

The following are examples of interpretive questions the teacher could ask at the cooking center while the students are making play dough:

Contrast Question: How is the dry measuring cup different from the liquid measuring cup? Why are they different?

Deriving Meaning Question: What does the word *blend* mean?

Purpose Question: What is the purpose of making play dough? Why would you want to make play dough instead of buying it ready-made as the product Play-Doh?

Cause and Effect Question: Why do the directions say to store the play dough in a covered, airtight container?

Evaluative Level of Comprehension

The **evaluative** level of comprehension requires a higher level of understanding. The students must judge the passage they have read. The evaluative level is the highest level of understanding; it requires students to ***read beyond the lines***. Having students determine whether a passage is true or false, deciding whether a statement is a fact or opinion, detecting propaganda or judging the qualifications of the author for writing the passage are examples of using the critical level of comprehension. The following are some examples of questions the teacher could ask students as they make play dough to encourage understanding at the evaluative level:

Checking Author's Reputation: The recipe for the play dough comes from a book of chemistry experiments. A chemist wrote the book. Do you think that a chemist would be a good person to write about play dough? Why or why not?

Responding Emotionally: Do you prefer to use the play dough we made in class or the play dough that the local stores carry?

Judging: Do you think the recipe for play dough that is on the recipe card will work? Why or why not?

Strategies for Promoting the Literal, Inferential and Evaluative Comprehension

Questioning: Questioning is vital strategy. When readers ask questions, even before they read, they clarify understanding and forge ahead to make meaning. Asking questions is at the heart of thoughtful reading. Vacca, et al. (2009) also recommend the following questioning strategies for extending students' understanding of the texts they read.

Reciprocal Questioning (ReQuest)

This strategy encourages students to think as they read in any situation that requires reading. Modeling appropriate questions—those that go beyond the literal level of comprehension—is vital.

Question-Answer Relationships (QARs)

This is a very important strategy that helps readers determine the most likely source of information needed to answer comprehension questions. As they point out, some questions can be thought of as textually explicit because they promote recall or recognition of *information actually stated in the text* as in literal-level questions. Other questions can be thought of as textually implicit because they provoke thinking, requiring students to provide information that is **not** actually stated in the text as in interpretive and evaluative levels of comprehension.

Strategies that Facilitate Comprehension Before, During and After Reading

Different strategies are important at different points of the reading process.

For example, **before reading** strategies include:

Activate prior knowledge: Readers attend better when they relate to the text. Readers naturally bring their prior knowledge and experience to reading but they comprehend better when they think about the connections they make between the text, their lives and the larger world.

Predicting: Making predictions based on the cover, the title and the first page or so is an effective strategy to keep students focused on the text. Predictions focus attention as children read to verify or reject earlier predictions, both as they read and after they read. They can do this through a picture walk with a story or by previewing content using title, table of contents and glossary for important vocabulary with informational texts. Both help students anticipate content and possible events in the story.

During reading students use strategies to monitor comprehension and maximize understanding. For example:

Mapping text structures: Students identify the text structures, whether narrative or expository. Story maps are effective for stories. For expository texts students can use the K-W-L strategy in order to record what they are learning.

Visualizing: Active readers create visual images based on the words they read in the text. These created "pictures" enhance their understanding.

Drawing inferences: Inferring is done when readers take what they know, garner clues from the text and think ahead to make a judgment, discern a theme or speculate about what is to come.

Determining important ideas: Effective readers grasp essential ideas and important information when reading. Readers must differentiate between less important ideas and key ideas that are central to the meaning of the text. This involves main ideas and important supporting details.

Repairing understanding: If confusing disrupts meaning readers need to stop and clarify their understanding. Readers may use a variety of strategies to "fix up" comprehension. This may involve rereading parts of the texts in order to better understand the author's meaning.

Using the parts of a book: Students should use all parts of the book, including charts, diagrams, indexes, and the table of contents, to improve their understanding of the content in the text.

Reflect: Stop and reflect on literal, interpretive, or evaluative questions.

After reading students reflect, relook and extend their knowledge of the text. For example readers:

Synthesize information: Synthesizing involves combining new information with existing knowledge to form an original idea or interpretation. Reviewing, sorting and sifting important information can lead to new insights that change the way readers think.

Reflecting: Reflection is an important comprehension strategy. It requires the reader to think about or reflect on what they have just read. It can be done through rethinking the content, through written activities such as in a journal writing activities or through visually representing.

Objective 0005: Understand comprehension strategies for literary and informational texts across the curriculum

For example:

- recognizing types and characteristics of literary and informational texts
- identifying characteristics and functions of literary elements and devices
- applying strategies for developing students' literary response skills
- demonstrating knowledge of genres, themes, authors, and works of literature written for children
- recognizing common patterns of organization in informational texts
- applying knowledge of strategies for promoting comprehension of informational texts

Objective five deals with comprehension strategies for varying texts structures.

The more students know about the organization of texts the better able they are to make meaning of them. Knowing the underlying structure of texts helps readers to set a purpose for reading, allowing them to anticipate possible events or content in the text they are reading, thereby enhancing comprehension.

Literary Text Structures

As pointed out earlier, comprehension strategies differ according to the literary type. Strategies for comprehending stories or poetry are different than those for comprehending informational text. Therefore it is important that students learn the characteristics of a variety of literary structures.

Stories have a specific structure including a clear beginning, middle and end. In the beginning of stories characters are introduced, a setting is introduced and a story problem or initiating event is identified. In the middle, the character attempts to solve the story problem. The story continues with multiple attempts at resolving the problem. This continues to a climax and the story ends with a resolution of the story problem. Story grammar is the knowledge about the basic parts of stories and how they tie together to form a well-constructed story. Important elements of stories are characters (those involved in the story), setting (where the story takes place), plot (sequence of events from the story problem introduction to the solution of the problem) and point of view (narrator of the story). Knowledge of these elements helps students anticipate story events and read for confirmation or rejection of the predicted events.

Poetry uses vivid and colorful words arranged in lines, stanzas or other shapes depending on the type of poetry. Poems uses poetic devices such as comparison (using similes or metaphors), alliteration (repetition of initial consonant sound), onomatopoeia (words that mimic sounds) or rhyme (repetition of ending sounds) to elicit a specific response or emotion. There are a variety of types, each with its own structure.

Informational texts convey information through the use of **expository text structures**. These include:

> **Description**: Describe a topic by listing characteristics, features, and examples. Details are used to support the main idea.

> **Sequence**: Organizes topic or events in numerical or the order in which they occurred.

Comparison: Discusses topic by explaining how two or more things are alike or different

Cause and Effect: Discusses topic by explaining the relationship between two or more events. The focus is on the triggering event/s (cause/s) and the resulting effect/s

Problem and Solution: A problem is explained and one or more solutions are offered

Informational books may also make use of a table of contents or glossary and other graphic organizers. Sometimes the pattern is clearly identified through titles, topic sentences or cue words (Tompkins, 2004).

Strategies for Developing Students' Literary Response Skills

Response and reflection are the hallmarks of literary comprehension. Reading response is an important part of the reading process. Here students continue to make text-to-self and text-to-world connections. Strategies such as journal writing, literature discussions, or visually representing help students examine the author's meaning.

Some strategies that extend knowledge enhance comprehension include:

Semantic Feature Analysis: Helps students think about similarities and differences between and among related concepts in the text.

Story Mapping Activities: Mapping activities require visually representing the story. Younger students use pictures, older ones use diagrams, maps, arrows, labels, etc.

Sketch-to-Stretch: This is a nonverbal response activity. Individual students draw a picture of a favorite or memorable event or scene from the story. The student shows the illustration to a small group, inviting classmates to provide their own interpretation of the drawing (Tompkins, 2009).

Compare-and-Contrast Chart: An important aspect of comprehension is the ability to make thoughtful comparisons across texts, between events within stories, and across other aspects of stories that students read. Activity begins with a grid, either a large one on chart paper or individual sheets of paper. Along one axis of the chart are listed the items to be compared. On the other axis, students brainstorm key characteristics that distinguish at least one item from another.

K-W-L charts: Provide an opportunity to reflect on and record what was learned from the text.

Response Journals: Journals are an effect way to extend comprehension in all types of literary text. Journals are a place for capturing reactions and thoughts related to the books students have read or take notes on important information.

Comprehension of informational texts involves reading to obtain information in the text. In order to maximize comprehension of informational texts it is important to understand how text is organized. Children need to identify key components of the organizational format and identify the type of information offered. Teachers guide children to notice and study the structure of text including the table of contents, titles, subtitles and headings.

Helping students focus on the main idea or the essential message in texts and the supporting details that make the main idea stronger. These may be stated explicitly or implied through factual information in the text.

Chats, tables, graphs, pictures and print and nonprint media are examples of materials writers use to present information. A graphic can expand a concept, serve as an illustration, support points, summarize data, organize facts, compare information or furnish additional information.

Strategies for promoting comprehension include:

Previewing and Skimming: This begins with previewing through questions about elements such as the table of contents, titles of chapters, headings and subheadings, highlighted text, index or glossary. Skimming is done by looking through the content quickly to get an overall sense of what the content is about.

Graphic Organizers: These highlight the key concepts and the children's prior knowledge. K-W-L is a good example of this strategy. In the K-W-L students complete what they *K*now and what they *W*ant to know before reading. Then later, after the reading, *L*earned is recorded as they discover the information. Other examples include webs or clusters.

Anticipation Guides: These include written statements for students to think about and discuss before they read. Statements are designed to activate prior knowledge and arouse curiosity about the issues addressed in the text.

Children's Literature

Children's literature is a vital part of the language arts curriculum. High-quality children's literature provides excellent models of good texts, enhancing both reading comprehension and children's own writing.

Genre refers to the category of literature. There are a variety of classifications, but the most common include fiction, nonfiction and poetry. Fiction includes traditional literature, modern fantasy, contemporary realistic fiction, historical fiction. Nonfiction includes informational books or biographies and autobiographies. There is also a variety of poetry types. Most genres can be further divided into a variety of subcategories. There is also a variety of formats across genre. These include picture books, in which the illustrations and the text work together to communicate the story, chapter books and multimedia versions.

Traditional literature includes tales that have been handed down from one generation to the next through oral stories. There are four types of traditional tales: folktales, fables, myths, and legends.

Folktales usually tell the adventures of animal or human characters. They contain common narrative motifs such as supernatural adversaries (ogres, witches, giants, etc.); supernatural helpers, magic and marvels, tasks and quests, and common themes such as reward of good and punishment of evil. Example: *Cinderella*

Fables are brief tales in which animal characters that talk and act like humans teach a moral lesson. Example: *The Tortoise and the Hare*

Myths explain something in life or in nature such as thunder and lightning and for human emotions and experiences such as love or death. The main characters may be animals, deities, or humans. Example: *How the Elephant Got its Trunk*

Legends are based on some fact but are exaggerated. For example the hero tales such as *John Henry* or *Johnny Appleseed*

Modern fantasy includes story with unrealistic or unworldly elements but that are written by an identifiable original author. Examples include *The Emperor's New Clothes* by Hans Christian Anderson, *Authur's Loose Tooth* by L. Hoban, or C.S. Lewis's *Narnia* series.

Contemporary realistic fiction includes stories that are consistent with the lives of real people in our contemporary world. The word *realistic* doesn't mean that the story is true, however; it means the story could have happened. Examples include *Dear Mr. Henshaw* by Beverly Cleary, *Amber Brown* books by Paula Danziger, or *Jacob Have I Loved* by Betsy Paterson.

Historical fiction tells realistic stories of history. Like contemporary realistic fiction, events reflect what has happened or could have happened. Realistic doesn't mean that the story is true however; it means the story could have happened. Examples: *Sarah Plain and Tall*, by Patricia MacLachlan, *Roll of Thunder, Hear My Cry* by Mildred Taylor, or *Number the Stars* by Lois Lowry.

Informational books are available on almost any subject. These include ideas, facts or principles related to the physical, biological or social world. Reference books include dictionaries, thesauri or encyclopedias.

Biographies and autobiographies are factual stories about people. In biographies authors tell about another's life. Autobiographies are stories about the author's life.

Poetry can be a difficult genre to define for children; there is no single accepted definition of poetry (Norton, 2007). There are multiple forms of poetry:

Narrative: poem tells a story

Lyric: statement of mood or feeling (e.g., song lyrics)

Limericks: five-line poems in which the first, second and fifth lines rhyme and have three pronounced beats each, and the third and fourth lines rhyme and have two beats each

Concrete: poem written in the shape of its meaning, forming a picture

Haiku: three unrhymed lines: the first and last lines have five syllables each, the second line has seven syllables

Objective 0006: **Understand skills and strategies involved in writing for various purposes across the curriculum**

For example:

- recognizing developmental stages of writing, including the use of pictures and developmental spelling

- analyzing factors to consider in writing for various audiences and purposes and in writing materials in various genres, formats, and modes

- demonstrating knowledge of the writing process and strategies for promoting students' writing skills

- demonstrating knowledge of the use of writing strategies and language to achieve various effects

- applying revision strategies to improve the unity, organization, clarity, precision, and effectiveness of written materials

- demonstrating knowledge of the use of research skills and computer technology to support writing

Objective six focuses on concepts related to writing in the elementary curriculum. This includes the developmental stages of children's writing and the key strategies and skills within each of the stages of the writing process.

Developmental stages of writing are evident in children's writing. Young children's writing begins as they make marks on paper. This begins with the earliest attempts of expression as children use pictures to convey meaning. These pictures become the story; children will "read" these as they communicate their meaning. As children begin to notice writing in their environment they make early attempts at "writing" through scribbling. These start out as random scribbles but eventually progress to a left-to-right, top-to-bottom orientation on the page. These scribbles later evolve into a child's first attempts at forming letters and numbers. Letters are pulled from those which are most important to the child, such as letters in his or her name. The letters will appear in random order or string together shapes, scribbles and familiar letter-like forms. As children become more phonemically aware and start in early phonics instruction, they begin to form their own spellings for words. One letter may represent the whole word and the words may be strung together without spaces in sentences. As children mature, their writing becomes more conventional.

The stages of spelling development most commonly agreed upon are identified by Bear, Invernizzi, Templeton, and Johnston (2007). These include the following stages: **emergent**, **letter-name**, **within-word**, **syllables**, and affixes and derivational relations. The earliest stage 1) emergent spelling, is characterized by random marks, representational drawing, mock letter-like writing and random letters and numbers. In stage 2, the letter-name spelling stage, children begin to represent the sounds in words with letters. In this stage, children use their knowledge of the names of letters of the alphabet to spell their words. This is characteristic of writers in the early grades of elementary school, and corresponds to early phonics instruction in short vowels, consonant sounds and consonant blends and digraphs. At stage 3, the within-word spelling phase, children's knowledge of the alphabetic principle is further developed. In this stage, children learn the long-vowel spelling patterns, diphthongs and r-controlled vowels. Stage 4 is the syllable and affixes spelling stage. At this stage students are learning to spell more complex words. Lessons in structural analysis support the spellers in this stage as they learn inflectional endings, syllabication, contractions, homophones and possessives. Finally, in the derivational-relations spelling stage, older children begin to learn concepts as consonant alternations, vowel alternations, as well as Greek and Latin roots of words and word origins.

Genres of Writing

There is a variety of writing modes and formats that all serve different purposes. One must determine the purpose and audience of writing in order to select the best form to use. The most common writing modes are 1) **narrative**, that which tells a story, 2) **expository**, which informs, 3) **descriptive**, which describes or paints a picture with words, and 4) persuasive, which is used to convince the reader of a position or point of view.

There is a variety of writing forms that may be used within each of the modes. For example, narrative writing may take the form of fictional stories or nonfictional stories such as biographies; persuasive writing may take the form of advertisements, letters to the editor or persuasive essays. Based on these, the most common writing genres taught in the K-5 curriculum are: 1) stories, 2) personal writing, such as response journals and letters, 3) informational writing, 4) poetry and 5) persuasive writing.

Stories have a specific structure used to tell a story and entertain the reader. Whether fictional or nonfictional, stories have a clear beginning, middle and end. They are told through a plot that involves characters in conflicts; tis is termed the *story problem*. Important elements are characters (those involved in the story), setting (where the story takes place), plot (sequence of events from story problem introduction to solution of the problem) and point of view (narrator of the story). Stories are told through both actions of characters and dialogue. All of these elements must be considered when composing stories.

Personal writing includes journal writing, which is used to record personal experiences, respond to literature or record and analyze information and letter writing. The most common types of journals are reading-response journals and learning logs, but may also include journals—personal, dialogue, or simulated. All are effective for learning across the curriculum. Letter-writing is used to develop and maintain relationships or to convey information. There is a variety of letter writing forms taught. These vary from the less formal, such as friendly letters and email, to the more formal, such as business letters and persuasive letters to the editor of a newspaper or magazine. Each has a specific structure (e.g. greeting, body, closing) varying from very informal (email) to more formal business letters and letters to editors.

Informational writing is valuable for both learning and sharing information across the curriculum as students study social studies, science and other curricular areas. As with other genres, informational writing has a specific structure. The most common organizational patterns are:

Description: Writers describe a topic by listing characteristics, features, and examples

Sequence: Writers list items or events in numerical or chronological order

Comparison: Writers explain how two or more things are alike or different

Cause and Effect: Writers describe one or more causes and the resulting effect or effects in this pattern

Problem and Solution: Writers present a problem and offer one or more solutions in this expository structure

Graphic organizers are also important as we teach students to use charts, tables, graphs, webs, etc. to convey meaning.

Poetry is used to entertain, create visual and oral images or to explore feelings. It includes a variety of poetic formulas. These include formula poems that provide a framework for writing (e.g., "I wish. . ." poems, "If I were. . ." poems, acrostic poems, etc.), free-form poems that allow the writer to put the poem together without concern about rhyme or other patterns (e.g., concrete/word picture poems, found poems, etc.), syllable/word-count poems such as haiku, cinquain or diamante poems, as well as the more traditional rhymed verse poems such as limericks and clerihews (Tompkins, 2008).

Persuasive writing is used to share opinions and support them by presenting facts in a clear, logical and convincing way, present an alternate viewpoint or persuade someone to do something. The structure of persuasive writing includes stating a position or opinion, developing the position or opinion by supporting facts or reasons and drawing conclusions to persuade the reader to accept their position or viewpoint. This can be done in the form of advertisements, posters, letters or essays.

Writing Process

The stages of the writing process are 1) prewriting, 2) drafting, 3) revision, 4) editing, and 5) publishing. The process is a focus on what writers do as they create a written piece.

Prewriting includes everything a writer does before writing. This includes considering the purpose for writing, deciding on what form or genre would be most appropriate for the specific writing purpose, the audience for whom the writing is being done, the topic, as well as generating and organizing ideas for writing. Children should be encouraged to select topics that are of interest to them and to consider the purpose of the writing before selecting the appropriate genre or form to write. Prewriting activities should help children to activate background knowledge as they explore ideas for writing. Appropriate activities include drawing, talking, reading, webbing ideas, dramatizing, etc.

Drafting is the second stage of writing. In this stage writers get their ideas down on paper in the form of a first draft. The emphasis here is on ideas and content rather than mechanics so it should be clearly labeled as a rough draft. This is where a writer gets the initial ideas down. Developing those ideas can then come in the revision stage.

Revision allows writers to look again at the ideas as well as seek feedback from others. The focus here is still on the ideas and content. Revision strategies are used during the revision stage of the writing process to improve the written product. Revision involves looking to see how you presented your ideas. One important strategy involves getting distance from the work. That distance is important for viewing the piece with a more objective eye. After rethinking what has been written it is important to get feedback from others in conferences or writer's workshop.

Changes are made based on the feedback given. This involves adding, deleting, consolidating, clarifying, and rearranging words and sentences to clarify meaning and expand ideas. Though the various genres have different structures they all should be clear, concise and effectively organized. The six-trait model is an effective framework for relooking at the written products. Spandel (2008) identifies the following traits:

1. Ideas: The main message or story line of the piece. It involves focusing or narrowing the topic, developing the main idea, using details that build understanding or hold the reader's attention.

2. Organization: The design and structure of the written piece. This includes an original title, an opening that attracts interest, transitions that connect the main ideas in the piece, clear ideas that are easy to follow and an effective ending.

3. Voice: A sense of the writer behind the words. It is the writer's personal imprint on the page. It shows concern for the reader and enthusiasm about the topic.

4. Word choice: Words should paint a picture in the reader's mind. This includes the use of strong verbs, specific nouns, descriptive adjectives, figurative language such as similes or metaphors and avoidance of overused words, slang or clichés.

5. Sentence fluency: The flow or rhythm of the language. Writers use a variety of well structured sentences that lend to the flow of the piece of writing. This includes a variety of sentence structures and beginnings.

These traits provide a framework for revision as students rethink their writing. The writer may find the need to return to the prewriting stage to do more research or to the drafting stage to do more writing. Once the content is complete and organized the writer moves on to polishing the final form.

Editing allows students put the writing in its final form. This is where the mechanical elements are addressed. Misspelled words, errors in grammar, capitalization and punctuation are addressed here. Students need to get distance from their written product before editing. They then proofread their writing (or the writing of another) in order to locate errors. This is the time to teach lessons on mechanics. Once the errors are corrected, they are ready to move to the final stage, publishing.

Publishing is the final stage of the writing process. The ultimate goal of publishing is to share the written product with the audience. This stage allows a celebration of the completed product. It can take the form of sharing from the author's chair or publishing a book for the classroom library.

Research skills and technology provide vital support for writing. There is a huge variety of resources that provide useful information as students develop their written products. It is important that we teach students both to locate and apply information effectively.

Students can use a number of resources to aid writing. These include dictionaries, the-sauri, encyclopedias, electronic information such as the internet of CD-ROM, almanacs, atlases, magazines and newspapers. It is important that students choose the resources appropriately. For example, a dictionary provides useful information about word meanings and spelling, encyclopedias provide information on a variety of topics about events or historical figures and a newspaper is useful for current news and events. Guiding students to the appropriate resource is vital.

Other skills related to the effective use of references are also important. This includes such concepts as locating information in reference texts by using organizational features such as the preface, appendix, index, glossary, table of contents, citations, end notes or bibliographic references. Students need to be knowledgeable about using features such as guide words, alphabetical and numerical order in order to obtain and organize information and thoughts.

While research skills are useful in many genres they are especially critical skills in writing informational research reports. Technology provides a wide variety of research options through the internet. Resources such as online databases, encyclopedias and other internet references are plentiful. Programs such as *Kid Pix*, *Kidspiration*, *VoiceThread* (to name only a very few) allow tools for gathering, organizing and presenting multimedia and written projects.

Other tools such as digital cameras, smart boards, electronic notebooks for note taking are also useful. Graphic organizers, such as data charts, allow students to record information and document sources. Elementary grade students learn basic keyboarding skills and become familiar with computer terminology such as software, memory, disk drive, hard drive, passwords, entry and pull-down menus, word searches, bookmarking, thesaurus and spell check as useful tools for researching, drafting, revising, editing, and publishing research reports.

Objective 0007:   Understand the conventions of standard English grammar, usage, and mechanics.

For example:

- demonstrating knowledge of the parts of speech

- demonstrating knowledge of elements of appropriate grammar and usage

- demonstrating knowledge of appropriate mechanics in writing

- identifying appropriate corrections of errors in sentence structure

- demonstrating knowledge of various types of sentence structures

Objective seven focuses on concepts related to the conventions of standard English.

Grammar is part of the syntactic system of language. Grammar involves principles of word and sentence formation that are the structure of language (Tompkins, 2009). Usage deals with socially acceptable correctness in applying those rules or principles of grammar. Usage is part of the pragmatic system of language. Grammar, usage and mechanics are taught as a part of the language arts curriculum.

In traditional grammar there are eight parts of speech. They are: 1) noun, 2) pronoun, 3) adjective, 4) verb, 5) adverb, 6) preposition, 7) conjunction and 8) interjection.

A **noun** is used to name a person, place or thing. There are two types of nouns, **common nouns** and **proper nouns**. Examples of common nouns include *boy, house,* or *dog.* Common nouns are not capitalized. Proper nouns name a specific person, place or thing as in *Brian, White House* or *Drew.* Proper nouns are capitalized.

Nouns may be **singular**, **plural**, or **possessive**. When a noun refers to one thing it is considered singular, as in *boy, dog* or *book.* For example, *The boy is gone.* When a noun refers to more than one it is said to be plural, as in *boys, dogs* or *books.* For example, *The* *boys are outside.* The plural is made by adding *–s.* There are exceptions when a plural noun ends in *x, z, s, ch* or *sh, y, o, f* or *fe.* There are also irregular plural forms such as *man/men, foot/feet,* etc.

A possessive noun shows possession. It shows who or what has something. Possessive nouns are formed by adding apostrophes which are explained in a later section. For example, *The dog is Brian's.* Most singular possessives are formed by adding an *apostrophe -s* (*'s*) such as in the sentence *The car is Candace's.* To form a possessive of a plural noun one adds just an apostrophe (*'*) if the noun ends in *-s,* such as in the sentence *The Kents' house.* An *apostrophe -s* (*'s*) for plural nouns not ending with *–s* such as in the sentence *The men's team won the game.*

A **pronoun** is used to take the place of a noun. For example, instead of saying *Jordan likes to play,* you could say *He likes to play.* Other examples of pronouns are *she, it, we,* or *they.* Singular pronouns take the place of singular pronouns; plural pronouns take the place of plural pronouns. **Possessive pronouns** take the place of nouns and show possession. For example, *The dog is his.* Other possessive pronouns include *her, their* or *our.* **Personal pronouns** represent specific people. For example *I, we, he,* or *she.*

An **adjective** describes, defines, or limits a noun or pronoun. For example, *blue, sticky,* or *big.* An **adverb** is used to modify a verb, adjective or other another adverb. It tells how, when, where, why, how often or how much. For example: *very, later, inside, well, really* or *badly.*

In general, we use adjectives as subject complements with linking verbs and adverbs with action verbs. For example: The sentence *Please be careful* uses adjective (*careful*) whereas the sentence *Please walk carefully* uses the adverb (*carefully*).

A **preposition** is a word that shows a relationship between the noun or pronoun and other words in a sentence. For example: *on, under,* or *above.* A **conjunction** is a word that connects a word and other words or phrases. For example: *and, or,* and *but.* **Interjections** are expressive words such as *wow, ah,* or *oh.* They are used to show strong emotion.

A **verb** is used to show action, as in *jump, run* or *hop,* or to show a state of being, as in *is, will* or *seem.* Students learn about present, past and past participle tenses of verbs. The use of regular verbs, such as *look* and *receive,* poses few problems since the past and past participle forms end in *–ed.*

The present, past and past participle forms of irregular verbs can cause problems however. Examples include *catch/caught, ring/rang/rung or swim/swam/swum*. These verbs are taught individually since there is no standard rule for irregular verb forms.

Sentence Structure and Types

Sentences can be classified by structure or by types. The structure of sentences includes **simple**, **compound**, **complex** or **compound-complex**, depending on the number and types of clauses used. Sentences can also be classified by the type. These include **declarative, interrogative, imperative** or **exclamatory** sentences.

A sentence is made up of one or more words and expresses a complete thought. Simple sentences are made up of a **subject** and a **predicate**. The subject is a noun or pronoun and the predicate is the verb and anything that completes or modifies the verb. Sentences may also include phrases or clauses. Phrases do not express a complete thought and do not contain a subject and a predicate. Clauses contain a subject and a predicate and may include a complete thought. Independent clauses contain a subject, a predicate and can stand alone as a complete thought. Dependent clauses contain a subject and a predicate but are not a complete thought.

The **four structures of sentences** are: **simple**, **compound**, **complex**, and **compound-complex**. A simple sentence is contains one independent clause. A compound sentence has two or more independent clauses. A complex sentence has one independent clause and one or more dependent clauses. Finally a compound-complex sentence two or more independent clauses and one or more dependent clauses.

There are also **four types of sentences**: **declarative**, **interrogative**, **imperative**, and **exclamatory**. Declarative sentences make statements. They begin with a capital letter and end with a period. An example would be, *I am going to the store*. Interrogative sentences ask a question and they end with a question mark. An example would be *Are you going to the store?* Imperative sentences make commands and end either with a period or an exclamation point. For example, *Go to the store*. Exclamatory sentences show strong emotion or surprise. For example, *Wow, you went to the store!*

Mechanics

Mechanics in writing usually refers to rules of capitalization and punctuation. The rules of capitalization and punctuation are taught throughout the K–5 curriculum.

Capitalization

The most common rules of capitalization include: 1) the first word in a sentence, 2) proper nouns or 3) the word *I* when used alone or in a contraction.

All sentences begin with a capital letter. This is true of all types of complete sentences.

Proper nouns are always capitalized. This includes names of persons, geographical places, organizations and the months of the year.

Example   *Derek Lowe* is a pitcher for the *Atlanta Braves,* who play in the *National League.* Their first game is in *March.*

The word I is also capitalized if it used alone or as a contraction.

Example   Anna and *I* live in Georgia or

Give me a minute and *I'll* go.

Punctuation

The most common components of punctuation include 1) ending marks such as periods, question marks, and exclamation points, 2) commas, 3) quotation marks, and 4) apostrophes.

End marks

The type of ending punctuation varies depending on the type or purpose of the sentence. The end marks are period (**.**), question mark (**?**) and exclamation point (**!**). As we saw earlier, different types of sentences end with different types end marks.

Commas

The following are the most common rules for commas taught in the K–5 curriculum:

In dates: In sentences with the month, day and year, a comma is placed between the day and the year.

> **Example**   *It is January 5, 2010.* If only the month and year appear in the sentence, no comma is needed. For example: *It is January 2010 already!*

In a series: When more than one adjective describes a noun, use a comma to separate and emphasize each adjective.

> **Example**   *the wet, smelly dog* or *the white, fluffy rabbit.*

In a letter greeting and closing:

> **Example**   In the greeting: *Dear Matthew,*
>
> In the closing: *Your friend,*

Between city and state:

> **Example**   *We live in Statesboro, Georgia.*

Before conjunctions forming compound sentences:

> **Example**   The children were sleeping, so I read my book.

After interjections at the beginning of sentences:

> **Example**   Oh, that was a great story.

Quotation marks

Quotation marks (" ") are used to set off quoted words, phrases and sentences.

> **Example**
>
> *"If everyone treated others as they want to be treated," said Ms. Smith, "the world would be a better place."*

Commas and periods at the end of quotations are always placed inside the quotation marks, even if they are not part of the quote.

Apostrophes

Apostrophes are used to make a noun possessive.

For example: The coat is Abby's.

Apostrophes are also used in contractions.

> **Example**
>
> *Cannot = can't*
>
> *Do not = don't.*

Objective 0008: Understand skills and strategies involved in speaking, listening, and viewing across the curriculum.

For example:

- applying knowledge of conventions of one-on-one and group verbal interactions

- analyzing ways in which verbal cues and nonverbal cues affect communication in various situations

- demonstrating knowledge of strategies for promoting effective listening skills

- recognizing types, characteristics, and roles of visual and oral media

- demonstrating knowledge of the structures and elements of oral, visual, and multimedia presentations for diverse audiences and for various purposes

Objective eight focuses on concepts related to speaking, listening and viewing. Listening talking and viewing are involved in all learning in all areas of the curriculum. Concepts related to oral and visual language are taught explicitly and incidentally through instruction in the other parts of language arts. They are also taught and reinforced in activities such as classroom routines (following directions, conversations and discussions).

Language uses a complex system for creating meaning through socially shared conventions. During the first months of life, babies are active listeners. Long before they can respond orally they communicate nonverbally by waving their arms, smiling or wiggling. They are also capable of communicating their needs and wants through non-verbal communication, including body language and crying. Through listening they develop the receptive language needed to begin communicating orally.

Oral communication then becomes the foundation for literacy. Proficiency in oral language can lead to success in written language. Therefore, speaking, listening and viewing are important parts of the elementary curriculum.

Learning opportunities in oral language should include a range of activities. These include informal conversations, projects involving cooperative learning, drama and role-play, storytelling and read-aloud, as well as oral language to both present information (oral reports, etc) and gain information (listening to instruction, viewing videos, etc).

While children have acquired basic oral language by the time they come to school, it is important to reinforce the basic concepts of verbal interactions. This includes things such as:

1. Asking and answering relevant questions

2. Displaying appropriate turn-taking behaviors

3. Speaking in appropriate volume and speed

4. Staying on topic

5. Actively soliciting the comments or opinions of others

6. Offering one's own opinion forcefully without being domineering

7. Providing reasons in support of opinions expressed

8. Clarifying, illustrating or expanding on a response when asked to do so

9. Employing a group decision-making technique such as brainstorming or a problem-solving sequence (e.g., recognizes problem, defines problem, identifies possible solutions, selects optimal solution, implements solutions, evaluates solution)

Both verbal and nonverbal cues are also important when communicating. Speakers use a variety of cues that help focus attention on important information. For example:

1. Emphasizes important information with words such as *you need to know. . . , let me emphasize. . .* , or *let me repeat. . .* to provide emphasis for important information.

2. Provides organizational cues such as *first we will. . . , next. . . , lastly. . . , or in review. . .*

3. Provides emphasis on information by repeating phrases, stressing key words, speak more slowly or more loudly, etc.

Nonverbal communication ranges from facial expression to body language. Gestures, signs, and use of space are also important in nonverbal communication. Multicultural differences in body language, facial expression, use of space, and especially, gestures, are enormous and can be open to misinterpretation. Helping children become aware of these can increase listening comprehension.

Listening Strategies

Listening strategies vary depending on purpose. Strategies for aesthetic listening differ from those used for efferent or critical listening.

Students listen aesthetically to stories or poems read aloud or view plays or videotapes of stories. Strategies for aesthetic listening include those such as:

- activating prior knowledge

- making predictions that help them anticipate upcoming story events, listening to confirm or reject predictions

- visualizing the story elements such as the characters or setting

- summarizing or retelling a story to reinforce the story elements

- reflecting on what was heard by writing about the story in a journal or discussing the story. This helps students make connections between the story and their lives, or other stories they have heard.

Students listen for efferent purposes as they listen to informational books read aloud, videos or informational presentations. The focus is on listening to take away information so the comprehension strategies are similar to those used for reading content area texts.

Efferent listening strategies such as organizing, summarizing, note-taking and monitoring are important. Teaching students to listen for the verbal and nonverbal cues discussed above are vital. Students should also be taught to using visual aids such as pictures or graphic organizers such as charts, diagrams, or boxes as important sources of information.

Critical listening skills are also important. We are exposed to much persuasion through commercials, politics, etc. Critical thinking is important in other areas of the curriculum as students learn about science, social studies and other areas of the curriculum as well. Teaching critical listening should involve lessons in propaganda and deceptive language.

Viewing and Visually Representing

Children learn through viewing from a very early age. According to Cox (2008), the United States is the most mass-mediated country in the world. Media is also an important component of effective communication. As with critical listening, critical viewing is important.

Multimedia presentations provide visual methods for enhancing the communication of factual information through the use of graphics, sound clips, video clips in order to deliver a message. Cox (pp. 427-428) presents a range of steps important in producing effective media. These include:

- Envisioning—discovering ideas and visions
- Arranging—brainstorming and recording ideas using graphic organizers such as webs, drawings and note taking.
- Storyboarding—breaking up the ideas into meaningful chunks of images and action
- Producing—use of storyboard to guide production
- Editing—through the camera or camcorder
- Presenting—publicizing the created piece

According to Cox, "participation in viewing and visually representing activities such as media, the visual arts, and drama performance provides great opportunities for developing language and literacy, communicating in social contexts, learning across the curriculum, and experiencing personal growth and development" p. (440).

References

Bear, D., Invernizzi, M., Templeton, S. & Johnston, F. (2007). *Words their way: Word study for phonics, vocabulary and spelling instruction.* (4th ed.). Upper Saddle River, NJ: Pearson.

Beck, I., McKeown, M., & Kucan, L. (2002). *Bringing words to life: Robust vocabulary instruction.* New York: Guilford Press.

Cox, C. (2008). *Teaching language arts: A student-centered classroom.* (6th ed.). Boston: Allyn & Bacon.

Davis, A. (2004). *Reading instruction essentials.* (3rd ed.). Boston: American Press.

Fox, B. (2010). *Phonics and structural analysis for the teacher of reading: Programmed for self-instruction.* (10th ed.). Boston: Allyn & Bacon.

Norton, D. & Norton, S. (2007). *Through the eyes of a child: An introduction to children's literature.* (7th ed.). Upper Saddle River, NJ: Pearson.

Report of the National Reading Panel. Teaching Children to Read: An Evidence-Based Assessment of the Scientific Research Literature on Reading and Its Implications for Reading Instruction. National Institute of Child Health and Human Development. (April 2000).

Spandel, V. (2008). *Creating young writers: Using the six traits to enrich writing process in primary classrooms.* (2nd ed.). Boston: Allyn & Bacon.

Tompkins, G. (2004). *Literacy for the 21st century: Teaching reading and writing in grades 4 through 8.* Upper Saddle River, NJ: Pearson.

Tompkins, G. (2007). *Literacy for the 21st century: Teaching reading and writing in pre-kindergarten through grade 4.* (2nd ed.). Upper Saddle River, NJ: Pearson.

Tompkins, G. (2008). *Teaching writing: Balancing process and product.* (5th ed.). Upper Saddle River, NJ: Pearson.

Tompkins, G. (2009). *Language arts: Patterns of practice.* (7th ed.). Upper Saddle River, NJ: Pearson.

Vacca, J., Vacca, R, Gove, M., Burkey, L., Lenhart, L., & McKeon, C. (2009). *Reading and learning to read.* (7th ed.). Boston: Allyn & Bacon.

DFCS - DEKALB CNTY MAIN
2300 PARKLAKE DRIVE
ATLANTA GA 30345
1-877-423-4746

GEORGIA DEPARTMENT OF HUMAN SERVICES
Division of Family and Children Services

NOTICE OF MISSED APPOINTMENT

000235
MARSHEA MASON
5918 HERITAGE WALK
LITHONIA GA 30058-3896

Case Number: T2392518
Client ID: 743040693

DATE: 01/06/2021

Report Medicaid Fraud: 1-800-533-0686

Recently you were asked to have an interview with us which was scheduled on 01/06/2021.

(Rev 06/16)

Social Studies

The Social Studies portion of the GACE Early Childhood Education Assessment covers principles, and methods of inquiry related to history, geography, U.S. government and civics, and economics. It comprises approximately 20 selected-response (multiple-choice questions) and 1 constructed-response assignment.

This chapter is designed to prepare you for the Social Studies portion of Test I. You will be guided through a review of the content related to the test objectives. In addition, you will learn a helpful approach to reading and analyzing social studies questions. By studying this review, you will greatly increase your chances of achieving a good score on the Social Studies portion of the GACE Early Childhood Education Assessment.

GACE Social Studies Objectives

The more you know about the skills tested, the better you will perform on the Social Studies test. The following list includes the objectives over which you will be tested:

- 0009   Understand important events, concepts, and methods of inquiry related to Georgia, U.S., and world history.

- 0010   Understand major concepts, principles, and methods of inquiry related to geography.

- 0011   Understand major concepts, principles, and methods of inquiry related to U.S. government and civics.

- 0012   Understand major concepts, principles, and methods of inquiry related to economics.

We will examine each of the objectives more closely. This section will include a review of the important aspects of each objective.

Objective 0009   Understand important events, concepts, and methods of inquiry related to Georgia, U.S., and world history.

In 1992 the Board of Directors of the National Council for the Social Studies defined Social Studies as the integrated study of humanities and the social sciences to promote civic competence. The main purpose of social studies is to help students develop the ability to make informed decisions for the public good as citizens of a culturally diverse, democratic society in an interdependent world. Social studies encompasses many disciplines, including history, geography, government and civics, and economics. The Georgia Performance Standards for Social Studies were designed to "develop informed Georgia citizens who understand the history of the United States and our place in an ever increasing interconnected world" (Georgia Department of Education, 2007). These standards were built around the belief that students must understand the past and how the past influences the present day and the future.

Objective 0009 involves the understanding of important events, concepts and methods of inquiry related to Georgia, U.S., and world history. Specifically, the objective includes: demonstrating knowledge of diverse people, events, issues, and developments; demonstrating knowledge of early Native American cultures; recognizing chronological relationships among the historical events; analyzing various perspectives, interpretations, and implications of the events, issues and developments; and, demonstrating knowledge of strategies and resources for historical inquiry.

Diverse people, events, issues, and developments in Georgia, U.S., and world history

It is important to demonstrate knowledge of the significant and lasting influence of diverse people, events, issues, and developments in the state of Georgia, the United States of America, and the world. Some examples of events and issues include slavery, the roots of democracy, the westward expansion, the Civil War, World Wars I and II, the Cold War, and the civil rights movement.

History of Georgia

The history of Georgia includes fifteen phases (London, 1999) and is tied to events that shaped American history and the world:

- Georgia's Earliest People

- European Exploration and the Colonization of Georgia

- The Royal Colony of Georgia and the Revolutionary War

- Georgia in the New Country

- Native Americans and Removal from Georgia

- Slavery and Days Before the Civil War

- The Civil War

- Reconstruction

- The New South: Southern Progress in the late 1800's

- Reform and the Progressive Era

- The fight for Civil Rights

- The Great Depression and World War II

- Changes after World War II and the Civil Rights Movement

- Protests, Changes and the End of the Twentieth Century

- The New Century

The first phase includes the study of Georgia's earliest people. The prehistoric culture would include the Paleo Indians, the Archaic Indians, the Woodland Indians, and the Mississippian Indians. The study would also include the Cherokee and the Creek Indian tribes, the largest early tribes in the area of what is now the state of Georgia.

The second phase, European Exploration and the Colonization of Georgia, includes the early explorations of Georgia by the Europeans such as Hernando de Soto. It also involves the colonization of Georgia by the English explorer, James Edward Oglethorpe. Oglethorpe and a group of settlers landed near the mouth of the Savannah River. Central to Georgia's colonization were two indigenous actors: Chief Tomochichi and Mary Musgrove. Mary Musgrove, born to a Creek Indian mother and an English trader, worked as the interpreter for Ogelthorpe in his negotiations with Chief Tomochichi of the Yamacraw Indians.

The third phase includes Georgia being made a Royal Colony and the period leading up to and including the Revolutionary War as it was fought in Georgia. Georgia was the thirteenth colony to declare independence from Great Britain, and several battles were fought in Georgia, including the Battle of Kettle Creek.

Georgia in the new country, the fourth phase, includes the years of hardship after the Revolutionary War, the War of 1812, economic development in Georgia, and Georgian life at the turn of the 19th century. The invention of the cotton gin in the 1700's by Eli Whitney and the invention of the mechanical reaper revolutionized farming, in the South.

The fifth phase is the story of the removal of Native Americans from Georgia at the beginning of the 1800's. Until 1828, the Cherokee and Creek Indians and colonists lived together in Georgia exchanging cultural information and building relationships. Once gold was discovered in the Northern Georgia mountains, and Indian land was coveted by colonists, the push to remove the Indians took on a new immediacy. In 1838, in one the saddest episodes of our history, the Cherokee were forcibly removed from their land in Georgia and marched over a thousand miles to Oklahoma on what is known as the *Trail of Tears*.

The antebellum period, the time just before the Civil War, and the institution of slavery comprises the sixth phase. The issues leading to the Civil War and the secession of Georgia from the Union in 1861 are covered. Key individuals during this period include Frederick Douglass, Harriet Tubman, Dred Scott, and John Brown, among others.

The seventh phase illustrates the central role Georgia played in the Civil War. Many of the war's most fierce and bloody battles were fought on Georgia soil. Georgia was left devastated by Sherman's "March to the Sea." This phase includes key events and people from 1861 until 1865.

The eighth phase includes post-Civil War Georgia, which was in ruins. Georgians faced famine, drought and anarchy. Georgia's government was bankrupt and owed the Confederacy $18 million. Under the orders of the occupying Union army, Confederate Georgia was abolished and President Johnson appointed a governor. The federal government required a repeal of the secession ordinance; the abolition of slavery; repudiation of $18 million debt to the Confederate government; and recognition of the federal government as supreme. Reconstruction (1865–1877) went through several incarnations, first as the *Presidential Reconstruction* overseen by President Johnson. But the Republicans in Congress had their own definition of reconstruction (*Congressional Reconstruction*), which included ratifying the 14th Amendment; giving black males the right to vote; and once black males could vote, electing a new state government.

The ninth phase was the era of the New South, the time after Reconstruction. Post-Reconstruction Georgia was controlled by a triumvirate of powerful politicians—the so called **Bourbon Triumvirate** of Joseph E. Brown, General John B. Gordon and General Alfred H. Colquitt. Between 1872 and 1890, either Brown or Gordon held one of Georgia's Senate seats, Colquitt held the other, and, in the major part of that period, either Colquitt or Gordon occupied the Governor's office. **Freedmen** (the popular term for former slaves) faced a bitter world, especially from the (formerly) wealthy plantation owners and white political infrastructure. After the war, planter-freedman relationships were far more adversarial than the pre-war master-slave relationships. Former slaves refused to work the long hours, before dawn to after dusk, for the pittance of wages they were offered. Conflict was the only possible result since planters typically wanted a work force that was pliable and freedmen wanted autonomy.

The tenth phase, The Progressive Era (1890s – 1920s) in Georgia, heralded political, economic, and social changes in science, technology, and medicine. The telephone, the phonograph, the automobile, and the x-ray changed the cultural landscape. In the state of Georgia, corporate institutions of notable worth began to to take root, with Coca-Cola as an iconic example. While there were deep divisions within the Democratic Party, there was one theme on which almost all Georgians agreed: segregation, and more importantly, white supremacy. Lynching provided the means to maintain the supremacy of white Georgians. Between Reconstruction and the start of the 20th century, Georgia frequently led the country in the number of people lynched. The **Ku Klux Klan**, an organization that fed on hate and whose main goal during reconstruction was white supremacy, virtually disappeared because the post-construction South was segregated by race after the 1870's. But terror was still an effective means of subjugation.

The late 1800's and the early 1900's, the eleventh phase, also saw a new era of Civil Rights. There arose the practice of convict leasing, where a company could lease prisoners and pay them meager wages, while keeping them ill-fed and poorly clothed. Most of the women and men in the convict-leasing program were black. Women suffered sexual abuse at the hands of the guards and it wasn't until Rebecca Latimer Felton called attention to the program that a commission was formed to investigate and the practice eventually was stopped. Not surprisingly, with reforms came a reaction from the white populace in the form of Jim Crow laws in Georgia and other states. At the start of the 20th century, Georgia was a strictly segregated society, emboldened by the Supreme Court's 1896 ruling in Plessy v. Ferguson that held that segregation was legal. Although blacks and sympathetic whites immediately began to chisel away at the ruling, African-Americans would have to wait another 70 years for the equality that had been constitutionally guaranteed them since 1868.

The twelfth stage encompasses the Great Depression and World War II. Throughout the first two quarters of the twentieth-century, Georgia would remain a rural, agricultural based society with relatively little wealth, almost all of which existed in the larger metropolitan areas. This period encompasses the mid-1920's until the late 1940's, including the Stock Market Crash, the election of Franklin Roosevelt and the New Deal, World War II, the Holocaust, and the attack on Pearl Harbor, the U.S. dropping of two atomic bombs on Japan, and the end of the war. The Nazi Holocaust involved the systematic state-sponsored murder of Jews and others.

World War II brought cultural changes to Georgia, as well as to the rest of the United States. Just as in World War I, World War II brought mass migration of African-Americans from the South to the North. Over 1.5 million African-Americans left states like Georgia for the industrial cities of the North. The Great Migration affected cities like Detroit where there was a promise of jobs and a new life. Competition for jobs and housing brought new tensions between whites and African-Americans and race riots ensued. The worst of the riots was in Detroit in June 1943.

The thirteenth phase, from the mid-1940's through the mid-1960's, involved cultural changes including the invention of and the popularity of the television; the rise of suburbia; and the push for civil rights. Having made minimal gains during the war, African-Americans were unwilling give up from those gains. The National Association for the Advancement of Colored People (NAACP) successfully challenged covenants requiring segregation in housing, interstate transport, and public facilities. Reverend Martin Luther King, Jr. emerged as one of the leaders of a powerful non-violent movement to desegregate the South. The Civil Rights Act was passed in 1964, and then the Voting Rights Act of 1965 which eliminated qualifying tests for voting such as poll taxes.

The end of the 1960s and the early 1970s, the fourteenth phase, included the struggle for women's rights and protests against the Vietnam War. In 1976, Jimmy Carter, former Governor of Georgia, became the first Georgian to be elected President of the United States. In the 1970s, as Atlanta's black population became a majority in the city, African Americans were elected to high office, including Andrew Young to the U.S. Congress in 1972 and Maynard Jackson to the mayor's office in 1973. Since then, African Americans have been elected to many offices in Atlanta and in southwestern Georgia. By the end of the twentieth century Georgia was one of the fastest growing states in the country.

The fifteenth phase encompasses the 1980s and onward into the first decade of the 21st century. The election of 1980 sent Carter back to Georgia where he and his wife, Rosalynn, founded the Carter Center in 1982. The center's mission reflected President and Mrs. Carter's passion for "advancing human rights and alleviating unnecessary human suffering." In 2002, Carter was awarded the Nobel Peace Prize for his work on behalf of human rights. He is the only President to win the prize after leaving office.

Georgia's prosperity in the late 20th and early 21st century was based mainly in the service sector and largely in and around Atlanta, due to its superior rail and air connections. Atlanta is home to the state's major utilities as well as the banking, food and beverage, and information technology industries. More than a century after the trademark "Coca-Cola" was registered to the Coca-Cola Company, Atlanta is recognized as one of the country's leading locations for corporate headquarters. Atlanta's image as a progressive city and its rapid economic and population growth propelled Georgia ahead of other states of the Deep South in terms of economic prosperity and convergence with national socioeconomic norms. The state continues to be a leader in the southern region.

History of the United States of America

The First Americans

European exploration began in earnest after Christopher Columbus landed in the New World in 1492. The Americas may have been "new" to Europeans, but indigenous peoples had been thriving in communities for thousands of years. The Paleo Culture was the earliest known collection of human beings in the New World. Most believe that they had crossed the land bridge from Siberia to Alaska. Much later (800 BCE–600 CE), groups such as the Adena-Hopewell Indians, who are known for creating large burial mounds and using metal tools, traded and moved across a large expanse of North America. The Mesoamerican civilizations (including the Mayans and the Aztecs) occupied Central America and much of Mexico. These peoples developed a strong agricultural system and extensive trade networks, followed a solar calendar, and participated in highly ritualistic religious and political ceremonies. The Aztecs founded present-day Mexico City in 1325. Spanish explorers, such as Juan Ponce de Leon, Ferdinand Magellan, and Vasco Núñez de Balboa sailed to Central and South America, and parts of North America. By 1519, when the Spanish explorer Hernan Cortés arrived in Mexico, the Aztec ruler Montezuma II reigned over 5 million people. There were over more tahn 30,000 indigenous people living in the land East of the Mississippi when Europeans first began exploring the continent. The Cherokee and Creek Indians were two of the Five Civilized Tribes to live peacefully on their ancestral lands in Georgia.

Explorers, Settlement, and Development in North America

Many European nations began aggressive exploration of the Americas in the late 15th century. The French were interested in establishing lucrative trade routes and formed close allegiances with many indigenous tribes to achieve this goal. The Spanish, interested primarily in precious metals, controlled much of Central and South America. The British worked to control the East Coast of North America for permanent territorial expansion.

Colonization, Jamestown, and the Massachusetts Bay Colony

In 1607, the London Group of the Virginia Company established the first English settlement at Jamestown, Virginia. Motivated by economic interest, these early settlers spent most of their time prospecting for gold and failed to adequately prepare for the winter months. Consequently, many Jamestown settlers did not survive and the settlement had difficulty thriving in the harsh realities of the New World.

The Pilgrims established a more successful settlement in New England's Massachusetts Bay Colony, by harnessing the strict work ethic embedded within their stringent religious convictions. The Pilgrims, known in England before their departure as Puritans, were an austere religious group influenced by the teachings of John Calvin. The Puritans fled the religious persecution of King George and landed in Plymouth on December 25, 1619. Before disembarking from the Mayflower, the Pilgrims signed the *Mayflower Compact*, an agreement whereby all signatories would follow the rules established by majority vote; the Compact was both a symbol of the democratic governance to come in America and considered by many to be the first constitution ratified in the colonies.

By 1733 the original 13 American colonies had been established, with Georgia as the 13th. Colonies such as Maryland, Rhode Island, and Pennsylvania were known for their religious tolerance, while colonies such as the Carolinas and Georgia prospered through the production of rice and tobacco, and many of the northern colonies participated in the manufacturing and trade of textiles.

Even as the colonies grew, the British Government continued to wield great influence over them as it was in Parliament's interest to control and expand British rule in America. Simultaneously, the British had to contend with other European powers interested in continued American conquest. These tensions came to a head during the French and Indian War (1754–1763) when the British fought the French and their native allies for control of North America. This protracted war resulted in British supremacy and control of North America.

The Slave Trade

Shortage of labor in the southern colonies and a drop in the number of people coming to the colonies as indentured servants forced the colonists to search for other sources of labor. Toward the end of the seventeenth century, larger numbers of Africans were enslaved and shipped to the New World. By the nineteenth century, millions of Africans had been taken from their native lands and sold into slavery. Slaves were packed into the lower regions of ships for the long transatlantic journey to the Americans. Many of them died during what has come to be known as the Middle Passage. After 1697, the English colonists began to buy large numbers of slaves and slave labor replaced the indentured servitude. Slave codes, a set of laws that protected slave owners and their property from rebellions and identified all non-whites or dark skinned people as slaves, were passed in the eighteenth century.

Religion and the Great Awakening

The *First Great Awakening* took the form of a wave of religious revivals that began in New England in the 1730's and swept across the colonies during the1740's. In the southern colonies, many slaves were converted to Christianity. Itinerant ministers advocated an emotional approach to religious practice, finding the established churches too rational in their practices. These evangelical, or "New Light," Presbyterian ministers promoted the growth of New Light institutions of higher learning, such as Princeton University, then known as the College of New Jersey. The divisions between the "Old Light" and "New Light" practices affected both the Presbyterian and Congregational churches, resulting in growing religious diversity within the colonies. The most significant effect of the First Great Awakening is that it was the first national event that affected all of the colonies.

In Georgia, German Protestants, known as **Salzburgers**, began a town called Ebenezer, now known as New Ebenezer. The town was laid out in a plan similar to that of Savannah. By 1741, the town had grown to a population of 1,200. The Salzburgers were successful in agriculture, cattle raising, lumbering, and silk culturing. These early settlers built the first saw mill in Georgia on Ebenezer Creek (1735); the first orphanage at New Ebenezer (1737), and the first rice and grist mill in the Georgia colony. The Salzburgers also established the first Sunday school in Georgia in 1734.

The Enlightenment

As the 18th century progressed, Americans were influenced by European thinking, culture, and society. Some Americans embraced the European intellectual movement known as the "Enlightenment." The key concept of the Enlightenment was rationalism—the belief that human reason was adequate to solve all of mankind's problems and, correspondingly, much less faith was needed in the central role of God as an active force in the universe.

A major English political philosopher of the Enlightenment was John Locke. Writing partially to justify England's 1688 Glorious Revolution, he strove to find in the social and political world the sort of natural laws Isaac Newton had recently discovered in the physical realm. He held that such natural laws included the rights of life, liberty, and property; that to secure these rights people submit to governments; and that governments which abuse these rights may justly be overthrown. His writings were enormously influential in America, though usually indirectly, by way of early 18th-century English political philosophers. The Enlightenment brought more focus on education and more schools and colleges were established. The Enlightenment drove scientific inquiry; Benjamin Franklin, for example, experimented with electricity and other aspects of science.

The American Revolution

After the Treaty of Paris in 1763 ended the French and Indian War, the British government's purse was heavily drained and the colonists' sense of total dependence on the British Army for protection was lessened. The preceding decade of war gave the colonists their first taste of quasi-independence, thanks to the wartime policy of *salutary neglect*, whereby the colonies operated and grew relatively unsupervised while the British were busy fighting off French forces. Through this strategic neglect, colonists began to depend and build upon their own resources for self-defense and small-scale self-government. When Parliament sought to defray the debts of war through a system of heavy direct and indirect taxation, the colonists' feelings of resentment for the heavy-handed legislation grew, fostering an urgent desire for independence from Britain.

The Stamp Act of 1765 imposed a direct tax on documents such as wills, marriage licenses, newspapers, and playing cards. It was enacted to help support the cost of British troops in the colonies. The subsequent "Stamp Act Congress" of the same year convened to protest this taxation and seek its repeal. The colonists were successful in their efforts and this small victory built self-confidence and an even greater desire for self-rule. In spite of the growing trend towards rebellion in the colonies, the British continued to tax, and colonists continued to dissent, protest, and subvert. The Declaratory Act and the Townshend Acts imposed more taxes on the colonists. A group called the *Sons of Liberty* formed to boycott British goods and organize protests. Samuel Adams was a founder of the Sons of Liberty. In March 1770, the Boston Massacre occurred. Tensions came to a head when a crowd of colonists in Boston—after harassing guards at the city's Customs House—were fired upon, making martyrs for the radical cause out of five men (including Crispus Attucks, a runaway Mulatto slave and one of the first patriotic heroes of the revolutionary cause) and wounding many others. In 1773, in a symbolic and purposefully incendiary act, colonists threw imported tea overboard into Boston Harbor, refusing to pay even reduced taxes to the British Government. This event is known as the Boston Tea Party. Parliament's response was to pass the Coercive Acts—known as the Intolerable Acts among patriots—which closed the port city of Boston until the tea had been paid for, increased the power of Massachusetts' royalist officials, and allowed for the quartering of troops anywhere. The Americans in turn called the First Continental Congress in 1774, a meeting where the attendants collectively called for a repeal of the Intolerable Acts and the immediate formation and gathering of local militias.

In April of 1775, the very first battle of the Revolution was fought at Lexington and Concord in Lexington, Massachusetts. The British had learned that the Patriots had stockpiled weapons in Concord, Massachusetts, and sent approximately 800 troops to seize the munitions. Upon learning of this secret attack, the Patriots sent three men on horseback to sound the warning. They were Paul Revere, William Dawes, and Dr. Samuel Prescott. In June, the Battle of Bunker Hill was in actuality fought on Breed's Hill in Boston. The Second Continental Congress convened in 1775, and eventually American independence was declared (and officially adopted through the Declaration of Independence, largely attributed to the work of Thomas Jefferson) on July 4, 1776.

A number of key developments precipitated the foundation of the National Government. The language in the Declaration of Independence was based on the philosophical argumentation of John Locke, who believed government should inherit powers from the people. Not wanting to recreate the centralized powers of the British government (the very powers the colonists had rebelled against), Americans designed a government that vested significant power in individual citizens.

New Governments: Articles of Confederation and the U.S. Constitution

Before independence had been achieved, important actions that eventually led to the signing of the Constitution had been set in motion. Written in 1777, but not ratified until 1781, the Articles of Confederation provided the first constitution for the fledgling nation. However, the Articles allowed each state too much freedom, creating a weak central government. In western Massachusetts, Shays' Rebellion (1786), in which poor farmers revolted against existing conditions, helped spur the development of a more unified Constitution that would broadened the powers of the national government. Soon after General George Washington and the colonial army defeated the British in 1787, delegates met in Philadelphia for the Constitutional Convention.

The delegates worked for two summers drafting our current national Constitution. Once finalized, supporters of the new Constitution, such as Alexander Hamilton and James Madison, circulated the *Federalist Papers* to rally support for the Constitution in the colonies. In 1791, the Bill of Rights, which enumerated rights of citizens such as freedom of speech and the right to a fair trial, was appended to the Constitution. By the end of 1791, all 13 colonies had ratified the new national constitution.

The War of 1812

Native American tribes of the Northwest and the Mississippi Valley were resentful of the government's policy of pressured removal to the West. The British authorities in Canada exploited their discontent by encouraging border raids against the American settlements. The British also interfered with American transatlantic shipping, including capturing ships and impressing sailors. President Madison asked for a declaration of war on June 1, 1812 and Congress complied. After three years of war, the British and Americans signed the Treaty of Ghent (1815). This treaty provided for the acceptance of the status quo that had existed at the beginning of hostilities, and both sides restored their wartime conquests to the other.

Manifest Destiny and Westward Expansion

In 1803, although the United States was still a young and somewhat unformed nation, the purchase of the Louisiana Territory from France (the Louisiana Purchase) reflected an ambitious agenda of territorial expansion. Thomas Jefferson's purchase of this land from Napoleon basically guaranteed uninhibited exploration and expansion beyond the Mississippi River. The following year (1804), Lewis and Clark embarked on a highly successful government-funded expedition of the new territory — in the name of scientific and geographic research.

In 1823, President James Monroe issued the Monroe Doctrine, a declaration that both asserted the new nation's dominance in the Western Hemisphere and instructed European nations to cease their interference on the American continents. Along with a focus on expanding boundaries for the sake of strengthening the economy and the international clout of the nation, Manifest Destiny—a sort of divine justification for moving westward into new lands—drove many individuals and their families to seek new lives, land, and opportunities in the unsettled West. While many Americans trail-blazed their way into new towns, settlements, and territories, millions of Native Americans were displaced, coerced into signing treaties, and forced to surrender their lands to the American government.

The question of whether to allow slavery in newly settled territories led to the Missouri Compromise of 1820. In this series of Congressional bills, Maine was admitted to the Union as a free state and Missouri as a slave state, to preserve the balance of slave and free states. Slavery would be prohibited in any future state created from the Louisiana Purchase, north of the 36° 30′ parallel, Missouri's southern border.

Native Americans and The Indian Removal Act

The Indian Removal Act of 1830 marked the first major legislative departure from the policy of officially respecting the legal and political rights of the American Indians. The act authorized the removal of Indian tribes from their desirable territories within state borders most notably those in the Southeast. Once gold was discovered in the mountains of Georgia and land east of the Mississippi was rapidly settled, it was clear that white Americans would not tolerate even peaceable Indians in competition for land. The Indian Tribes were granted unsettled Western prairie land in exchange for their valued homesteads. President Andrew Jackson, known as a great Indian-fighter, vigorously promoted this new policy. And while the Act provided only for the negotiation with tribes east of the Mississippi and required payment for their lands, the United States resorted to force to gain the Indians' compliance to accept the offer and move West.

Several northern tribes were peacefully resettled in the West, but in the Southeast members of the Five Civilized Tribes (Chickasaw, Choctaw, Seminole, Cherokee, and Creek) refused to trade their cultivated farms for the promise of strange land in the Indian Territory, even though they were promised permanent title to that land. These Indians lived in homes, had representative government, children in missionary schools, and trades other than farming. Over 100,000 tribesmen were forced to march westward under U.S. military coercion in the 1830's; up to 25 percent of the Indians, many in manacles, perished en route. The trek of the Cherokee in 1838–39 became known as the infamous *Trail of Tears*. Even more reluctant to leave their native lands were the Seminole Indians of Florida who fought resettlement for seven years in the second of the Seminole Wars. And, as the frontier pushed aggressively westward, the "guaranteed" titles to the western lands were no longer guaranteed.

Slavery and the Civil War

In 1849, westward expansion was driven by the search for gold, discovered in California. The gold rush greatly expanded the state's population and led California to apply for admission to the union as a free state. Due to Southern concern for the growing inevitability of Northern—and therefore free-state—control, this application sparked a crisis which led to the Compromise of 1850, a law that allowed new territories to decide the matter of slavery for themselves, based on the principle of "popular sovereignty." In further debates over the expansion of slavery into the territories, the Illinois Senator Stephen A. Douglas argued in the Kansas-Nebraska Act that any territory desiring to exclude slavery could do so simply by declining to pass laws to protect it. Abraham Lincoln—who became both a Unionist and the President of the United States in 1860—while not advocating the abolition of slavery, argued that the country must restrict slavery's extension into the territories. The controversy continued in the aforementioned Kansas-Nebraska Act of 1854, which repealed the Missouri Compromise and allowed the people of those territories to decide for or against slavery by popular sovereignty. Fierce fighting later broke out in Kansas as pro- and anti-slavery forces battled for control. The nation's controversy over the issue of slavery was only heightened by the passage of the Fugitive Slave Act of 1850 and the Dred Scott Case of 1857. At the passage of the Fugitive Slave Act, many northerners and abolitionists were outraged, as the law required citizens to capture and return escaped slaves, under penalty of fine and imprisonment, without the option of a jury trial. In the case of the former slave Dred Scott, the Supreme Court ruled that slaves who resided temporarily in free states or territories were still slaves, and that Congress did not have the authority to exclude slavery from a territory. According to the ruling, a person only became a free citizen of the United States through birth or the process of naturalization. Tension continued to brew between the North and South as the balance of power remained precarious and unstable, and in 1861, eleven southern states seceded from the Union with the intention of forming their own nation and government, known as the Confederacy.

On April 12, 1861, confederate troops fired on Union-held Fort Sumter in Charleston, South Carolina, thereby marking the official beginning of the Civil War. At its outbreak, both the Union and the Confederacy held desirable advantages. The northern states had a larger population and greater control of factories, industries and railroads. On the other hand, the Southern states were defending territory largely unfamiliar to Union forces.

During the first year of war confederate forces won several battles. However, the Battle of Gettysburg in 1863 marked a turning point, as the Confederate Army sustained a crippling loss of manpower in only two days. In that same year, another blow was dealt to the South when President Lincoln issued the Emancipation Proclamation, declaring that all slaves residing within the Confederacy would be free. Later, this freedom would be extended to all slaves living within the United States. African American soldiers were allowed to enlist after the Emancipation Proclamation. The 54th Massachusetts Infantry was an African American regiment led by Colonel Robert Gould Shaw. As the war raged on and hundreds of thousands of men lost their lives, Union troops, under the leadership of General William Tecumseh Sherman, blazed a ruthless path of destruction through the states of Georgia and South Carolina, working in tandem with the strategies of Union Commander Ulysses S. Grant and draining the resources and supplies of the Confederate Army. As Union soldiers surrounded the South Carolina capital of Richmond, Confederate General Robert E. Lee was finally forced to surrender to General Grant at Appomattox Courthouse on April 9, 1865.

Casualties of the Civil War numbered upwards of 600,000, devastated many areas and the economy of the South, and left bitter and lingering resentment. President Abraham Lincoln was assassinated by John Wilkes Booth just three days after the Confederate surrender. Violence against and oppression of former slaves continued, equality was not proffered as promised, and decades of reconstruction for the entire country—on every level—were necessary to repair the rifts and forge both new regional and national identities.

The Reconstruction Era

While the Civil War raged across southern soil, the economy of the South was weakening and eventually collapsed. This physical and geographical, psychological and economic, devastation led to the period known as *Reconstruction* (1865–77). Before the war officially ended, President Lincoln had announced his plans for Reconstruction. After his assassination, Vice President Andrew Johnson carried out Lincoln's plans with minor changes.

Lincoln's government appointed military governors to temporarily oversee the operations of individual rebel states as they were slowly reincorporated into the Union. The Emancipation Proclamation announced the ruin of the southern economy, as at its crux lay the practice of slavery. There was no money left over after the war effort, and this lack of capital crippled the South's ability to manufacture. Industrialization and the spread of railways—so rampant in northern states—were slow to get going. Many southerners headed west in the search of a new life and greater opportunities.

For the roughly 4 million freed slaves, the reality of a Union victory fell far short of the promises of freedom and equality. In spite of the passage of the Reconstruction Acts, aimed at improving and protecting conditions for former slaves, and the Civil Rights Act of 1866, which officially granted blacks citizenship and denied all states the power to restrict or deny them rights, violent oppression and exploitation continued. The 13th, 14th, and 15th Amendments to the Constitution, which abolished slavery, extended citizenship to blacks, and banned race as a voting condition, respectively, produced little real change.

In the aftermath of the Civil War, bitterness and resentment were vented as hostility and violence, and many blacks lived in fear and lacked almost any improvement in opportunities. It would take years for the impoverished South to rebuild. Meanwhile, the new southern climate, a climate of instability and racial oppression both old and new, continued well into the 20th century.

The first women's rights' meeting was held in Seneca Falls, N.Y., in 1848. Elizabeth Cady Stanton was a featured speaker at the Seneca Falls Convention; she proposed resolutions for women's rights in legal and political matters. Among these resolutions was the issue of *suffrage* (the right to vote). The movement had ardent supporters, but there were also many others who felt that women did not require these rights. Therefore, the Civil Rights Act of 1866 and the 13th through 15th Amendments to the Constitution failed to include Native Americans and women. Later, laws were made more comprehensive and extended to protect all people, regardless of race, color, or sex.

Industrialism, World War I and the Progressive Era

Even while the North and South battled during the Civil War, the seeds of Industrialism were being sown across the country in the form of railroad ties. By 1900, almost 200,000 miles of railroad track crisscrossed the continent, allowing for easy trade and a growing industrialized economy. Urbanization followed industrialization as people relocated to cities, searching out factory jobs.

The American economy rapidly grew, but only a small percentage of the population controlled the newly minted wealth. Industrialists, such as John D. Rockefeller and Andrew Carnegie, created huge and immensely profitable corporations. However, most laborers endured harsh conditions for which they received little pay. As a result, clashes between unions and management became increasingly common.

Elected President in 1900 as a Progressive candidate, much of Theodore Roosevelt's work aimed at restraining corporate monopolies (or trusts) and promoting economic competition. The Progressive Era also attempted a purification of politics, which many believed had become exceedingly corrupt. Journalists, known as muckrakers, exposed corruption and greed. Important political reforms, aimed to challenge the decadence of the Industrial or Gilded Age, included the passage of the income tax laws, prohibition, and women's suffrage.

In 1914, when World War I broke out in Europe, many Americans favored neutrality. However, by 1917 Germany had begun brutal attacks on Britain's merchant ships with submarines called U-boats. After one particular submarine attack in which two Americans were killed, President Woodrow Wilson began lobbying Congress to declare war. Three million U.S. troops were drafted and quickly deployed to European battlefields. Although the U.S entered the war late, America's presence had a decisive impact on the outcome. After the war's end in 1918, Wilson, an idealist, formulated a peace plan to make the world "safe for democracy." This plan included the formation of the League of Nations, an international organization whereby the member nations would unite to ensure peace and security for all. In the end, the United States did not join the League.

The post–World War I period was marked by prosperity. For the first time in U.S. history, suburbs began to grow more rapidly than central cities. New technology, such as streetcars, commuter trains, and automobiles opened the suburbs to working-class families.

After World War I, large numbers of southern and rural blacks began migrating to northern cities to find jobs. Unfortunately, the boom years of the twenties ended just as quickly as they had been ushered in. As the decade progressed, a depressed farm economy, the failure of over 5,700 banks nationwide, a decline in new construction, and other factors culminated in the Great Depression after the stock market crash of October 29, 1929 (commonly known as Black Tuesday).

Women were granted the right to vote in 1919, at the end of World War I. Women's efforts on the home front during World War II had strengthened the case for gender equality, as women assumed men's roles both at home and at work while soldiers fought abroad. Though the return of these soldiers from World War II and the subsequent decade of the 1950s saw a return to more traditional and binding gender roles, by the 1960s—a decade marked by social upheaval—new demands from historically marginalized groups, and mass protestation of the Vietnam War strongly indicated that radical changes were afoot.

Immigration

By the mid-nineteenth century, immigration was recognized as contributing to the nation's growth. Over a million Germans, Irish, and British migrated to the United States by 1850 due to developments in Europe including the *Great Potato Famine* in Ireland. By 1890 immigration patterns changed with the majority of immigrants originating from Italy, Russia, including the Baltic States, Poland, and Finland and Austria-Hungary. Between 1890 and 1920, more than 18 million Europeans immigrated to the United States.

The *Chinese Exclusion Act of 1882* was the first legislation to impose restrictions on immigration. Anti-Chinese sentiment had existed ever since the great migration from China during the gold rush, where white miners and prospectors imposed taxes and laws to inhibit the Chinese from success. Racial tensions increased as more and more Chinese emigrated, occupied jobs, and created competition on the job market. By 1882 the Chinese were hated enough to be banned from immigrating; the Chinese Exclusion Act, initially only a ten-year policy, was extended indefinitely, and made permanent in 1902. In June 1917, Congress imposed a literacy test for immigrants and excluded many Asian nationalities. In 1921 Congress passed the Emergency Quota Act that restricted the immigration of Italians, Greeks, Poles, and eastern European Jews. Congress also passed the National Origins Act of 1924 which reduced the number of southern and eastern European immigrants and cut back their annual immigration total.

The Great Depression and the New Deal

By 1932, 24 percent of the American population was unemployed. Elected in the midst of this crisis, Franklin Roosevelt enacted huge reforms collectively known as the New Deal, including agricultural and business regulation, public works projects, farm relief, and ultimately the establishment of the Social Security system. The New Deal put millions of people back to work and helped turn the struggling economy around; however, many historians credit America's eventual involvement in World War II as the most important aspect of the country's economic turnaround.

World War II

World War II was divided into two large campaigns: the European Campaign and the Pacific Campaign. Between 1938 and 1941, America provided aid to the Allied forces as they fought against the advancing Fascist armies of the Axis powers (Germany, Italy, and Japan). However, since many Americans and politicians supported isolationism, the belief that the U.S. should not participate in war outside of the Western Hemisphere, U.S. troops were not involved in either campaign. Not until after the events of Dec. 7, 1941, when Japanese fighter planes attacked Pearl Harbor, did President Roosevelt lead America directly into the war.

The U.S. achieved major victories in the Pacific campaign at the Battle of Midway (June 1942), Iowa Jima (1945), and Okinawa (1945). American and British troops began their most successful and aggressive push against the still formidable Germany and the other Axis forces on D-Day—June 6, 1944. By the end of the summer the Axis powers had retreated and surrendered.

Once again, the U.S. focus returned to Japan. Back at home, scientists from the *Manhattan Project* had developed the first atomic bomb, which was successfully tested in New Mexico on July 16, 1945. In an attempt to hasten a Japanese surrender and to demonstrate American power to the world, President Truman ordered the use of a single atomic bomb to be dropped on Hiroshima on August 6, 1945. When Japan refused to surrender, a second bomb was dropped on Nagasaki three days later. Japan surrendered the very next day. It has been estimated that about 210,000 people died that year from the effects of the bombs.

Postwar Era, Civil Rights and the Cold War

The term "superpower" was first used to describe America at the end of World War II. Increased industrial output during the war had stimulated the economy, impressive demonstrations of America's military strength as well as nuclear technology had secured the title of "world's greatest army," and—unlike most of Europe and the East—the war had not ravaged American cities and infrastructure. However, the Soviet Union and its allies quickly emerged as challengers to America's "superpower" status. By 1948, Poland, Romania, Bulgaria, Hungary, Albania, and Czechoslovakia had all become part of the growing Soviet block. In September 1949, the Soviets detonated their first nuclear bomb. Cold War tensions led to a rise of anti-communist sentiment at home, leading to the imprisonment of leaders of the American Communist party. Hearings led by Senator Joseph McCarthy, sought to root out supposed communists in government. Abroad, the struggle between communism and capitalism led to the *Truman Doctrine*, which argued that the United States had to support populations who were resisting Communist movements, and to a policy of U.S. opposition to the expansion of communism (the theory of containment).

In the 1950s, the civil rights movement gathered momentum, beginning with the case of *Brown v. Board of Education of Topeka, Kansas*. The National Association for the Advancement of Colored People (NAACP) assigned Thurgood Marshall to the case. He successfully argued on behalf of Brown and against segregation, winning the Supreme Court ruling in 1954 that "separate but equal" public schools were unconstitutional. This move toward desegregation was resisted in many parts of the South, with federal troops being sent in at times to enforce the Supreme Court's decision. The Civil Rights Movement was emboldened after the ruling and campaigned to end segregation entirely. In 1967, President Johnson appointed Thurgood Marshall as the first African American Supreme Court Justice.

Rigid separation along racial lines, and laws supporting such division, had been in place since after the Civil War. Although outlawed in practice, slavery as a cultural institution was still a way of life in the South and the separation of education (and its inherent inequality) can be traced back to the Jim Crow laws, laws which divided practically every aspect of life into two categories: black and white. Lynching was another brutal way used to maintain the status quo because it kept black people in constant fear. These divisive laws and practices, which dominated for decades, lie at the root of the civil rights movement a century later.

Dr. Martin Luther King, Jr., was a Baptist preacher who preached a philosophy of nonviolence. He advocated a peaceful way of protesting against racial injustices by organizing bus boycotts, sit-ins, and freedom rides, which eventually led to the passage of the Civil Rights Act and the Voting Rights Act of 1964 signed by President Lyndon Johnson. The most famous bus boycott was the Montgomery bus boycott of 1955. Rosa Parks, a seamstress and secretary for the NAACP, was arrested for refusing to relinquish her seat in the middle of a bus to a white man. While African Americans were allowed to sit in the middle of the bus, they had to give up their seat to a white person if no other seat was available. Arrested at the next stop, she was charged with violating the segregation laws. Civil rights leaders organized the Montgomery bus boycott as a response to her arrest, whereby over the next year, more than 50,000 African Americans in Montgomery avoided the city bus system until the Supreme Court declared that bus segregation was unconstitutional.

The 1960s saw the true rise of the women's liberation movement. The women's movement gained momentum in 1963 with the publication of Betty Friedan's book *The Feminine Mystique*, which attacked the middle-class "cult of domesticity" and argued that society did not allow women to use their individual talents. The National Organization for Women (NOW), founded in 1966, called for equal employment opportunities and equal pay. It later advocated the Equal Rights Amendment to the Constitution, changes in divorce laws, and the legalization of abortion. The Equal Rights Amendment has not yet passed.

Kennedy's "New Frontier," Vietnam, and Social Unrest

The Presidential election of 1960 pitted Senator John F. Kennedy against Vice President Richard M. Nixon. The campaign marked the first time that debates between presidential candidates were televised. In a series of four debates, Senator Kennedy appeared able, articulate, and energetic. In the campaign, Kennedy spoke of moving aggressively into the new decade, for "the New Frontier is here whether we seek it or not." In his first inaugural address he concluded with an eloquent plea: "Ask not what your country can do for you—ask what you can do for your country." Throughout his brief presidency, Kennedy's special combination of grace, wit and style sustained his popularity and influenced generations of politicians to come.

John F. Kennedy's *New Frontier* and Lyndon B. Johnson's *Great Society* were two of the most comprehensive social policy agendas since the *New Deal*. They sought to solve a number of the problems from poverty and unemployment to discrimination and the Space Race. While they varied in their approaches to these and other issues and the amount of success they had at dealing with those issues, both programs played an important role in shaping American public policy. The United States is what it is today in part thanks to these two programs.

In the Cuban Missile Crisis President Kennedy faced his biggest foreign policy challenge. With photographic evidence of the construction of missile sites in Cuba, President Kennedy announced a blockade of Cuba. He called on the Soviet premier, Khrushchev to dismantle the missile bases and remove all weapons capable of attacking the United States from Cuba. Khrushchev backed down and withdrew the missiles and President Kennedy lifted the blockade.

President Kennedy appointed his brother, Robert Kennedy to serve as the Attorney General. The Justice Department, under the leadership of Robert Kennedy, pushed for civil rights, with desegregation of interstate transportation in the South, integration of schools, and supervision of elections. In a nationally televised address on June 6, 1963, President John F. Kennedy urged the nation to take action toward guaranteeing equal treatment of every American regardless of race. Soon after, Kennedy proposed that Congress consider civil rights legislation that would address voting rights, public accommodations, school desegregation, nondiscrimination in federally assisted programs, and more. On August 28, 1963 civil rights and church organizers brought together over 250,000 protestors to march in support of jobs and freedom. It was here that the Reverend King, still a relatively unknown civil rights activist, gave his "I Have a Dream" speech, which that galvanized the marchers and launched him onto the national stage.

When President Kennedy was assassinated in November 1963, Lyndon Johnson became president. Despite Kennedy's assassination, his proposal culminated in the Civil Rights Act of 1964, signed into law by President Lyndon Johnson just a few hours after House approval on July 2, 1964. It created the Equal Employment Opportunity Commission to enforce the law and eliminated the remaining restrictions on black voting. Reverend King, continued to demonstrate peacefully for civil rights, winning the Nobel Peace Prize in 1965, at the age of 35. In 1968 he was assassinated in Memphis.

Americans were deeply divided over the war in Vietnam. This was the first war that played nightly on television, and therefore came into America's living rooms. Thousands of Americans protested the war. Violent confrontations erupted between National Guard troops and student protestors on college campuses.

When Richard Nixon was elected President in 1968 he increased bombings in Vietnam to try and force the communists to negotiate. However, thousands more were killed and injured in the war. A cease-fire was finally declared in January 1973 after more than

57,000 Americans and 2,000,000 Vietnamese had been killed. On March 29, 1973 the last U.S. combat troops left South Vietnam. The North Vietnamese forces pushed back the South Vietnamese until, in April 1975, Saigon fell to the North Vietnamese. The North Vietnamese government occupies all of the country now.

Watergate, Carter, and the New Conservatism

On June 17, 1972, in the heat of the presidential campaign, a security officer for the Committee for the Reelection of the President, along with four other men, broke into Democratic headquarters at the Watergate apartment complex in Washington, D.C. The men were caught by authorities as they were searching through files and installing electronic eavesdropping devices. Thus began the Watergate scandal that would bring down a presidency. A grand jury indicted several of President Nixon's top aides in March 1974 and President Nixon himself was named as an unindicted co-conspirator. Americans were riveted to television while House Judiciary Committee debated the impeachment of the president. Nixon was charged by the committee with obstructing justice, misusing presidential power, and failing to obey the committee's subpoenas. On August 8, 1974, Nixon announced his resignation, which would take effect at noon the following day. Vice-President Gerald Ford was sworn in as president. On September 8, 1974, President Ford granted Nixon an unconditional pardon, even though Nixon had not been indicted of any crime. Watergate had a serious impact on the American people. The affair led Americans to be more cynical about their government.

James Earl "Jimmy" Carter was the first Georgian to become president of the United States and the first president from the Deep South since the Civil War. He was born in Plains on October 1, 1924, and grew up on his parents' southwest Georgia peanut farm. In 1976 Carter was nominated by the Democrats to run against President Ford. Many Americans were still upset about Watergate and President Ford's pardon of Richard Nixon. Carter ran on the basis of his integrity and lack of Washington connections. Carter narrowly defeated Ford in the election.

President Carter is recognized for meetings he hosted and led at Camp David between leaders of Israel and Egypt which led to the Camp David Accords. President Carter acted as mediator, negotiating the first peace treaty between these two warring nations. In the Accords, which was achieved in 1982, Israel promised to return occupied land in the Sinai to Egypt in exchange for Egyptian recognition. The agreement to negotiate the Palestinian refugee problem proved ineffective, however.

Carter also developed a foreign policy emphasizing world-wide human rights. He negotiated a controversial treaty with Panama that provided for the transfer of ownership of the canal to Panama in 1999 and guaranteed its neutrality.

On November 4, 1979, a mob of Iranian students stormed the U.S. embassy in Tehran and took the diplomatic staff hostage. In April 1980, after months of fruitless negotiations with students and officials of Iran's revolutionary government (which had sanctioned the takeover), Carter ordered a military rescue operation, which failed dramatically. The hostage crisis contributed to a general public perception of the Carter administration as weak and indecisive, and the failed rescue mission reinforced Reagan's charge that the Democrats had allowed the country's military to deteriorate badly. Many blame the Iran hostage crisis for Carter's loss of the 1980 election. The hostages, in fact, were not released until President Reagan's Inauguration Day in January 1981, after extensive negotiations with Iran.

The *New Conservatism* is marked by the election of President Ronald Reagan. Reagan's priority was to cut taxes. His "supply-side" economic approach was meant to leave more money in the hands of the people; they would invest rather than spend the excess on consumer goods. The theory was that greater productivity, more jobs, and greater prosperity would ensue resulting in more income for the government despite lower tax rates. However, the federal budget deficit increased from $59 billion in 1980 to $195 billion by 1983, while the Reagan Administration sought to reduce government interference with business.

Reagan's foreign policy was fueled by his anti-Soviet rhetoric and his strong anti-communist beliefs. Reagan's massive military spending program, which was the largest in American peacetime history, is touted as a major factor in the ultimate downfall of the Soviet Union. However, some observers argued that the buildup—through the strain it imposed on the Soviet economy—was actually responsible for a host of positive developments in Reagan's second term, including a more accommodating Soviet position in arms negotiations, a weakening of the influence of hard-liners in the Soviet leadership, making possible the glasnost ("openness") and perestroika ("restructuring") policies of moderate Soviet leader Mikhail Gorbachev after 1985, and even the dissolution of the Soviet Union itself in 1990–91.

In 1988, Vice President George H.W. Bush won the Republican nomination. He defeated Democrat Michael Dukakis, but the Republicans were unable to make any inroads in Congress. Bush's presidency is best remembered for the Persian Gulf Crisis. On August 2, 1990, Iraq invaded Kuwait, an act that Bush denounced as "naked aggression." The United States banned most trade with Iraq, froze Iraq's and Kuwait's assets in the United States, and sent aircraft carriers to the Middle East. On August 6, after the U.N. Security Council condemned the invasion, Bush ordered the deployment of air, sea, and land forces to Saudi Arabia; he called the operation "Desert Shield." The allied air assault began on February 23. Four days later, President Bush announced the liberation of Kuwait and ordered offensive operations to cease. The United States established the terms for the cease-fire, which Iraq accepted on April 6.

Road to the Twenty-First Century

The Cold War mentality and anti-communist fervor continued throughout the 1980s. In 1989, while the conservative Reagan was in office, the Soviet Union finally collapsed. The subsequent decade was marked by economic growth, fueled in large part by the emergence of the Internet and the technology boom. Globalization—a theory by which the entire planet is deeply connected through the exchange of goods and knowledge— also followed these new technologies.

Elected to two terms, William Jefferson Clinton, the 43rd president, signed the Family and Medical Leave Act as well as the North American Free Trade Agreement (NAFTA). He also signed a series of executive orders that set aside vast expanses of public lands, especially in the West. Clinton also set in motion a massive overhaul of the nation's welfare system—the first such revamp since FDR had created it in the 1930's.

The terror bombings of the World Trade Center and Pentagon on September 11, 2001, marked a turning point in American politics and international relations. Much of George W. Bush's presidency between 2000 and 2008 was marked both domestically and internationally by the Bush-declared U.S. War on Terror.

In November 2008, in the 232nd year since the founding of the United States, a record number of voters elected Barack Obama as the nation's 44th president—and he became the first African American to hold the office. His election coalition included minorities, college-educated whites, and young voters aged 19 to 26. In a *Time* magazine article written just before the election, *Atlantic Monthly* contributing editor Ta-Nehisi Cotes wrote: "Consider this fact: the most famous black man in America isn't dribbling a ball or clutching a microphone. He has no prison record . . . Words like hope, change, and progress might seem like naïve campaign sloganeering in a dark age. But think of the way those words ring for a people whose forebears marched into billy clubs and dogs, whose ancestors fled north by starlight, feeling the moss on the back of trees."

World History

Prehistory

The earth is approximately 6 billion years old. The earliest known humans are called hominids. They lived in Africa 3 to 4 million years ago. All modern humans are believed to have descended from one group of hominids, the Homo sapiens who appeared in Africa between 200,000 and 150,000 years ago.

Early humans lived in hunter-gatherer societies, often nomadic and dependent on local natural resources such as edible plants and game animals. Over time, other forms of social organization developed, such as semi-nomadic livestock herding and subsistence farming, village-based subsistence farming, city-states, kingdoms, and empires. Societies have been classified by their level of technological development based on whether their tools were made of stone, bronze, iron, or more advanced materials. This has led to the designations of Stone Age, Bronze Age, Iron Age, etc. During these periods, civilizations arose in the ancient Middle East to which modern Western civilization can trace its writing system and law codes. These civilizations include Sumeria, Israel, Egypt, Assyria, Babylonia, and Medo-Persia.

Ancient and Medieval Times

Of pivotal importance in Western history is the rise of ancient Greek civilization, beginning with the conquest by Alexander the Great in the 4th century BCE of much of the former territory of the previous Middle Eastern empires. This led to the spread of the Greek culture and language. Ancient Greek culture and learning has had an enduring influence on western development in many areas: the sciences, philosophy, scholarship, political thought, and games and sportsmanship, along with lasting literary contributions, notably the epic poems of Homer.

Elements of democracy were developed under the Greeks. The Greek city-state, or polis, was an important political feature made up of a city or town and its surrounding countryside. The polis was the center of an individual's social and political life. During the Hellenic Age (612–339 BCE) an aristocrat named Draco codified the laws for the Athenian polis and posted them for the public. Though his laws were harsh (the term "draconian" derives from his name due to the strict nature of his rules), his contribution to democracy was the idea that the law belonged to all citizens.

Three of the most important philosophers in terms of the development of western thought lived during the period of Classical Greece. Socrates was interested in human behavior and ethics. The "Socratic Method" uses logically constructed questions to challenge ideas. His student, Plato, believed in a more personal and transcendental approach to the body, mind, and world affairs. Plato's pupil, Aristotle, was a man of logic, reason, and direct observation. The world's first democracy was founded at Athens around 500 BCE.

The civilization of Rome thrived on preserved and adapted aspects of Greek culture, but over time achieved even greater dominance and influence in the Middle East and the Mediterranean region. By conquering the Greek dynasty ruling over Egypt in 31 BCE, Rome, under a single government, became the undisputed regional power and, in time, went on to conquer much of the known world. Rome was the first empire to extend the ancient Middle Eastern and Greek cultures northward into Europe.

Julius Caesar, the powerful Roman reform leader (ca. 102–44 BCE), is known for his military conquests and for the institution of a calendar system still in use today (with a few minor changes). The peace of this period led to a flourishing of the visual arts and higher learning, values and concepts at the core of aesthetic and intellectual progress, from the Middle Ages, through the Renaissance, and into our modern world.

The first and second centuries CE (Common Era), was a period known as Pax Romana (Latin for "Roman Peace"). Named because it was a time of political peace with no major wars or internal conflicts to threaten the empire, the Pax Romana was a time of much development of new architecture and an extensive system of roads, as well as a postal system, that facilitated transportation and thus favored the expansion of trade. Roman law was based on fairness and constancy, aspects still in demand and debate today.

Sometime during the reign of the Roman Emperor Augustus, Jesus of Nazareth (Jesus Christ) was born. Although crucified around 30 CE, Jesus' followers (later called Christians) grew in great numbers and the diffusion of this new faith contributed in large part to the eventual fall of Rome. Beginning in the third century, Rome also began a long decline as the succession of emperors grew unstable and the army began to have trouble maintaining control over outlying provinces. In the fifth century, invading Germanic tribes conquered Rome. Remnants of imperial power survived, however, in the Eastern Empire, with its capital in Constantinople (now Istanbul) and in the Roman Catholic

Church. The Germanic invaders also preserved and adopted much of what was left of the Roman Empire.

Even after Rome's power was broken, its impact was still felt in its former European territories. The Church and the feudal system filled the vacuum of power resulting from Rome's fall. In the feudal system of social organization, nobles ruled over peasants, called serfs, who worked the land. Among the nobles, the less powerful, called vassals, swore oaths of loyalty to the more powerful nobles, with the promise of military protection in exchange for their support. The feudal system included group contracts in addition to individual ones. Entire towns of peasants could have contractual agreements with nobles. Charters allowed peasants to govern their own affairs. Tradesmen formed guilds to regulate the price, quality, and quantity of goods produced. This system, with many variations, was the dominant economic and social system in Europe throughout the Middle Ages.

The Middle Ages, also known as the Dark Ages, were marked by political instability in the early centuries after Rome's fall. The Emperor Charlemagne ruled from 768 to 814, building a huge but also vastly fractured empire (The Holy Roman Empire) stretching across Europe. The Crusades, holy wars fought between Christians and Muslims, were fought with both religious and economic motives. After Jerusalem was captured and claimed by European Crusaders at the end of the 11th century, Saladin, King of Egypt and Syria, recaptured the Holy Land in 1187 and it remained under Islamist control through the 20th century. The sharp decrease in the spread of knowledge, widespread illiteracy, and disasters such as the population-decimating Black Plague of the 14th century, contributed to the stagnation of the era. Stability was highly valued in the midst of such problems, and medieval worldviews emphasized finding security by accepting one's status on "the great chain of being." In time, however, increasing political stability and the growth of trade and commerce set the stage for the early modern era of Western history.

Late Middle Ages and the Renaissance

The modern era began around 1450 with the period known as the *Renaissance* (French for "Rebirth"). A cultural movement, the Renaissance began in Florence, Italy, with a renewed interest in, and veneration for, classical Greek and Roman aesthetics. This initial interest led to a flourishing of the arts as well as an interest in the exploration of the human experience. It was a time of creativity and change in Europe. Artists, such as Michelangelo and Leonardo da Vinci, explored the human body to create more realistic paintings. The growth of commerce, banking, and industry favored the spread of knowledge among the rising middle class. The invention of the printing press in Mainz, Germany, by Johann Gutenberg in the mid-fifteenth century, revolutionized the way, and to what extent, information was disseminated, helping to raise literacy rates across Europe and beyond. William Shakespeare wrote 37 plays during this time, and Cervantes wrote "Don Quixote."

Closely following the grandeur of the Renaissance, the Reformation challenged the dominance and corruption of the Roman Catholic Church and led to the development of Protestantism, which more closely reflected the values of Northern European cultures and the middle class. A German monk, Martin Luther, posted ninety-five arguments against Papal authority and the practices of selling indulgences and salvation. His explanation of sola fide—justification by faith alone—led to his excommunication from the Roman Catholic Church. Thus began what became known as the Protestant Reformation. In England, Queen Elizabeth I (r. 1558-1603) valued political unity and stability over religious unity and harmony and imposed a strictly controlled system upon the Anglican Church. Elizabeth's rule was a success on both the domestic and foreign fronts and she supported exploration abroad. At this time, not only England but also Spain and Portugal began exploring the globe and founding overseas colonies. The interests in discovering new knowledge, and the attitude of challenging traditional views, have continued as western traditions.

The renewed interest in classical learning spurred a great increase of scientific knowledge in the 17th century. Sir Isaac Newton's discovery of the laws of gravity and motion, based on previous studies of Galileo's work, established a foundation for the study of physics in place for the next two hundred years. This period was also marked by political change as the feudal system slowly gave way to the development of monarchies in Western Europe. In this form of government, power was centralized in the hands of the king (or monarch) rather than divided among the nobles. In France, there was an absolute monarchy, where the King ruled by divine right and without any check on his actions other than his own conscience. The other major form of monarchy, constitutional monarchy, existed in England. In a constitutional monarchy the King, (or Queen), ruled along with the larger body of Parliament. Advances continued in the fields of science, politics, education, and commerce; these advances further removed Europe from its medieval past and favored the growth of the middle class.

Revolution and the New World Order

The 18th century saw the development of ideas based on rational thought, reason, logic, and the application of scientific knowledge for the betterment of society. This period, known as the Enlightenment, further challenged medieval ideals of stability and order by championing progress and planned change. John Locke was an Enlightenment thinker who wanted to reform government. He believed that the government should protect the natural rights of the people. Natural rights can be defined as those rights belonging to all humans from birth. The growing pressures for progress caused strained relationships between the ruling class and the middle class; such conflict eventually exploded in France, in the French Revolution of 1789. Before the French Revolution, the concept of an individual citizen's rights did not exist. There had merely been certain privileges allowed to, and afforded by, class.

Soon thereafter, the Industrial Revolution and colonialism transformed the face of Europe and many other regions of the world. In the 19th century, the unprecedented explosion of industry and technology destroyed the agricultural traditions and society of Europe, led to the process of rapid urbanization, and western civilization expanded its power throughout the rest of the world.

Britain led the Industrial Revolution since it had the necessary natural resources and plenty of workers for its new factories and mines. Iron and coal were key components of industrialization. Iron, which could be made faster and stronger by using coal, was used to build machines and steam engines. The textile industry was the first to use machines to weave cloth, which had previously been hand-spun in homes. The machines were large and expensive, so spinners and weavers worked in large rooms. These became the first factories. Steam engines provided speedy transportation for people and goods. The engines were used in boats along canals and in steam locomotives, which led to the development of the railroad system.

While Spain and Portugal were losing their colonies in the Americas, many European countries expanded into Africa, Asia, and the Pacific, including areas that had never before been colonized by Western nations.

The competition over resources in overseas colonies was one of the major reasons for World War I, which, in spite of its name, was mainly a European war. Finally sparked by the assassination of the heir to the throne of Austria-Hungary, it soon claimed the lives of millions. In addition, in countries such as Great Britain and Germany, the immense scale of the war meant that for the first time, enlisted men from all walks of life—not only professional soldiers—became casualties of war. In France, about half the men of an entire generation were lost and in one single battle (the Battle of the Somme); the British suffered more than 60,000 casualties on the first day alone.

Germany, the major instigator of World War I, fell far short of its attempt to create a global empire. At the end of World War I, German-controlled colonies fell into the hands of Great Britain and France. Germany became economically poor and remained repressed for the next two decades. Bitterness in Germany over the loss of the war, inflation, and the cost of war reparations were factors in the successful cultivation of nationalism and the eventual rise of Adolf Hitler to power. Hitler's Third Reich and Nazi regime eventually killed a staggering 50 million people, including 6 million Jews and 20 million Soviets. World War II began in 1939 when Hitler invaded Poland. Germany was joined by Japan and Italy to form the Axis powers, which fought against the Allied Forces, mainly Great Britain, the United States, and the Soviet Union. (France, perhaps remembering the dead of World War I, surrendered to Germany early in the war and formed the collaborative Vichy government.) World War II came to an end in Europe in May of 1945 after the Battle of the Bulge, and Russian advancement and subsequent occupation of Berlin. The war ended in the Pacific with Japan's surrender on August 14.

Almost immediately after World War II, the Cold War, a contentious conflict fought between the superpowers and nuclear threats of the United States and the Soviet Union, began. The process of decolonization (the process where formerly European and U.S. colonies rejected foreign rule and protested further interference) also began. Great Britain's most important colony, India, broke away in 1948 under the famously nonviolent leadership of Mohandas Gandhi. Britain was also unable to prevent the establishment of the Jewish state of Israel in formerly British Palestine in that same year. Most of Britain's African colonies became independent in the 1950s and 1960s. In the meantime, Europe was divided by a figurative Iron Curtain between capitalist Western Europe and Soviet-controlled Eastern Europe.

China, in which a Communist revolution under Mao Zedong (also known as Mao Tse-tung), succeeded following the great devastation caused by the Japanese occupation during World War II, was solidly in the Soviet camp for many years but remained independent during much of the Cold War. Japan, though not allowed to assemble a military as a condition of its defeat in World War II, became a U.S. ally and a dominant Asian economic power.

The U.S. and the Soviet Union waged war through their allies in Korea and Vietnam. The Cold War came to an end in several phases between 1989 and 1991, when the Soviet Union essentially collapsed. The end of the Cold War—which involved conflict on practically every continent—did not, however, bring peace to the world. In the formerly Soviet-controlled state of Yugoslavia, long buried ethnic rivalries led to civil war, genocide, and an eventual split into three separate countries.

On the continent of Africa, many formerly French and British colonies began to break apart along tribal lines, often leading to terrible bloodshed, such as Tutsi genocide in Rwanda in 1994. The South African revolution and struggle against the apartheid (Afrikaans for "separateness") regime, led in large part, and over decades, into the 1990s by Nelson Mandela, were relatively peaceful, though the country was rife with inequality, oppression and exploitation — and continues to mend. Most of Africa is still subject to poverty, disease, and war. In the Middle East, ongoing and complicated international conflicts (such as the two Gulf Wars), religious fundamentalism, and various political regimes, along with the continually contentious issue of the state of Israel, have led to the spread of radical political Islam. Such extremist groups have wreaked much havoc in the world, including in the terror attacks on the World Trade Center and Pentagon on September 11, 2001.

Over the past half century, as the many advances in technology have brought people closer together and made people more conscious of the global scale, the process and effects of globalization have become embedded into our everyday lives. Advances in medicine and health care are lengthening life spans the world over and the process of industrialization continues to reach countries of the third world, creating, strengthening, and at times complicating ties to world powers. Such a multi-layered process creates ever more detailed patterns of crisscrossed and vested interests and the modern world still grapples with exploitation, oppression, and equality — issues both moral and economic. The historical tradition of recognizing individuals for their contributions, discoveries, and revolutionizing force continues, only with 21st century advancement, this information is less privileged and more readily available to a connected global audience via the Internet and other improved forms of communication. Global figures perform on a world stage. Improved means of travel, along with changing immigration patterns and policies, designed to meet the realities of our 21st century world, are redefining geographic, ethnic, and cultural boundaries. Nationalism remains an issue of patriotism and identity and it is still a useful political tool, but the rigid lines that have been used for centuries to define people and places seem to be expanding to include amalgams, yet another reflection of our mixed, enmeshed, and entangled global community.

Recognizing chronological relationships among historical events

Students of history understand that there is a complex relationship between sequential events. An example of a complex relationship is that of the migration of African-Americans from Georgia in search of better paying jobs, during each of the world wars and the subsequent race riots that took place in some urban areas after the wars. While some would argue that the riots were largely due to overcrowding (seemingly an isolated cause), others might argue that, while overcrowding was a factor, it was the fact that African-Americans, having left the socially oppressive and segregated South, were unwilling to retreat from their gains.

Historical understanding includes the use of reasoning, resulting in a thorough exploration of cause-effect relationships to reach defensible historical interpretations through inquiry. This is true with all levels of history, such as discussed above in the previous section (Georgia history, United States history, and world history). Another example, this time in world history, would be the relationship between the Industrial Revolution and the emergence of a new category of people who depended on their jobs for income and who thus need job security. From the practices employed during industrialization, came new theories of the relationship between work and the worker (e.g., marxism, socialism and capitalism). Without those practices and the subsequent historical analysis, comparing pre-industrialization work to that of industrialization, the important concepts which help us think about the socio-political systems most likely would not have emerged.

Demonstrating knowledge of early Native American cultures in North America and their interactions with early explorers

Demonstrating knowledge of the early Native American cultures in North America necessitate an understanding of the interactions between early settlers and native cultures. According to Ferrell and Natkiel (1993), the early European explorers did not find an unpopulated wilderness when they arrived in North America. Around 2 million Native Americans were widely scattered across the "New World." There were hundreds of different tribes speaking about 500 different languages. It is now understood that between about 40,000 and 8000 BCE, early Asiatic peoples crossed the Bering Strait land bridge. They eventually moved southward and spread over the North and South American continents. These people were mainly fishers, hunters, and gatherers. They were primarily nomadic or inhabitants of small towns. The Mound Builders of the Mississippi River Valley were sedentary farmers. They did, however, create temples and tombs that were common in Central and South America.

Christopher Columbus described these first Americans as "Indians" because he thought he had sailed to the Orient rather than discovered a New World. The "Indians" were confused and astonished when they met the first explorers.

According to Davis (1998), there were several stages of relations between these native people and the Europeans. The first stage involved an exchange of plant and animal life between old and new worlds. Geographic isolation had come to an end. The Native Americans introduced crops to the Europeans, such as potatoes, beans, squash, and maize. These crops had a great nutritional impact on the Europeans. The Europeans introduced wheat, rice, bananas, sugar, and white grapes and these were soon grown across the new country. Domesticated animals were brought by colonizers and these animals had an impact upon the tribal lifestyles. The grazing animals, however, were responsible for destroying large acres of cropland. The animals were also utilized for transport and clothing.

"The Columbian Exchange" was one of the devastating effects of the relationship between the Native Americans and the Europeans. The native people had little immunity to European disease. Diseases, such as measles, influenza, diphtheria, tuberculosis, smallpox, and the common cold swept throughout the New World in epidemic proportions.

The second stage of relations between the Europeans and the native peoples involved trade and cultural interchange. The settlers and the Native Americans lived side by side. The first colonist relied on the help of local tribes for survival. The Indian Squanto showed the Puritans in New England how to fertilize the land and plant corn. This is celebrated today with Thanksgiving. In Virginia, the Powhatan Confederacy helped the colony to succeed. Pocahontas was an important mediator between the Indians and the English. European goods included tools, clothes, cloth, blankets, guns, and alcohol were exchanged for Native expertise, land and hunting skills. Missionaries brought Christianity to Indians using coercion at times to convert them. Since Indian religions used deities based in the natural world, it was devastating and disruptive of their native traditions when more and more game was hunted with no thought of the consequence to the ecology of the area. The Indian way was based in ecological balance so they only thinned herds that required it and celebrated their kill with religious sanctity that showed their respect to the natural world.

The last phase of relations of European and Indian contact involved friction and warfare. The colonies wanted to expand, and the Native Americans slowly retreated as the white settlements extended westward. Indian lands were removed, as the settlers wanted more and more of them. One of the most shameful events in the history of the United States was the "Trail of Tears."

Analyzing various perspectives, interpretations, and implications of events, issues, and developments in Georgia, U.S., and world history

Just as one studies history, it is necessary to analyze various perspectives and interpretations of events, issues, and developments in the state of Georgia, the United States, and in the world. Events and issues are written from different perspectives and interpretations. Perspectives and interpretations change as time moves on. It is also important to examine the implications of events, issues, and developments. The occurrence of events does not happen in isolation, but rather has implications for future events.

Employing a historical perspective includes a rich understanding of events, ideas, and people from the past. That knowledge encompasses an understanding of the diversity of race, ethnicity, social and economic status, gender, region, politics, and religion within history. Historic understanding includes the use of historical reasoning, resulting in a thorough exploration of cause-effect relationships to reach defensible historical interpretations through inquiry.

Demonstrating knowledge of strategies and resources for historical inquiry

The ability to understand and apply skills and procedures related to the study of history involves knowledge of the use of systematic inquiry. Inquiry is essential for use in not only examining a single discipline, such as history, but also integrated social studies. Being able to engage in inquiry involves the ability to acquire information from a wide variety of resources, and organize that information, which leads to the interpretation of information. Inquiry involves the ability to design and conduct investigations, which in turn leads to the identification and analysis of social studies issues.

Also, this understanding includes knowledge about and the use of the various resources used in systematic social science inquiry. Those resources include primary (e.g., letters, diaries, speeches, photos, and autobiographies) and secondary sources (e.g., encyclopedias, almanacs, atlases, government documents, artifacts, and oral histories).

However, there are instances where secondary source materials can function as primary sources. One example is Lytton Strachey's famous history of nineteenth century England, *Eminent Victorians*, published in 1918. *Eminent Victorians* is a secondary source, a history of English society and culture in the 1800s based on Strachey's research and analysis of primary sources. And yet, to a present-day scholar *Eminent Victorians* itself as a primary source for use in analyzing the mores and attitudes of Lytton Strachey and the early twentieth-century English society of which he was a part.

Objective 0010   Understand major concepts, principles, and methods of inquiry related to geography.

Objective 0010 includes the understanding of major concepts, principles, and methods of inquiry related to geography. Specifically, the objective includes: applying knowledge of basic concepts of geography; demonstrating knowledge of major physical and human-constructed features of the earth; analyzing interactions between physical systems and human systems; applying knowledge of maps, globes, and other geographic tools; and, demonstrating knowledge of strategies and resources for geography inquiry. (Ambrose & Brinkley, 1999; Davies, 1998; Ferrell & Natkiel, 1993; London, 1999)

Applying knowledge of basic concepts of geography (e.g., location, movement of people, interaction among peoples)

The geographer's craft is all about space—not outer space, but physical space. Geographers look at space and investigate patterns—a geographer might look at the space of your bedroom and ask several questions: How are things distributed? What processes operate in that space? How does this space relate to other nearby spaces? Such a way of identifying, explaining, and predicting the human and physical patterns in space and the interconnectedness of various spaces are known to geographers as the spatial perspective. The field of geography has several subfields that branch from two main fields: human (cultural) geography and physical geography. Human geography takes as its subject humans and the cultures they create relative to their space. Physical geography looks at the planet earth—its water, air, animals, and land (i.e., all that is part of the four spheres—the atmosphere, biosphere, hydrosphere, and lithosphere).

The five themes of geography created in 1984 by the National Council for Geographic Education and the Association of American Geographers were to facilitate and organize the teaching of geography in the K-12 classroom. These themes have been supplanted by the National Geography Standards, which we will discuss, but the original five continue to provide an effective way of organizing your understanding the field of geography.

The Five Themes of Geography

Location

Most geographic study begins with learning the location of places. Location can be absolute or relative. Absolute Location refers to a position on the global grid. Technically, a location is absolute when it has only one possible reference point. That is why latitude and longitude work; only one place is 85 degrees north, 37 degrees west on the planet.

Your home address is another absolute location. There is only one 28 North Main Street in Williamsport, Pennsylvania. In addition to absolute location, anything can have a relative location, or its location as described in relation to places around it. The relative location of Nashville, Tennessee, could be described as being "south of Louisville, Kentucky," for example. "Hillsboro High School is located 9 miles southwest of McGavock High School" is another example of a relative location. While a site's absolute location will not vary, 28 North Main Street in Williamsport, Pa., will always be 28 North Street, in Williamsport, the site relative to the Joe's Corner Grocery store may change, if Joe's Corner Grocery becomes Slidell's Barber Shop, for instance.

The global grid is an invisible map of latitude and longitude lines. Lines of latitude, measured in degrees, run north and south from the equator, which lies at 0 degrees latitude. The North Pole is 90 degrees north latitude, while the South Pole is 90 degrees south latitude. Lines of latitude never intersect, so geographers often call lines of latitude parallels. Because lines of latitude encircle the earth and never intersect, the circumferences of lines of latitude decrease as they move away from the equator in both directions. Therefore, the equator has the largest circumference of all the lines of latitude. Latitude exerts a large amount of control over any given area's climate—probably the single most important factor. Latitude dictates the intensity and duration of sun exposure to an area. When an area is closer to the sun, the days are longer and the sun's rays are stronger. This heats the climate.

Lines of longitude are measured in degrees east and west of one line of longitude known as the prime meridian, which runs through Greenwich, England, and is located at 0 degrees longitude. The line of longitude on the opposite side of the prime meridian is known as the International Date Line. The International Date Line is aligned with the 180-degree longitude line for some latitudes but not for others. This reflects the political influence on time zones. For example, the International Date Line was moved to put all of Russia ahead of Greenwich Mean Time.

Place

The fourth geographic theme is place, which is a unique combination of physical and cultural attributes that give each location on the earth its individual "stamp." Place describes the human and physical characteristics of a location. Physical characteristics include a description of such things as the mountains, rivers, beaches, topography, and animal and plant life of a place. Human characteristics include the human-designed cultural features of a place, from land use and architecture to forms of livelihood and religion to food and folkways to transportation and communication networks.

Human components of place include religion, language, politics, and artwork, whereas the physical attributes include climate, terrain, and natural resources. The combination of these two parts of place, the human and physical are what differentiate each location from another, almost like fingerprints.

Humans also develop a sense of place, which is a person's perception of the human and physical attributes of a location that give it a unique identity in our minds. For example, you probably remember a set of smells, sounds, and images from your ninth-grade English classroom. Think of how that sense of place differs from the total set of memories you have of your childhood bedroom or a favorite vacation spot. People can even develop a sense of place for a location they have never visited—through movies, television, and interactions with others who have traveled or heard of the places. You probably have never been to Siberia, but I bet you think it is a place you never want to visit because of its harsh climate!

Human-Environment Interaction

This theme considers how humans adapt to and modify the environment. Humans shape the landscape through their interaction with the land; this has both positive and negative effects on the environment.

Region

Region divides the world into manageable units for geographic study. Regions have some sort of characteristic that unifies the area. Regions can be formal, functional, or vernacular/perceptual. Formal regions are those that are designated by official boundaries, such as cities, states, counties, and countries. For the most part, they are clearly indicated and publicly known. Functional regions are defined by their connections. For example, the circulation area for a major city area is the functional region of that paper. Vernacular regions are perceived regions, such as "The South," "The Midwest," or the "Middle East"; they have no formal boundaries but are understood in our mental maps of the world.

Formal regions (sometimes referred to as uniform regions) are areas that have common (or uniform) cultural or physical features. A country is a formal region, or an area of places linked by a shared government. A climate region is a formal region because it links places that share a climate. A map showing where Christianity is practiced is showing a formal region, or a group of places sharing that religion.

A functional region (sometimes referred to as a nodal region) is a group of places linked together by some function's influence on them. Often the influencing function diffuses, or spreads, from a central node, or originating point. Functional regions are created through the movement of some phenomenon, like a disease, or a perceived interaction among places, like pizza delivery routes. For example, a functional region might appear on a map of Delta Airlines' flights from Atlanta, Georgia. A mapmaker would plot all the places to which Delta travels from its hub in Atlanta—the node. Then the mapmaker would draw a boundary enclosing all those places into one functional region. The area affected by the spread of a flu epidemic is a functional region. A functional region could even show the transmission of a rumor from its source to all the people who hear it. Remember, functional regions are defined by the places affected by the movement of some phenomenon from its source or node of other places.

The third type of region is a perceptual (or vernacular) region. The boundaries of a perceptual region are determined by people's beliefs, not a scientifically measurable process. For example, the space in which the "cool kids" sit at lunch would be a perceptual region because its boundaries are totally determined by the region maker's perception of who is cool and who is not—something that could be debated by any other person in the room. Another example of a perceptual region is the South in the United States. People differ in their perceptions of which places are considered part of the South.

Movement

Humans move . . . a lot! In addition, ideas, fads, goods, resources, and communication all travel distances. The fifth theme studies movement and migration across the planet. Geographers analyze the movement occurring in a space—movement of information, people, goods, and other phenomena. Geographers also evaluate how places interact through movement, a process known as spatial interaction. Although everything is theoretically linked to everything else, nearer things are usually related more to each other than to faraway things. Thus, the extent of spatial interaction often depends on distance.

In evaluating movement and spatial interaction, geographers often evaluate the friction of distance, which is the degree to which distance interferes with some interaction. For example, the friction of distance for a working-class Ohio man wanting to visit a dentist in Ethiopia is quite high, meaning that the distance gets in the way of this interaction occurring. However, the friction of distance has been reduced in many aspects of life with improved transportation and communication infrastructures.

Today, the friction of distance is not as much of a problem for a business in Kentucky to sell something to a business in Taiwan, for example. Businesses can now communicate over the Internet, buying and selling their goods in transactions that would have taken months to complete just 30 years ago. This increasing sense of accessibility and connectivity seems to bring humans in distant places closer together, a phenomenon known as space–time compression. Note that space–time compression is reducing perceived distance, which is the friction of distance thought by humans, not the actual distance on the land.

Related to space–time compression is the effect of distance decay, in which the interaction between two places declines as the distance between the two places increases. Imagine putting a magnet on your desk and putting an iron nail on it. The farther you pull the iron nail away from the magnet, the less of a pull effect the magnet has on the nail, right? It is the same with distance decay; as the distance between two entities increases, the effect of their interaction decreases.

However, improved transportation and communication technologies have reduced the effect of distance decay on most human interactions. In 1850 on any given day, a person living in Atlanta probably never interacted with someone from 30 miles outside the city. Now a person in Atlanta can interact with people from all over the world via the Internet and improved transportation.

Applying knowledge of maps (e.g., political, physical, topographic, resource), globes, and other geographic tools (e.g., compass rose, legend, map scale)

A map is a two-dimensional model of the earth or a portion of its surface. The process of mapmaking is called cartography. All maps include a somewhat simplified view of the earth's surface. Simplification is when a cartographer gets rid of unnecessary details and focuses on the information needing to be displayed on the map. When designing a map of Europe for high school students to use to help them memorize the names of countries and capitals, a mapmaker would present a simplified map of Europe's political states and

boundaries, eliminating details such as vegetation or climate. Another example of simplification involves a cartographer designing a map of London's underground subway for
tourists. Such a cartographer might eliminate unnecessary details such as unrelated buildings and streets from their maps because tourists do not need these details to understand
London's subway tracks. Tourists are simply interested in getting on and off the correct
subway stops.

Distortion and Map Properties

It is impossible to take the earth's round surface and put it onto a flat surface without
some form of distortion, or error, resulting from the "flattening" process. Think of distortion as caused by a process similar to trying to flatten an orange peel. Sorry to inform you
of this, but all the maps you have memorized are wrong. As it is often said, "All maps lie
flat, and all flat maps lie." Yes, that's right; every map is, in some way, wrong. The globe is
the most accurate representation of the earth.

Each map has four main map properties: shape, size (area), distance, and direction.
Shape refers to the geometric shapes of the objects on the map. Size (area) refers to the
relative amount of space taken up on the map by the landforms or objects on the map.
Distance refers to the represented distance between objects on the map. Direction refers
to the degree of accuracy representing the cardinal directions—north, south, east, and
west—and their intermediate directions—northwest, northeast, southwest, and southeast.
Less accurate are the relative directions that people commonly use to describe a location,
such as right, left, up, and down, among many others.

All four properties cannot be accurately represented, so a cartographer must choose
which of the properties to distort. Cartographers make this decision by considering the
map's purpose. When designing a map for navigational purposes, the cartographer would
keep direction and distance accurate; size (area) and shape are not as important.

The Process of Mapmaking: Projection

In making a flat map of the round earth, geographers use geometric shapes. They can
choose a cylinder, cone, or flat plane to touch to the earth and construct a map. To visualize this process, imagine that the globe has a light in it and is in a dark room. When the
chosen geometric shape, such as a flat plane, is placed on the globe, the globe reflects
onto this geometric shape, forming a flat image, or projection, of the round earth. The
resulting projection reflects the geometric surface used in constructing it.

The projection is distorted in some way, however, depending on the geometric shape used to make the map. Geographers have different labels for maps that reflect the different properties distorted by the maps:

- Equal-area (or equivalent) projections: maps that maintain area but distort other properties

- Conformal (or orthomorphic) projections: maps that maintain shape but distort other properties (it is impossible to have a projection that is both conformal and equal area)

- Azimuthal projections: maps that maintain direction but distort other properties

- Equidistant projections: maps that maintain distance but distort other properties

The Mercator projection is a conformal projection created using a cylindrical surface, and the Albers projection was created using a conic surface. Azimuthal projections are flat-plane-constructed maps of each hemisphere. Great-circle routes are apparent on azimuthal projections.

Uses of Projections

Consider the different maps you have seen in your lifetime. You probably have used a Robinson projection in your social studies class to memorize points on the world map because the Robinson projection shows the world according to slight distortion of all four properties, rather than getting just one correct and drastically distorting others. Before the Robinson projection was invented, social studies teachers often used the Mercator projection. Though the Mercator projection shows the shapes of the continents and landforms accurately, it drastically distorts the size (area) of the continents. For example, Greenland is almost as large as Africa on the Mercator. Moreover, schools in the former Soviet Union used the Mercator projection to teach its children because the map made the USSR look larger than its enemies. A geographer created the Peter projection to show relative sizes of the earth's continents accurately (equal area), but because it distorts shape, it is not conformal.

Types of Maps

Most maps include a compass which indicates which way is north, south, east and west. They also include a scale so you can estimate distances. Different maps also include:

- Climate maps provide information about precipitation (rain and snow) of a region. Cartographers, or mapmakers, use colors to show different climate or precipitation zones.

- Economic or resource maps feature the type of natural resources or economic activity that dominates an area. Cartographers use symbols to show the locations of natural resources or economic activities. For example, oranges on a map of Florida tell you that oranges are grown there.

- Physical maps illustrate the physical features of an area, such as the mountains, rivers and lakes. Colors are used to show relief—differences in land elevations. Green is typically used at lower elevations; orange or brown indicate higher elevations and blue indicates a body of water.

- Political maps indicate state and national boundaries and capital and major cities. A capital city is usually marked with a star within a circle.

- Road maps show major along with some minor highways, as well as roads, airports, railroad tracks, cities and other points of interest in an area.

- Topographic maps include contour lines to show the shape and elevation of an area. Lines that are close together indicate steep terrain, and lines that are far apart indicate flat terrain.

Geographers examine how people shape their world—how they settle the land, form community, and how they permanently change the landscape. The various branches of geography taken as one give the geographer the tools to understand the vastness of the earth.

Physical geography is a branch of geography concerned with the natural features of the earth's surface. Physical geography concentrates on such areas as land formation, water, weather, and climate. Population geography is a form of geography that deals with the relationships between geography and population patterns, including birth and death rates. Political geography deals with the effect of geography on politics, especially on national boundaries and relations between states. Economic geography is a study of the interaction between the earth's landscape and the economic activity of the human population.

The use of maps requires students to identify different types of maps, such as political, physical, topographic and resource. Additional graphics that students use in geography include charts, graphs, and picture maps.

Demonstrating knowledge of major physical and human-constructed features of the earth

A Geographic tour

Geographers examine how people shape their world—how they settle the land, form community, and how people permanently change the landscape. The various branches of geography taken as one give the geographer the tools to understand the vastness of the earth.

Physical geography is a branch of geography concerned with the natural features of the earth's surface. Physical geography concentrates on such areas as land formation, water, weather, and climate. Population geography is a form of geography that deals with the relationships between geography and population patterns, including birth and death rates. Political geography deals with the effect of geography on politics, especially on national boundaries and relations between states. Economic geography is a study of the interaction between the earth's landscape and the economic activity of the human population.

If characteristics of an area become unacceptable to residents, then their lifestyle may change as they decide to move from there and relocate to another area. Since transportation is easier today, people can move more easily than they could have in earlier times.

Economic reasons affect relocation decisions. For example, families consider finances and the economic level required to live comfortably in an area. Many people change locations in order to raise their standard of living or to go to a less expensive area.

Cultural reasons affect some individuals and help them decide to relocate. For example, a family may decide to move to an area to live with others who are more similar to them. Individuals may like the culture of one area better than another. In Georgia, for example, one who loves the ocean and its way of life may decide to move from Atlanta and settle in Brunswick.

Physical reasons can also affect a person's decision to relocate. One must understand how people rely on the environment, how they alter it, and how the environment can limit what people are able to do. Sometimes people move to a place where they can satisfy their physical wants or needs. People can also modify their environment or bring needed goods to their area without having to relocate.

Demonstrating knowledge of strategies (e.g., interpreting maps) and resources for geographic inquiry

Students need to be able to apply research skills when they begin geographic inquiry. For example, learning to read a map can be as basic as using tools such as the compass rose and the legend, or more difficult when, for example, using a topographical map to find a peak greater than 5,000 feet.

The ability to understand and apply social studies research skills requires systematic inquiry. Recognizing the difference between economic and geographic sources and where to find them is an important step in research. Organizing information and understanding the various ways to present and interpret information provides the scholar with the important tools to communicate her findings. Inquiry involves the ability to design and conduct investigations, which in turn leads to the identification and analysis of geographic issues in social studies.

Objective 0011   Understand major concepts, principles, and methods of inquiry related to U.S. government and civics.

Objective 0011 includes the understanding of major concepts, principles, and methods of inquiry related to U.S. government and civics. Specifically, the objective includes: demonstrating knowledge of the functions of government and the basic principles of the U.S. government as a republic; identifying the roles and interrelationships of national, state, and local governments in the United States; recognizing the roles and powers of the executive, legislative, and judicial branches of government; demonstrating knowledge of the Declaration of Independence, the U.S. Constitution, and the Bill of Rights; identifying the rights and responsibilities of U.S. citizenship; and, demonstrating knowledge of strategies and resources for inquiry related to government and civics. (Ambrose & Brinkley, 1999; Davies, 1998; Ferrell & Natkiel, 1993; London, 1999)

Demonstrating knowledge of the functions of government and the basic principles of the U.S. government as a republic

America was founded on a strong set of ideals and values. Many of these values are expressed in three essential founding documents: the Declaration of Independence, the U.S. Constitution, and the Bill of Rights.

The purposes and objectives of the U.S. government were written into the Constitution's short preamble: "We the People of the United States, in Order to form a more perfect Union, establish Justice, insure domestic Tranquility, provide for the common defense, promote the general Welfare, and secure the Blessings of Liberty to ourselves and our Posterity, do ordain and establish this Constitution for the United States of America." The remaining seven articles of the Constitution delineate how the government shall be organized and function. The U.S. Constitution creates a strong central government, and also provides a system of checks and balances among the three branches of government: the legislative, executive, and judicial branches.

For the Founders, a system of checks and balances was key to reconciling the power of each branch of government. The legislative branch makes laws and has the power to declare war. The legislative branch is composed of the Senate and the House of Representatives. At the federal level, there are 100 senators, who serve six-year terms, and 435 state representatives, who serve two-year terms.

The executive branch enforces laws. At the federal level, the president signs bills into law and serves as the Commander-in-Chief of the Armed Forces.

The judicial branch interprets the constitutionality of laws. At the federal level, the Supreme Court seats nine members who are appointed for life by the president with consent of the Senate. Each branch of the government checks the power of the other two branches and all three branches must work together to properly govern and create laws.

Identifying the roles and interrelationships of national, state, and local governments in the United States

According to the Constitution of the United States of America, all governmental powers stem ultimately from the people. Local matters are generally handled by local governments. The issues that affect all citizens are the responsibility of the federal government. This governmental relationship called Federalism, is unique.

The Tenth Amendment declares, "Those powers not delegated to the United States by the Constitution, nor prohibited by it to the States, are reserved to the States respectively, or to the people." The federal and state governments have powers that may in practice overlap, but when they conflict, the federal government is supreme.

The following powers are reserved for the federal government:

1. Regulate foreign commerce.
2. Regulate interstate commerce.

3. Mint money.

4. Regulate naturalization and immigration,

5. Grant copyrights and patents.

6. Declare and wage war and declare peace.

7. Admit new states.

8. Fix standards for weights and measures.

9. Raise and maintain an army and a navy.

10. Govern Washington, D.C.

11. Conduct relations with foreign powers.

12. Universalize bankruptcy laws.

The state governments have the following powers:

1. Conduct and monitor elections.

2. Establish voter qualifications with the guidelines established by the Constitution.

3. Provide for local governments.

4. Ratify proposed amendments to the Constitution.

5. Regulate contracts and wills.

6. Regulate intrastate commerce.

7. Provide for education for its citizens.

8. Levy direct taxes.

Recognizing the roles and powers of the executive, legislative, and judicial branches of government

These branches have separate functions, but they are not entirely independent. These functions are outlined in Articles I, II, and III of the main body of the Constitution.

The Legislative Branch

Legislative power is vested in a bicameral (two houses) Congress, which is the subject of Article I of the Constitution. The expressed or delegated powers are set forth in Section 8 and can be divided into several broad categories.

Economic powers include:

1. Lay and collect taxes.

2. Borrow money.

3. Regulate foreign and interstate commerce.

4. Coin money and regulate its value.

5. Establish rules concerning bankruptcy.

Judicial powers are as follows:

1. Establish courts inferior to the Supreme Court.

2. Provide punishment for counterfeiting.

3. Define and punish piracies and felonies committed on the high seas.

War powers of Congress include:

1. Declare war.

2. Raise and support armies.

3. Provide and maintain a navy.

4. Provide for organizing, arming, and calling forth the militia.

Other general peace powers consist of the following:

1. Establish uniform rules on naturalization.

2. Establish post offices and post roads.

3. Promote science and the arts by issuing patents and copyrights.

4. Exercise jurisdiction over the seat of the federal government (District of Columbia).

Congress is also given power by the Constitution to discipline federal officials through impeachment and removal from office. The House of Representatives has the power to charge officials (impeach), and the Senate has the power to conduct the trials. The first impeachment of a president was that of Andrew Johnson.

The Senate also has the power to confirm presidential appointments (to the cabinet, federal judiciary, and major bureaucracies) and to ratify treaties. Both the Senate and the House of Representatives are involved in choosing a president and vice president if there is no majority in the Electoral College. The House of Representatives votes for the president from among the top three electoral candidates, with each state delegation casting one vote. The Senate votes for the vice president. This Senate has exercised this power only twice, in the disputed elections of 1800 and 1824.

The Executive Branch

The Executive Branch is centered on the office of the President of the United States. The President is the chief executive. Article II of the Constitution includes the powers and duties of the president. The constitutional responsibilities of the chief executive include the following:

1. Serve as commander in chief.

2. Negotiate treaties (with the approval of two-thirds of the Senate).

3. Appoint ambassadors, judges, and other high officials (with the consent of the Senate).

4. Grant pardons and reprieves for those convicted of federal crimes (except in impeachment cases).

5. Seek counsel of department heads (cabinet secretaries).

6. Recommend legislation.

7. Meet with representatives of foreign states.

8. See that federal laws are "faithfully executed."

It should be remembered that the president is the country's leading general. He/ she can make battlefield decisions and shape the military policy of the country. The president's powers with respect to foreign policy are paramount. Civilian control of the military is a fundamental concept embodied in the naming of the president as commander-in-chief.

The president also has broad powers in domestic policy. The president's budget is the most significant domestic policy tool. This budget must be submitted to Congress. Although Congress must approve all spending, the president has a great deal of power in budget negotiations. The president can use considerable resources in persuading Congress to enact legislation, and the president also has opportunities, such as in the "State of the Union" address, to reach out directly to the American people to convince them to support presidential policies.

The Judicial Branch

It is stated in Article III of the Constitution that "the judicial power of the United States shall be vested in one Supreme Court and in such inferior courts as the Congress may from time to time ordain and establish." The Constitution makes two references to a trial by jury in criminal cases (in Article III and in the Sixth Amendment).

Demonstrating knowledge of the Declaration of Independence, the U.S. Constitution, and the Bill of Rights

Declaration of Independence

The Declaration of Independence is a statement that was approved on July 4, 1776, by the Second Continental Congress. It was officially signed on August 2, 1776. The Declaration announced that the thirteen American colonies, then at war with Great Britain, were now independent states. The colonies were thus no longer a part of the British Empire.

The Declaration of Independence was primarily written by Thomas Jefferson. It is a formal explanation of why Congress voted on July 2, 1776, more than a year after the beginning of the American Revolutionary War, to declare independence from Great Britain In the United States, we celebrate the birthday of our country on July 4, the day the wording of the Declaration was approved by Congress.

Three Georgians signed the document. They were Lyman Hall, George Walton, and Button Gwinnett. Their signatures appear on the left side of the document, below the signature of John Hancock.

The Declaration of Independence has 1,458 words. It can be divided into three parts. These are: The introduction, or Preamble; the body; and the conclusion. The introduction, or Preamble, describes how the colonists felt about democracy. The second part, or body, lists twenty-seven grievances against King George III and his government. These were the reasons that caused the colonists to seek independence from Great Britain. The third part, the conclusion, declares the colonies to be an independent nation for all future times.

It was very dangerous and risky for the men who signed the Declaration of Independence. If the colonies had lost the war, the men could have been shot for treason. The colony of Georgia thus began to make preparations for war. Georgians sent food and ammunition to the Continental Army and strengthened the home militia.

The U.S. Constitution

For ten years after the Declaration of Independence, the thirteen states worked together under the loose regulations of the Articles of Confederation. Congress had little power under the Articles. Congress could declare war, coin money, establish post offices, and send or recall ambassadors to other nations. However, Congress could not levy taxes to fund a national government. Congress also could not control the trade of goods between one state and another or between a state and other countries. States could set up their own tariffs, which were not always fair. There was no president for the country and there was no court system. There was only a loose union in which each state retained its own independence. Also, if a power was not clearly given to the Congress, it belonged to the states. The Articles of Confederation were weak and they were not strong enough for a new nation.

In the summer of 1787, there was a convention held in Philadelphia with fifty-five delegates, representing every state except Rhode Island. The purpose of the meeting was to revise the Articles of Confederation. This constitutional convention was a "closed-door" meeting. The delegates included prominent people like Benjamin Franklin, James Madison, John Adams, and Georgia Washington. The four men from Georgia were William Few, Abraham Baldwin, William Pierce, and William Houstoun. Some of the delegates went home before the work was finished.

The delegates realized that the Articles of Confederation could not be revised and that a new plan of government had to be created. George Washington was the chairman of the convention. After a summer of debate, thirty-nine delegates proposed a new constitution for the United States of America on September 17, 1787. James Madison drafted much of the final document.

Only nine states had to ratify the Constitution. Georgia was the fourth state to ratify it on a cold day, January 2, 1788.

Articles I, II, and III of the Constitution provided for the legislative, executive, and judicial powers. Article IV guaranteed citizens of each state the privileges and immunities of the other states; this was to help prevent discrimination against visitors. If a person commits a crime in one state and escapes to another state, the state in which that person is hiding must give the person up to the state from which the criminal escaped. The Fourth Article also provides protection to the states.

The Bill of Rights

The delegates at the convention knew that the Constitution would need some changes as the country grew. They provided a way for the Constitution to be amended.

George Mason of Virginia had objected to the fact that the constitution contained no bill of rights. When the first Congress met in 1789, the agenda included the consideration of 12 amendments to the Constitution written by James Madison. The states approved 10 of the 12 on December 15, 1791. Those 10 amendments make up the Bill of Rights.

First Amendment	Right to freedom of worship, speech, press, and assembly.
Second Amendment	Right to keep and bear arms.
Third Amendment	Right against quartering of troops.
Fourth Amendment	Right against unreasonable searches and seizures.
Fifth Amendment	Rights of accused person: grand jury, due process, just compensation.
Sixth Amendment	Right to jury trial.
Seventh Amendment	Rights in suits; decisions of facts in case decided by jury; judge's role limited to questions about the law.
Eighth Amendment	Prohibition of cruel and unusual punishment.
Ninth Amendment	Rights retained by people.
Tenth Amendment	Rights retained by states.

Other Amendments to the Constitution

An amendment is either an addition to the Constitution or a change in the original text. Making additions or revisions to the Constitution is no small feat. Since 1787, more than 9,000 amendments have been proposed, but only 27 have been approved with states' permission.

Eleventh Amendment	A citizen of one state may sue a citizen of another state only if that person has the state's permission.
Twelfth Amendment	Election of the president.
Thirteenth Amendment	Abolishment of slavery.
Fourteenth Amendment	Definition of *citizen*; protection of the citizen against states' abridging rights.
Fifteenth Amendment	Suffrage rights not denied or abridged by "race, color, or previous condition of servitude."
Sixteenth Amendment	Income tax.
Seventeenth Amendment	Senators elected by popular vote.
Eighteenth Amendment	Prohibition of intoxicating liquors.
Nineteenth Amendment	Women's suffrage.
Twentieth Amendment	Beginning and ending of terms of elected officials (members of Congress, vice president, president); presidential succession.
Twenty-first Amendment	Repeal of Eighteenth Amendment.
Twenty-second Amendment	Limitation of president to two terms in office.
Twenty-third Amendment	District of Columbia given vote in presidential elections.
Twenty-fourth Amendment	Repeal of poll tax in federal elections.
Twenty-fifth Amendment	Appointment of vice president if vacancy in that office occurs; procedure in case of presidential disability.
Twenty-sixth Amendment	Establishment of voting age at 18.
Twenty-seventh Amendment	No change in compensation for representatives and senators can take effect until an intervening election of representatives.

Identifying the rights and responsibilities of U.S. citizenship

Essential democratic principles include those fundamental to the American judicial system, such as the right of due process of law, the right to a fair and speedy trial, protection from unlawful search and seizure, and the right to avoid self-incrimination. The democratic values include life, liberty, the pursuit of happiness, the common good, justice, equality, truth, diversity, popular sovereignty, and patriotism. Furthermore, the ideals of American democracy include the following essential constitutional principles: the rule of law, separation of powers, representative government, checks and balances, individual rights, freedom of religion, federalism, limited government, and civilian control of the military.

It is a responsibility for citizens to be active in maintaining a democratic society. Active citizens participate in the political process by voting, providing services to their communities, and regulating themselves in accordance with the law. Citizens of the United States need also to assume responsibilities to their communities, their states, the nation, and the world.

Demonstrating knowledge of strategies and resources (e.g., Internet, mass communication) for inquiry related to government and civics

The ability to understand and apply skills and procedures related to the study of government and civics involves knowledge of the use of systematic inquiry. Inquiry is essential for use in examining topics. Being able to engage in inquiry involves the ability to acquire information from a variety of resources, and organize that information, which leads to the interpretation of the information. Inquiry involves the ability to design and conduct investigations, which in turn leads to the identification and analysis of the issue being studied.

This understanding includes knowledge about and the use of the various resources used in systematic social science inquiry. Those resources include primary and secondary sources, encyclopedias, almanacs, atlases, government documents, artifacts, and oral histories. The resources of the Internet and mass communication are utilized.

Objective 0012   Understand major concepts, principles, and methods of inquiry related to economics

Objective 0012 involves the understanding of major concepts, principles, and methods of inquiry related to economics. Specifically, the objective includes: recognizing basic economic concepts and the purposes and functions of currency; demonstrating knowledge of the basic structure of the U.S. economy and the ways that the U.S. economy relates to and interacts with the economies of other nations; recognizing the roles and interactions of consumers and producers in the U.S. economy; identifying the functions of private business, banks, and the government in the U.S. economy; identifying the knowledge and skills necessary to make reasoned and responsible financial decisions as a consumer, producer, saver, and borrower in a market economy; and, demonstrating knowledge of strategies and resources for inquiry.

Recognizing basic economic concepts (e.g., scarcity, supply and demand, needs and wants, opportunity cost, productivity, trade) and the purposes and functions of currency

Since one of the most important governmental values in America involves restraining individual power, politicians must continually seek reelection. Economics, politics, and government are all enmeshed. The American economy is built upon the theories of capitalism. American citizens have the right to own, maintain, and sell private property. The price of this property depends upon the fluctuations of a free market. Although the government does provide some regulations, a market economy is mostly driven through supply and demand—if there is great demand for a commodity and the supply of that commodity is small, then the price will go up. *Scarcity* is a key term in understanding supply and demand economics. Scarcity describes the constant state of affairs in which individual desires may be endless, but resources are always limited. Because of scarcity people must compete over resources, giving each resource a specific value.

Economics could be defined as the study of choices. Because resources and money are both limited, all economic transactions require specific choices. *Opportunity cost* is defined as the value of what was not chosen because every economic choice rejects alternative options. Often when people think of economics they think only in terms of price and profit; however, opportunity cost could also include non-monetary units such as time or energy.

The *capitalist system* encourages innovation, competition, and an entrepreneurial spirit with the aim of increasing productivity and profit. Entrepreneurs start new economic ventures by organizing labor, capital, and resources. Entrepreneurs compete against each other and the best ideas, inventions, and businesses survive and thrive. When entrepreneurs embark on a new project they take on a certain degree of risk because not all projects will be successful.

Demonstrating knowledge of the basic structure of the U.S., economy and ways in which the U.S. economy relates to and interacts with the economies of other nations

Free enterprise is an economic and political doctrine of the capitalist system. This concept is based on the premise that the economy can regulate itself in a freely competitive market through the relationship of supply and demand, and with minimum governmental intervention. This allows for competition among businesses.

The system of free enterprise has led to globalization. Globalization can be defined as a continuous increase of cross-border financial, economic, and social activities. It implies some level of economic interdependence among individuals, financial entities, and nations. As a result of globalization, trade barriers have been eliminated and tariffs imposed on imported products have been largely discontinued. In a global market, it is difficult to determine the origins of products. For example, Toyota from Japan and Ford from the United States joined forces to build cars using parts and labor from Mexico.

The concept of economic interdependence describes a close connection between producers and consumers of goods and services within a nation or across nations. This economic interdependence has guided nations to establish large markets of free trade zones like the North American Free Trade Agreement (NAFTA) and the European Union (EU) trade agreement.

The United States has rich mineral resources. These include gold, oil, coal, and uranium deposits. Farming makes the United States one of the top producers of wheat, sugar, tobacco and corn (maize). America produces cars, airplanes, and electronics. The top trading partners of the United States include the countries of Canada, China, Mexico, Japan, Germany, UK, South Korea, France, Taiwan, the Netherlands, Brazil, Malaysia, Italy, Singapore, and Ireland.

Recognizing the roles and interactions of consumers and producers in the U.S. economy

Goods and services are the things that generally satisfy human needs, wants, or desires. Goods are tangible items, such as food, cars, and clothing; services are intangible items such as education and health care. A market is the interaction between potential buyers, or consumers, and sellers, or producers, of goods and services. Money is usually the medium of exchange. Supply of a good is the quantity of that good that producers offer at a certain price. The collection of all such points for every price is the supply curve. Demand for a good is the quantity of a good that consumers are willing and able to purchase at a certain price. The demand curve is the combination of quantity and price, at all price levels.

Identifying the functions of private business, banks, and the government in the U.S. economy

It is important for students to identify the functions of private business, banks, and the government in the U.S. economy. Private businesses compete with each other through our system of free enterprise. This is based on the premise that the economy can regulate itself in a freely competitive market through the relationship of supply and demand, and with minimum governmental intervention. One of the main benefits of the system of free enterprise is the competition among businesses.

The main economic institutions of the United States are banks, credit unions, the Federal Reserve System, and the stock market. Banks are one of the main economic institutions of the United States. Banks serve anyone in the general public. Small groups of investors who expect a certain return on their investments own the banks. Only the investors have voting privileges; customers do not have voting rights, cannot be elected board members, and do not participate in governing the institution. The **Federal Deposit Insurance Corporation** (FDIC) insures the banks. Typically, banks do not share information, ideas, or resources.

Macroeconomics is the study of the economy at the world, regional, state, and local levels. Some of the topics include reasons and ways to control inflation, causes of unemployment, and economic growth in general. This is different from microeconomics, which deals with specific issues related to the decision-making process at the household, firm, or industry levels.

Identifying the knowledge and skills necessary to make reasoned and responsible financial decisions as a consumer, producer, saver, and borrower in a market economy

A **market** is the interaction between potential buyers and sellers of goods and services. Every consumer makes buying decisions based on his or her own needs, desires, and income. Every producer decides personally what goods or services to produce, what price to charge, what resources to employ, and what production methods to use. Profits motivate the producers. Competition is central to a market economy. Supply and demand may affect the availability of resources needed for production, distribution, and consumption.

After production, the producer ideally distributes the product to the places where consumers need/want the product, and have the money to pay for the goods or services. In the United States, there is a large and active government sector, but there is a greater emphasis on the market economy.

Demonstrating knowledge of strategies (e.g., interpreting graphs and tables) and resources for inquiry related to economics

The ability to understand and apply skills and procedures related to the study of economics involves knowledge of the use of systematic inquiry. Being able to engage in inquiry involves the ability to acquire information from a variety of resources, and organize that information, which leads to the interpretation of that information. Inquiry involves the ability to design and conduct investigations, which in turn leads to the identification and analysis of social studies issues. In addition, this understanding includes knowledge about and the use of the various resources used in systematic social science inquiry. Those resources include primary and secondary sources.

References

Ambrose, S. & Brinkley, D. (Eds.) (1999). *Witness to America*. New York: HarperCollins.

Davies, P. (1998). *The history atlas of North America*. New York: Macmillan.

Ferrell, R.H. & Natkiel, R. (1993). *Atlas of American history*. Greenwich, CT: Brompton Books.

London, B.B. (1999). *Georgia: The history of an American state*. Montgomery, Alabama: Clairmont Press.

Mankiw, N.G. (2008). *Georgia Southern Economics 2105*. Mason, Ohio: Thomson South-Western.

Savage, T.V. & Armstrong, D.G. (2008). *Effective teaching in elementary social studies*. Upper Saddle River, NJ: Pearson.

Urdang, L. (Ed.) (1996). *The timetables of American history*. New York: Simon & Schuster.

Books Used

The Best Teachers' Test Preparation for the Texes Examinations of educator Standards

The Best Teachers' Test Preparation for the Michigan Test for Teacher Certification

The Best Teachers' Test Preparation for the Florida Teacher Certification Examinations

Mathematics

The mathematics portion of the GACE Early Childhood Education test assesses problem solving processes, as well as concepts and skills relating to numbers and mathematical operations, measurement and geometry, algebra, and data analysis. It is composed of 25 selected-response (multiple-choice questions) and 1 constructed-response assignment.

This review is designed to prepare you for the mathematics portion of Test II. You will be guided through a review of the content related to the test objectives. In addition, you will learn a step-by-step approach to analyzing and accurately answering math problems. By studying this review, you will greatly increase your chances of achieving a good score on the Mathematics portion of the GACE Early Childhood Education Assessment.

I. GACE Mathematics Objectives

Remember, the more you know about the skills tested, the better you will perform on the test. The objectives on which you will be tested are contained in the following list:

- 0013 Understand processes and approaches for exploring mathematics and solving problems.

- 0014 Understand concepts and skills related to numbers and mathematical operations.

- 0015 Understand principles and skills of measurement and the concepts and properties of geometry.

- 0016 Understand concepts and skills related to algebra.

- 0017 Understand concepts and skills related to data analysis.

Now that you know what the objectives are, let's look at them more closely. This section will provide a review of the important information about each of the objectives.

Objective 0013: Understand processes and approaches for exploring mathematics and solving problems.

The first objective deals with problem solving skills, as well as different ways of exploring mathematical concepts. Here, we will review a number of specific concepts associated with mathematical problem solving. However, it is important to note that this objective involves process skills that are typically embedded in mathematical content. This means that the actual GACE questions associated with this objective will also involve other skills that will be reviewed later in this chapter. As we examine each process skill, we will explore examples that illustrate each concept.

1. Problem-Solving Strategies

Problem-solving strategies are purposeful methods of reading and solving mathematical word problems. A problem-solving strategy is different from the operation/s used to solve a problem, such as addition, subtraction, multiplication or division. These operations may be used as part of a strategy, but an operation alone is not a strategy. In any context, a strategy is a systematic way of planning a solution or response, and this is no different with mathematics. There are a number of strategies that can be used to solve problems, including:

- Guess and check

- Draw a picture or diagram

- Look for a pattern

- Estimate

- Simplify the problem

- Work backwards
- Create a table or graph

While multiple strategies might result in the same ultimate solution to a problem, there is usually one strategy that is most effective, depending on the content presented. In order to determine which strategy is best, you must read the problem carefully and consider which strategy is most logical. When reading the word problem, ask yourself which strategy would work best. Can the problem be simplified? Is an exact answer needed, or will an estimate work? Is there a discernible pattern? Would a picture or diagram be helpful?

Read the following examples and see if you can determine the most effective strategy for solving each problem.

Example 1   Virginia is washing the windows of a tall office building. Beginning on the first story, she washes all the windows on one story of the building before moving up to the next. If she completes three stories each day, how many days will it take her to reach the 13th floor?

Example 2   Aliya and Jenny shared a bag of fruit-flavored candies. The bag contained 33 pieces of candy. Jenny ate twice as many candies as Aliya. How many candies did Aliya eat?

Example 3   When the cold weather arrived, Mrs. Stearns knew that she would need more tissues in her classroom, so she brought a new box of 50 tissues to school on Monday. That day, she gave out just three tissues. The next day, she gave out five tissues. On Wednesday, she gave out eight tissues. On Thursday, she gave out 12 tissues. At this rate, how many school days will it take to use up the box of tissues?

Example 1 Explanation:

Each of these problems above is best solved using a different strategy. Example 1 involves a physical or spatial situation, so the "Draw a Picture or Diagram" strategy is most helpful. In order to solve this problem, a simple diagram can be constructed, as shown below in Figure 4.1:

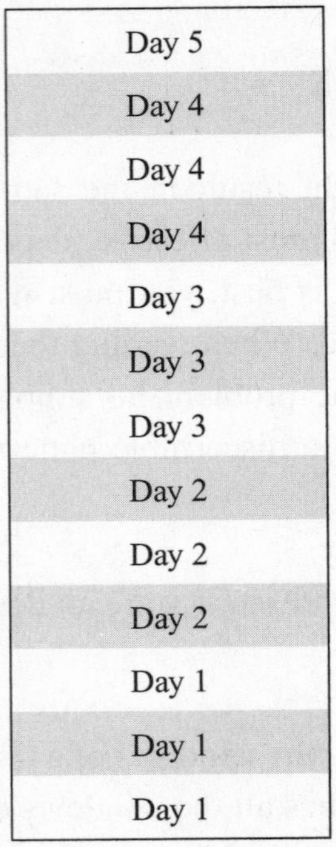

Day 5
Day 4
Day 4
Day 4
Day 3
Day 3
Day 3
Day 2
Day 2
Day 2
Day 1
Day 1
Day 1

Figure 4.1: Building Diagram

Each level of the diagram represents a story of the building. Since Virginia completes three stories per day, a new day begins after each set of three levels. Using the diagram, it can be determined that Virginia will reach the 13th floor of the building on Day 5. While drawing a picture or diagram can be helpful for visual learners in solving many different types of problems, the physical situation here is a clue that this strategy is most effective in finding a quick solution.

Example 2 Explanation:

In Example 2, we are given only one exact number, the total number of candies in the bag that Aliya and Jenny shared. Without another exact number, we cannot simply perform an operation to find the number of candies Aliya ate, but we know that Jenny ate twice as many as Aliya did. Since we are given the relationship between the two numbers, we know the formula for solving the problem. If x equals the number of candies Aliya ate, then the formula for our problem would be $x + 2x = 33$. The best way to solve this problem is simply to start replacing x with different numbers to see if they work with our formula. This is the "Guess and Check" strategy for problem solving. It isn't always necessary to identify a specific formula to use with this strategy. Here, we could simply ask ourselves, "What number can be doubled and added to itself to equal 33?" Then we simply start trying out numbers to determine what works. On paper, the "Guess and Check" process might look like this:

$$\cancel{9 + 2(9) = 27}$$

$$\cancel{10 + 2(10) = 30}$$

$$11 + 2(11) = 33$$

Example 3 Explanation:

In Example 3, we are provided with several different figures regarding the number of tissues distributed by Mrs. Stearns. Here we are asked, based on the numbers provided, to predict when Mrs. Stearns will have distributed all of the 50 tissues in her box. In order to solve this problem, we need to look at the relationships between the numbers we are given. The numbers are: 3, 5, 8, and 12. The series of numbers provided here, along with a situation that requires us to use those numbers to make a prediction, indicates that we should use the "Look for a Pattern" strategy in order to solve this problem. By looking closely at the numbers we are given, we can see that with each day, the difference in the number of tissues given increases by one tissue. Therefore, the pattern here is +2, +3, +4, etc. We can complete this pattern until we reach a total equal to or greater to 50.

The first five numbers are 3, 5, 8, 12, and 17. Their sum is 45. The next number in this sequence is 17 + 6 = 23. Note that 45 + 23 = 68, which is greater than 50.

Therefore, we know that it will take 6 school days for Mrs. Stearns to use up her box of tissues.

Remember, when choosing a problem-solving strategy, you should read the problem carefully and examine the information provided to determine which strategy is most effective.

2. Mathematical Arguments

Another skill associated with processes and approaches for exploring mathematics and solving problems is the ability to explain and justify mathematical arguments. When evaluating a mathematical argument, you should be able to provide evidence for why a mathematical statement is true or false. This requires logical reasoning skills and a basic understanding of mathematical concepts such as principles of geometry, measurement and computation, number sense, and relationships between numbers and operations. In other words, you must understand and be able to explain the general "rules" of mathematics. While many math "facts," are committed to memory, logic and reason are required for solving any math problem that goes beyond simple computation or recall. Multiple-choice questions involving the evaluation of mathematical arguments may ask you to identify an error or step in a mathematical process, or they may simply require you to provide a "logical" answer that may or may not involve calculation. Consider the following examples:

Example 1   Yasar is studying the growth of six small flowering plants over a period of several weeks. At the end of the observation period, he measures the plants and discovers that two plants are 12 inches, and the other four are 13 inches, 10 inches, 14 inches, and 11 inches. What should he do to find the average height of the plants?

Example 2   Caleb and Taylor spent Saturday baking cookies for their teachers. When all the dough was gone, they had baked 150 cookies. How could they be sure that they will be able to divide the cookies equally among their six teachers without actually dividing?

Explanation of Example 1

Example 1 asks us to identify the process by which we would determine the average height of the plants under study. In order to answer this question, we must know the rule for finding average or *mean* of a set of numbers. To find the average, we add the numbers together and then divide by the total number of figures. In this case, we need not solve the problem itself, but simply describe how the problem should be solved. Had the problem required us to report the average height in feet, we would also need to convert inches to feet after finding the average height in inches.

Explanation of Example 2

Example 2 asks use to describe how Caleb and Taylor know, without actually dividing, that 150 cookies can be divided equally among their six teachers. To solve this problem, we must understand the rules of divisibility. These rules provide us with simple strategies that can be used to test any number in order to determine divisibility. According to the rules of divisibility, a number is divisible by 6 if it divisible by 2 **and** 3. A number is divisible by 2 if it ends in 0, 2, 4, 6, or 8. 150 ends in 0, so we know that it is divisible by 2. A number is divisible by 3 if the sum of the digits is divisible by 3. The sum of the digits of 150 is 6, which is divisible by 3. Therefore, 150 is divisible by both 2 and 3, and, therefore, 6.

3.   Mathematical Communication

Mathematical communication requires using the language and vocabulary of mathematics to express ideas. All mathematical problems involve an understanding of the basic vocabulary used to describe numbers and figures, as well as the basic operations, concepts, and processes of mathematics. Effective mathematical communication skills will be needed to perform successfully on all of the GACE objectives that appear in this chapter. However, we will look at a few examples here to describe how mathematical communication might evaluated:

Example 1   Which of the following terms does NOT describe a rectangle?

    a.   polygon

    b.   quadrilateral

    c.   square

    d.   parallelogram

Example 2 $120 \div 12 = 10$

In the problem above, what does the number "10" represent?

    a.   the dividend

    b.   the quotient

    c.   the sum

    d.   the divisor

Explanation of Example 1:

This problem requires us to understand how a number of geometric figures are defined. First, we must know that a rectangle is a four-sided shape with four right angles. Then, we must determine the meaning of the other terms to decide which of them does not apply to a rectangle. Any closed plane figure made up of lined segments is considered a polygon, so a rectangle is clearly a polygon. A quadrilateral is any polygon with four sides and four vertices, which also applies to the rectangle. A parallelogram is a quadrilateral with two sets of parallel sides, with opposite sides being of equal length. Therefore, a rectangle is also a parallelogram. Finally, a square is a special kind of rectangle with four equal sides. Since a rectangle does not necessarily have four equal sides, it is not a square. Therefore, the answer is choice c.

Explanation of Example 2:

Example 2 evaluates our knowledge of the vocabulary associated with the process of division. The term "sum" refers to the total achieved when adding, so it does not apply to division. The dividend is the number that is being divided into equal groups. Here, that number is 120. The divisor is the number that we are dividing the dividend by. In the example, we are dividing 120 into groups of 12. In this problem, 10 is the answer, or quotient (choice b).

4.   Mathematical Connections

Mathematical connections refer to the relationships among the materials, models, methods, and technologies used to solve mathematical problems, as well as the interconnections among different mathematical concepts. An understanding of mathematical connections also involves an awareness of how mathematics relates to other content areas as well as everyday life. As with the use of reasoning and mathematical communication, the ability to recognize connections and relationships is important for success in a wide variety of mathematical contexts. Many of the concepts and examples that you will encounter throughout the rest of this chapter involve an understanding of such connections. However, once again we will isolate a few examples that clearly illustrate the evaluation of mathematical connections.

Example 1   At the local grocery store, Vidalia onions are sold individually from a bin and pre-packaged in groups of two or three, depending on size. Onions in the bin are priced at $0.58 cents per pound. The pre-packaged onions are priced at $1.88. Which is a better deal: three pounds worth of onions from the bin from or three pre-packaged onions weighing a total of 48 ounces?

MATHEMATICS

CHAPTER 4

Example 2

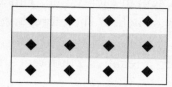

Zahra used counters to create the array above to represent a multiplication problem. Then, Mr. Sandlin asked her to separate the counters into rows of three counters each. What number sentence would represent his request?

Explanation of Example 1

The first problem demonstrates a number of mathematical connections. We are asked to apply our knowledge of mathematical concepts in the "real-life" context of grocery shopping. This requires that we understand how mathematical skills can be applied outside of the classroom. In order to solve this problem, we also need to understand the relationship between the unit and total price of the onions, as well as the relationship between pounds and ounces. We know that the pre-packaged onions are priced at $1.88 for three, and that these weigh in at 48 ounces. Because we know that there are 16 ounces in one pound, we can divide 48 by 16 to determine that the pre-packaged onions weight three pounds. To determine the price of three pounds of onions from the bin, we multiply $0.58 by three, and find the total price to be $1.74. Since both quantities weigh three pounds, we can see that purchasing onions from the bin is the better buy.

Explanation of Example 2

The second problem illustrates how mathematical connections can require an understanding of how to apply various materials and models to solve problems. This problem also requires that we understand the relationship between multiplication and division. The figure in Example 2 is an array, which is used to teach and represent multiplication and division problems. As shown, the array would be represented by the following number sentence:

$$3 \times 4 = 12$$

The product, or total, in determined by multiplying the number of groups by the number in each group. Note that this particular array is arranged in **three** rows of **four**, which means that there are three groups, with four counters in each group. This determines the order of the numbers in the multiplication number sentence. Therefore, even though

$4 \times 3 = 12$ yields the same product, it requires a different array.

The problem asks us to determine the number sentence that would represent the separation of these counters into rows of three counters each. If we rearranged the array according to Mr. Sandlin's request, it would look like this:

Here, we separated, or divided, the 12 counters into four rows of three each. The number sentence that represents 12 counters separated into rows of three is:

$12 \div 3 = 4$

Solving this problem requires us to understand the inverse relationship between multiplication and division, as well as the models and materials we can use to represent multiplication and division.

Objective 0014: Understand concepts and skills related to numbers and mathematical operations.

This objective involves a wide variety of basic skills relating to numbers and operations. These skills involve an understanding of the properties and values of numbers, the relationships between numbers, the organization of the base-ten number system, and operations involving whole numbers, common and decimal fractions, and percentages. Here, we will consider individually seven basic concepts that are addressed by this objective.

1. Number Sense

Number sense is essential to a deep conceptual understanding of mathematics. It involves an intuitive awareness of the way that numbers "work" within the base-ten system. As Burton et al. (1992) suggest, "This 'friendliness with numbers" goes far beyond mere memorization of algorithms and number facts and implies an ability to recognize when operations are required and when they have been correctly performed" (p. 8). Consider the example below:

Example 1   Which operational symbols correctly complete the number sentence below?

$$90 \underline{\quad} 15 = 24 \underline{\quad} 18$$

Explanation of Example:

This problem requires us to understand the relative value of numbers (larger/ smaller) in order to determine what operations are required in order to complete the number sentence. If the solution was not readily apparent, you may have employed the "Guess and Check" strategy discussed earlier to determine the correct answer by substituting trying different operations until success is achieved. The solution requires us to divide 90 by 15 and subtract 18 from 24. When the division symbol is added to the left of the equal sign, and the subtraction symbol to the right, we achieve a result of six on both sides.

2.   Place Value

Place value is, quite literally, the value of a number based on its position, or place. We use a base-ten, or decimal, place value system, which has several basic characteristics, as described by Smith (1997):

- Exactly ten numerals: 1, 2, 3, 4, 5, 6, 7, 8, 9, and 0.

- Position determines value. Ones are placed on the right. The next position, the tens place, is the base. The values increase in multiples of 10: hundreds, thousands, ten thousands, and so on.

The base-ten system applies to whole numbers as well as decimals. As we place numerals to the left of the decimal point to indicate values less than one, the values of the numerals **decrease** in the same way that whole numbers **increase.** The "th" at the end of the position name indicates that we are referring to a decimal rather than a whole number: tenths, hundredths, thousandths, and so on. Consider the following example:

Example What will happen to the following number if the 3 and the 8 change places?

481,672.35

    a. The digit 8 will represent the hundredths place.

    b. The digit 8 will represent the tens place.

    c. The digit 3 will represent the ten thousands place.

    d. The digit 3 will represent the thousands place.

Explanation of Example:

In the example above, we must determine what will happen to the value of the number if the positions of the numerals 3 and 8 are interchanged. We know that the 8 is in the ten thousands place, and the 3 is in the tenths place. Therefore, if we switch the two numbers, the 3 will represent the ten thousands place, as indicated by choice c.

3. Equivalent Forms

An understanding of equivalent forms requires the ability to describe a specified quantity as a common fraction, decimal fraction, and percentage. In order to use these forms interchangeably, one must recognize the value of decimal fractions in the base-ten system, and be able to connect that value to its common fraction and percent equivalent. The example below illustrates how knowledge of equivalent forms might be evaluated:

Example Chris, James and John shared a pepperoni pizza. The table below shows how much each of them ate:

Chris	0.5
James	30%
John	$\frac{1}{5}$

According to the chart above, who ate the most pizza?

Explanation of Example:

The problem above requires us to use fractions, decimals and percents interchangeably. In order to determine who ate the most pizza, we need to convert the unlike quantities into a single form so that we can compare them. The two non-percent values are easily converted into percents. 0.5, read as five tenths, is equivalent to 50 percent. $\frac{1}{5}$ is equivalent to $\frac{20}{100}$ or 20 percent. Fifty percent is greater than the other two values. Therefore, we know that Chris ate the most pizza.

4. Operations

Mathematical operations include addition, subtraction, multiplication and division. An understanding of these operations involves an awareness of the relationships between the mathematical operations and the ability to use the basic four operations to perform calculations with variables and numbers. Variables represent the unknown in a mathematical problem, and they can be represented by a "blank," as seen in simple equations at the primary level, or by letters, as seen in more advanced equations involving algebraic skills.

Recognizing how to interpret and use the symbols that represent the four basic operations is an important part of understanding operations, but we also need to be aware of the order in which the operations should be applied in a mathematical expression. The order of operations that, when solving an expression, to follow what Suggate et. al (1998) term the "rules of precedence" (p. 37). These are:

1. Carry out operations within parentheses (or brackets)

2. Perform multiplications and divisions, in the order in which they appear.

3. Complete the addition and subtraction calculations.

The following examples illustrate the range of skills associated with mathematical operations:

Example 1 Which of the following words is least likely to be found in a word problem involving division?

    a.   equally

    b.   groups

    c.   altogether

    d.   each

Example 2 Rubén wants to distribute a large box of 500 pencils equally among his 22 homeroom students. Before he passes them out, he needs to set aside two pencils for each of the students in Stephanie's homeroom, but he isn't sure how many students she has. Which expression accurately represents the mathematical operations that Rubén must perform to distribute the pencils?

    a. $\dfrac{500}{2(22 + x)}$

    b. $\dfrac{500 - 2(x)}{22}$

    c. $\dfrac{22 + 2(x)}{500}$

    d. $\dfrac{500(x)}{22}$

Example 3 Solve for y.

$$y = 10 + 3 \times (5 - 3) + 6 \times 3 - 12 \div 2$$

Explanation of Example 1:

The first problem requires us to understand the relationship between the basic operations in order to determine which words apply to the situation described. In order to solve the problem, we must be able to recognize that multiplication is repeated addition that combines equal groups into a larger group, while division separates one group into smaller equal groups. Therefore, "equally," "groups," and "each" are all words that are likely to be found in a division problem. The word "altogether" (choice c) indicates a total or larger sum, so it would not be consistent with the operation of division.

Explanation of Example 2:

The second example evaluates our ability to use the operations with variables. In order to solve this problem, we must examine the operations required to solve the problem. We know that the problem involves division because we are told that the pencils must be distributed equally. However, the total number of pencils is not our dividend, because we must "set aside," or subtract, a certain number of pencils from the total quantity before dividing. In order to determine how many pencils to subtract, we need to multiply the number of students in Stephanie's class by 2. Because we do not know how many students she has, we represent that unknown number with "x." The equation that represents the process of determining the dividend is:

$$500 - 2(x)$$

Once the dividend is determined, we can divide by 22, the number of students in Rubén's class, to determine the final answer. Therefore, the correct answer is b.

Explanation of Example 3:

To work out the expression in Example 3, we must follow the order of operations. The table below illustrates how we can use the order of operations to solve for y.

$$y = 10 + 3 \times (5 - 3) + 6 \times 3 - 12 \div 2$$

Order of operations	Calculations	Expression
Parentheses	$(5 - 3) = 2$	$y = 10 + 3 \times 2 + 6 \times 3 - 12 \div 2$
Multiplication and Division	$3 \times 2 = 6$ $6 \times 3 = 18$ $12 \div 2 = 6$	$y = 10 + 6 + 18 - 6$
Addition and Subtraction	$10 + 6 + 18 = 34$ $34 - 6 = 28$	$y = 28$

5. Properties

In addition to the recognized order of operations, there are also rules for the way that the four operations interact with each other in a mathematical or number sentence. These properties of numbers are described below:

I. Commutative Law

Suggate et. al (1998) summarize this property with the question, "Can I change places with you?" (p. 38). When you think of "commuting," you probably imagine traveling back and forth between destinations, such as from school to home, or home to work. In traveling, you are changing positions from one place to another, and back again. Similarly, in mathematics, numbers that "commute" can exchange positions without changing the value of the expression. Addition and multiplication are said to be commutative because the numbers linked by these operations can be interchanged without changing the result of the expression.

The expressions below illustrate this property:

$$4 + 5 = 9 \qquad\qquad 7 \times 8 = 56$$
$$5 + 4 = 9 \qquad\qquad 8 \times 7 = 56$$

No matter which order the numbers are presented in the addition or multiplication problem, the result is the same. However, this is not true of division and subtraction.

II. Associative Law

This property addresses the way in which we combine, or "associate" numbers that are related to each other through operations. This law might be summarized as "Does the order of action matter?" (Suggate et al., p. 37). Consider the following expression:

$$15 + 10 + 25$$

We solve this problem by combining two numbers at a time. There are two ways that we can combine the numbers to add them:

$$(15 + 10) + 25 \qquad\qquad 15 + (10 + 25)$$

$$= 25 + 25 \qquad\qquad\qquad = 15 + 35$$

$$= 50 \qquad\qquad\qquad\qquad = 50$$

Whether we solve the problem by starting with the first two numbers or the second two numbers, the result is the same. This property also applies to multiplication. Addition and multiplication, which is simply repeated addition, are said to be associative because it does not matter in which order the operations are executed. Again, this law does not apply to subtraction and division.

III. Distributive Law

This property addresses the question, "Can this be split up?" (Suggate et al., 1998, p. 38). When we discussed the order of operations, it was noted that operations inside parentheses should be executed first. However, sometimes it is possible to remove the parentheses and "distribute" the numbers to simplify the calculation. For example, consider how you might use mental math to solve a two-digit by two-digit multiplication problem.

$$34 \times 15$$

To solve this problem mentally, you might begin by using multiples of ten (30×15). Then, you could work the simple problem that remains (4×15) and add the two products together to find the answer. This process is shown below:

$$34 \times 15$$

$$= (30 + 4) \times 15$$

$$= (30 \times 15) + (4 \times 15)$$

$$= 450 + 60$$

$$= 510$$

This example shows how the multiplier can be *distributed* across the expression without changing the result of the expression. This also applies to division, as a divisor can also be distributed across the expression. Thus, multiplication and division are said to be distributive over addition and subtraction.

IV. Identity Properties

The identity properties of addition and multiplication are perhaps the most straight-forward of the principles outlined here. The identity property of addition, also called *the property of zero*, tells us that the sum of any number or variable and zero is always that number or variable. Symbolically, this property can be represented as:

$$x + 0 = x$$

Similarly, the identity property of multiplication states that any number or variable multiplied by one is that number or variable. This can be represented as:

$$x(1) = x$$

Now that we have examined the properties that describe how the mathematical operations interact with each other in a mathematical or number sentence, let's look at an example of how this might expressed as a test question:

Example $5(4 + 8) = 60$

Which property is best represented by the expression above?

    a.   commutative property of addition

    b.   distributive property of multiplication

    c.   associative property of addition

    d.   identity property of multiplication

Explanation of Example:

This example best illustrates the distributive property of multiplication. The parentheses here can be removed and the expression rewritten as shown below:

$$(5 \times 4) + (5 \times 8) = 60$$

$$20 + 40 = 60$$

6. Calculations

In the context of this objective, calculations simply refer to computations using whole numbers, decimals, and fractions. You may be required to perform these calculations as a simple problem, or in the context of a word problem, as demonstrated in Objective 0013. Consider these examples:

Example 1   Solve.

$$88 \times \frac{1}{4}$$

Example 2   Jake is creating a memory book of family pictures. He needs 0.25 meters of ribbon to create a border on each page. If he has 4 meters of ribbon, how many pages can he decorate?

Explanation of Example 1:

We can multiply a whole number by a common fraction by converting the common fraction to a decimal fraction, or we can divide by the reciprocal. These two methods are illustrated below:

$$88 \times \frac{1}{4} \qquad\qquad 88 \times \frac{1}{4}$$
$$= 88 \times 0.25 \qquad = 88 \div 4$$
$$= 22 \qquad\qquad\quad = 22$$

Explanation of Example 2:

The second problem requires us to perform division with decimals. We can easily solve this problem manually, as shown below:

$$\frac{4}{0.25} = \frac{4 \times 100}{0.25 \times 100} = \frac{400}{25} = 16$$

7. Estimation

Estimation is an important skill for mathematical reasoning, because it allows us to predict the result of calculations and evaluate the accuracy of our computations. Estimation requires an understanding of place value, because we use the base-ten system to round numbers to the nearest ten, hundred, thousand, and so on, depending on how precise we desire the estimate to be. The example below involves the use of estimation skills:

Example   If the numbers below are rounded to the hundreds place and then added together, what will the sum be?

   5,823   87   7,865   786

Explanation of Example:

The problem requires us to use our knowledge of place value to round the numbers to the hundreds place in order to provide an estimated sum:

   5,800   100   7,900   800

When added, the rounded numbers total 14,600.

Objective 0015:   Understand principles and skills of measurement and the concepts and properties of geometry.

This objective assesses the ability to use measurement tools, procedures and units. It also addresses a variety of geometric concepts, including plane and solid figures and coordinate systems. Let's take a closer look at the concepts of measurement and geometry that are associated with this objective.

1. Measurement

As Smith (1997) explains, measurement involves using units to describe physical quantities (such as length, height, weight, volume) as well as nonphysical quantities (such as time, temperature, or money). We call the procedures we use to assign units to physical quantities *direct* measurement. The use of measurement tools such as clocks, calendars, temperature, and money is *indirect* measurement.

When we use direct measurement, we can use both standard units, such as centimeters, feet, or pounds, and nonstandard units. Standard units include both customary and metric units. Inches, feet, yards, miles and pounds are examples of customary units. When we use nonstandard units, we estimate units using everyday items or personal references of measurement, such as the length of our finger or the width of our hand.

In order to demonstrate an understanding of measurement, we must be able to select and use the appropriate procedures, tools, and units for measuring length, perimeter, area, capacity, weight, time, and temperature. The examples that follow represent the types of questions involve measurement skills.

Example 1   About how much does a large bagel weigh?

        a.   4 grams

        b.   4 kilogram

        c.   4 ounces

        d.   4 pounds

Example 2   Kris is constructing a picture frame using two feet of plywood trim. If the length of the frame, l, is to be 2 inches greater than the width, w, write an equation that can be used to determine the width of the garden.

Example 3   The train left Savannah at 11:35 A.M. and arrived in Jacksonville at 2:15 P.M. There was a half-hour layover at the Jesup station. How long did the trip take?

Explanation of Example 1:

The first problem asks us to determine a reasonable weight for a bagel. One gram is about the weight of one paper clip. Since a bagel is heavier than four paper clips, 4 grams is not a reasonable choice. A pineapple, which is heavier than a bagel, weighs about one kilogram, so 4 kilograms is not a reasonable choice, either. A pint of milk weighs about one pound, so 4 pounds can also be ruled out as a choice. This leaves the best answer, 4 ounces. A slice of bread weighs about one ounce, and since a bagel is typically denser than loaf bread, it is reasonable to assume that a large bagel might weigh 4 ounces.

Explanation of Example 2:

This problem requires that we know how to find the perimeter of a rectangle by adding the length of the four sides. The perimeter is equal to the length of the wood used to make the frame, which is 2 feet, or 24 inches. To find the perimeter, we add two times the length plus two times the width, represented by the expression $2l + 2w = 24$. Since we need to determine the width, we solve for w. Our problem tells us that the length (l) is 2 inches greater than the width, so we can substitute this into the expression:

$$2(w + 2) + 2w = 24$$

Explanation of Example 3:

11:35 to 2:15

This problem asks us to determine elapsed time from A.M. to P.M. Note that this problem includes some irrelevant information, so it's important to read carefully. We are told that a 30-minute layover occurred, but this is already figured into the total length of the trip, so we do not need to consider this in our calculations. To determine the time that has passed, we can use a counting-up strategy. Counting up from 11:35 A.M. to 2:15 P.M., we find that the trip was 2 hours and 40 minutes long.

2. Geometric figures

Identifying geometric figures involves classifying plane (2-D) and solid (3-D) geometric figures. Examples of 2-D figures include: triangle, rectangle, rhombus, quadrilateral, and parallelogram. Examples of 3-D figures include: sphere, cone, cube, and cylinder. In addition, you must demonstrate the ability to measure the component parts of geometric figures (e.g., angles, segments) and find the volume of simple geometric solids.

Example 1

Which of the following describes the figure above?

    a.   hexagon

    b.   trapezoid

    c.   polygon

    d.   quadrilateral

Example 2

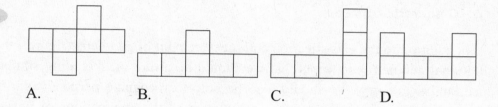

    A.   B.   C.   D.

Which of the nets above can be folded to make a cube?

Example 3   Grant and Weston built a rectangular bird feeder. The width was 4 inches. The length was twice the width and the height was three times the width. What is the volume of the box?

Explanation of Example 1:

This example requires us to identify an irregular plane figure. The figure shown has seven sides and angles, so it is not a hexagon, which is a six-sided figure. A trapezoid is a quadrilateral with two unequal parallel sides, and this figure is neither. This figure is an irregular heptagon, and because it is a closed shape with straight sides, is a polygon.

Explanation of Example 2:

Example 2 presents a variety of nets, which are "unfolded" versions of three-dimensional shapes. In order to determine which of these nets would form a cube, we must be familiar with the shape of the cube, and be able to visualize the folding process. When folded, nets B, C, and D would leave gaps in the cube. Choice A is the only option that will form a complete cube.

Explanation of Example 3:

The third example asks us to find the volume of a rectangular prism, based on the information provided. In order to solve this problem, we need to know that, in order to find the volume of a rectangular prism, we multiply length times the width times the height. We know that the width is 4 inches. If the length is twice the width, then the length is 8 inches. The height is three times the width, or 12 inches. Therefore:

$$V = 4 \times 8 \times 12$$

$$V = 384 \text{ cubic inches}$$

3. Geometric concepts

In addition to the classification and measurement of geometric figures, there are some additional geometric concepts that we should be aware of, including similarity, congruence, and symmetry. We should also be able to recognize perpendicular, parallel, and intersecting lines, and demonstrate knowledge of the applications of measurement and geometry in everyday life.

Example

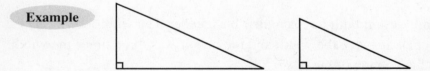

Which describes the two figures pictured above?
   a.   Symmetrical
   b.   Congruent
   c.   Similar
   d.   Quadrilateral

Explanation of Example:

In the example above, we see two right triangles. These figures are not symmetrical because a line cannot be drawn that separates them into two mirror images. The figures are not congruent because they are not identical in shape and size, nor are they four-sided figures, or quadrilaterals. However, even though the figures are not the same size, they are similar because they share the same angles.

4. Coordinate systems

In the coordinate system, two perpendicular lines, the *x*-axis, or horizontal line, and the *y*-axis, or vertical line, are used to define a grid upon which we locate points. At the elementary level, students begin to identify and graph ordered pairs in the first quadrant in the coordinate plane. This provides a foundation for understanding the coordinate system, which will eventually be used to graph algebraic functions. The example below demonstrates how a basic knowledge of the coordinate system might be evaluated:

Example

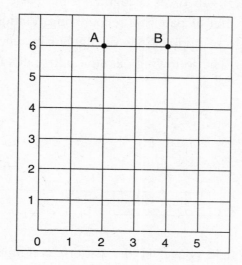

In the grid above, what is the ordered pair at point B?

Explanation of Example:

In order to determine the ordered pair of point B, we begin by identifying its location on the *x*-axis. The point is located 4 units to the right of the origin. Then, we identify the position on the *y*-axis. Point B is located 6 units above the origin. Therefore, the ordered pair that represents the location of point B is (4, 6).

Objective 0016:   Understand concepts and skills related to algebra.

Objective 0016 deals with algebraic concepts. An understanding of patterns is essential to mastering the skills associated with algebra. According to Suggate et al. (1998), "Algebra is a very powerful way of expressing patterns concisely. It is concerned with generalities and finding equivalences among expressions" (p. 100). Therefore, the primary concepts addressed by this objective include patterns, expressions, and algebraic functions. Algebraic skills are closely tied to problem solving, as many word problems require us to recognize and extend patterns or create algebraic expressions can be used to find a solution. Let's take a closer look at the basic algebraic concepts addressed by the GACE Early Childhood Education Assessment.

1. Patterns

In algebra, a pattern is a sequence governed by a rule that can be expressed in words or symbols. An understanding of patterns involves recognizing the basic characteristics of patterns, identifying correct extensions of patterns, recognizing relationships among patterns, and demonstrating knowledge of applications of algebra in representing relationships and patterns in everyday life. The following example illustrates the concept of pattern characteristics and extensions:

Example

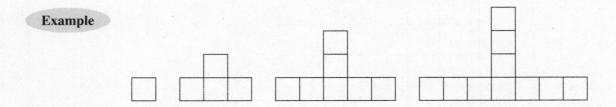

Look at the four models above. If the pattern continues, how many squares would be needed to build the 6th model?

Explanation of Example:

The example asks us to extend the pattern based on the information we are given. The first step in extending the pattern is to recognize the relationships between the four models by counting and recording the number of squares in each one. The creation of a simple table is a useful aid in recording what is known and what must be determined:

Model	1	2	3	4	5	6
Squares	1	4	7	10	?	?

By looking at the table, we can see that the number of squares increases by three each time a new model is constructed. Following this rule, we can determine that the 5th model would contain 13 squares, while the 6th model would contain 16 squares. Since this problem requires us to extend the pattern only twice beyond what is illustrated, we could solve it without the use of the table. However, creating a table is a reliable way of recording patterns and ensuring accuracy as the pattern is extended, particularly as the number of extensions increases.

2. Algebraic Expressions

Understanding algebraic expressions requires knowledge of the concepts of variable, function, and equation. These concepts are essential to the expression of algebraic relationships, the application of algebraic methods to solve equations and inequalities, and the use of algebraic functions to plot points, describe graphs, and determine slope.

At the elementary level, algebraic expressions typically contain numbers, operational symbols and variables. The expression is part of the number sentence, or equation, which includes the equal sign. In elementary mathematics, functions are algebraic equations that express rules or patterns to determine the relationship between values. For example, if the number of green beads of a necklace is 3 fewer than 5 times the number of red beads, we could represent this function as:

$$G = 5R - 3$$

Using this rule, we could determine the number of green and red beads, given the quantity of either color. We could use this rule to express the relationship between x and y in order to plot points using the coordinate system and create a graphic representation of the function. The example that follows illustrates the use of algebraic functions to plot points and determine slope.

Example

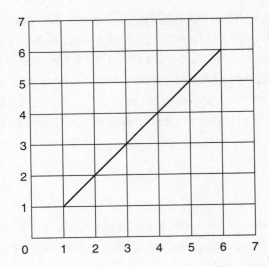

Which function is illustrated in the graph above?

a. $y = 2x + 3$

b. $y = x - 1$

c. $y = \dfrac{x}{2}$

d. $y = x$

Explanation of Example:

In the example above, we are asked to determine the function represented by the graph that is pictured in the figure. To determine the relationship between the x and y variables, we can plot some points along the line. Focusing on the first quadrant alone, we could plot the following ordered pairs: (1, 1), (2, 2), (3, 3), and so on. This tells us that the value of x is equal to the value of y. Therefore, the function is $y = x$.

Objective 0017:   Understand concepts and skills related to data analysis.

Understanding how to represent and interpret data is an important skill, not only in mathematics, but in other content areas and in everyday life. In our information-rich society, we are constantly confronted with questions that often require us to collect, organize and interpret data. As Cathcart et al. (2001) note, "Teaching about data analysis must be more than just creating and read graphs. Instruction must help children to understand, interpret, and apply reasoning in studying data" (p. 354). Therefore, this objective involves not only answering questions about graphs, but also drawing logical conclusions from the data represented.

Organizing, Interpreting and Analyzing Data

Specifically, this objective involves the ability to organize and interpret data in a variety of formats, such as tables, frequency distributions, line graphs, and circle graphs. Identifying the best format for displaying different types of data is also important. When presented with data in any type of graph, we should be able to identify trends and patterns in the data and describe it using standard measures such as mean, median, mode, and range. Finally, we should also be able to draw valid conclusions based on the data presented and demonstrate knowledge of how data analysis applies to everyday life. Let's look at example of a question involving data analysis skills:

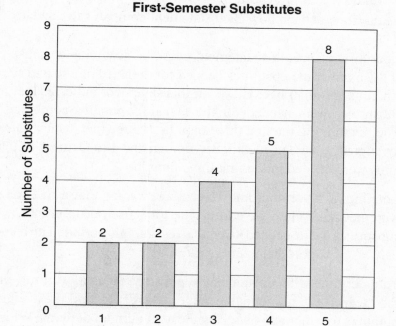

The principal of Goodyear Elementary is trying to determine how much he needs to budget for substitute teacher pay for the upcoming school year. The graph above shows the number of substitutes needed for each of the first five months of the school year, beginning in August. Which of the following statements regarding teacher substitutes is consistent with the data depicted above?

a. Fewer than five substitutes were needed during the first three months of the school year.

b. More than half of the substitutes required between August and December were needed for the last two months of the semester.

c. The mean number of substitutes for the five-month period above is 2.

d. Four substitutes were needed in the 5th month of the semester.

Explanation of Example 1:

The example above requires us to use the graph to draw some conclusions about the data presented. We are asked to determine which of the statements is consistent with the data presented. Let's look at each how each statement compares to the data:

a. Upon first glance, this statement might be deceiving, because we might look at the number of substitutes needed for the third month and see that it is four, which is less than five. However, this statement indicates that fewer than five substitutes were needed for the first three months combined, which is not true. Examining the first three months, we see that 2 substitutes were needed in August, 2 were needed in September, and 4 in October. A total of 8 substitutes were needed in the first three months.

b. Looking at November and December, we see that a total of 13 substitutes were needed. When we add up the total from each month, we find that 21 substitutes were needed over the five-month period. Thirteen is more than half of 21, so this statement is true.

c. To determine if this statement applies to our data, we must understand that the mean is the numerical average. In order to find the average, we add the numbers together and divide by the total number of items. When we divide 21 by 5, we get 4.2. Therefore, the average is not approximately 2, as the statement indicates.

d. This statement tests our ability to distinguish the x-axis from the y-axis. If we confused the two, we might notice the 5 and the 4 together in the fourth data set, and assume the statement is true. However, if we are familiar with the x-axis and their titles, we know that we must move horizontally to the 5th position on the x-axis before moving up the y-axis to determine the number of substitutes needed in the 5th month, which equals 8.

II. Strategies for Success on the Mathematics Portion of Test II

In order to make the most out of the time allotted it is important to approach the problems strategically. The following is a recommended plan of attack to follow when solving math problems.

A Four-Step Approach

It has long been recognized that a strategic approach to problem-solving can enhance success and promote mathematical thinking and reasoning skills. Smith (1997) describes Polya's (1962) simple four-step strategy for solving problems. This method is a "common sense" approach to solving problems that can be applied in mathematics, as well as other contexts. Following these steps each time you encounter a new problem will help you choose the best solution and achieve greater success.

Step 1: Understand the problem.

- In order to understand the problem, you must first step carefully read the **entire** problem. Even if the problem is a simple computation with no other information, you should study it carefully before beginning any calculations.

- After you have read the problem, take time to think about what the problem is asking you to do. Note the key words and/or mathematical symbols that identify your task.

- Determine what information you have and what you need to solve the problem. Eliminate any unnecessary information.

Step 2: Devise a plan.

- Once you've determined what the problem is asking, you should develop your strategy for solving it.

- Examine the task at hand carefully and determine the most effective way to solve the problem. Consider the following strategies:

  - Guess and check

  - Draw a picture or diagram

  - Look for a pattern

  - Estimate

  - Simplify the problem

  - Work backwards

  - Create a table or graph

- Consider how you will execute your plan. What data should be represented in your diagram, table, or graph? If you work backwards, with what data should you begin? If an estimate is used, will further calculation be needed? Would it be more efficient to work out the problem and compare your answer to the choices provided, or should you systematically rule out each incorrect answer? Determine the most efficient way to yield an accurate answer.

Step 3: Carry out the plan.

- Once you have identified your task and the best strategy for completing it, you are ready to carry out your plan. Think through each part of the task and carefully apply your chosen strategy to solve the problem.

Step 4: Look back.

- After you determine your solution to the problem, consider whether or not it makes sense. Look again at the question you identified in Step 1 and make sure that your result answers that question. If your task involved an operation, check your work using the inverse operation. Rephrase your answer in the form of a statement and reflect on whether it sounds logical.

Additional Tips

- Read all directions carefully.

- Identify and underline key words and phrases.

- Use the context of the sentence to find the meaning of an unfamiliar word.

- Make your final response and move on. Don't linger over or get frustrated by the very difficult problems. If you have carefully followed the four-step approach and are still uncertain about the solution, answer as best you can and move on. You are not penalized for guessing.

- If you have time at the end of the testing period, go back to the problems that were difficult and review them again.

The four-step approach to problem solving, along with the additional tips offered here, will help make the test-taking process efficient and increase the accuracy of your responses. To help you further master these test-taking strategies, along with the skills outlined in the objectives, the remainder of this chapter provides practice using the types of questions you will likely encounter on the GACE mathematics test. Each question is tied directly to one of the five GACE objectives identified and explained in the section above.

Test Practice

The practice problems that appear in this section will help you evaluate your understanding of the skills addressed in this chapter. You will commonly encounter questions that will ask you to:

1. Use processes and approaches for exploring mathematics and solving problems. (Objective 0013)

2. Use concepts and skills related to numbers and mathematical operations. (Objective 0014)

3. Use principles and skills of measurement and the concepts and properties of geometry. (Objective 0015)

4. Use concepts and skills related to algebra. (Objective 0016)

5. Use concepts and skills related to data analysis. (Objective 0017).

The practice questions are designed to review the skills addressed in this chapter in order to prepare you for the practice test that is designed to mirror the format of the GACE Early Childhood Education Assessment. Before you begin answering the questions that follow, take some time to review the mathematics skills outlined by the test objectives. Then, try to answer the ten questions without looking back in the chapter and remember to practice using the four-step approach to answering the questions. An explanation of each practice question will be provided.

1. Daphne visited the local pet store. One aisle contained all the dogs on one side and all the parrots on the other. Daphne counted 26 tails and 78 feet. How many dogs and parrots did the pet store have?

   Which of the following is the best strategy to use to solve the problem above?

   a. Estimate.

   b. Draw a diagram.

   c. Guess and check.

   d. Look for a pattern.

2. Cole and Deb are collecting used books for the community rummage sale. Cole brings 25 books to sell, and Deb brings 15. Their 40 books will be added to the 20 that have been donated by others.

   If the scenario described above were expressed as a number sentence, what term could be applied to the number "25"?

   a. addend

   b. minuend

   c. sum

   d. dividend

3. Which equation illustrates the associative property of multiplication?

   a. $1x = x$

   b. $(s + 9) + d = s + (9 + d)$

   c. $x + 0 = x$

   d. $8(4 \times 3) = (8 \times 4)3$

4. Solve.

   $$6\frac{4}{5} - 1\frac{2}{3} = \underline{\quad\quad}.$$

5. Patrick is buying colorful ribbon to make nametag lanyards for a conference. Each lanyard requires 24 inches of thread. He needs to make 150 lanyards. How many yards of ribbon should he buy?

6.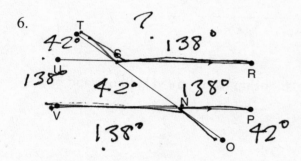

   In the diagram above, ∠PNO measures 42°. What is the measure of ∠RST?

7. Nekia has a number in mind. If she adds 3 to that number, divides it by 3, and multiplies the resulting number by 2, she will get 6.

   Write an algebraic expression using x as the unknown number that can be used to solve the word problem shown above.

8.   Use the graph to answer the question.

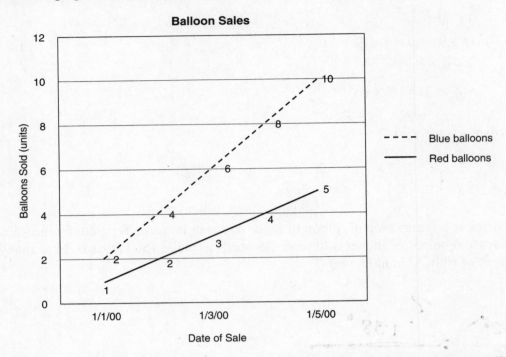

Which algebraic expression shows the relationship between red balloons and blue balloons?

a. $r = \dfrac{b}{2}$

b. $r = b - 2$

c. $b = \dfrac{r}{2}$

d. $r = b(2)$

9.   Use the chart below to answer the question.

Before ordering new books for the school library, Mrs. Smith conducted a survey of elementary students' preferred genre. Which of the following statements is consistent with the data presented above?

a.   More than half of the students prefer Science Fiction or Fantasy.

b.   About 25 percent of the students prefer Non-Fiction or Historical Fiction.

c.   About $\frac{1}{4}$ of the students prefer Realistic Fiction.

d.   More students prefer Mystery than Non-Fiction.

10.   After completing and presenting a culminating task in small groups, the students in Mr. Fernandez's Math class were given a unit test. The students' scores were: 75, 95, 100, 65, 70, 90, 80, 85, 90, 100, 85, 70, 90, 95, and 60. In this data set, 85 is the:

a.   mean

b.   median

c.   mode

d.   range

Explanations of Practice Problems:

Objective 0013:   Processes and Problem Solving

1. This problem requires knowledge of problem-solving strategies. We must find the value of two unknown quantities, which can be accomplished with the guess-and-check approach (choice c). With two types of animals, birds with two feet and dogs with four feet, and given 26 tails and 78 feet, we must determine how many dogs and parrots there are. Creating a simple table to record our guesses can help organize our attempts to solve the problem.

Dogs	Parrots	Tails	Feet
10	16	$10 + 16 = 26$	$4 \times 10 + 2 \times 16 = 72$
11	15	$11 + 15 = 26$	$4 \times 11 + 2 \times 15 = 74$
12	14	$12 + 14 = 26$	$4 \times 12 + 2 \times 14 = 76$
13	13	$13 + 13 = 26$	$4 \times 13 + 2 \times 13 = 78$

The correct answer is 13 dogs and 13 parrots.

2. Here, we are asked to examine a word problem to identify the correct mathematical term for a given value. The word problem could be expressed in the following number sentence:

$$25 + 15 = 40$$

In this number sentence, the numbers being added, or addends, are 25 and 15. 40 is the sum. Therefore, the correct answer is addend. (answer choice a)

Objective 0014:   Numbers and Mathematical Operations

3. This question asks us to identify which equation illustrates the associative property of multiplication. Recall that this property addresses the way in which we combine, or "associate," numbers that are related to each other through operations. The first choice illustrates the identity property of multiplication, which states that any number multiplied by 1 is that number. The second equation, which shows how addends can be combined, illustrates the associative property of addition. The third choice shows the identity prop-

erty of addition, which states that zero added to any number is that number. The last equation, which demonstrates the combination of multipliers within a number sentence, is the correct choice.

4. This problem requires us to subtract mixed numbers with unlike denominators. When we subtract fractions with unlike denominators, we must first make the denominators equal to each other by finding the least common denominator. The least common denominator of 5 and 3 is 15. To make the denominators equal, we multiply $\frac{4}{5}$ by 3 to get $\frac{12}{15}$. Then we multiply $\frac{2}{3}$ by 5 to get $\frac{10}{15}$. Then, we can subtract using our new denominator.

$$6\frac{12}{15} - 1\frac{10}{15} = 5\frac{2}{15}$$

Since this fraction cannot be further reduced, $5\frac{2}{15}$ is our final answer.

Objective 0015:   Measurement and Geometry

5. To solve this problem, we must know how to convert inches to yards. First, we determine how many inches of ribbon is needed for the lanyards:

$24 \times 150 = 3600$ inches

Then, we determine how many yards are needed:

3600 inches/ 36 = 100 yards

6. This question requires us to understand corresponding angles, which are the matching angles created when two lines are crossed by another line. In the diagram, ∠PNO measures 42°. Therefore, we know that ∠PNT measures 138°, because the angles on one side of a straight line always add up to 180°. Since ∠PNT and ∠RST are corresponding, we know that ∠RST measures 138°.

Objective 0016:   Algebra

7. This problem asks us to create an equation to represent the operations described in the problem. It is important to carefully read the problem to determine the correct order

of operations. Here, we are told that Nekia adds 3 to the original number, divides by three, and multiples the *result* by 2 to get 6. Therefore, the equation would be:

$$\frac{x+3}{3} \times 2 = 6$$

8. Here, we are provided with a graph that illustrates the relationship between the number of red and blue balloons sold. The table below shows the values presented in the graph:

R	B
1	2
2	4
3	6
4	8
5	10

By looking at this table, we can see that the number of red balloons is determined by dividing the number of blue balloons by 2. Therefore, the correct equation is $r = \frac{b}{2}$.

Objective 0017:   Data Analysis

9. This question requires us to analyze a circle graph, which is used to represent a part to whole relationship. We must recognize the relationship between percentages and fractions in order to determine which of the statements is consistent with the data presented. Looking at the distribution of the percentages, we can see that just less than half, not more than half, of the students prefer Science Fiction or Fantasy. If we imagine the circle divided into four portions, we realize that the sector of the graph that represents the number of students who chose Realistic fiction is less than $\frac{1}{4}$ of the whole represented. The Mystery sector is not larger than the Non-Fiction sector, so we cannot say that more students prefer Mystery than Non-Fiction. However, when we combine the sectors representing Non-Fiction and Historical Fiction, we can see that the two portions comprise about $\frac{1}{4}$ of the total responses. Therefore, the correct choice is b.

10. Here, we are asked to examine a data set and describe it using standard measures of mean, median, mode, and range. In order to determine the significance of the number 85, we have to analyze the data to find the standard measures. We can rule out choice d, the range, because we can see that the scores range from 60 to 100, which indicates a range of 40. The mode can also be quickly eliminated as a choice, because the most frequently occurring score is 90. This leaves us with the mean and the median. To find the mean, we add all the numbers together and divide by 15, the total number of scores. This results in a mean or average score of 83.3. To find the median, we list the numbers in order to find the number that falls in the center of the data set. If we list the 15 numbers in order, beginning with 60 and ending with 100, we find that 85 is the median score.

References

Burton, G. et. al (1992). *Curriculum and evaluation standards for school mathematics*

addenda series, grades K-6: Fifth-grade book. Reston, Virginia: The National Council of Teachers of Mathematics.

Cathcart, G. et. al (2001). *Learning Mathematics in Elementary and Middle Schools.*

Columbus, OH: Prentice Hall, Inc.

Polya, G. (1962). *Mathematical Discovery*. Volume 1: New York: Wiley.

Smith, S. (1997). *Early Childhood Mathematics*. Needham Heights, MA: Allyn & Bacon.

Suggate, J., Davis, A., and Goulding, M. (1998). *Mathematical Knowledge for Primary Teachers.*

CHAPTER

Science

5

The Science portion of the GACE Early Childhood Education assessment tests you on the characteristics and processes of science, as well as the concepts and principles of earth science, physical science, and life science. It is composed of approximately 20 selected-response (multiple-choice questions) and one constructed-response assignment.

This review is designed to prepare you for the Science portion of Test II. You will be guided through a review of the content related to the test objectives. In addition, you will learn a helpful approach to reading and analyzing science questions. By studying this review, you will greatly increase your chances of achieving a good score on the Science portion of the GACE Early Childhood Education Assessment.

I. GACE Science Objectives

Remember, the more you know about the skills tested, the better you will perform on the test. The objectives on which you will be tested are contained in the following list:

- 0018 Understand the characteristics and processes of science.
- 0019 Understand concepts and principles of earth science.

- 0020 Understand concepts and principles of physical science.

- 0021 Understand concepts and principles of life science.

Now that you know what the objectives are, let's look at them more closely. This section will provide a review of the important information about each of the objectives.

Objective 0018:   Understand the characteristics and processes of science.

The first objective deals with science process skills, as well as the characteristics of scientific knowledge and inquiry. Here, we will review a number of specific concepts associated with the characteristics and processes of science. As we examine each process skill, we will explore examples that illustrate each concept.

1. Scientific Knowledge and Values

Scientific knowledge can be classified in at least three different ways: factual, conceptual, and procedural (Carin et al., 2005). This particular objective focuses primarily on procedural knowledge, or learning about the attitudes, values and skills that are essential to the process of scientific inquiry. There are many important attitudes that are associated with science, including curiosity, honesty, openness, and skepticism. Let's examine more closely each of these values of science:

- **Curiosity**: Like inquisitive children who learn about the world through exploration, scientists study natural phenomena because of a desire to better understand the world around them. As Carin et al. (2005) note, "This dynamic, almost compulsive involvement of children and adults in searching for answers provides the fuel for investigation" (p. 27).

- **Honesty**: In order for scientific knowledge to be a reliable and accurate representation of inquiry, honesty is essential. Scientists are expected to keep careful records of investigations and observations and not alter the records later. Honesty also requires verifiable evidence. We must be able to distinguish observations from ideas and speculation about those observations. Conclusions and claims must be supported with evidence.

- **Openness:** Although some scientific facts, details and principles are very old and yet still applicable today, the landscape of scientific knowledge is constantly changing as we discover new ways of learning about the world. Therefore, in order to embrace scientific inquiry, we must be open to new ideas and willing to work cooperatively to address scientific questions.

- **Skepticism:** In order to engage in scientific inquiry, we must adopt a questioning attitude that enables us to reflect on and change our ideas and the ideas of others. As new explanations come to light, we have to reevaluate our original conclusions. Even similar scientific investigations do not often produce exactly the same results. Therefore, we must be able to evaluate conclusions by offering reasons for findings and considering other possible explanations. An attitude of skepticism allows us to recognize that there are unexpected differences in the subject of inquiry or the way the investigation was conducted.

The following example illustrates how an understanding of scientific knowledge and values might be demonstrated:

Example   Cherry conducted a simple experiment on the effect of sunlight on plant growth. She predicted that less sunlight would cause slower growth. The first time she conducted the experiment, she used two identical bean sprouts that she had on hand. One plant received six hours of sunlight each day, while the other plant received only three. She was careful to record the exact amount of time each plant spent in the sunlight, and the amount of water received. After four weeks, her hypothesis was supported. The second time she conducted the experiment, she purchased two small potted bean plants. After four weeks, Cherry found no measurable difference in the size of the potted plants. What is the best explanation for why the two similar experiments yield different results?

    a.   Differences in the methods used to care for the plants.

    b.   Differences in the plants that were studied.

    c.   Differences in the quality of sunlight over time.

    d.   Differences in the accuracy of observations or measurements.

Example Explanation:

In order to identify the best possible explanation for why the results of the two experiments differed, we must carefully examine the information provided. The text tells us that Cherry was careful to use the same methods to care for the plants and record observations, therefore choices a. and d. can be reasonably eliminated. The experiments did take place at two separate times, so it is possible that a time change could impact the available amount of sunlight each day, but we are told that the amount of sunlight given remained the same for both experiments. This leaves choice b. as our most likely answer. We are told that the first attempt involved bean sprouts, while the second attempt utilized purchased bean plants that were already sprouted. Therefore, it is likely to assume that there was some unrecognized difference between the bean sprouts and the bean plants that may have affected the results of the experiment.

2. Principles of Scientific Inquiry

Understanding the principles of scientific inquiry requires that we recognize, first and foremost, that scientific investigations may take many different forms and can be conducted in many different ways. Science involves many diverse people engaging in many different types of work. However, there are some common characteristics among the tasks that are considered essential to scientific inquiry. According to the National Research Council (1996), "Full inquiry involves asking a simple question, completing an investigation, answering the question, and presenting the results to others" (p. 122).

Processes: There are a number of processes that are essential to scientific investigations. These include hypothesizing, observing, measurement, classification, inferring, predicting, and experimenting. Investigations may be descriptive, classificatory, or experimental (Carin et. al, 2005). A controlled experiment is a type of investigation that involves the manipulation of a single condition in order to determine its effect on the outcome.

In order to present the results of scientific inquiry, clear and active communication is essential. Scientists must be able to inform others about their work, offer their ideas for analysis and evaluation by other scientists, and articulate the significance of findings in the context of other scientific discoveries around the world.

Tools: In addition to the common characteristics of scientific investigations, there are also certain tools and instruments that are commonly used for observing, measuring and manipulating objects in scientific activities. For example, scientists use technology, such as computers, cameras, microscopes, telescopes, and satellites, to increase their power to observe and measure things accurately. Scientific investigation also involves choosing and measuring materials and following accepted safety procedures.

The question below provides an example of how principles of scientific inquiry might be addressed on the GACE Early Childhood Education Assessment:

Example   In visiting kindergarten classrooms, the principal noticed that students in Mr. Flowers' class were less likely to use the available art supplies in completing their work than the students in Mrs. Croy's class. After speaking with the teachers, she discovered that Mr. Flowers' rewarded his students each time they used art supplies, while Mrs. Croy did not. Which principle of scientific inquiry is the principal demonstrating?

    A.   Forming a hypothesis

    B.   Identifying variables

    C.   Analyzing data

    D.   Communicating results

Explanation of Example

In this question, our task is to identify a principle of scientific inquiry in the context of a real-life situation. A hypothesis is a possible explanation that forms the basis of a scientific investigation. In the scenario provided, the principal does not state a tentative explanation before investigating, so choice a. can be eliminated. We are provided with the trend observed by the principal, but no specific data regarding student art supply use is provided. Therefore, it cannot be said that the principal is analyzing data (choice C.) in this particular example. There is also no indication that the information was shared, therefore, we can also rule out choice D. The correct answer is B. By determining the differences in the way the two teachers are encouraging the use of art supplies, the principal is identifying variables.

3. Science Concepts

Just as there are certain general characteristics of scientific investigations, there are also a number of unifying concepts of science:

- **System**: A system is a group of independent but interrelated objects of components that form a whole. The solar system and ecosystems are examples of systems that are introduced to elementary students. In order to understand the concept of system, we must be able to observe and describe how different components influence one another in things with many parts.

- **Change**: The world around us is constantly changing. Recognizing and investigating these changes is a part of the process of inquiry. Applying the concept of change requires us to recognize patterns of change in different natural phenomena and identify them as steady, repetitive, or irregular. Some changes, such as the phases of the moon, are steady and repetitive, while others, such as weather on a daily time scale, are less predictable. Records, tables, and graphs are helpful in identifying patterns of change.

- **Model:** Models, or representations, are commonly used in science to study phenomena that are physically inaccessible because of size, distance, or safety. In elementary science, we must be prepared to use many different types of models, including geometric figures, number sequences, graphs, diagrams, sketches, number lines, maps, and stories, to represent different objects and events in the real world. We must also recognize that there are limitations to the information that models can provide, as often representations may not match their original counterparts.

- **Scale:** This concept shares a connection to scientific models, as it involves understanding the relationship between the size of something and a representation of it. At the most basic level, scale involves understanding the relative size of things in order to make comparisons. For example, when we speak of billions, such as when discussing the number of stars in the universe, we should have an idea of the magnitude of that figure. We must also be able to use the representation to conceive of the actual size or distance being depicted.

The example below demonstrates how knowledge of science concepts might be evaluated:

Example   Mr. Jackson asked his students these questions about the class aquarium:

- What do the fish do in the aquarium?

- How do the fish and the plants interact?

- What is the role of the snail?

Which unifying scientific theme is best represented by his questions?
   a.   Model
   b.   Change
   c.   Scale
   d.   System

Explanation of Example:

In this scenario, Mr. Jackson is asking his students about the interactions of the organisms within the classroom aquarium. The individual organisms are part of the aquarium system. Therefore, the scenario is most representative of the concept of system (d.).

4. Scientific Data Analysis

Data Analysis is another important part of scientific inquiry. In order to communicate the results of a scientific investigation, the data that has been collected must be organized into diagrams, tables and graphs. To present data clearly and accurately, we should be able to use numerical data in describing and comparing objects and events. Data tables, bar graphs, histograms, and line graphs are all useful in organizing data. By putting data into tables and graphs, we can make connections between the data and the investigative procedures, make comparisons between data sets, and see patterns and trends (Carin et al., 2005).

The example below demonstrates how the concepts and skills related to data analysis can be presented in the context of science content.

Example

	Jan	Feb	Mar	Apr	May
2005	2.5	5.5	7.5	4.4	1.9
2006	5.1	5.5	2.9	2.5	2.8
2007	4.0	2.6	1.3	1.8	2.0
2008	2.9	4.7	5.2	3.2	2.8

The table above shows how much rain fell in a city from January to May over a period of four years. What conclusion can be drawn from the information provided?

a. Total rainfall from January to May has decreased steadily each year.

b. 2005 was the rainiest year during the four-year period.

c. During this period, February was rainier than January, March, April or May.

d. Rainfall increases from January to May.

Explanation of Example

In this problem, we are asked to draw a conclusion based on the data provided. To determine the correct answer, we can examine each statement to determine if it accurately represents the data. By looking at the data, we can easily see that rainfall does not generally increase from January to May, so we can eliminate the most obvious incorrect choice, d. If we add the rainfall measurements from January to May for each year, we find that the total rainfall amounts do not represent an increase over time. Therefore, we can also eliminate choice a. Choice b is a little more challenging. When adding the rainfall amounts for each year included in our data, we find that 2005 saw the most rainfall for the months shown. However, we do not know how much rain fell during the other months of these years, and, without that data, we cannot conclude which year was the rainiest overall. However, if we add the rainfall amounts for each month over the four-year period, we find that the month of February saw the greatest amount of rainfall. Therefore, choice c is the correct answer.

5. Scientific Connections

Making scientific connections is another important component of understanding the characteristics and processes of science. We must be able to recognize relationships between science, mathematics, technology, society and everyday life. This includes possessing the computation and estimation skills necessary for analyzing data and following scientific explanations. The example above demonstrates one way that we use mathematics in the collection and analysis of scientific data. The problem below provides another example of how scientific connections might be evaluated:

Example Reka notices that in the winter, when her skin is dry, she tends to shoot sparks when she touches objects. Which scientific concept explains this phenomenon?

    A.   Chemical bonding

    B.   Friction

    C.   Thermodynamics

    D.   Static electricity

Explanation of Example:

This problem involves something that all of us are likely to have experienced at some time: "shooting sparks" when we touch objects, which tends to occur most frequently during the winter months. Here, we are asked to identify the scientific concept that explains this phenomenon. The correct choice is D, static electricity, which involves the collection of electrically charged particles on the surface of a material. In this case, our dry, winter skin becomes highly positively charged, especially when our clothes contain polyester, which can become negatively charged.

Objective 0019:   Understand concepts and principles of earth science.

Earth Science involves many different concepts, including rocks, minerals, and fossils, earthquakes and volcanoes, constructive and destructive earth processes, the sun, planets, and stars, the atmosphere, and weather. The GACE Early Childhood Education Assessment addresses several specific topics that are important to the elementary science curriculum. Here, we will examine in detail these topics, which include the solar system and universe, the composition of the earth and its systems, earth processes, and fossils.

1. The Solar System and Universe

An understanding of the solar system begins with observations of the night sky. By examining the sky, we can begin to recognize the attributes of stars, such as their vast numbers, variations in size and color, and positional patterns or constellations. Thorough knowledge of the solar system requires the ability to compare and contrast the characteristics of stars and planets, and describe the ways that technology is used to identify and analyze distant objects.

In addition to the general characteristics of stars and planets, more specific knowledge is required regarding the earth and its moon. By understanding the position of the earth and how it moves in the solar system, we can describe the day and night cycle, and explain the changes that occur with the seasons. It is important to recognize how the revolution of the earth around the sun and the tilt of the earth on its axis impact seasonal changes. Finally, we must be able to identify the phases of the moon, including the new moon and full moon, the first quarter and third quarter, as well as the phases in between.

The example below illustrates how knowledge of earth science concepts might be evaluated:

Example   Each night, Kitty observes the night sky through a telescope. After several months of observations, she notices that the Big Dipper can always be seen in the northern sky, while the position of Venus has shifted from west to east. Which statement best explains why Venus changes position, but the Big Dipper does not?

      A.   All planets rotate in a counter-clockwise motion.

      B.   Stars are too far away for us to see their motion or detect their relative positions.

      C.   Constellations orbit the sun at the same speed as the earth, but the orbits of the planets vary.

      D.   The patterns of stars in constellations do not change.

Explanation of Example:

The example above evaluates our understanding of the characteristics of stars and planets. In order to answer this question correctly, we must recognize that we can observe differences in the positions of planets, while the patterns of stars in constellations do not appear to change. Except for the sun, all of the stars are more than 40 trillion kilometers away from us. Although the patterns of stars in the sky do change, the stars are so far away from us that we cannot see those changes occur within the span of our lifetime (Comins, 2009). Therefore, the correct answer is b.

2. The Composition of the Earth and its Systems

An understanding of the composition of the earth requires knowledge of the structure and processes of the earth's lithosphere, hydrosphere, and atmosphere and the interactions among these systems. The lithosphere consists of the earth's crust, mantle, and core, including rocks and minerals. The hydrosphere is made up of the earth's water, which includes oceans, lakes and rivers. The atmosphere is the blanket of gases surrounding the Earth.

Recognizing the physical attributes of rocks and soils is important to a thorough understanding of the earth's lithosphere. We must recognize that the hard material that makes up the earth surface is rock. The grains and crystals that make up this hard material are minerals. Minerals come in many different varieties, and rocks can contain more than one type of mineral. We can classify rocks and minerals in many different ways, including by shape, color, and texture, as well as hardness. Water and wind can change rocks and minerals over time through weathering and erosion.

Water and wind are important concepts in understanding the interaction among the earth's spheres, which can be seen primarily through the water cycle and weather patterns. An understanding of the water cycle begins with knowledge of how water changes states from solid (ice) to liquid (water) to gas (water vapor/steam).

This leads to an understanding of the water cycle (evaporation, condensation, and precipitation).

Knowledge of the water cycle is necessary in order to understand how to predict and communicate weather data, and to predict weather patterns and seasonal changes. Thermometers, rain gauges, barometers, wind vanes, and anemometers are all useful weather instruments that can provide information about weather conditions. Weather maps are also important in identifying fronts, temperature, and precipitation in order to describe weather conditions. These observations and records of weather conditions can help us predict weather patterns throughout the year. However, it is important to differentiate between weather, the day-to-day conditions of the atmosphere, and climate, the pattern of weather conditions in a particular place over time.

The example below illustrates how an understanding of the composition of the earth and its systems might be assessed.

Example   Talc is the softest mineral, while diamond is the hardest. The scale used to test hardness of minerals for identification is:

    A.   the Mercalli Scale.

    B.   the Moh's Scale.

    C.   the Richter Scale.

    D.   the Igneous Scale.

Explanation of Example:

The example requires specific knowledge about the test used to classify minerals by their hardness. The correct answer is b. The Moh's scale lists ten standard minerals in order of their hardness. A mineral with a higher rating will scratch a mineral with a lower rating.

3. Earth Processes

Understanding earth processes requires one to recognize the natural and human-caused constructive and destructive processes that shape the earth's surface. Constructive processes, such as deposition, cause some features of the earth's surface. Deposition occurs when natural processes, such as earthquakes and volcanoes, deposit sediment. Destructive processes, such as erosion, weathering, and the impact of organisms, can also shape the earth's surface.

The example below demonstrates how knowledge of earth processes might be evaluated.

Example 1   Where a river flows from an area of harder rock to an area of softer rock, the softer rock may wear away, eventually forming a:

    A.   delta.

    B.   waterfall.

    C.   sand dune.

    D.   mountain.

Explanation of Example 1:

This example requires an understanding of constructive and destructive processes. The scenario describes a destructive process, by which rock is being worn away by water. Answer choices a, c, and d are all products of a constructive process by which matter is deposited on the earth surface. Choice B, waterfall, is the only surface feature that could result from the weathering described here.

4. Fossils

A final component of earth science, fossils, is related to the composition and processes of the earth. Understanding fossils involves the knowledge of how fossils are formed and how they provide evidence of organisms that lived long ago. As Coyne (2009) observes, "The formation of fossils is straightforward, but requires a very specific set of circumstances" (p. 21). Typically, fossils are formed when animal or plant remains are covered with sediment at the bottom of a body of water. Once buried in sediment, the hard parts of fossils are replaced with dissolved minerals, leaving behind a cast that is pressed into the rock by the deposited sediment (Coyne, 2009).

The example below illustrates how knowledge of fossil concepts might be addressed.

Example   Trace fossils provide evidence of past behavior of organisms. Which of the following is not an example of a trace fossil?
- A.   Footprints
- B.   Burrows
- C.   Teeth
- D.   Tracks

Explanation of Example:

As described by Bromley (1996), traces are "structures produced in rocks, sediments and grains by the life processes of organisms" (p. xv). Trace fossils are the preserved remains of those structures, including footprints, tracks, burrows, borings, etchings, and fecal matter. These fossils provide insight into the behaviors of organisms that lived long ago. Trace fossils are contrasted with bone fossils, which are skeletal structures or other bodily remains, such as teeth or shells. Therefore, the correct answer is c.

Objective 0020:   Understand concepts and principles of physical science.

This objective addresses the physical properties and processes of the world around us. Physical science involves the characteristics of matter and energy. Let's look more closely at the specific physical science topics addressed by this GACE Early Childhood Education Assessment objective.

1. Properties of Matter

Knowledge of the properties of matter is essential to an understanding of physical science. Matter is made up of atoms, the tiny particles that make up every substance. Elements are simple substances made up of only one kind of atom. There are 118 known elements. Elements join to form compounds. Water, for example, is a compound made up of two hydrogen atoms and one oxygen atom. Molecules, which are made up of at least two atoms, are the smallest units of a compound.

Elements have unique physical properties. Physical properties, such as density, boiling and freezing points, can be measured and observed, and remain the same for a particular element. For example, we know that, under normal atmospheric conditions, water boils at 100 degrees Celsius, or 212 degrees Fahrenheit, and freezes at 0 degrees Celsius, or 32 degrees Fahrenheit. Density is the amount of mass per unit volume, or "a measurement of how closely packed together the matter is" (Halaw, 2008, p. 98). We can measure density by dropping an object in a container of water to determine how much water is displaced. We can also calculate density mathematically by dividing an objects mass by its volume.

We should also be aware of the changes that impact the properties of matter. Physical changes such as separating mixtures and manipulating objects by cutting, tearing, or folding, do not change the composition of the substance undergoing the change. Physical changes involve a change in shape, phase, or location (Halaw, 2008). For example, changes in state of water that result from temperature differences are examples of physical change.

Chemical changes occur when "two or more materials react and a new substance that has a different properties than the original materials forms" (Halaw, 2008, p. 110). Chemical changes can often be recognized by the formation of bubbles or smoke, or a change in color. Burning paper and baking a cake are examples of chemical changes. It is important to recognize that, when a chemical change occurs, the products of that change have the same mass as the original substances. This is due to the law of conservation of matter, which states that matter cannot be created or destroyed.

The question below provides an example of how the properties of matter might be addressed on the GACE.

Example 1   Which of the following represents a compound?

        A. O_3

        B. CO_2

        C. O_2

        D.   Fe

Explanation of Example 1:

This question evaluates our understanding of the properties of matter. Compounds are made up of more than one element. Choices A and C are made up of multiple oxygen atoms, but since oxygen is the only element present, they are not considered compounds. Choice D, Fe, is the chemical name for Iron, one of the periodic elements. Therefore, the correct choice is B, which is the chemical name for the compound carbon dioxide, which is made up of one carbon atom and two oxygen atoms.

2. Energy

Energy is another important physical science concept. Energy is the capacity to do work. Energy has many forms, including heat, light, electricity, chemical, nuclear, sound, and mechanical motion (Halaw, 2008).

Heat: All matter has heat, or thermal, energy. The amount of heat energy determines how quickly atoms and molecules move within a sample of matter. A change in temperature indicates a change in heat. There are many ways to produce heat energy, such as burning, rubbing (friction), and mixing one thing with another. As Halaw (2008) observes, "Heat energy moves in predicable ways. It flows through materials and across space from warmer objects to cooler ones" (p. 114). There are three processes of energy transfer: conduction (direct transfer), convection (transfer through fluid or the atmosphere), and radiation (transfer through space).

Light: Light is another form of energy. Light is a form of electromagnetic energy. As Halaw (2008) explains, "Light consists not only of the visible light and colors we see, but also other forms of electromagnetic energy, like ultraviolet light, infrared right, and microwaves that travel through the universe" (p. 112). Most of our light energy comes from the sun.

We can identify different materials based on the way that they interact with light. A material is said to be transparent if most of the light that interacts with material is transmitted. Other objects can be viewed through transparent materials, and the material has virtually on impact on the appearance of the object. Opaque materials absorb or scatter all the light that interacts with them. You cannot see through an opaque material. Translucent materials transmit some light, and appear to be the color that is transmitted through them.

Lenses and prisms are useful in investigating the properties of light. A convex lens is thicker at the center than at the edges. A convex lens makes light rays converge, or come together, to form an inverted image that can be seen on a screen. A concave lens is thicker at the edges than the center. A concave lens makes light rays diverge, or separate, to form a smaller "virtual" image that cannot be displayed on a screen (Macaulay and Ardley, 1998).

Electricity: Electricity, like light, is also a form of electromagnetic energy. We have already examined one form of electricity, static electricity, in a previous example. Electricity is the movement of electrons through a conductor. Conductors allow electrons to move easily from atom to atom. Insulators do not allow electrical currents to flow. Glass, wood, paper and plastics are examples of insulators. Copper and aluminum are examples of good conductors of electricity. For this reason, copper and aluminum are used in most electrical circuits and systems. A circuit is the path that electricity follows. In order for electrons to travel, the circuit must be closed. Electricity can travel in series circuits, in which electric current may travel in only one path, or parallel circuits, in which more than one path is available.

Sound: Sound is another form of energy. Sound is produced by vibrating objects and can be varied by changing the rate of vibration. The number of vibrations per second is known as the frequency. Increasing the frequency of vibrations creates a higher-pitched sound, while decreasing the frequency of vibrations creates a lower-pitched sound. Sound moves in waves and requires a medium such as air, water, or metal, in which to travel.

Mechanical Energy: The last type of energy we will examine is mechanical energy. This is the kind of energy that is found in objects in motion. In order to understand mechanical energy, we must recognize the role of force, which is a push or pull that causes an object to move. Gravity is a force that affects all objects. All objects exert gravitational force on other objects. The strength of the gravitational attractive force between two objects depends on their size and the distance between them. Some forces, such as friction, can hinder motion. Friction acts in opposite direction to movement.

Mechanical energy can be observed in the work of simple machines, such as the lever, pulley, and inclined plane. As Tiner (2006) explains, "A machine transmits a force from one place to another. A simple machine allows a person to overcome a resistance at one point by applying a force at some other point" (p. 34).

The sample question below provides one example of how knowledge of energy might be addressed.

Example

The picture above shows firefighters attempting to put out a house fire. Which of the following describes a way that the firefighters might feel heat as a result of conduction?

A.   During the fire, the temperature increases in the areas between the burning home and the houses on either side.

B.   The heat from inside the burning house can be felt from outside the window.

C.   The metal ladder becomes hot to the touch when it comes into contact with the flames.

d.   The fire occurs on a summer day when the sun's solar energy creates high temperatures.

Explanation of Example:

This example requires us to use our knowledge of the processes by which heat energy is transferred. We are asked to identify which of the statements describes the process of conduction, which occurs when heat is transferred directly from one material to another. Only choice C describes a situation in which heat is directly transferred from the fire itself to another material, in this case, the metal ladder. The other choices provided indicate an indirect transfer of heat energy through the atmosphere (convection) or empty space (radiation).

Objective 0021:   Understand concepts and principles of life science.

The final science objective deals with the study of living things. The GACE life science objective involves classifying different types of living things, understanding their basic needs and characteristics, and exploring principles of heredity, interaction, and survival. Let's look more closely at the topics addressed by this objective.

1. Classification and Basic Needs

In order to compare and describe living things, scientists sort them into groups based on their characteristics. For example, animals are classified by what they eat (herbivore, omnivore, carnivore), the type of skeleton they have (vertebrate and invertebrate), how threatened their species is in the wild (endangered vs. non-endangered), and how they are adapted to live in their environment (fish, amphibian, reptile, bird, mammal, and crustacean).

Plants are also sorted into groups based on their characteristics. Plants can be sorted in many different ways, vascular and non-vascular, flowering and non-flowering, and spore-producing and seed-producing. Some common names for different types of plants include flowers, herbs, shrubs or bushes, and trees. For each type of plant, there are numerous ways to further classify according to their characteristics. However, almost all plants have in common roots, stems, leaves, and flowers.

Both plants and animals have basic needs that must be met for survival. Animals require air, water, food, and shelter from the elements. Plants need air, water, light and nutrients in order to survive.

The question below provides an example of how classification skills might be assessed:

Example   The Kamchatka Lily and Yellow Pond Lily are among the few species of wild flowers that are found in Alaska. Which of the following is **most** important in determining where a plant can grow and survive?

    A.   animals

    B.   climate

    C.   tides

    D.   wind

Explanation of example:

In order to answer this question, we must be aware of the basic needs of plants. Herbivorous animals may impact adult plant growth cycles, but plants will grow regardless of the presence of animals. Plants require water to survive, but ocean tides are inconsequential. Plants require air, and winds can be helpful in transporting seeds, but the presence of wind is not essential. The correct answer is B. Climate has the greatest impact on the presence of air, water, light, and nutrients, and therefore, is the most important factor that determines where a plant can grow.

2. Heredity and Life Cycles

Heredity is another important life science concept. Understanding the principle of heredity begins with the recognition that offspring can resemble parents in inherited traits and learned behaviors. Inherited human traits include characteristics like skin, hair, and eye color, color-blindness, dimples or freckles, and curly or straight hair. Behaviors that we learn from our environments are often specific to our cultures, such as preferences, tastes, and verbal and non-verbal communication.

Genes play an important role in the transfer of traits. An understanding of genes begins at the cellular level. Within each of the millions of microscopic cells of which we are made, there exists a nucleus, and within each nucleus are forty-six chromosomes. These chromosomes are made of a molecule called DNA. Genes are small segments of DNA. Genes hold the information needed for the cell to generate proteins, which eventually produce specific physical traits.

Life cycles are one characteristic that all living organisms share. A life cycle is the series of changes that an organism experiences, including birth, growth, reproduction and death. Life cycles vary among living organisms. For example, all frogs develop predictably from eggs, to tadpoles, to froglets/ metamorphs, and, finally, to frog. Plant life cycles also vary depending on the type of plant. Many plants begin as seeds, which sprout roots, grow leaves, and develop into small plants that grow larger over time. Fungi are living organisms that are separate from plants and animals, but they, too, have a specific pattern of reproduction and growth.

The question below provides one example of how knowledge of heredity and life cycles might be evaluated.

Example   Which of the following is **not** an inherited trait of humans?

    A.   Eye color

    B.   Attached earlobes

    C.   Favorite food

    D.   Height

Explanation of Example:

This question requires knowledge of the principles of heredity. We know that inherited traits are physical characteristics passed down through genes. Each of the choices above is a physical trait that can be inherited except for choice C. While we may notice that we often share the same favorite foods as our family members, our preferences for specific types of foods are learned from our environment, and are often specific to individual cultures.

3. Environmental Interactions

Another aspect of life science involves the interaction of organisms with one another and their environment. This concept also includes the flow of energy and matter within an ecosystem. Organisms have specific roles within their ecosystems. For example, plants are classified as producers because they produce their own food through photosynthesis. Animals are consumers because they eat plants and other animals. Consumers can be herbivores, carnivores or omnivores. Bacteria and fungi are considered decomposers because they eat dead plants and animals and break them down into the nutrients that plants need.

Together, these organisms comprise a complex web of interactions. Energy flows from the sun, to producers, to consumers and decomposers. Ecosystems can change as a result of natural occurrences or human activities. These changes may reduce available resources, such as food, water, space or shelter, which means that fewer organisms can survive. As organisms are dependent on the roles of other organisms for survival, a change that affects one group of organisms will impact all other organisms in some way.

Human activities that result in environmental pollution, such as littering, can be particularly harmful to the environment. Animals can swallow or become entangled in trash items left behind by humans, and they can consume toxic substances. Overdevelopment can also destroy habitats and reduce available resources. We can reduce our impact on the environment by conserving resources, disposing properly of trash, and recycling.

In addition to changes in the environment, there are other factors that affect the survival of organisms. For example, many animals have developed adaptations to ensure survival. These include variation of behaviors, such as hibernation or grazing patterns, and external features such as camouflage and protection. In spite of these adaptations, natural factors, such as disease or environmental changes, may lead some organisms to become extinct. However, human intervention has the greatest impact on the survival of organisms. When humans destroy or alter plant or animal habitats, the organisms may not be able to adapt to the changes.

Example   A meerkat is a small mammal that lives in the Kalahari desert. Meerkats have black patches of fur around their eyes. Which survival factor does this adaptation address?

      A.   Protection

      B.   Water

      C.   Climate

      D.   Food

Explanation:

The correct choice is C. The desert climate exposes this animal to extreme temperatures and direct sunlight. The black patches of fur around the meerkat's eyes prevent the harsh sunlight from shining directly in the meerkat's eyes.

II. Strategies for Success on the Science Portion of Test II

In order to make the most out of the time allotted it is important to approach the problems strategically. The following is a recommended plan of attack to follow when answering science content questions.

A Four-Step Approach

According to the National Research Council (1996), "Full inquiry involves asking a simple question, completing an investigation, answering the question, and presenting the results to others" (p. 122). This four-step approach is based on these principles of scientific inquiry.

Step 1: Ask

- First, identify what question is being asked. Restate the question in your own words. This step is important because it will help you focus on the task at hand as you answer the question.

Step 2: Investigate

- Examine the data by carefully reading the **entire** problem.

- Determine what information you have and what you need to answer the question.

- Think about what you already know about the topic and recall any relevant scientific principles or concepts.

Step 3: Answer

- Look at each answer choice and compare it to the principles and concepts you identified in step 2.

- Evaluate each answer to determine if it is logical, based on what you know about the topic.

- Rule out incorrect choices and select the best answer.

Step 4: Evaluate

- Mentally "present" your results to yourself by evaluating your answer. Look again at the question you identified in Step 1 and make sure that your result answers that question. If your task involved mathematical calculations or formulas, check your work.

Additional Tips

- Read all directions carefully.

- Identify and underline key words and phrases.

- Use the context of the sentence to find the meaning of an unfamiliar word.

- Make your final response and move on. Don't linger over or get frustrated by the more difficult problems. If you have carefully followed the four-step approach and are still uncertain about the solution, answer as best you can and move on. You are not penalized for guessing.

- If you have time at the end of the testing period, go back to the problems that were difficult and review them again.

To help you further master these test-taking strategies, along with the skills outlined in the objectives, the remainder of this chapter provides practice using the types of questions you will likely encounter on the GACE science test. Each question is tied directly to one of the four GACE objectives identified and explained in the section above.

Test Practice

The practice questions that appear in this section will help you evaluate your understanding of the skills addressed in this chapter. You will commonly encounter questions that will ask you to:

- Demonstrate an understanding of the characteristics and processes of science (Objective 0018).

- Apply concepts and principles of earth science (Objective 0019).

- Apply concepts and principles of physical science (Objective 0020).

- Apply concepts and principles of life science (Objective 0021).

The practice questions are designed to review the skills addressed in this chapter in order to prepare you for the practice test that is designed to mirror the format of the GACE Early Childhood Education Assessment. Before you begin answering the questions that follow, take some time to review the science concepts outlined by the test objectives. Then, try to answer the eight questions without looking back in the chapter and remember to practice using the four-step approach to answering the questions. An explanation of each practice question will be provided.

Questions

1. A gardener plants two rows of squash. She puts fertilizer on one row but does not put fertilizer the other. Both rows receive the same amount of water and sunlight. She checks the growth of the squash at the end of each week. What is a constant in this experiment?

    A. Amount of water

    B. Squash without fertilizer

    C. Squash with fertilizer

    D. Plant growth

2. Which of the following would you most likely examine using a hand lens?

    A. A virus

    B. Rock crystals

    C. Moon phases

    D. An ant

3. How is weathering different from erosion?

    A. Erosion breaks down rock into smaller pieces, while weathering moves soil, rock and sediment from place to place.

    B. Weathering creates soil, and erosion transfers that soil away from the point at which the weathering occurred.

    C. Weathering breaks down rock into smaller pieces, while erosion moves soil, rock and sediment from place to place.

    D. Weathering causes erosion, which creates sediment.

4. Which of the following lists Earth, Jupiter, Mercury, and the Sun in order from smallest to largest?

    A.   Mercury, Earth, Jupiter, Sun
    B.   Sun, Jupiter, Earth, Mercury
    C.   Jupiter, Mercury, Earth, Sun
    D.   Earth, Sun, Jupiter, Mercury

5. Canned soft drinks feature tabs that make them easier to open. The ring that pops the tab on a soft drink is an example of what kind of simple machine?

    A.   Wheel and axle
    B.   Pulley
    C.   Inclined plane
    D.   Lever

6. Pictured here are two ice cubes in a glass. As the ice cubes melt, their molecules will:

    A.   Release heat energy and move farther apart.
    B.   Absorb heat energy and move farther apart.
    C.   Release heat energy and move closer together.
    D.   Absorb heat energy and move closer together.

7. Several state parks recently began allowing hunting for deer. Which of the following would be a logical reason for such a decision?

    A.   Lack of undergrowth to support smaller mammals
    B.   An increase in the coyote population
    C.   Flooding in low-lying and coastal areas
    D.   A recent decrease in deer density

8. A curlew is a large shorebird that can be found on the Georgia coast. It probes the shoreline for worms and other invertebrates that are buried in the sediment. Which of the following best represents the likely shape of the curlew's beak?

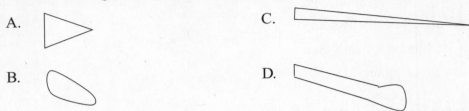

A.

C.

B.

D.

Explanations of Practice Problems:

Objective 0018: Characteristics and Processes of Science

1. In this experiment, the independent variable is the fertilizer. Plant growth is the dependent variable. Both rows of squash receive the same amount of water and sunlight, therefore, both of these are constants in this experiment. The correct answer is A.

2. A hand lens is a magnifying glass with a handle. It contains a convex lens that can be used to produce an enlarged image of small items in the laboratory or in nature. However, the magnification of a hand lens is relatively weak compared to a powerful microscope. A typical laboratory microscope could be used to closely examine tiny insects, small pieces of body tissue, and other objects that can be seen with the naked eye. A virus is too small to be seen with an ordinary microscope, and requires an electron microscope, which can magnify an object up to 500,000 times. Telescopes are needed to observe distant objects, such as the moon. A hand lens would be most effective in examining a rock. The correct answer is B.

Objective 0019:   Earth Science

3. Weathering is the breakdown of rocks into smaller pieces. Physical weathering occurs when water breaks apart rocks by flowing over and through cracks or freezing inside those cracks and then expanding. Chemical weathering occurs when chemicals dissolve in rainwater and change the composition of rocks (Halaw, 2008). Once rocks are weathered, erosion occurs as soil and rocks are moved to new locations by wind, water and ice. The correct answer is C.

4. While the sun is of average size compared to other stars in our galaxy, it is far bigger than any of the planets in our solar system. In fact, it is far larger than the rest of the solar system put together. Jupiter is the largest planet in the solar system, about 11 times larger than Earth. Mercury is about the size of our moon, about three times smaller than Earth (McNab and Younger, 1999). Therefore, these celestial bodies listed from smallest to largest would be Mercury, Earth, Jupiter, and the Sun. The correct answer is A.

Objective 0020:

5. A wheel and axle is a lever that rotates in a circle around a center point. inclined plane is essentially a ramp, a slanted plane set at an acute angle against a horizontal surface. A pulley is made from a wheel and a rope. A lever uses force to move a load around a pivot or fulcrum. The tab on a soft drink features a ring that is attached to the can by a small rivet. When the tab is pulled upward, the ring acts as the lever, and the rivet as the pivot or fulcrum, allowing the ring to depress the pre-scored opening. The correct answer is D.

6. When water is in its solid state, the molecules are packed close together. When ice melts as the water molecules absorb heat energy, the molecules begin to move faster and farther apart. The correct answer is B.

Objective 0021:

7. Organisms within an ecosystem comprise a complex web of interdependence. A disruption in the flow of energy impacts all the organisms within this web. Deer are examples of primary consumers. They feed on the producers at the base of the food chain. Their predators are secondary consumers. In this ecosystem, an increase in secondary consumers, such as coyotes, would result in a decrease in the number of deer. In this case, additional human predators would not be needed to reduce the deer population. Flooding could displace deer or disturb deer habitats, but seasonal weather patterns are not likely to cause an increase in deer density. A decrease in the number of deer would not result in the need to further reduce population density. However, when there are too many deer, too much forest and undergrowth are eaten, which decrease the food and shelter available to small mammals that make their home there. The correct answer is A.

8. Bird beaks are uniquely adapted to enable birds to the type of food that they are able to eat, based on the habitats in which they live. The curlew, also called the Long-Billed Curlew, survives on worms and other invertebrates found in the sediment along

the shoreline. In order to obtain food, the curlew must prod the sand to dislodge its buried prey. Short, dull, or flat beaks would make this task difficult, if not impossible. A long, slender, slightly down-curved beak is ideal. The correct answer is B.

References

Bromley, R. (1996). Trace fossils: Biology, taphonomy and applications. London: Chapman and Hall.

Carin, A., Bass, J. and Contant, T. (2005). *Teaching science as inquiry*. Upper Saddle River, NJ: Pearson.

Comins, N. (2009). *Discovering the essential universe*. New York: W.H. Freeman and Company.

Coyne, J. (2009). *Why Evolution is true*. New York: Viking Penguin.

Macaulay, D. and Ardley, N. (1998). *The New way things work*. London: Dorling Kindersley Limited.

McNab, D. and J. Younger (1999). *The Planets*. London: BBC Worldwide Ltd.

National Research Council. (1996). *National science education standards*. Washington, DC: National Academy Press.

Tiner, J.H. (2006). *Exploring the world of physics*. Green Forest, AR: Master Books.

Health, Physical Education, and the Arts

6

The Health, Physical Education, and the Arts portion of the (GACE Early Childhood Education exam assesses basic principles and practices related to health and safety and physical education, as well as the basic elements, concepts and techniques associated with the arts. It is comprised of approximately 15 selected-response (multiple-choice) questions.

This review is designed to prepare you for the Health, Physical Education, and the Arts portion of Test II. You will be guided through a review of the content related to the test objectives. By studying this review, you will greatly increase your chances of achieving a good score on this portion of the GACE Early Childhood Education Assessment.

I. GACE Health, Physical Education and the Arts Objectives

The objectives on which you will be tested are contained in the following list:

- 0022 Understand basic principles and practices related to health and safety.

- 0023 Understand basic physical education principles, practices, and activities.

- 0024 Understand basic elements, concepts, and techniques associated with the arts.

This section will provide a review of the important information about each of the objectives.

Objective 0022: Understand basic principles and practices related to health and safety.

For example:

- demonstrating knowledge of the primary functions of the human body systems, the processes of human growth and development, and the basic principles of human nutrition

- recognizing the differences between communicable and noncommunicable diseases and strategies for preventing or treating them (e.g., vaccinations, hand washing, regular exercise, antibiotics)

- recognizing characteristics of interpersonal relationships (e.g., within families, among peers) and strategies for maintaining healthy interpersonal relationships (e.g., using conflict resolution and positive character development skills)

- identifying strategies for maintaining personal emotional and physical health (e.g., stress management, sleep, proper diet)

- recognizing the effects of substance abuse, factors contributing to substance abuse (e.g., media advertising, peer pressure), and strategies for resisting pressure to use alcohol, tobacco products, and other drugs

- identifying safety practices to avoid accidents and injuries

The first objective addresses basic concepts relating to health and safety. Here, we will review a number of specific concepts associated with this objective.

Human Body Systems

The body has a system of interrelated subsystems working together to keep the body functioning properly. Cells are the building blocks of the human body, and tissues are groups of similar cells working together to perform a specific job. An organ consists of many kinds of tissues working together for a larger purpose, and a group of organs working together is called an organ system. There are several organ systems in the human body.

Circulatory System

The heart pumps blood in the circulatory system. The blood passes through the right chambers of the heart and through the lungs, where it acquires oxygen, and back into the left chambers of the heart where it is pumped into the aorta, which branches into increasingly smaller arteries throughout the body. Beyond that, blood passes through tiny, thin-walled structures called **capillaries**. In the capillaries, the blood gives up oxygen and nutrients to tissues and absorbs metabolic waste products containing carbon dioxide.

Finally, blood completes the circuit by passing through small veins, joining to form increasingly larger vessels until it reaches the largest veins, which return it back to the right side of the heart.

Respiratory System

Respiration results from the expansion and contraction of the lungs for gas exchange in the body. In the lungs, oxygen enters tiny capillaries, where it combines with hemoglobin in the red blood cells and is carried to the body's tissues. At the same time, carbon dioxide passes through capillaries into the air contained within the lungs. Inhaling draws air that is higher in oxygen and lower in carbon dioxide into the lungs; exhaling forces air that is high in carbon dioxide and low in oxygen from the lungs.

Digestive System

Food provides the energy required for sustenance of the human body. After the fragmenting of food by chewing and mixing with saliva, digestion begins. Chewed food passes down the esophagus into the stomach, where gastric and intestinal juices continue the digestion process. Thereafter, the mixture of food and secretions makes its way down the alimentary canal using peristalsis (the rhythmic contraction of the smooth muscle of the gastrointestinal tract). The smallest units of food are ultimately absorbed into the blood stream and transported throughout the rest of the body for utilization.

Immune System

The body defends itself against foreign proteins and infectious microorganisms by means of a complex immune system. The immune system is composed of a dual system that depends on recognizing a portion of the surface pattern of the invader and the generation of lymphocytes and antibody molecules to destroy invading molecules.

Skeletal System

The human skeletal system consists of more than 200 bones held together by connective tissues called ligaments. The bones are attached to the skeletal muscles; contractions of these skeletal muscles affect movements.

Nervous System

The nervous system controls muscular contractions. The nervous system has two divisions: the somatic, which allows voluntary control over skeletal muscle, and the autonomic, or involuntary, which controls cardiac and glandular functions.

Nerve impulses carried by cranial or spinal cord nerves that connect the brain to skeletal muscles cause voluntary movement. Involuntary movement, or reflex movement, occurs in direct response to outside stimulus. Various nerve terminals, called receptors, constantly send impulses to the central nervous system. Each type of receptor routes nerve impulses to specialized areas of the brain for processing.

Other systems include the reproductive system, consisting of the male and female reproductive organs, the urinary system, and the excretory system, which is made up of the lungs, large intestine and the kidneys.

Recognizing how these systems operate together is central to a basic understanding of human body functions.

Human Growth and Development

Another aspect of human health involves the processes by which we grow and develop. Calabresi (2007) provides a basic overview of the growth process:

- The first two years of life are a time of rapid physical and mental development.
- Physical growth begins at birth and continues through puberty.
- Humans are usually fully grown by the age of 20.

- When physical growth ceases, cell production continues. The new cells replace old cells but do not cause further growth.

- Cell production decreases as we age, which causes signs of aging, such as reduced bone and muscle strength, memory problems, wrinkling, and gray hair.

A teacher does not have to be an expert in anatomy and physiology to see the physical changes that accompany students' growth and maturity. The preschool child has trouble grasping pencils and crayons in a manner that facilitates handwriting; however, even most two-year-olds can grasp crayons sufficiently to make marks on papers and thus enjoy the creative excitement of art. Physiological changes play a significant role in the development of children as they increase their control of bodily movements and refine their motor skills. Their ability to engage in simple to complex classroom and playground activities increases as they develop. Teachers must adjust and adapt classroom and playground activities to be developmentally appropriate for students' various skill levels.

Girls, on average, reach maturational milestones before boys. Physical changes may cause embarrassment to both females and males when they draw unwelcome attention.

These changes almost always create some discomfort as adolescents find the body they were familiar and comfortable with to be quite different, sometimes seemingly overnight.

To facilitate this transition, teachers need to make children aware that these changes are part of their natural development.

Many major factors relate to and are necessary to build both social and emotional health. It is critically important for teachers to develop a basic understanding of the principles of human development and its multiple dimensions (e.g., physical, mental, emotional, and social). Additionally, teachers must appreciate a dynamic and interactive view of human development. This approach to understanding human development is one that recognizes that human beings do not develop in a vacuum. People exist in an environment that, friendly or unfriendly, supportive or non-supportive, evokes and provokes reactions from individuals. Moreover, human development is not a one-way street with the environment doing all the driving. People also act in certain ways to shape and form their environment.

A constant interaction occurs between people and their environments. Thus, effective teachers must be sensitive to and knowledgeable of both personal characteristics of students (internal factors) and characteristics of their environment. Internal factors, beyond the general characteristics that humans share as they grow and mature, also include students' personality characteristics, their self-concept and sense of self-esteem, their self-discipline and self-control, their ability to cope with stress, and their general outlook on life (attitude).

Empowerment has many components, one of which is self-concept. A good definition of self-concept is what we think and believe to be true about ourselves, not what we think about others and not what they think about us. Related to self-concept is self-efficacy.

Simply stated, self-efficacy is the confidence you have in your ability to cope with life's challenges. Self-efficacy refers to your sense of control over life or over your responses to life. Experts say that ideas about self-efficacy get established by the time children reach age four. Because of this early establishment of either a feeling of control or no control, classroom teachers may find that even primary grade students believe that they have no control over their lives, that it makes no difference what they do or how they act. Therefore, it is all the more important that teachers attempt to help students achieve coping skills and a sense of self-efficacy.

Nutrition and Exercise

Good nutrition and exercise are essential to health. Statistics show that Americans get more overweight each year. Even though countless books and magazine articles are available on the subject of weight control, often the only place a student gets reliable information about diet is in the classroom. The unfortunate reality is that people who are overweight on average do not live as long as those who are not. Being overweight has been isolated as a risk factor in various types of cancer, heart disease, gallbladder problems, and kidney disease. Chronic diseases such as diabetes and high blood pressure are also aggravated by, or caused by, being overweight. Conversely, being underweight presents a great many dangers to health as well. Our society often places too much emphasis on losing weight and being thin. Women are especially prone to measuring their self-worth by the numbers they read on the bathroom scale. Young girls are especially susceptible to these messages and eating disorders can result.

According to the National Institute of Mental Health (2009), ideal weight and a good body fat ratio should be the goals when trying to lose weight. A correlation may exist between body fat and high cholesterol. Diet and exercise are the key to maintaining a good body fat ratio. Exercise helps keep the ratio low, improves cholesterol levels, and prevents heart disease. In order to lose weight, calories burned must exceed calories consumed.

Metabolism is a set of chemical processes that occur in the body to keep it functioning, growing, responding to the environment, and maintaining life balance. Basal Metabolic Rate (BMR) is the pace at which the body burns the vast majority of calories efficiently at rest. Adjustments in the BMR are slow, occur over time, and are dependent upon the demands put upon the body physically (i.e., exercise) and calorie consumption. If calorie intake is restricted too much, the body goes into starvation mode and operates by burning fewer calories in order to conserve energy. Just a 250-calorie drop a day combined with a 250-calorie burn will result in a loss of one pound a week. Crash diets, which bring about rapid weight loss, are not only unhealthy but also ineffective. Slower weight loss is more lasting. Aerobic exercise is a major component to successful weight loss. Exercise speeds up metabolism and causes the body to burn calories efficiently. Timing of exercise may also enhance the benefits. Exercise before meals speeds up metabolism and helps suppress appetite. Through education, people will be better able to realize that maintaining a healthy weight is crucial to a healthy life and should be a constant consideration.

Along with exercise, a healthy diet is vital to good health, learning, academic achievement, and longevity. The elements of good nutrition, the role of vitamins, elimination of risk factors, and strategies to control weight are all part of a healthy lifestyle. In the spring of 2005, the U.S. Department of Health and Human Services changed the food pyramid to guide Americans to improve their eating habits (U.S. Department of Health and Human Services, 2006). As shown in Figure 6-1, the food pyramid has six divisions reminding us of what kind of foods need to be proportioned in our diet. The climbing figure reminds us all to be active.

Figure 6-1. USDA Food Pyramid

Source: U.S. Department of Agriculture, *Steps to a Healthier You*, *www.mypyramid.gov*.

The food groups indicated on the pyramid (left to right) are as follows:

1. Grains (e.g., bread, cereal, rice, and pasta); 6–11 daily servings

2. Vegetables; 3–5 daily servings

3. Fruits; 2–4 daily servings

4. Oils; use sparingly

5. Milk (yogurt and cheese); 2–3 daily servings

6. Meat and Beans; 2–3 daily servings

Nutrients are divided into two main groups: macro-nutrients (carbohydrates, proteins, and fats) and micro-nutrients (vitamins and minerals). Most foods contain a combination of the two groups. Complex carbohydrates (e.g., vegetables, fruits, whole grain breads, and cereals) are the preferred energy source for the body and should comprise up to one-half of the diet. These foods provide fiber, which helps digestion, reduces constipation, and reduces the risk of colon cancer. Proteins (e.g., milk, eggs, meat, fish, and beans) are one of our most essential nutrients because the body uses it to build and repair itself in more ways than any other food. Fats (e.g., olive and canola oils) are important to the body for regulating blood pressure, forming cell structures, transporting vitamins, and triggering immune system responses. Vitamins are essential given they perform highly specific metabolic processes in the cells and aid with many other functions such as growth and maintenance of the body. Minerals (e.g., calcium, iron, potassium, and zinc) help build strong bones and teeth, aid in muscle function, and help the nervous system transmit messages.

Keeping a balance of nutrients consistently in the body combined with hydration will keep systems functioning appropriately and minimize overall health risk. A world of nutrition information is available to teachers in *Dietary Guidelines for Americans*, published by the United States Department of Health and Human Services (2006).

Disease Prevention

School health services typically include a set of policies and programs that assess and protect the health of students. Specifically, the school nurse leads this collaborative effort to direct patient care, screen and diagnose symptoms, promote health counseling services, participate in health promotion and disease prevention, and maintain relationships with allied health professionals and community health service providers. School administrators have the legal responsibility for the safety of all students and for the supervision of the health services program offered in school.

Immunizing children against certain communicable diseases (e.g., polio, diphtheria, measles, mumps, rubella, chicken pox, and hepatitis) is a vital part of preventing the spread of disease. In addition to any formal instruction in health, teachers should integrate health-related issues the content areas (e.g., social studies, science, art, and music). Examples of topics that can be integrated easily into other content areas are:

1. the effects of pollution on health and occupational-related disease (e.g.,

2. "black lung" disease)

3. the health care options available to people in different parts of the world and

4. in different economic circumstances

5. differentiation between communicable and noncommunicable diseases

6. the importance of washing hands frequently

Older children should be able to explain the transmission and prevention of communicable diseases, and all children should learn which diseases cannot be transmitted through casual contact.

Students as young as kindergartners and first grade can learn how to recognize advertisements that might lead them to unhealthy behavior (e.g., for candy or sugar-laden cereal). By third or fourth grade, children should be able to demonstrate that they are able to make health-related decisions regarding advertisements in various media. Teachers can encourage students to: 1) avoid alcohol, tobacco, stimulants, and narcotics, 2) get plenty of sleep and exercise, 3) eat a well-balanced diet, 4) receive the proper immunizations, and 5) avoid sharing toothbrushes, combs, hats, beverages, and food with others.

Healthy Interpersonal Relationships

The social domain of health is manifested in our ability to practice good social skills and maintain comfortable relationships with others. Socially healthy people are effective at communicating respect for others, being tolerant and patient, and accepting differences without compromising relationships. Successful teachers are able to listen intently and recognize the needs and issues of others. Ultimately, effective educators recognize ways they enrich and are enriched by their relationships and use these skills to role-model appropriate behaviors.

To become effective communicators, students need a variety of learning opportunities to practice interpersonal skills in a variety of situations they are likely to encounter (e.g., communicating empathy, resisting peer-pressure, managing conflicts, and asking for help). As a result of practicing such methods, a natural link is established for students to express their healthy intentions when the correct situation/environment arises. Educators should constantly look for ways in which to practice assertive communication including stating a position, offering a reason that makes sense or is healthy, and acknowledging others' feelings.

Stress Management

Stress is the product of any change, either negative or positive. Multiple components and situations can cause stress. Some of these are:

- Environmental factors such as noise, air pollution, and crowding

- Physiological factors such as sickness and physical injuries

- Psychological factors such as self-deprecating thoughts and negative self-image

In addition to the normal stressors that everyone experiences, some students may be living in dysfunctional families, some may be dealing with substance abuse and addictions, and some may be experiencing sexual abuse.

People have numerous sources of stress in their lives, and it is important that students and teachers learn acceptable ways to cope with stress. The first step is to recognize the role that stress plays in our daily lives. A teacher might lead a class through a brainstorming activity to help the students become aware of the various sources of stress affecting them. Next, the teacher could identify positive ways of coping with stress, including positive self-talk, physical exercise, proper nutrition, adequate sleep, balanced activities, time management techniques, good study habits, and relaxation exercises.

Students facing stress often experience a wide range of emotions. They may be sad, frustrated, or afraid. Effective teachers realize that students' emotions play a significant role in students' classroom performance and achievement. Thus, they should seek to create a classroom environment supportive of students' emotional needs. They should have appropriate empathy and compassion for the emotional conflicts facing students, as well as a realistic awareness that students need to attain crucial academic and social skills that will give them some control over their environment as they become increasingly independent individuals and, eventually, productive citizens.

Substance Use and Abuse

Drug and alcohol problems can affect anyone, regardless of age, sex, race, marital status, place of residence, income level, or lifestyle. However, there are certain identifiable risk factors for substance abuse. These factors include individual, familial, social, and cultural characteristics.

Some of the personal characteristics that have been linked to substance abuse are: aggressiveness, emotional problems, inability to cope with stress, and low self-esteem.

Feelings of failure and a fragile ego can also contribute to this problem. The presence of physical disabilities, physical or mental health problems, or learning disabilities can add to the student's vulnerability to substance abuse. In many ways, students who are at-risk for academic problems are also susceptible to substance abuse problems.

Associated with substance abuse among youth are several family characteristics. First, and perhaps most important, is the alcohol or other drug dependency of a parent or both parents. This characteristic might relate to another significant factor: parental abuse and neglect of children. Antisocial and/or mentally ill parents are also factors that put children at risk for drug and/or alcohol abuse. Other conditions like family unemployment or underemployment, and parents with little education or who are socially isolated can also become risk factors. Single parents without family or other support, family instability, a high level of marital and family conflict or violence, and parental absenteeism due to separation, divorce, or death can also increase children's vulnerability to substance abuse.

Finally, other important factors to consider are the lack of family rituals, inadequate parenting, little child-to-parent interaction, and frequent family moves. These factors describe children without affiliation or a sense of identity with their families or the community.

Any of these family factors could lead to a substance abuse problem in a student. Living in an economically depressed area with high unemployment, inadequate housing, a high crime rate, and a prevalence of illegal drug use are social characteristics that can put an individual at risk for substance abuse. Cultural risk factors include minority status involving racial discrimination, differing generational levels of assimilation, low levels of education, and low achievement expectations from society at large. All the recognized risk factors are only indicators of the potential for substance abuse. They are not necessarily predictive of an individual's proclivity to drug or alcohol abuse. Some children who are exposed to very adverse conditions grow up to be healthy, productive, and well-functioning adults. Yet, knowing the risk factors, teachers are better able to identify children vulnerable to substance abuse and employ prevention education strategies. If teachers recognize these risk factors in some of their students, there are certain things that teachers can do to increase the chances that the child will resist the lures of illegal and dangerous alcohol and drug abuse.

Sometimes it can be difficult to tell if someone is using illegal drugs or alcohol. Usually, people who abuse drugs or alcohol (including young people) go to great lengths to keep their behavior a secret. They deny and/or try to hide the problem. However, certain warning signs can indicate that someone is using drugs or drinking too much alcohol. These include: 1) lying to teachers and family members, 2) avoiding people who are long-time friends or associates, 3) having slurred speech, 4) complaining of headaches, nausea, or dizziness, 5) having difficulty staying awake in class and, 6) bloodshot, glazed over, and/or squinting eyes.

These examples are insufficient to confirm a substance abuse problem, but in combination and when displayed consistently over time, they are strong indicators. Teachers should record their observations and keep written reports of the behavioral changes they witness. Moreover, they should report their suspicions to the appropriate school authorities.

Objective 0023:   Understand basic physical education principles, practices, and activities.

For example:

- Identifying the components of health-related fitness (e.g., cardiovascular endurance, muscular strength, flexibility) and appropriate activities for promoting each of the different components

- Demonstrating knowledge of activities that promote the development of locomotor, nonlocomotor, manipulative, and perceptual awareness skills in children

- Applying knowledge of basic rules and strategies for developmentally appropriate physical activities, cooperative and competitive games, and sports

- Recognizing the role that participation in physical activities can play in promoting positive personal and social behaviors

Principles of Physical Education and Physical Activity

In 1986, the National Association for Sport and Physical Education (NASPE) appointed a committee to develop a working definition of the characteristics that physically educated people ought to exhibit (National Association for Sport and Physical Education, 2009). As a result of this initiative, NASPE introduced the following definition. A physically educated person is someone who:

1. has learned skills necessary to perform a variety of physical activities

2. knows the implications of and the benefits from involvement in physical activity

3. participates regularly in physical activity and is physically fit; and values physical activity and its contribution to a healthy lifestyle

With this definition in mind, NASPE developed the National Standards for Physical Education:

Standard 1: Demonstrates competency in motor skills and movement patterns needed to perform a variety of physical activities.

Standard 2: Demonstrates understanding of movement concepts, principles, strategies, and tactics as they apply to the learning and performance of physical activities.

Standard 3: Participates regularly in physical activity.

Standard 4: Achieves and maintains a health-enhancing level of physical fitness.

Standard 5: Exhibits responsible personal and social behavior that respects self and others in physical activity settings.

Standard 6: Values physical activity for health, enjoyment, challenge, self-expression, and/or social interaction.

In order to help students achieve these standards, physical education teachers must have an understanding of the human body, and how physical activity can impact it.

Knowledge of anatomy and physiology can guide teachers in the selection and implementation of games and physical activities appropriate for development. Anatomy describes the structure, position, and size of various body parts and organs. Because our bones adapt to fill a specific need, exercise is of great benefit to the skeletal system.

Bones that anchor strong muscles thicken to withstand the stress put on them. Weight-bearing bones can develop heavy mineral deposits while supporting the body. Because joints help provide flexibility and ease of movement, it is important to know how each joint moves. Types of joints are ball and socket (e.g., shoulder and hip), hinge (e.g., elbow and knee), pivot (e.g., head of the spine), gliding [e.g., carpal (wrist) and tarsal (ankle) bones], angular (e.g., wrist and ankle joints), partially movable (e.g., vertebrae), and immovable (e.g., bones of the adult cranium).

Muscles are the active movers in the body. In order to properly teach any physical education activity, the functions and physiology of the muscles must be understood.

Because muscles move by shortening or contracting, proper form should be taught so the student can get the most out of an activity. It is also important to know the location of each muscle. This knowledge will help in teaching proper form while participating in physical education activities.

Understanding the concept of antagonistic muscles, along with the related information concerning flexors and extensors, is also vital to the physical educator. Imagine trying to teach the proper form of throwing a ball if you do not understand the mechanics involved.

Knowledge of anatomy and physiology is also necessary to teach proper techniques used in calisthenics as well as all physical activities. Without this knowledge, exercise itself can cause harm to the body.

Exploration of movement activities through fun activities constitutes the main focus of the physical education curriculum in the early grades. However, the curriculum can provide for more organized activities like yoga or low-impact aerobic exercise. Aerobic exercise involves both muscle contractions and movement of the body. Aerobic exercise requires large amounts of oxygen and when done regularly, will condition the cardiovascular system. Some aerobic exercises are especially suited to developing aerobic training benefits, with a minimum of skill and time involved.

Examples of good aerobic activities are walking, running, swimming, and bicycling. These activities are especially good in the development of fitness because all of them can be done alone and with a minimum of special equipment. In order to be considered true aerobic conditioning, an activity must require a great deal of oxygen for the body to utilize, it must be continuous and rhythmic, it must exercise major muscle groups and burn fat as an energy source, and it must last for at least 20 minutes in an individual's target heart rate range. Children can participate in low-impact aerobics training but parents and teachers must monitor their performance. Children will probably try to keep up with adults, and initially they may not have the strength, flexibility, and/or skill to keep pace. This could lead to undue fatigue, needless muscle soreness, and/or injury.

Benefits of an Active Lifestyle

Our bodies thrive on physical activity, which is any bodily movement produced by skeletal muscles and resulting in energy expenditure. Physical fitness enables a person to meet the physical demands of work and leisure comfortably. A person with a high level of physical fitness can enjoy a better quality of life and minimize the development of life-threatening diseases.

Unfortunately, Americans tend to be relatively inactive. Lack of activity can cause many problems, including weak muscles and heart, poor circulation, shortness of breath, obesity, coronary artery disease, hypertension, type II diabetes, osteoporosis, and certain types of cancer. Overall, mortality rates from all causes are lower in physically active people than in sedentary people. In addition, physical activity can help people manage mild-to-moderate depression, control anxiety, and prevent weakening of the skeletal system.

By increasing physical activity, a person may improve heart function and circulation, respiratory function, and overall strength and endurance. All of these lead to improved vigor and vitality. Exercise also lowers the risk of heart disease by strengthening the heart muscle, lowering pulse and blood pressure, and lowering the concentration of fat in both the body and the blood. It can also improve appearance, increase range of motion, and lessen the risk of back problems associated with weak muscles, weak bones, and osteoporosis.

Every person should engage in regular physical activity and reduce sedentary activities to promote health, psychological well-being, and a healthy body weight. On most days of the week, children should engage in at least 60 minutes of physical activity. Proper hydration is also important during physical activity. To help prevent dehydration during prolonged physical activity or when it is hot, people should consume water regularly during the activity and drink several glasses afterwards.

Development of Motor Skills

Physical changes play a significant role in the development of children as they gradually gain control of the movements and functions of their bodies. As they develop physically, children refine their motor skills, enabling them to engage in increasingly complex movement lessons and/or activities. For teachers to be able to identify patterns of physical development, they must first assess the level at which students can control specific movement patterns and then create educational activities that are developmentally appropriate for their students' physical abilities.

Children between the ages of three and four have already mastered standing and walking. At this stage, children are developing gross motor skills, including the ability to hop on one foot and balance, climb stairs without support, kick a ball, throw overhand, catch a ball that has bounced, move forward and backward, and ride a tricycle. Children between the ages of three and four are also developing fine motor skills, such as using scissors, drawing single shapes, and copying shapes like capital letters. By age four or five, when most children enter school, they are developing the gross motor ability to do somersaults, use a swing, climb, and skip. These skills require a multitude of movement patterns with increasing coordination. In addition, children at this age can begin to dress themselves using zippers, buttons, and possibly tying their shoes. They can also eat independently using utensils. Children at this age are increasingly capable of copying shapes, including letters and numbers. They can cut and paste and draw a person with a head, body, arms, and legs. These fine motor skills develop quickly in children of this age. By age six, children can bounce a ball, skate, ride a bike, skip with both feet, and dress themselves independently.

As the student develops year by year, the physical skills (both fine and gross motor) become increasingly complex and involve more muscles and more coordination. By age nine, children can complete a model kit, learn to sew, and cook simple recipes. By age ten, children can catch a fly ball and participate in all elements of a softball game.

Recognizing the basic milestones that most children will achieve by a certain age will assist teachers in making decisions about academic lessons and tasks. In addition, teachers may be able to identify children who may not be reaching their developmental milestones with the rest of the class. In short, the physical ability of students to engage in simple to complex activities in school gradually increases as they develop. Physical educators must adjust and adapt classroom and playground activities to be developmentally appropriate for the specific skill levels of students.

During play activities, a child engages in meaningful movement patterns that utilize large muscle groups in the body. Movement education is the process by which a child is helped to develop competency in those general movement patterns. It has been defined as learning to move and moving to learn. Movement competency requires the student to manage his or her body through space, time, and direction with the ability to accomplish basic and specialized physical tasks and traverse various obstacles. Basic movement skills are necessary for a child's daily living, whereas specialized skills are required to perform sports and other complex activities that have very clear techniques. Of course, basic skills must be mastered before the child can develop specialized ones.

Perceptual motor competency is another consideration in teaching body management. Perceptual motor concepts that are relevant to physical education include those that give attention to balance, coordination, lateral movement, directional movement, awareness of space, and knowledge of one's own body. Basic skills can be divided into three categories, locomotor, non-locomotor, and manipulative skills. A more complex movement pattern might include skills from each category.

Locomotor skills describe the type of movement children have to master in order to travel or move within a given space. These include walking, running, leaping, jumping, hopping, galloping, sliding, and skipping.

Nonlocomotor skills are used to control the body in relation to the force of gravity. These are typically done while in a stationary position (i.e., kneeling or standing). Some of these activities include: pushing, pulling, bending, stretching, twisting, turning, swinging, shaking, bouncing, rising, and falling.

Manipulative skills are used when a child handles, moves, or plays with an object. Most manipulative skills involve using the hands and feet, but other parts of the body may be used as well. Hand-eye and foot-eye coordination are improved when manipulating objects. Throwing, batting, kicking, and catching are important skills to be developed using balls and beanbags. Starting a child at a less challenging level and progressing to a more difficult activity is an effective method for teaching manipulative activities. Most activities begin with individual practice and evolve to partner activities. When teaching throwing and catching for example, the teacher should emphasize skill performance, principles of opposition, weight transfer, eye-focus, and follow through. Some attention should be given to targets when throwing because students need to be able to catch and throw to different areas and levels. For detailed information on developmentally appropriate physical education activities for K–5 children visit the PE Central website at *www.pecentral.org*.

Promoting Physical Fitness

Children in early childhood are not concerned with physical fitness; instead, they are interested in having fun. Based on this premise, a physical education program for this age group should reflect this interest. The child who is actively involved in fun physical activities will get the same benefits as children in a highly structured physical fitness program.

To that end, it is important for K–5 physical educators to understand that programming activities that focus on the enjoyment of moving their bodies is much more important than being groomed for success at a specific event or sport. Movement education enables the child to make choices of activity and the method they wish to employ. Teachers can structure learning situations so the child can be challenged to develop his or her own means of movement. The child becomes the center of learning and is encouraged to be creative in carrying out the movement experience.

In this method of teaching, the child is encouraged to be creative and progress according to his/her abilities. The teacher is not the center of learning, but offers suggestions and stimulates the learning environment through guided discovery. Student-centered learning works especially well when there is a wide disparity of motor abilities. If the teacher sets standards that are too high for the less talented students, they may become discouraged and lose motivation. On the other hand, if the teacher sets standards that are too low, the more talented students will become bored and also lose interest. Providing an array of options for learners is the best way to facilitate movement games and activities. This way, learners can identify which option or challenges are most appropriate and perform up to their developmental level with little assistance and/or cues from the teacher.

Movement education attempts to develop the children's awareness not only of what they are doing but how they are doing it. Each child is encouraged to succeed in his or her own way according to his or her own capacity. If children succeed at developing basic skills in elementary school, they will have a much better chance at acquiring the specialized skills required for sports, events, and specific activities later on in the secondary school setting.

To teach a basic or specialized movement skill to a variety of learners, the instructor must present and use explanation, demonstration, and drill. Other students can do demonstrations, provided the teacher monitors the demonstration and gives cues for proper form. Drills are excellent to teach specific skills but can become tedious unless they are done in a creative manner. Using game simulations to practice skills is also an effective method to maintain interest during a practice session.

Teachers must remember to use observation and feedback when teaching a skill or activity. Of course, positive feedback is much more conducive to skill acquisition than negative feedback. The typical "old school" intimidation tactics of physical education coaches will not work for children at this age. Appropriate feedback means correcting with suggestions to improve. For example, if a student playing kickball continually misses the ball or kicks the ball out of play, he or she is aware that something is not right. The teacher should indicate what the problem is and tell the student how to be successful when kicking the ball into the play area.

Many physical education professionals have advocated for the "Teaching Games for Understanding" model as a sound philosophy regarding movement games education. It is a socio-constructivist teaching and learning approach to physical education that emphasizes the learners' engagement in the construction of knowledge, skills, and experience. This student-centered model is built upon critical thinking, problem-solving, observation, and debriefing the experience for specific learning outcomes (i.e., teamwork, sportsmanship, and skill performance). Strategies of this model can be implemented across a variety of physical education curriculum including adventure education, cooperative learning, fitness education, tactical games, and sports education.

Managing Instruction

Because of the active nature of physical education, managing a large class of kids in a loud gymnasium or outdoor learning environment is no easy task. Therefore, a major goal of the physical education teacher is to have all students listen to directions prior to activity. The instructions should be short, to the point, and as clear as possible. A teacher who talks longer than 20 seconds during any single instructional period will soon find the class beginning to lose interest. This leads to an environment difficult to manage. For this reason, teachers should alternate short instructional episodes (including one or two points of focus) with longer periods of activity. Minimizing instructional content will reduce both student frustration and difficult situations to manage. Most students and teachers enjoy a learning environment that is organized, efficient, and allows a maximum amount of class time to be devoted to learning skills.

Management behavior routines must be enforced regularly by the instructor (especially early on); otherwise, the environment will always be chaotic and difficult to manage.

Effective physical educators identify a consistent keyword to use with learners that commences a new activity (i.e., "Begin" or "Ready Go"). This implies encouraging children to listen to the entire set of instructions before preparing for the next exercise.

Since the keyword is not given until all directions have been issued, students cannot begin until they hear the selected keyword.

Similarly, a consistent signal should be established for stopping an activity (i.e., "Freeze" or "Clap once... Clap twice... Clap three times..."). Whatever the signal, it must be practiced everyday so learners come to know the signal and it becomes second nature. Using an audio signal (i.e., whistle blast) and a visual signal (i.e., raising the hand overhead) may also be effective, since some children may not hear the audio signal if they are engrossed in loud activity. Whereas a loud audio signal may be used to stop a class, a voice command should always be used to start the class. If children do not respond to these signals, the procedure must be practiced. Remember, if a teacher settles for less than full attention, students will fulfill those expectations of being chaotic and unmanageable.

Physical education teachers should also know how to divide students into teachable groups quickly. Simple games, such as "Back-to-Back" or "Foot-to-Foot" in which individuals get back-to-back (or foot-to-foot, etc.) with a partner as quickly as possible, can be used to accomplish this. Students without a partner are instructed to go to the center of the teaching area (marked by a cone or spot) to immediately find someone else without a partner. If students are staying near a friend, teachers can tell the class to move throughout space using a locomotor skill and then find a different partner each time the body part is called.

If arranging students in groups larger than two people, Whistle Mixer works effectively. When the whistle is blown a certain number of times, students form groups corresponding to the number of whistle blows and sit down to signify that they have the correct number of people in their group.

Physical education teachers need to use a consistent approach for dealing with undesirable behavior. "Time-Out" is generally used to deal with inappropriate behavior. The timeout approach moves children out of the class setting and places them into a designated area when they misbehave. Being placed in the time-out area does not imply that the student is a "bad person," but rather that he/she has forgotten to follow the rules. When placing students in time-out, teachers should communicate to children that they are loved individuals, but their misbehavior is unacceptable, hence, the reason they are in time-out.

To minimize incidence of undesirable behavior, teachers are encouraged to develop a set of expectations and rules for the class. The plan's expectations should be no more than five items, posted in the teaching area for easy reference. The rules should be discussed regularly so children clearly understand what are the expected behaviors and consequences.

A set of consequences might be as follows: First misbehavior—the student is warned quietly on a personal basis to avoid embarrassment. Sometimes, students are unaware that they are bothering others and a gentle reminder is all that is needed to refocus the behavior. Second misbehavior—the student is told to go to a designated time-out spot. The student must stay there until ready to reenter the activity and demonstrate the desired behavior. It is acceptable for the student to go to the area for a short period and almost immediately return to the activity since the assumption is that they have agreed to stop misbehaving. Third misbehavior—the student goes to time-out for a longer period or the remainder of the period. In addition to negative consequences, teachers are also asked to identify positive consequences. The reward system is used to reward those students that follow the rules and comply with instructions, and as a way to motivate others to exhibit appropriate behavior.

Adaptive Physical Education

The Americans with Disabilities Act of 1990 (including ADA Amendments Act of 2008) requires the placement of students in the least restrictive environment. For most "handicapped children," the least restrictive environment is the regular classroom, which includes participation in physical education activities. The challenge in teaching physical education to handicapped children is tailoring activities to fit each child. For example, blind or partially sighted students can participate in dance, and some gymnastic and tumbling activities.

These students can also participate in some other activities with modifications. A beeper ball together with verbal cues can be used for T-ball or even for softball. If a beeper is not available, the teacher can put the student in position and assist in aiming and cueing when to hit the ball. For students using assistive devices like walkers or crutches, they can be allowed to hit the ball from a seated position and use the crutch to bat. If the child is unable to run, allow a substitute runner. Many games and activities can be modified for the handicapped child. Sometimes all it takes is a little ingenuity to change activities so handicapped students can enjoy participating.

Objective 0024: Understand basic elements, concepts, and techniques associated with the arts.

For example:

- Identifying the basic elements, concepts, and terms associated with dance, music, drama, and the visual arts (e.g., pathways, rhythm, plot, perspective

- Recognizing the basic techniques, processes, tools, and materials for creating, performing, and producing works in the various arts

- Applying knowledge of diverse strategies for promoting critical analysis, cultural perspectives, and aesthetic understandings of the arts

- Recognizing how the arts can be used as a form of communication, self-expression, and social expression

- Demonstrating knowledge of the connections among the arts as well as between the arts and other areas of the curriculum and everyday life

- Recognizing the role and function of the arts in various cultures and throughout history

The final objective in the Health, Physical Education and the Arts section focuses on the arts in the elementary school. The arts include four disciplines: visual arts, music, drama and dance. Each is organized by basic foundations, creative expression/production, response/critical analysis, making connections and cultural/historical context. These are addressed below by discipline.

Visual Arts

Young children's earliest experiences with the visual arts are much more scientific than artistic in nature. A child making marks by moving a crayon or marker across a surface is concentrating on the sensory experience rather than on self-expression or symbolism. The child is most interested in the texture of the surface, the colors that appear, and the shapes that emerge. It is not until age three or four that the child may notice a similarity between an actual object and a mark that has been made. At this point, the child artist begins to realize that the colors and shapes being applied can symbolize people, objects, and events in reality.

Children of all cultures may experiment in their drawings with variations of the *mandala,* a circle intersected by lines, and the *tadpole person,* a circle representing a human head with lines protruding to represent arms and legs. Around age five, children move into drawing individual symbols to represent people and objects. A house, for example, may be consistently represented as a square with a triangle on top, regardless of the appearance of the house in reality.

The use of symbolized drawings continues through the early elementary years, when children typically become enamored with repeating a particular theme in their drawings. A scene with a house, a tree, and hills in the background, or one with a spaceship, a planet surrounded by rings and a quarter moon may be repeated many, many times with little variation as the child artist works toward his/her own ideas of perfection. As children move into the middle and later elementary years, they strive increasingly to achieve photographic realism in their artwork. The frustration they may experience at this point will convince some children that they do not have artistic abilities and make them very reluctant to engage in art activities.

By relating art production in the elementary curriculum to art products created by artists from other historical eras and cultures, children are introduced to art appreciation and the basic elements and principles of art. An analysis of the elements and principles of arts follow.

Elements and Principles of Art

Art is a way of communicating and expressing ideas, emotions, and experiences. In order to communicate their own ideas and to understand the communications of other artists, children must have knowledge of and be able to use the elements of art. The elements and principles of art are used by artists to create paintings, drawings, and/or designs; they are the basic principles of design.

Elements of Art

The elements of art are the individual components that combine to create artwork—line, shape, space, value, color, and texture (Wallace, 2006). Most works of art have some small aspect of each element. A description of each element follows.

1. **Line** refers to marks from a pen or brush used to highlight a specific part of a painting or a structure. More subtle lines can also be used to accomplish the opposite effect.

2. **Shape** represents a self-contained, defined area of a two- or three-dimensional area creating a form. There are two basic types of shapes: geometric and organic. The term *geometric shapes* refers to squares, triangles, circles, and rectangles. The term *organic shapes* includes more natural-looking shapes like leaves, animals, and clouds.

3. **Space** describes the emptiness around or within objects. Space can be used to create perspective, to create objects or people in different planes, and to create a sense of depth. Positive space is the main area or object of focus in an artwork. Smaller objects in a painting seem farther away, while larger objects will appear to be closer.

4. **Value** refers to the darkness or lightness of an artwork. Values are commonly used to create the two-dimensional quality of artwork. Values also indicate the source of light in a work and provide a three-dimensional view of figures by suggesting shadows. Values can also represent the mood of the artist and

the artwork. Darker values are used to represent sadness, mystery, or formality, while lighter values usually represent contentment and relaxation.

5. **Color** represents reflected light and the way it bounces off objects. There are three primary colors (red, yellow, blue); three secondary colors (green, orange, violet); and an unlimited amount of tertiary colors, which are colors that fall between the primary and secondary colors, and compound colors. Compound colors are colors containing a mixture of the three primary colors. There also warm colors (such as yellow, orange, and red) and cool colors (such as blue, green, and purple). Artists use all these color combinations to create the environment of the painting.

6. **Texture** describes the surface quality of a figure or shape. A shape can appear to be rough, smooth, soft, hard, or glossy. Texture can be physical (felt with the hand, e.g., a buildup of paint) or visual (giving the illusion of texture, e.g., the paint gives the impression of texture, but the surface remains smooth and flat).

Principles of Art

The principles of art describe the guidelines that artists follow to create art and to deliver their intended message. Artists use the elements of art to communicate the principles in their creations. The principles of art include emphasis, balance, rhythm, contrast, movement, and harmony (Wallace 2006). A description of these components follows.

1. **Emphasis** is the technique of making one part of a work standout from the rest of the artwork. It guides viewers to pay attention to specific details or components of the artwork. Often the lines and texture lead viewers to the target feature. Lines in paintings and sculpture can point or lead to the focus of attention. By making texture different in one area from the rest of the artwork, the artist can also make the target area stand out.

2. **Balance** refers to the positioning of objects in such a way that none of them overpower the other components of the artwork. Size, space, color, shape, and lighting can be used to create balance. A large shape, for example, that is close to the center can be balanced by a smaller shape that is close to the edge. A large light-toned shape can be balanced by a small dark-toned shape. There are two main kinds of balance: symmetrical and asymmetrical. Symmetrical balance occurs when two halves of a figure coincide creating a mirror image. The line of symmetry is the line that divides the figure in two. The easiest way to identify symmetric figures is to fold the figure in half, and if these two halves are identical, then we can say that the figure is symmetrical. Asymmetrical balance occurs when two sides of an artwork are different. For example,

the artwork of the American flag—horizontal lines of different sizes, a smaller rectangle in the upper left corner with stars—makes it asymmetrical.

3. **Rhythm** describes the type of patterns used in the artwork. For example, placing a repetition of objects evenly spaced presents a regular type of rhythm. Elements increasing or decreasing in size in an artwork presents a progressive rhythm.

4. **Contrast** is used to create interest through the combination of elements. Contrast is used to break the monotony or repetitious pattern in a work of art. Rembrandt's paintings are well-known for using value (lightness and darkness) to create contrast. He also used lighter values to highlight portions of the paintings.

5. **Movement** refers to the way that artists produce the appearance of motion. In painting, artists use the element of line to simulate the movement of wind or water. This technique leads viewers to perceive the effects of motion and action through the artwork.

6. **Harmony** is used to represent a sense of completeness in the artwork. It shows the unity of the artwork. For example, texture and color can be combined to provide a sense of balance and harmony.

While the elements and principles of art provide the foundations of artwork in all media and styles, they also have application in other disciplines and in contemporary occupations. **Line**, **shape**, **space**, and **balance** are terms with parallel meanings in the field of mathematics, while **texture** and **color** are also basic objects in science observations.

Similarly, **rhythm** and **harmony** are used to describe synonymous concepts in both art and music. Mathematical concepts such as symmetry, angle, distance, and convergence are illustrated in artwork and must be explicitly understood by artists. Artists regularly explore science concepts related to light, water, and temperature in their work.

Engagement in art also requires artists, whether adults or children, to think critically and to problem-solve. Artists must carefully consider how to communicate emotions and ideas in their work, how to convey change and movement, and how to use symbolism. Artists of all ages must also learn to evaluate their own efforts and the work of others.

While art at its most basic is self-expression, the skills and dispositions required of artists have application in other fields and occupations. Architects and interior designers, for example, draw upon the elements and principles of art, as well as other technical skills, to create aesthetically pleasing designs for buildings, landscaping, and interior spaces. Commercial artists may use their abilities in advertising, animation of comics or cartoons, or illustrating print media.

Visual Arts Activities for K–5

Throughout the elementary grades, students engage in a variety of art activities such as drawing, painting, designing, constructing, crafts, sculpting, weaving, and finger painting. In grades 3 and 4, students continue perfecting the skills from K through 2 and begin working with new techniques like printmaking, sponge painting, graphics, film animation, and environmental design. In grade 5, students develop their art from personal experience and direct observation and are expected to demonstrate technical skills.

The elementary curriculum encourages the integration of visual art in the regular classroom, as well as specialized activities in the art room. Appropriate art activities should first of all focus on the self-expression of young artists. While the developing fine motor and perceptual skills of young children may lead to art products that have little resemblance to reality, it is important that children are encouraged to experiment, explore, and express their own ideas through their own efforts. Teacher-made models, pre-cut outlines and templates that standardize art products are not appropriate for elementary age children.

Art materials for the elementary art program include scissors, wet and dry brushes, fabrics, wrapping papers, film, computers, clay, glue, construction paper, crayons, beads, and multiple household items that can be used to create art. Safety is a primary concern during art activities, and toxic substances or potentially dangerous tools should not be allowed in the classroom. While elementary children enjoy variety in the materials they use in their art projects, teachers should recognize that the introduction of new materials leads children to explore the properties of those materials rather than to engage in creative expression. A regular rotation of familiar materials in classroom art projects is most likely to encourage artistic engagement.

Art techniques such as painting and drawing are familiar activities to most elementary teachers. Other techniques and materials used in the visual arts curriculum may be less known. Some of these activities are:

1. **Printmaking:** This is the artistic process of making a print in which color (paint or ink) is applied to an object; the object is then pressed onto a surface. When the object is lifted, a print is left on the surface.

2. **Ceramic:** The use of clay to create ceramics is one of the oldest forms of art. Figurines, tiles, and tableware are made by applying high heat to fresh clay and then cooling the object until it becomes solid.

3. **Textiles**: The textile arts are those that use plant, animal, or synthetic fibers to construct practical or decorative objects, including stitchery, weaving, dying and printing, lace making, knitting, crocheting, and embroidery.

4. **Basket weaving:** This ancient art uses unspun fibers (pine straw, animal hair, hide, grasses, thread, or wood) to create baskets or other forms for artistic or utilitarian purposes.

5. **Metalworking:** The traditional metalworking is the artistic process of working with metals to produce individual pieces, assemblies, or structures, including jewelry.

6. **Photography and filmmaking:** This relatively modern art creates still or moving pictures by recording radiation on a sensitive medium, such as a photographic film or an electronic sensor.

7. **Sculpture:** A sculpture is a three-dimensional artwork made by shaping or combining hard material such as marble, rock, glass, wood, or metal. Some sculptures are created directly by carving in a solid material; others are assembled, built together and fired, welded, molded, or cast.

8. **Computer-generated art:** This relatively new form of art is created through the manipulation of pixels, either through drawing and painting software or through electronic images stored in the computer. The computer screen serves as the canvas and colored light is the medium.

Identifying Characteristics of Style in Works of Art

A **style** is an artist's manner of expression. When a group of artists during a specific period (which can last a few months, years, or decades) have a common style, it is called an **art movement**. Art movements are found predominantly in Western cultures and occur in both visual art and architecture.

There are eight main historical periods, with various artistic styles and art movements within each. Although some periods have only one or two unique art styles, the twentieth century has produced 36 unique styles. Descriptions of some of the best-known styles throughout history follow (Witcombe, 1995).

The **Prehistoric** period is characterized by paintings that represent the daily activities of a group of people. The best-known representation of this type of art is the Caves of Altamira, in modern Spain. The Paleolithic peoples of Europe produced small, stylized stone carvings of women as symbols of fertility. These small statues have been found most often in modern France, Italy, and Austria.

The **Ancient** period produced a large number of masterpieces from varied civilizations, such as the Sumerians, Babylonians, Assyrians, Egyptians, Greeks, and Romans. These civilizations skillfully carved even the hardest rocks, such as granite and basalt, into narratives of battles and historical records. Egyptian statues, like their architectural monuments the pyramids, were often of colossal size in order to exalt the power of the society's leaders and gods. The art of ancient Greece has its roots in the Minoan civilization on the island of Crete, which flourished from about 2500 to 1400 BCE. The palace at Knossos held characteristic wall paintings revealing a civilization enamored with games, leisure, and the beauty of the sea.

The mainland of the Greeks of the **Classical** period, about 1,000 years later than the ancient period, was fascinated by physical beauty. Fashioned in the human image, with a universal ideal of perfection and guided by a master plan, the Greeks recreated their Olympian gods in their idealized and gracefully proportioned sculptures, architecture, and paintings. In the **Hellenistic** period (330–30 BCE), the populace, fascinated by physical beauty, appreciated these various objects of art for their beauty alone. The culture of Rome excelled in engineering and building, skills intended to efficiently organize a vast empire and provide an aesthetic environment for private and public use. The Romans built temples, roads, bathing complexes, civic buildings, palaces, and aqueducts. One of the greatest of their artistic and engineering accomplishments was the massive-domed temple of all the gods called the Pantheon, which is today one of the most perfectly preserved of all buildings from the classical period.

The **Medieval** period (500–1400 CE) also produced large numbers of artistic masterpieces. The Romanesque style of art and architecture was preeminent from about 800 to 1200 CE. By then many local styles, including the decorative arts of the Byzantine Empire, the Near East, and the German and Celtic tribes, were contributing to European culture. Common features of Romanesque churches are round arches, vaulted ceilings, and heavy walls that are ornately decorated—primarily with symbolic figures of Christianity. Realism had become less important than the message. The Gothic architecture flourished during this period with the creation of magnificent ribbed vaulting and pointed roofs. The cathedrals in this style are some of the purest expressions of an age. They combine a continued search for engineering and structural improvement with stylistic features that convey a relentless verticality, a reach toward heaven, and the unbridled adoration of God. Soaring and roomy, the construction of the Gothic cathedrals employed such elements as flying buttresses (structure to reinforce a wall) and pointed arches and vaults; a number of sculptures and stained-glass windows that were, for the worshippers, visual encyclopedias of Christian teachings and stories.

Renaissance (14th to 16th century) artists developed new forms and revived classical styles and values, with the belief in the importance of the human experience on Earth and realism. Great sculptors approached true human characterization and realism as they revived elements of Greek architecture. Like the painters of the period, Renaissance architects took a scientific, ordered approach and emphasized perspective and the calculated composition of figures in space. Art became more emotional and dramatic, and because of this, the use of color and movement increased, compositions were more vigorous, and references to classical iconography and the pleasures of an idyllic golden age increased. Typical examples of this emotional, dramatic art are Michelangelo's magnificent Sistine Chapel frescoes and his powerful sculptures of David and Moses; Leonardo da Vinci's *Mona Lisa*; Raphael's *School of Athens* fresco; and the increasingly dramatic and colorful works of the Venetian and northern Italian masters Titian, Correggio, Giorgione, and Bellini.

Baroque style emerged in the 17th century in Europe. The baroque style used exaggerated motion, and elaborate and detailed artwork. The movement produced drama, tension, exuberance, and grandeur in sculpture, painting, literature, and music. **Rococo art** characterizes the art of the early eighteenth century. Artists of the Rococo era turned the agitated drama of the baroque style into light, pastel-toned, swirling compositions that seem placed in an idyllic land of a golden age.

Nineteenth-century art was characterized by three elements—romanticism and idealism, realism, and impressionism. In the first half of the nineteenth century, landscape painting in England reached a zenith with the works of John Constable and Joseph Mallord William Turner. Turner's awe-inspiring landscapes form a bridge between the spirit of romanticism and the expressionistic brushwork and realism of the Barbizon School in France, whose chief painters were Charles Daubigny and Jean-Baptiste-Camille Corot. Beginning with Barbizon, the French painters of the nineteenth century concentrated increasingly on the reporter-like depiction of everyday life and the natural environment in a free, painterly (gesture and brushwork) style.

Realism rejected traditional means of composing a picture, academic methods of figure modeling and color relations, and accurate and exact rendering of people and objects in favor of an art that emphasized quickly observed and sketched moments from life, the relation of shapes and forms and colors, the effects of light, and the act of painting itself. The realist pioneers were Gustave Courbet (*The Stone Breakers, A Burial at Ormans*), Jean-François Millet (*The Sower, The Angelus*), and Honoré Daumier (*The Third-Class Carriage*).

Impressionism began with Edouard Manet in France in the 1860s. French artists continually blurred the boundaries of realism and abstraction. They used light and color to capture the impression of images as opposed to the real "real image." The landscapes and everyday-life paintings of impressionist artists like Claude Monet, Camille Pissarro, Auguste Renoir, Alfred Sisley, and Edgar Degas gave way to the more experimental arrangements of form and color of the great postimpressionists: Paul Gauguin, Vincent van Gogh, Georges Seurat, and Henri de Toulouse-Lautrec. Auguste Rodin produced powerful sculptures with the freedom of impressionist style.

Twentieth-century art provided new avenues for artistic expressions. **Surrealism** is one of the new trends in painting that emerged in the 20th century. Inspired by the psychoanalytic writings of Sigmund Freud and Carl Jung, artists made the subconscious and the metaphysical important elements in their work. The influence of psychology is especially evident in the work of the surrealist artist Salvador Dali. Salvador Dali created non-realistic paintings as revealed in dreams, free of conscious controls of reason and conventions.

Cubism and abstract paintings of Pablo Picasso also emerged during the twentieth century. This new type of art represents the most direct call for the total destruction of realistic depiction. Artists challenged common realistic conventions to create new representations of reality or imagination. Cubism is the most important and influential movement of European paintings and sculptures in the early 20th century.

Muralists and social realists between WWI and WWII created art that was physically interesting and whose subjects were accessible to the average person. John Sloan, George Bellows, Edward Hopper, Thomas Hart Benton, Grant Wood, and John Stuart Curry were among those who celebrated the American scene in paintings, frequently in murals for public buildings, and through widely available fine prints. The great Mexican muralists, who usually concentrated on political themes—Diego Rivera, José Clemente Orozco, and David Siqueiros—brought their work to the public both in Mexico and in the United States. **Photorealism** also emerged as a new form of art in which paintings resemble photos, lifelike—often portraits, still lifes, and landscapes.

Graffiti is a new and controversial type of art form that emerged in inner cities in America. The controversial nature of this new form of art is caused by the way that the expression is conducted. Traditionally, spray painting and using brushes, the artists create the work on the surface of private and public buildings with or without the approval of the owners. For some people, graffiti is a nuisance while for others, it becomes a liberating response to the pressure of modern-day living.

Art in Other Cultures

The progression of art in **China** is divided into periods according to the ruling dynasty and the development of technology. The earliest Chinese art products were made from pottery, jade, and, eventually, bronze. Porcelain art forms were introduced in early imperial China and were refined to the extent that in English the word *china* came to mean high-quality porcelain. Buddhism arrived in China in the first century BCE and strongly influenced artists throughout the country. Calligraphy and painting were popular art forms at this time, with artists working primarily on silk until paper was invented. While classical sculpture was the dominant art form of the Tang dynasty, landscape painting, almost Impressionistic in its portrayal of distance, was dominant during the Song dynasty. Color painting and printing were emphasized during the Ming dynasty and reached their peaks during the Qing dynasty when painters known as **Individualists** began to use free brushwork to express their ideas more openly.

Beginning in the 19th century, Chinese artists were increasingly influenced by Western ideas and techniques. In the early 20th century, **social realism** was the dominant theme of Chinese artists. During the Cultural Revolution of the mid-20th century, art schools were closed and exhibitions were prohibited. Following the Cultural Revolution, however, art exchanges were established with other countries and artists began to experiment with various themes and methods. Of particular note is artist Wang Yani, a child prodigy whose work since 1975 has exemplified *xieyi hua,* a freehand style.

Traditional **African** art was generally intended to both please the viewer and to uphold moral values. Because traditional African art was based in religious and ethical meanings, the human figure was the primary subject. African art was most often created and exhibited or used in ritual contexts that dealt with important moral and spiritual concerns (Ray, 1997).

Native American, or American Indian, art encompasses a broad variety of media and techniques including pottery, woodcarving, weaving, stitchery, painting, beadwork, and jewelry-making. Art forms and symbols vary considerably across Native American tribes. Tribal artisans relied on available natural resources to determine the media in which they worked. Generally, art was used to beautify everyday objects and to create objects of spiritual significance. For a comprehensive analysis of the history of art visit: *http://witcombe.sbc.eduARTHLinks.html.*

Integration of the Arts in the Content Areas

The arts can be easily integrated with other academic content areas. In reading, children draw to represent the main idea of a story. Later in writing, they begin adding words to their drawings. Art appreciation activities also provide an appropriate context for children to notice and discuss details in a painting. Through observation and description, children practice new vocabulary and use descriptive language. Scientific principles like light, color, and texture can be easily introduced through artwork. Likewise, art concepts of space, proportion, and balance can be introduced through mathematics. Artworks in all media provide meaningful contexts for the discussion of culture and history.

Evaluating Works of Art

To judge the quality of a work of visual art, students should be given basic criteria for evaluation. The main principle of the criteria can be derived through questions similar to the ones presented below:

- What is the purpose of the artist? Does the work achieve the purpose?

- Has the artist spoken with a unique voice, regardless of style, or could this artwork just as easily be the work of someone else?

- Is the style appropriate to the expressed purpose of the work?

- Is the work memorable and distinctive?

- Was it created to meet social or cultural needs?

- Has the artist used the elements and principles of art effectively?

After answering such questions, a student might be able to determine the specific timeframe of the painting and the style in which it was painted. When addressing these questions, students should be able to describe a work of art using terms such as line, color, value, shape, balance, texture, repetition, rhythm, and shape. They should be able to discuss some of the major periods in the history of the visual arts. It is important that students be able to confront a work and judge its aesthetic merits, regardless of their ability to recognize it from memory.

Music

The main goal of music education is to introduce students to the concepts and skills involved in experiencing music, and the aesthetic and personal dimensions of music. It is expected that teachers will guide children in music understanding and discrimination, music's role in society, and the context in which it is created. Children are expected to study music structure, increase listening awareness, and develop sensitivity to its expressive qualities. Teachers of music should be able to teach children how to sing in tune, keep a steady beat, listen to different styles of music appropriately, and perform music expressively. Teachers should learn and use music terminology and the elements of music as well as the appropriate methodology to integrate music in the content areas.

Terminology for Music Education

One of the key elements in music education is to introduce children to the vocabulary and concepts they need to describe and analyze music. Some of the key music concepts for children in K-5 include:

- **Tone** is the musical sound of the voice; it may describe the quality of the sound. For instance, one might say that someone sings with a "nasal tone," a "thin tone," or a "full tone." A synonym for tone is **timbre**.

- **Tempo** stands for the word "time" and it describes the speed or pace of a song or music. The tempo is described as the number of beats per second (BPS).

- **Pitch** describes the vocal or instrumental production of sounds. Pitch can be described as high or low. It is often confused with volume. Volume can be loud or soft, while pitch is described as high or low. Vocal pitch can be classified from the lowest to the highest, as bass, baritone, tenor, alto, mezzo soprano, or soprano. Placido Domingo and the late Luciano Pavarotti are examples of famous tenors.

- **Meter** is a musical term used to describe the rhythm of a composition based on the repetitive patterns or pulses of strong and weak beats. Children can easily be taught to count the beats of a song by tapping the foot or clapping.

Elements of Music

Essential to the understanding of music are the key elements upon which all music is based. The key elements are rhythm, melody, harmony, form, and expression.

Rhythm is the varied lengths of sounds and silences in relation to the underlying beat. Usually children (K–3) confuse beat and rhythm, trying to make them the same thing. Beat is the pulse that is felt in the music and rhythm is typically called the melodic rhythm or word rhythm found in the song. Audiate (to hear music inside one's head) the song *Happy Birthday*; the beat is the underlying pulse and the melodic rhythm is the words to the song. Now audiate *The Star-Spangled Banner*; the beat may or may not be faster or slower (the speed of the underlying pulse of music is called tempo).

The beginning of *The Star-Spangled Banner* has the same melodic rhythm as the beginning of *Happy Birthday*. *Happy Birthday* begins with "Happy birthday to you" and has the same melodic rhythm as "Oh say can you see." After this beginning the two songs do not have the same melodic rhythm.

Melodic rhythm is identified using musical notation (the writing of music), which includes various types of notes and rests (see Figure 6-2).

Melody is the succession of sounds and silences that may move upward, downward, or stay the same. The "tune" or the singable part of the song is the melody. A **musical staff** (see Figure 6-3), consisting of five parallel lines and four spaces, is needed to read a musical tune. The pitches are represented by symbols called notes placed on the staff. There are seven letters found in the musical alphabet (A, B, C, D, E, F, G). The **clef signs** at the beginning of the song determine the pitch level, either higher or lower. Typically,

Figure 6-2. Notes and Rests

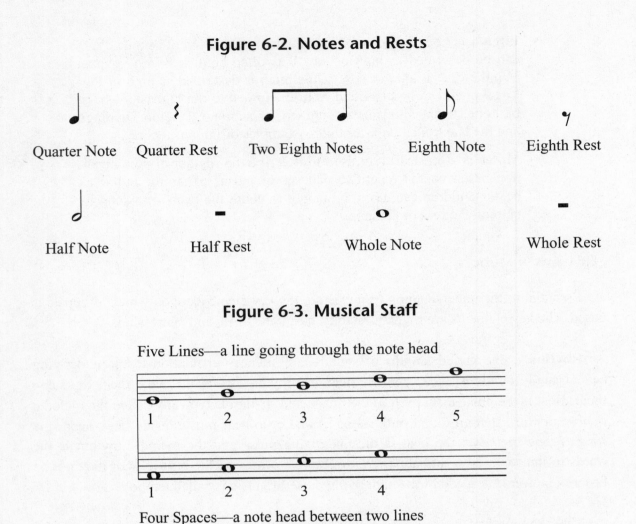

Quarter Note   Quarter Rest   Two Eighth Notes   Eighth Note   Eighth Rest

Half Note   Half Rest   Whole Note   Whole Rest

Figure 6-3. Musical Staff

Five Lines—a line going through the note head

1   2   3   4   5

1   2   3   4

Four Spaces—a note head between two lines

the **treble clef** is the singing range of women and the right hand on the piano; and the **bass clef** is the singing range of men and the left hand on the piano (see Figure 6-4).

Harmony is usually the accompaniment or supportive sounds to a melody. These accompaniments are typically played by a pitched instrument, such as a piano, guitar, or autoharp. Another way to produce harmony is through the use of singing rounds, such as

Row, Row, Row Your Boat.

Form is the structure or design of the music. A phrase, which is a musical line that contains groups of pitches, is similar to a sentence in language. Several musical phrases make up a song just like several sentences make up a paragraph. These phrases can

Figure 6-4. Musical Staff with Clefs and Notes

Treble Clef

C D E F G A B C D E F G

C B A G F E D C B A G F

Bass Clef

define a song. Musical forms are analogous to mathematical patterns. Common forms in elementary music are binary (AB), ternary (ABA), theme and variation (A A1 A2 A3 A4 etc.), and rondo (ABACA).

Expression consists of dynamics and timbre. Dynamics is a term used by musicians to represent the louds and softs in music. Typically, younger children (K–2) confuse dynamics with pitch level or melodic direction. The word "up" in music is usually associated with pitch level (the music moves up or goes higher) whereas, in the home if children are asked to turn up the music or television, the word "up" is associated with a dynamic level (louder). Dynamics are expressed using the Italian language (see Table 6-1).

Table 6-1. Dynamics

Italian Term	Dynamic Level
Piano	Soft
Mezzo piano	Medium soft
Mezzo forte	Medium loud
Forte	Loud

Timbre is defined as tone color in music. This tone color refers to the quality of sound that distinguishes one voice or instrument from another. Kindergarten children distinguish between the four human voices—speaking, whispering, calling, and singing; whereas, first- and second-grade students can identify the timbre of classroom instruments (woods, metals, and skins). Students in grades 2–5 can identify the timbre of singing voices (soprano, alto, tenor, baritone, bass) and orchestral instruments (strings, woodwinds, brass, percussion, and keyboard).

Music in the Classroom

Music is the arrangement of sounds for voice and musical instruments and, like dance, requires training and repetitive practice. Making music is part of our daily activities. Mothers sing to their babies. Children beat sticks together, make drums, and sing during their play. Adults whistle or sing along with tunes on the radio or portable music device. Sound and music naturally draw people together. Music is an important part of culture, religious practice, and personal experience for all people. Some people become professional musicians, whereas other whistle, sing or play for their own enjoyment and nothing more.

It is important that students have the opportunity to experience as many ways to make music as possible. It is through the acquisition of basic skills in singing and playing instruments that people grow in their ability to express themselves through music. As students develop skills, they are also exposed to basic musical concepts such as melody, harmony, rhythm, pitch and timbre (tone). With experience, students come to make decisions about what is acceptable or not acceptable within a given cultural or historical context and thereby develop their own aesthetic awareness. Music making is a natural part of the human experience.

Vocal Performance

Children's vocal ranges vary from one child to the next. The voice ranges of girls and boys remain about the same until the boys' voices begin to change, which is usually sometime during middle school.

For young children to learn to sing well they must sing songs that will not strain the undeveloped vocal chords by singing too high or too low. Typically, the classroom teacher sings too low for children and as a result children strain their voices or do not sing along with the teacher. The best singing range for students in K–2 is from D–A (see Figure 6-5). Students in grades 3–5 can sing a little higher, usually from D–D (see Figure 6-6). Children in K–5 have a breathy tone quality and should not be asked to sing louder or project their voice. If a louder sound is necessary, add more children. If an adult asks children to sing louder, children will typically yell instead of sing and therefore damage their voice.

Figure 6-4. Singing Range of Students in K–2

Figure 6-5. Singing Range of Students in 3–6

When selecting music for students in K–5, make sure that most of the pitches fall within the desired range listed above. Avoid songs that are too low, which will cause strain and harm to the voice. There are several music collections from around the world that are appropriate for children. When choosing this music, try to choose recordings that are as authentic to the culture as possible.

The materials used for a quality music program in any grade should reflect various musical periods and styles, cultural and ethnic diversity, and a gender balance. The goal of a quality music program is to make students aware that music is both a part of and a reflection of many cultures and many ethnic groups. The teacher should include diverse styles (basic musical languages) and genres (categories). Dividing music into categories can be difficult. Styles are constantly emerging. Many songs can be categorized by multiple genres. Nevertheless, the main groupings are classical, gospel, jazz, blues, rhythm and blues, rock, country, electronic, electronic dance, melodic music, hip hop, rap, punk, reggae, and contemporary African music.

There is a difference between the study of simple instruments and the study of orchestral instruments. The instruments that the classroom teacher normally uses in K-5 include the **rhythmic instruments**, **melodic instruments,** and **harmonic instruments**.

Rhythmic Instruments

Rhythmic instruments include instruments such as triangles, tambourine, blocks and sticks. After the students have a chance to move along with music and after singing games and action songs, they may be ready to try rhythmic instruments. The students need opportunities to experiment with triangles, tambourines, sticks, and blocks, among others, in order to experience the sounds they make. Students might try striking the tambourine with the hand to get one sound and with the knee to get another, for instance. After this experimentation, the teacher and class will be ready to try something new.

Another approach to music instruction is having students listen to a piece of music and then decide on the instruments they want to play. The musical selection is then played again with student accompaniment. This more creative approach is appropriate for young children who cannot read music or even for music readers who want to produce their own performance techniques.

Melodic Instruments

Melodic instruments include melody bells and simple flutes. Bells are instruments that the child strikes with a mallet. The child may use the bells before they learn an instrument like flutes. Teachers can introduce these melodic instruments with the music instruction in the upper elementary grades but the formal teaching of these musical instruments is generally not done until middle school.

Harmonic Instruments

Harmonic instruments include chording instruments like the autoharp. The rectangular wooden base of an autoharp has wire strings stretched across it. The child can press the wooden bars and strum the wires to produce chords. Students can experiment with harmony using the autoharp. They will find that sometimes a variety of chords "sound right" but that at other times only one chord works.

Music and the Content Areas

Music does not exist in a vacuum. The historical or cultural context of a piece of music, and the development of various instruments, is vital for understanding musical expressions. Students should be able to discuss the context of music by making connections among social studies, reading or language arts, and the fine arts. For example, when students are reading stories about the American Revolution, they should be aware that it occurred during the period known as the classical period in music history. Listening to a piece of music by Franz Joseph Haydn or Wolfgang Amadeus Mozart should be discussed in the context of the Old World. The teacher may also compare the classical works to a colonial American tune by William Billings as an effective way to help students understand the historical, cultural and societal contexts of music.

Similarly, the music of the Beatles, the assassination of John F. Kennedy, the Hippie movement, and the war in Vietnam all took place within the same approximate time frame. The teacher can ask students to find contrasts and similarities among these artistic and social events and look for ways that the historical context affected music or ways that music affected and reflected history.

These examples from American history are easy for most students to grasp. However, the objective seeks to have teachers and students consider the role of music in history and culture beyond the American experience. By having students listen to music from Mexico, the Caribbean islands, China, Japan, Germany, Australia or Africa when they are studying these cultural groups, the students' learning experience is enriched and becomes more memorable for them. It is even more valuable for students to view performances of music and dance of theses cultures. Seeing the costumes and the movement are an important part of understanding the culture.

Evaluating Musical Performance

People respond to music naturally. They do not need prompting or help to respond to it. However, to share their thoughts and feelings about music, students must learn how to put their responses into musical terminology. Some people call music a language, but it does not function as a spoken language. It does not provide specific information, instruction, or reactions. Rather, music sparks thoughts, feelings, and emotions.

To put their experiences into words, musicians and artists have developed vocabularies and approaches to discussing music and art. This does not mean there is only one way to respond to or talk about music. However, it is easier for students to understand music and musicians if they can use the kind of vocabulary and approaches that musicians use to discuss their work.

People cannot express themselves or effectively communicate if they do not understand the structures and rules that underlie the "language" that they are trying to use. Although music does not provide the kind of specific communication that spoken language does, it has its own structures. When students are able to think about and discuss music, they gain a deeper understanding of the music and can better express their responses to that music.

The aesthetic experience is what draws people to music. The experience is one that most people have had, but one that some people cannot easily describe. In fact, words seem clumsy when it comes to something that can be so profound and wonderful. The type of music, the period, or the performer does not necessarily limit the aesthetic experience. It is possible to have an aesthetic experience when listening to a child sing or while listening to a professional orchestra performing a symphony by Beethoven. The important thing is to share the aesthetic experience. It is part of what makes music and art special.

There are many ways to encourage exploration of and growth through aesthetic responsiveness. A common experience is a crucial starting point. After students listen attentively to several pieces of music, the teacher might ask them to describe how each piece made them feel. It is often best to write their responses down before starting a discussion. Then, the teacher might ask them to explain why each piece of music made them feel the way they described.

Through this kind of sharing, along with teacher insights and readings about how other people have responded to music, students come to a deeper understanding of their personal responses to music, other arts forms, and possibly the world. In addition, teachers should provide students with practical ways to express their responses or reactions to what they experience in life outside the musical or artistic genres.

In addition to having aesthetic experiences, recognizing their value, and being able to discuss or share those experiences, teachers and students must attempt to foster an appreciation for the arts and their ability to create meaning. The arts provide an opportunity to explore and express ideas and emotions through a unique view of different life experiences.

Drama

Drama and theatre activities offer students opportunities to experience an art form in many different ways. Drama helps students learn about themselves and their world, develop social skills, strengthen both their verbal and nonverbal communication skills, creatively problem-solve, analyze, and collaborate.

Drama means "to do, act." As such, drama and theatre are an experiential way to connect to content. Students are engaged physically, mentally, and emotionally. In today's classroom, infusing these techniques into the curriculum allows for hands-on learning that is meaningful and lasting. Children learn not only about drama or theatre but also through the art form if it is partnered with another content area.

Drama offers multiple approaches to gaining knowledge. Whether a student's preferred learning style is visual (verbal), visual (nonverbal), aural, or tactile/kinesthetic, infusing lesions with drama expands ways of knowing. Multiple approaches to knowledge acquisition and retention help to insure that all children learn. Even students who are generally less successful may thrive in classrooms where drama is a regular part of their learning environment. Teaching and learning through and with dramatic art is a unique and effective approach to instruction at all educational levels and with students of varying degrees of academic achievement.

Educators teaching elementary school age children will find that understanding child drama and the continuum of activities that defines it will help them to determine what type of activity is best to use at any given time. While the following comparison helps to distinguish the two major components of this progression, it is important to recognize that one is not better than the other; they are simply different in composition and purpose. Creative drama, children's theatre, and the activities between them offer ample opportunities for integration and demonstrate that the arts are powerful partners for learning.

Elements of drama, or the key components of dramatic presentation, include literary elements, technical elements and performance elements.

- **Literary elements** include those elements of story structure discussed in the Reading and Language Arts chapter. These include concepts such as plot or storyline, characters, monologue, dialogue, setting, theme and conflict.

- **Technical elements** include scenery, costumes, props, make-up, music and sound.

- **Performance elements** include acting (pretending to be a character), storytelling, speaking style, vocal expression, as well as nonverbal communication such as gestures, facial expressions, and movement.

At one end of the drama/theatre spectrum is creative drama. In this format, process is more important than product; the benefit to the participant is paramount. Creative drama is frequently used in classrooms because it is informal drama that can work in any setting and with any number of children. Scenery, costumes, and/or props are not required. These activities move from teacher-centered to student-centered, from shorter to longer activities and sessions; from unison play to individual play and from simple beginning activities to more complex story work. Participants need little, if any, previous experience with this approach to curriculum.

The following are definitions for the many types of activities that are components of creative drama.

- **Beginning Activities:** These are warm-up activities such as name games chants listening games, and other simple exercises designed to relax and motivate participants.

- **Games:** These are more challenging than beginning activities and often focus upon developing players' concentration, imagination, and teamwork skills. Frequently, they are played with students seated or standing in a circle.

- **Sequence Games**: The teacher takes a story or similar materials and divides it into particular events or scenes, placing each on an index card. These are randomly distributed to players. When a student recognizes his/her cue being performed, that student goes next. Index cards should have the cue at the top and the new action at the bottom, preferably in a different font or color. The teacher should keep a master list, in order of cues. This helps students if the correct sequences is interrupted or lost.

- **Pantomime**: Players use their bodies to communicate rather than voices. Pantomime sentences and stories, creative movement exercises, and miming games are common examples.

- **Improvisations**: These are spontaneously created performances based upon at least two of the following: who (characters), what (conflict), where (setting), when (time), and how (specifics of interpretation). Performed either in pantomime or with dialogue, improvisations should not be planned or rehearsed. Interesting episodes that emerge may be further developed through story creation. Role-playing improvisations deal with problem solving. Students are exposed to differing points of view by replaying and switching roles.

- **Stories**: A number of activities can be based upon stories and can range from simple to complex. In *noisy stories* for example, students help tell the story by making sounds or saying words associated with characters when the story is read aloud. *Story creation* activities require that players develop stories. These activities can be stimulated by various items including props, titles, students' previous writings, or true events. In *open-ended stories* students are provided with story beginnings. They write the stories then share their creations either orally or through performance. *Story drama* is the most complex informal dramatic activities. In story drama students take on the role of characters in a piece of children's literature and retell the story by acting out the story events. Students act out the story using their own words, not by performing from a memorized script. This is especially effective for teaching social studies concepts using historical realistic literature.

Several types of activities bridge the gap between creative drama and theatre. These include Theatre-in-Education (TIE), readers' theatre and puppetry. Each can be integrated into classroom practice.

- **Theatre-in-Education (TIE)**: Originating in Britain, Theatre-in-Education is performed by actor-teachers and students. Using material based upon curriculum or social issues, players assume roles and, through these, explore and problem-solve. TIE's structure is flexible and its focus is educational.

- **Readers' Theatre**: Readers' theatre is a dramatic presentation by a group of readers. It offers performance opportunities without elaborate staging or memorization of script. Traditionally, this type of performance has players sitting on stools and using notebooks or music stands to hold scripts. A narrator may be used and readers may or may not play multiple roles. This type of performance is wedded to children's literature.

- **Puppetry**: Puppets can range from simple paper bag or sock creations to elaborately constructed marionettes. Puppets can be used for creative drama and theatre activities. Likewise, puppet stages can be as simple as a desktop or table, or they can be intricately constructed with artistically designed settings and theatrical trappings.

Children's theatre is product-oriented and audience-centered. This theatre for young people can be performed by and for children, by adults for youth, or with a combined cast of adults and children. In addition, actors can be either amateurs or professionals. Here, dialogue is memorized, the number of characters in the play determines the cast size, and scenery and costumes are generally expected production elements.

Educators may take their students to see plays or they may wish to stage plays in their classrooms or other school facility. In addition to the familiar format, plays for children can also be done as participation plays or as story theatre. These last two are especially adaptable to educational venues.

- **Traditional Theatre:** In this most commonly used form of theatre, performers and audience are separate entities. Actors use character and story to communicate and the audience responds with feedback (e.g. laughing, applauding). Typically, actors perform on a stage and are supported by others who contribute the technical elements of theatre.

- **Participation Theatre**: Children are given opportunities to use their voices and bodies within the context of the play. They might be asked for their ideas, invited to join the actors, or given chances to contribute to the play in meaningful ways.

- **Story Theatre**: In this format, actors can function as both characters and narrators, sometimes commenting upon their own actions in role. They can play one role or multiple parts. If used, scenery is minimal and costume pieces can suggest a character. Story theatre is classroom friendly and is linked to children's literature.

Children benefit from exposure to theatre, whether as participant or audience member. Opportunities abound for developing vocal skills, vocabulary, imagination, knowledge of dramatic structure and types of conflict, physical skills and empathy. Theatre offers innovative instructional options for teaching across the curriculum.

Theatre is not a new art form. It emerged in ancient Greece as part of religious celebrations. The fact that theatre has evolved over the centuries is a testament to its nature. It is both experimental and transitional, allowing innovative elements to be absorbed into the mainstream while continuing to look for new artistic inventions. This is not its only dichotomy. Theatre is a profession for some and an avocation for others. It is a communal and a collective art form. Regardless of its structure, theatre engages through both visual and auditory stimulation. Also, because it uses live actors performing for an audience that is "in the moment" with them, it can be repeated but it will never be exactly the same.

How does theatre help students learn? Plays reflect culture, allowing us to travel to different places and time periods, learning about the conditions, people and viewpoints that have shaped the world of the play. They challenge learners to explore and to deepen their understanding. Theatre introduces children to some characters who are like them and some who are not. It enriches and broadens a child's way of knowing.

Using drama in the classroom may result in a lively educational environment. Teachers should welcome the energetic chatter and movement indicating students who are learning. They should also recognize that, in this type of experience, there might not be one correct answer or interpretation. Part of the joy and challenge of using drama in the classroom is that it pushes students to think creatively and independently. If teachers view themselves as co-explorers in this process, the journey they take with their students is both productive and fun!

Dance

Dance is physical movement of the body combined with artistic expression. As such it is closely tied to both the music and physical education curriculum. Like movement in physical education addressed earlier in this chapter, dance includes both locomotor (actions that cover space such as walk, run, skip, etc.) and nonlocomotor movements (actions of the body that do not cover space such as bend, twist, stretch or swing).

Elements of Dance

As with the other arts there are basic elements and concepts related to dance. These include space, time and force (Edwards, 2006).

- **Space**: Space is the area covered by the dance movements. There are three concepts related to space. These include **direction** (forward, back, to the side, up, down, etc.), **level** (the distance from the dance floor), and **pathways** (the patterns that body makes as it moves through space or on the floor) and **shape** (the design of the body as it exists in space).

- **Time**: Time includes **tempo** (how fast or how slow movement is), **beat** (whether even or uneven), and **duration** (how long or short the movement is).

- **Force**: Force deals with the use of energy while moving the body.

Roles of Dance

Dance plays important roles among the peoples of the world. As far back into ancient times as written records or artwork exist, we have evidence that all cultures dance. From the earliest artwork to that of today, the dancing figure is the artistic subject of many cultures. When we consider why people draw, paint, or sculpt, we learn that they portray what is important to them, what their community or culture values. Dance is important enough to be represented in the art of most cultures from antiquity to today.

There are many ways in which dance is a mirror of culture. Dance may be looked at as a social activity, as a performing art, and a creative pursuit.

Cultural Values

When a culture values strength and power, their dance will show it. When a culture values the community over the individual, it is clear in the dance. When a culture values order and hierarchy in social structure, the dance will give evidence of the same structure. With an observant eye, one can learn a great deal about a culture by studying its dances. This section speaks to many dance-evident cultural values such as religion, gender roles, sexuality, concepts of beauty and aesthetics, community solidarity, and creativity.

Religion

Most cultural dances are historically connected to religion. All over the world we can observe dances of devotion and worship of the deities where movements might include bowing in reverence, lifting arms to the heavens, and gestures of receiving of divine benefits. We can observe dances that tell stories of the power and conquests of deities (e.g., Egyptian, Greek, Indian, Japanese). These movements may include a wide, strong stance with fisted hands and stamping feet. It is also common to see the important stories of the gods told through dance and mime.

We can observe dances that appeal to the gods for survival. For hunting success (e.g., Native American, Inuit), movements may include pantomime of the animal and hunter and the inevitable killing of the animal. For fertile fields and lavish harvest (e.g., Hebrew, Egyptian, European), movements may include pantomime of the planting, tending and harvesting, as well as lifting or expanding actions that suggest crop growth. For victory in war (e.g., Chinese, Roman, African), movements may include use of swords, spears, or shields and the miming of conflict and victory. In most cultures the power of the dance to cause the gods' positive response is unquestioned.

We can observe dances that ask for divine blessings on life events. For the birth of a child (e.g., African, Polynesian), the movements may include childbearing actions, cradling and "offering" the child up to the deity, and crawling, walking, and running to indicate growth of the child. For initiation into adulthood (e.g., Native American, African) the movements may include shows of strength and manhood for the male and swaying and nurturing gestures for the female. For marriage (in most cultures), movements are jubilant, reflect traditional gender roles for men and women, and may include movements that suggest sexuality and fertility. For funerals (e.g., Egyptian, Cambodian, Zimbabwean), movements may reenact the life story of the deceased and may include grieving as well as celebration of an afterlife. For many cultures, dance is the primary connection between people and their gods.

Gender Roles

How should a man move? How should a woman move? Each culture answers these questions in dance. Most often the rules are unwritten, but they are clear nonetheless. In the dances of the Polynesian culture of the Cook Islands, for example, men keep a pulsing rhythm in their bodies by taking a wide stance and pumping knees open and closed. Their movements are always strong and powerful. The women stand with feet together and sway softly from side to side with undulating hips and rippling arms. In their dances, the man and woman never touch. In fact, they often dance in separate gender groups. In the ballroom dancing of European and American cultures, the man leads the woman by holding her and guiding her. She follows his lead. They move in perfect synchrony and reflect the Western cultural ideal of a flawless heterosexual union (led by the man) that is effortless and perfect. Each culture defines gender-specific movements that speak volumes about the roles of men and women through its dance.

Beauty and Aesthetics

All cultures define beauty in their own way. Dances clearly reflect that ideal (aesthetic) of beauty. Some African dances, for example, feature plump and fleshy women dancers who embody health, fertility, the earth, and beauty to their people. In the European traditional form of ballet, however, the skeletal ballerina is spotlighted to reflect the fragile, ethereal, romantic ideal of female beauty. Another contrast can be made between the traditional court dances of Bali and American Modern dance. In Bali, the court dances have existed for centuries. Dancers train for many years to perform with great serenity, balance, and symmetry. They embody the ideal beauty of Balinese culture. In contemporary America, modern dance can express the very different aesthetic of a driving, off-balance asymmetry. Each image mirrors a cultural definition of what is beautiful. We can all discover many different kinds of beauty through experiencing the dances of various cultures.

Dance as a Social Activity

Social dance has a relatively short history in the human race. Dance has always drawn people together as communicants in a common religion and as celebrants of community events in the context of religion. However, the practice of dance for the primary purpose of gathering people together to enjoy each other's company is only centuries old, rather than millennia-old. When we look at the history of social dance we can clearly see changes in social structure and accepted behavior through changes in the dances.

Folk Dances around the World

Folk dances are cultural dances that have remained quite stable for a long period of time. The music has remained constant and the movements have changed little over the years. Folk dances usually reflect the national traditions of various cultures. They evoke pride in people's traditions and culture by keeping alive the dances of their ancestors. Folk dances are usually about the group, not the specific dancer or couple. Folk dance is a solid connection to the past and a vehicle for "belonging." When one dances a dance, one belongs to the group that has danced that dance through the ages. For some cultures that are being absorbed into western society and swallowed by global culture, such as the Inuits of northern Canada, languages, traditional crafts are lost and ancient religion are gradually lost, but the dances are the last to go. People cling to their dances as the last remnant of a shared past. For the Punjab Indians who immigrated to England in the past century, the dances of their Indian culture are so important to their understanding of their cultural heritage that all children study the dances and the people perform them at social gatherings. People dance their own culture's folk dances to understand who they are and from where they came. It is also valuable to learn the folk dances of other cultures. When we dance the dances of others, we learn about them and gain respect for them by "dancing in their shoes."

Social Dances of Western Cultures

Social dances of Western cultures are usually about the couple and heterosexual courtship. In contrast with folk dance, social dances usually change over time. Through several centuries in Europe and America, changes in social dance have created a fascinating mirror of changing social attitudes toward courtship and gender. When the waltz emerged in full force on the European scene in the nineteenth century, it was soundly condemned as scandalous because the couple was, for the first time, dancing fact to face in an embrace. However, the man continued to lead the dance and the woman followed. Each new social dance has met with similar resistance as the changes in social attitudes toward gender and sexuality have initiated new ways of moving. Embraces become closer, sexual movements become more suggestive, and clothing becomes more revealing as times and social attitudes change.

It is possible to clearly track changes in social attitude in America by looking at the social dances of various times. The Lindy Hop of the late 1920s and 1930s is a good example. The earliest swing dance, the Lindy Hop emerged from the heart of the African-American culture of Harlem. Its popularity grew and the mainstream white culture was fascinated. White Americans began to flock to Harlem to learn the Lindy Hop. In this time of great separation between the races, the Lindy Hop forged new connections between people of different skin color. Social strictures began to marginally break down.

Another example of the power of social dance to reflect changing social attitudes is the Twist. During the 1960s in America, the Twist emerged and took the social dance scene by storm. Its impact was felt in the fact that the couple did not have to synchronize their movements. In fact, the dancers no longer had to touch each other. Each one danced alone. This dance reflects an important social change in the 1960s America when women's liberation and the civil rights movements announced that each person had equal rights regardless of gender or race. The Twist was a revolutionary dance that allowed the individual to pursue her/his own movement. Neither dancer lead nor followed, mirroring society at the time.

Dance as a Performing Art

Dance has played another role in history—the role of performing art. In various cultures elite groups of people are designated as dancers/performers. Their occupation is to dance before audiences. There are several examples of performing styles, old and new, among various cultures.

In Japan, Kabuki emerged as a performing art from a long history in the streets. Traditionally, men play all women's roles in elaborate makeup and costume. Highly controlled, stylized movements and lavish costumes represent favorite stories and characters. The theater art is studied for a lifetime and the popularity of top Kabuki actors/dancers can equal the level of movie stars in Japan.

In India, the Baharata Natyam is a centuries-old dance rooted in the Hindu religion. A solo female dancer who is highly trained in the intricate form of storytelling performs the Bharata Natyam. The dancer utilizes the entire body, but especially the hands and eyes, in a very colorful and expressive dance.

From South Africa comes a style of dance called Gumboots. Out of the dark and silent goldmines and the oppressive lives of the slave laborers emerges a style of dance performed by groups of men wearing miners' gumboots. The dancers leap, turn, and stamp their boots in well-grounded group formations. Their rhythmic and exuberant dance tells of solidarity within adversity and of the workers' amazing endurance.

Finally, out of Irish step-dancing traditions and American innovation comes the Riverdance phenomenon. In this vertically lifted, stylized Irish dancing, the dancers hold their arms tightly at their sides while making quick explosive movements of their legs. They balance mainly on their toes while creating lightning-fast tap rhythms with their hard-soled shoes in kaleidoscopic group patterns.

In Europe and America, the primary performance styles of dance are ballet, modern, jazz, and tap dance.

Ballet, a stylized form in which the body is elongated and extended into space, emerges from the royal courts of Renaissance Europe. Female dancers, or ballerinas, study for years to be able to dance "en pointe," on the tips of their toes. The romantic ballet literally elevates the ballerina to an otherworldly figure unhampered by gravity. Ballet has a long history as an elite form of dance that contains elements of the affectations of royalty. Modern forms of ballet, however, have stretched the limits of the traditional form to include many more movement possibilities.

Modern dance emerged around the turn of the twentieth century, primarily in the United States, as a reaction against the style restrictions of ballet. It was a "freer" form of dance in which the dancer explores and creates dance with very few stylistic limits. Modern, and now postmodern, dancers and choreographers use many existing movement styles and combine them in innovative ways to create new forms.

Jazz and tap dance emerged in America from a similar source. They both meld the dance styles of Europe, Africa, and various other cultures. Both grow from the fertile cross-cultural ground of nineteenth and twentieth century America to create new dance blends and hybrids. Jazz dance is a performing style that also borrows from American social dance and uses contemporary music, physical power, body-part isolations, and gravity to create strong and rhythmic dances. Tap dance uses metal taps attached to the toes and heels of dance shoes to create intricate and complex rhythms. These four western performing styles have greatly influenced each other throughout the twentieth and into the twenty-first centuries. Choreographers and dancers borrow from each other, style lines become blurred and new blends between styles are common and exciting. Performing forms are constantly changing through time, but each has a cherished tradition.

Dance as a Creative Pursuit

Arguably the earliest creative act of a human being is movement. Long before mastering poetry, visual art, or music a child creates movement. Fundamentally, in all creative pursuits, we are practicing problem solving. Creative problem solving includes: contemplating a problem, considering various solutions, trying various solutions, choosing one solution, altering and fine-tuning the solution, and finally, evaluating the solution. Development of creative problem solving skills is important. Education programs profess the importance of problem solving, and the arts are no exception. The more we use creative movement in the classroom, the greater the learning potential. As students create they learn about the world, about others, and about themselves.

The Body as the Medium

Dance is an art that requires only the human body, standard equipment for all children. No pen, paintbrush or musical instrument is needed. As children explore the basics of movement (body, space, time, and relationship), they gain the movement vocabulary to express themselves more and more eloquently. Mastery of the body as a creative medium should be a primary goal in dance education.

Dance Content

Usually, dances are about something. They often have identifiable content. Most dances create meaning in some form, even when quite abstract. When a human being creates a dance, he or she may be expressing such diverse ideas as: community, literary conflict, properties of magnets, regular or irregular rhythms, mathematical patterns, or visual design. A dancer/choreographer may be exploring feelings such as: alienation, comfort, precision, smooth or bumpy flow, anger, or peace. A choreographer may also be sharing experiences through dance by telling story or by creating an environment that arises from their life experiences. Students are encouraged to create meaning in dance by expressing ideas, exploring feelings, or sharing experiences learn a great deal about themselves while developing their creative problem-solving skills.

Dance in the Classroom and Across the Curriculum

Why isn't there more dancing in the schools? General classroom teachers may feel inadequate to teach dance but maybe they define dance too narrowly as merely patterns of intricate steps. Dance in the elementary schools should be about creative movement. Any sensitive teacher can guide students through creative movement that builds upon classroom learning.

For example, in language arts, students can learn spelling and vocabulary words by spelling words with their body or acting out the meaning of the word. They can embody the concept of opposites, for example by exploring (along or with a partner) heavy/light, near/far, curved/angular, or symmetrical/asymmetrical. Students can also dance the character or mime the story they are studying.

Movement in math and science can also extend content knowledge. Creative movement studies can use repetition and rhythm to count in multiples or can use partner body sculptures to reflect symmetry and asymmetry, for example. In science, the difference between hot and cold can be represented through creative movement (i.e., heat moves, cold doesn't). They can also explore concepts such as gravity, creating a group machine, demonstrating the flow of electrical currents and circuits, or moving within the properties of various types of clouds.

Social studies supply many rich ideas for creative movement also. Some movement ideas include drawing a map of the classroom and creating a movement "journey" or exploring various occupations, transportation forms, or types of communities through creative movement. Folk dances are always a powerful means to experience other cultures.

Dance is a powerful teaching tool that can bridge the disciplines. Throughout history dance has been rich with meaning and passion. It expresses the depths of humanness across cultures.

References

Americans with Disabilities Amendments Act (2008). Information and technical assistance on the Americans with Disabilities Act. *www.usdoj.gov/crt/ada/adahom1.htm* (accessed July 16, 2009).

Calabresi, L. (2007). *Human Body.* New York: Simon & Schuster Books for Young Readers

Edwards, L. C. (2006). *The creative arts: A process approach for teachers and children.* (4th ed.). Upper Saddle River, NJ: Pearson.

National Association for Sport and Physical Education (2009). Physical activity guidelines published by the national association for sport and physical education. *http://www.aahperd.org/naspe/standards/nationalGuidelines/PEguidelines.cfm* (accessed February 17, 2010).

National Institute of Mental Health (2009). Eating disorders: Facts about eating disorders and the search for solutions. *www.nimh.nih.gov/Publicat/eatingdisorders.cfm*(accessed June 21, 2009).

PE Central. (2009). The premier website for health and physical education. *www.pecentral.org* (accessed May 27, 2009).

Ray, B. C. (1997). African art: Aesthetics and meaning. *http://www2.lib.virginia.edu/artsandmedia/artmuseum/africanart/index.html* (accessed June 26, 2009)

U.S. Department of Agriculture (2009). My food pyramid: Steps to a healthier you. *www.mypyramid.gov* (accessed June 7, 2009).

U.S. Department of Health and Human Services (2006). Dietary Guidelines for Americans. *www.health.gov/DietaryGuidelines/* (accessed June 29, 2009).

Wallace, L. (2006). Utah Education Network (UEN). *http://www.uen.org/* (accessed July 31, 2009).

Witcombe, C. L. (1995). *Art history*. Sweet Briar College, VA. *http://witcombe.sbc.edu/ ARTHLinks.html (accessed July 31, 2009).*

Practice Test 1

GACE Early Childhood Education

This test is also on CD-ROM in our special interactive TestWare® for the GACE Early Childhood Education Test. It is highly recommended that you first take this exam on computer. You will then have the additional study features and benefits of enforced timed conditions and instantaneous, accurate scoring. See page 7 for instructions on how to get the most out of our GACE Early Childhood Education book and software.

ANSWER SHEET
PRACTICE TEST 1

1 _____	25 _____	45 _____	73 _____	97 _____
2 _____	26 _____	50 _____	74 _____	98 _____
3 _____	27 _____	51 _____	75 _____	99 _____
4 _____	28 _____	52 _____	76 _____	100 _____
5 _____	29 _____	53 _____	77 _____	101 _____
6 _____	30 _____	54 _____	78 _____	102 _____
7 _____	31 _____	55 _____	79 _____	103 _____
8 _____	32 _____	56 _____	80 _____	104 _____
9 _____	33 _____	57 _____	81 _____	105 _____
10 _____	34 _____	58 _____	82 _____	106 _____
11 _____	35 _____	59 _____	83 _____	107 _____
12 _____	36 _____	60 _____	84 _____	108 _____
13 _____	37 _____	61 _____	85 _____	109 _____
14 _____	38 _____	62 _____	86 _____	100 _____
15 _____	39 _____	63 _____	87 _____	111 _____
16 _____	40 _____	64 _____	88 _____	112 _____
17 _____	41 _____	65 _____	89 _____	113 _____
18 _____	42 _____	66 _____	90 _____	114 _____
19 _____	43 _____	67 _____	91 _____	115 _____
20 _____	44 _____	68 _____	92 _____	116 _____
21 _____	45 _____	69 _____	93 _____	117 _____
22 _____	46 _____	70 _____	94 _____	118 _____
23 _____	47 _____	71 _____	95 _____	119 _____
24 _____	48 _____	72 _____	96 _____	120 _____

PRACTICE TEST 1

1. The Spaniards Francisco Pizarro and Hernán Cortés conquered, respectively, which of the following two civilizations?

    A.   Mayan and Aztec

    B.   Inca and Aztec

    C.   Toltec and Olmec

    D.   Taino and Quechua

2. The earliest European colonization efforts in North America began with the founding of

    A.   Virginia and Massachusetts.

    B.   Texas and New Mexico.

    C.   Saint Augustine and Roanoke.

    D.   New York and New Jersey.

3. The Earth, spherical in shape, is artificially divided into 24 time zones to account for its rotation around the axis and its varying exposure to the sun. What is the degree of separation between these time zones?

    A. $10°$

    B. $20°$

    C. $30°$

    D. $15°$

4. The tallest mountains in the world are part of the

    A.   Andes Range.

    B.   Himalayas Range.

    C.   Karakoram Range.

    D.   Kunlun Range.

5.   The United States has 50 states and at least four territories. Based on these figures, what is the maximum number of senators who can serve in the U.S. Senate?

    A.   50

    B.   100

    C.   54

    D.   435

6.   A census of the population in the U.S. is conducted every 10 years. Based on census results, identify the agency or entity that can be affected by population changes.

    A.   House of Representatives

    B.   U.S. Senate

    C.   Justices of the Supreme Court

    D.   The Executive Branch

7.   Identify the syntactic structure that represents the following sentence—*Mary gave me a dollar*.

    A.   noun, intransitive verb, predicative nominative

    B.   noun, intransitive verb, predicative adjective

    C.   noun, transitive verb, indirect object, direct object

    D.   noun, transitive verb, direct object

8.   **Scenario:** Joe is a third grader having difficulties with American idioms. He often gets confused with expressions like "Keep an eye on the baby" and "Keep your nose clean." Joe is having problems dealing with

    A.   academic English.

    B.   denotative language.

    C.   connotative language.

    D.   metaphors and similes.

9. **Scenario:** Mr. Figueroa introduced a cooperative learning activity for fourth graders wherein the students were to identify the syntactic classification for selected words. Accent marks were used to indicate the appropriate pronunciation of a word and also to give a clue for its meaning. The students were also to write a sentence with each of the words assigned.

Word	Word Classification	Example of Sentence
Example: in•sert´	Verb	I insert a key to open my door.
sub•ject´		
sub´•ject		
in´•sert		
con´•vert		
con•vert´		

In addition to promoting vocabulary development, what is the main phonological component presented through this activity?

A. The use of sight words for decoding

B. The importance of using accents to guide pronunciation of words in English

C. The semantic value of word stress

D. The importance of contrasting similar words to help in their spelling

10. Identify the rationale for the popularity of onset and rime to teach spelling skills in English.

A. It is used to compensate for the grapheme-phoneme inconsistency of English.

B. It is used to teach words as sight words.

C. It is the best approach to teach words with multiple syllables.

D. It is the best approach to teach the spelling pattern for prefixes and suffixes.

11. What is the main reason for introducing the letter-sound correspondence of the *m, b, t, p,* and *s* prior to the letters like the *x* or *q*?

    A. Children might have more interest in the first set of sounds.

    B. The first set of graphemes occurs more frequently in reading.

    C. Children have muscular control and can pronounce nasal sounds.

    D. The last set of graphemes can create language interference.

12. During the pre-reading stage of the shared book experience, teachers can increase interest in the story by

    A. encouraging students to make predictions based on the title and the pictures.

    B. encouraging students to draw a picture representing the main idea of the story.

    C. encouraging students to draw pictures representing the characters of the story.

    D. introducing students to the author's biography and other books written by the author.

13. Silent sustained reading (SSR) is designed to promote

    A. reading fluency.

    B. reading comprehension.

    C. word analysis.

    D. decoding skills.

14. Kindergarten students can identify the main idea of a story by

    A. drawing a picture representing the story.

    B. writing a short paragraph summarizing the story.

    C. verbalizing the main points of the story and writing a chronology of events in the story.

    D. developing a detailed analysis of the story line.

15. Reciprocal teaching is a technique used with struggling readers and is designed to

   A.   promote reading fluency.

   B.   promote reading comprehension in the content areas.

   C.   establish an environment where students can practice oral language skills.

   D.   introduce cooperative learning activities.

16. What is the key advantage of using interactive writing journals for emerging writers?

   A.   Students can communicate silently in class.

   B.   Students learn that writing can be used for communication.

   C.   Students can correct each other's writing samples.

   D.   Students can learn about personal information from teachers and peers.

17. Connectors are used in writing to create cohesive and coherent compositions. Connections like "on the contrary," "conversely," and "on the other hand" are commonly used in compositions addressing

   A.   opinion.

   B.   sequencing.

   C.   contrast.

   D.   results.

18. Use the information below to answer the question that follows.

**Citizens of Peoplefine
Rate Their Mayor**

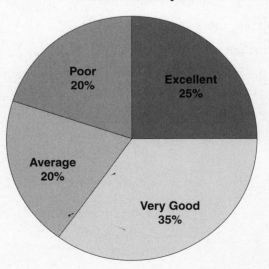

Poor 20%

Excellent 25%

Average 20%

Very Good 35%

Each adult resident of the town of Peoplefine, Georgia, was surveyed to determine the efficiency of the mayor. The categories were "Excellent," Very Good," Average," and "Poor." Using the pie chart, if a combined total of 1,440 residents rated the mayor as either "Excellent" or "Very Good," how many adult residents are there?

A. 2,400

B. 2,800

C. 3,200

D. 3,600

19. Divide 6.2 by 0.05.

A. 124

B. 1.24

C. 12.4

D. 0.124

Use the figure below to answer the following question.

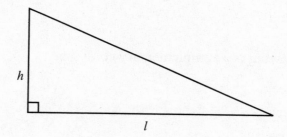

20. Which formula can be used to find the area of the triangle?

A. $A = \dfrac{(l \times h)}{2}$

B. $A = \dfrac{(l + h)}{2}$

C. $A = 2(l + h)$

D. $A = 2(l \times h)$

Use the figure below to answer the following question.

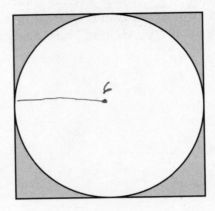

21. What is the approximate area of the shaded region, given that

    1. the radius of the circle is 6 units

    2. the square inscribes the circle

    A.   106 square units

    B.   31 square units

    C.   77 square units

    D.   125 square units

22. Which of the following is a complementary color pair?

    A.   Blue and green

    B.   Red and green

    C.   Yellow and red

    D.   Purple and red

23. Flying buttresses, pointed arches, and stained glass windows are characteristic of which historic style of architecture?

    A.   Romanesque

    B.   Renaissance

    C.   Byzantine

    D.   Gothic

24. Some of the musical instruments typically introduced in K–4 are

    A. tambourine, triangle, and sticks.
    B. flute, clarinet, and trumpet.
    C. violin, guitar, and guitarrón.
    D. bongos, piano, and harp.

25. Identify the most appropriate first step to take in helping a child experiencing heat exhaustion.

    A. Get the child out of the heat and initiate CPR.
    B. Get the child to a shaded area and give him/her water to drink.
    C. Get the child out of the heat and seek medical attention immediately.
    D. Get the child to a shaded area and pour ice water on top of the child.

26. Activities that develop gross motor–visual skills almost always involve the use of a

    A. ball.
    B. balance beam.
    C. trampoline.
    D. exercise mat.

27. For an aerobic workout to be effective, exercise should be performed at an individual's targeted heart rate for a minimum of

    A. 10 minutes.
    B. 20 minutes.
    C. 45 minutes.
    D. 5 minutes.

28. The most appropriate and safest way to provide exercise for kindergarten and first-grade students is through

    A. jogging and walking.
    B. contact sports.
    C. games that require endurance.
    D. games that require physical activity.

29. Identify the test designed to measure flexibility in children.

    A. Pull-up test
    B. Sit-and-reach test
    C. Grip strength test
    D. Push-up test

30. **Scenario:** Ms. Pachuta uses a fish tank filled with water to teach students how to make predictions about the ability of objects to float or sink. Students have fun with this activity, but they don't really know the scientific principle demonstrated in it, which can be best described as the

    A. mass and amount of matter in an object.
    B. concept of density and its relation to mass and volume.
    C. properties of matter.
    D. concept of weight and its connection with gravitational forces.

31. What is the role of evaporation and condensation in the water cycle?

    A. They recycle and redistribute the water in an ecosystem.
    B. They keep the ecosystem clean of pollutants.
    C. They provide water for vegetation and animals.
    D. They change water from liquid to vapor.

32. The capability of predatory animals to develop new physical traits to improve their ability to capture prey represents an example of

    A. intelligent creation.
    B. adaptation.
    C. metamorphosis.
    D. reproduction.

33. How many of the following planets (Mercury, Venus, Mars, Jupiter, Saturn, Uranus, or Neptune) have a year that is shorter than that of Earth?

    A. 4
    B. 8
    C. 2
    D. 1

34. **Scenario:** Ms. Cena asked her students to bring their raincoats outside to observe the clouds. Once outside, her students observed cumulus clouds. Based on their observation, what kind of weather were they experiencing that day?

    A. A sunny day

    B. A cloudy day

    C. A rainy day

    D. A snowy day

35. Identify the number of syllables and the number of phonemes present in the word *thought*.

    A. Two syllables and three phonemes

    B. One syllable and three phonemes

    C. Three syllables and six phonemes

    D. Two syllables and three phonemes

36. All of the following are characteristics of emergent readers EXCEPT:

    A. Use illustrations in the texts they are reading to aid in their comprehension

    B. Develop awareness of the story structure

    C. Represent the stories read through the use of visual images and drawings

    D. Engage in self-correction when text does not make sense to them

37. When teaching English to ELLs of Spanish background, Ms. Rico introduced a list of Greek and Latin prefixes common to Spanish and English. She explained the spelling patterns and the meaning of each of the prefixes. She presented examples of words that contain the prefixes, and led students to decode these based on the meaning of the prefixes. What decoding strategy is Ms. Rico using?

    A. Contextual

    B. Structural

    C. Pictorial

    D. Syntactic

38. Perform the indicated operation: $(-36) - 11$.

    A. 47
    B. 25
    C. −47
    D. −25

39. Simplify: $6 \cdot 2 + 3 \div 3$.

    A. 18
    B. 5
    C. 10
    D. 13

40. If a can weighs 14 oz., how many cans would you need to have a ton? (Round your answer to the nearest ones place and pick the best answer.)

    A. 2,285
    B. 2,286
    C. 2,287
    D. 2,300

41. Which of the following is LEAST likely to lead to illness and disease?

    A. Stress
    B. Hydration
    C. Dietary sugar
    D. Isolation

42. To apply the concept of time zones, students need to have a clear understanding of the

    A. International Date Line.
    B. Earth's yearly revolution.
    C. concept of the meridians of longitude.
    D. concept of the parallels of latitude.

43. Identify the statement that best describes the country of Iraq.

   A. It is a linguistically and ethnically homogeneous Muslim nation.

   B. It is a Muslim nation with multiple ethnic groups within its borders.

   C. It is located in Southeast Asia.

   D. It is a province of Pakistan.

44. The Mayflower Compact was one of the earliest agreements to

   A. establish a political body and to give that political body the power to act for the good of the colony.

   B. rules for farming and trading.

   C. a plan to implement plantation systems.

   D. a policy for settlement.

Use the information in this scenario to answer the next three questions.

Scenario: Mr. Jetter organized a lesson to introduce sixth-grade students to the concept of marine habitats. As a focus activity he presented two 25-gallon aquariums. Aquarium A has a variety of aquatic plants, 10 snails, and 25 unique varieties of small fishes. Aquarium B contains a variety of aquatic plants, three snails, and five small fish of the same variety. To implement the lesson, he organized the students in groups of five. Once the groups were formed, students were asked to discuss the appropriateness of the combination of aquatic plants and number of animals. The ultimate goal is to predict the success of the habitats, including successful breeding among animals.

45. What is the main science objective of Mr. Jetter's lesson?

   A. Guide students to communicate with peers.

   B. Promote scientific inquiry and problem-solving skills using scientific data.

   C. Work in cooperative groups.

   D. Keep students engaged and interested in the scientific concepts presented in class.

46. After a lengthy discussion, students agreed that Aquarium B had a better chance to establish and maintain a successful habitat. What information led students to arrive at this conclusion?

    A. The size of the aquarium

    B. The ratio of plants to animals

    C. The number of plants

    D. The number of fish

47. Students also agreed that Aquarium B has a better chance of successful breeding among the fish. What information did students use to arrive at this conclusion?

    A. The ratio of plants to fish

    B. The number of fish in each tank

    C. The size of the tanks

    D. The types of fishes in each tank

48. By second grade, students are generally guided to discontinue the practice of pointing to the words being read. What is the rationale for this change of strategy?

    A. Students get tired of pointing to the words while reading.

    B. Students find this practice annoying and typical of younger children.

    C. This practice can interfere with the development of reading fluency.

    D. This practice is archaic and does not seem to help in the reading process.

49. Characteristics of emergent writers include the following EXCEPT

    A. dictating of an idea or a complete story.

    B. using initial sounds in their writing.

    C. using pictures and scribbles.

    D. using conventional spelling in their writing.

50. What causes earthquakes?

    A. Thermal activity in the core

    B. The movement of continental plates

C.   The melting of rocks and minerals

D.   The movement or rotation of Earth

51.   A two-year-old child using a crayon to scribble on manila paper is focusing on

A.   expressing his thoughts and ideas.

B.   drawing personal symbols that represent objects in the environment.

C.   the texture of the paper and the color and shape of the marks being made.

D.   repeating themes to achieve photographic realism.

52.   What song has the same rhythm as *Happy Birthday*?

A.   *America*

B.   *The Star-Spangled Banner*

C.   *Take Me Out to the Ballgame*

D.   *America the Beautiful*

53.   Based on the Individuals with Disabilities Education Act (IDEA), children with crutches or any other types of assistive devices should

A.   not be allowed to participate in physical education activities.

B.   be allowed to participate in physical education activities like any other student.

C.   be provided with appropriate modification for participation in physical education activities.

D.   be provided with a special physical education class designed for them.

54.   The Virginia House of Burgesses was established in Jamestown to

A.   function as the official body of the U.S. government.

B.   regulate trading among colonies.

C.   function as a form of representative government.

D.   regulate the establishment of religions.

55. A globe is a scale model of the Earth shaped like a sphere. A globe shows sizes and shapes more accurately than a

    A.   compass rose.

    B.   Mercator projection map.

    C.   map scale.

    D.   thematic map.

56. Two paper bags are each filled with four blue marbles and four red marbles. What is the probability of selecting a blue marble from the first bag and a blue marble from the second bag?

    A. $\dfrac{1}{4}$

    B. $\dfrac{2}{16}$

    C. $\dfrac{1}{2}$

    D. $\dfrac{4}{8}$

57. How many lines of symmetry do all non-square rectangles have?

    A.   0

    B.   2

    C.   4

    D.   8

58. Identify the most appropriate strategy(ies) to meet the needs of children at the emerging stage of writing development.

    A.   Identify errors in the writing sample and guide children to self-correct.

    B.   Provide a prompt and guide children to write a composition based on it.

    C.   Read stories and ask children to retell the story while you write it down.

    D.   Allow the child to read for at least 30 minutes every day.

59. Xylophones, metallophones, and glockenspiels are instruments associated with what classroom musical approach?

   A. Orff

   B. Kodály

   C. Mariachi

   D. Tejano

60. The most appropriate exercises for kindergarten and first-grade students are

   A. jogging and walking.

   B. contact sports.

   C. games that require endurance.

   D. fun games that require physical activity.

61. Germaine, a fourth-grade student, notices that the shape of South America is similar to the shape of Africa. To demonstrate this, he cut out the South American map, placed it next to the map of Africa, and found an almost perfect match. He was amazed by his discovery and asked the teacher if Africa was once part of South America. What type of theory or scientific principle can the teacher introduce to make Germaine's discovery a teachable moment?

   A. Theory of evolution of the species

   B. Theory of intelligent design

   C. Theory of transcontinental migration

   D. Theory of plate tectonics

62. Mr. Obama uses monosyllabic words to present the concept of onset and rimes. Identify the pair of words that best represents this concept.

   A. want-ed—walk-ed

   B. very—berry

   C. think-ing—eat-ing

   D. s-ank—b-ank

63. Newly fluent readers can read with relative fluency and comprehension. Which cuing system is NOT one they would use to obtain meaning from print?

    A. Semantic cuing systems
    B. Structural cuing systems
    C. Visual cuing systems
    D. Punctuation cuing systems

64. Identify the mathematical property involved in the following problem: $(6 + 2) + 5 = 6 + (2 + 5)$.

    A. Distributive property
    B. Associative property of addition
    C. Property of zero
    D. Associative property of multiplication

65. Probably as a response to the war in Iraq and Afghanistan, the Organization of Petroleum Exporting Countries (OPEC) cut the production of oil. As a result of this action, the cost of gasoline increased to almost $3.00 per gallon in 2005. What is the economic principle or statement that is best represented by this situation?

    A. During war, the prices of fossil fuels increase.
    B. The American economy is dependent on foreign oil.
    C. The law of supply and demand determines the prices of goods and services.
    D. OPEC was boycotting the United States.

66. In the problem, $5 + 6 \times \dfrac{3}{2}$, what is the first operation that should be performed according to the order of operations?

    A. Exponent
    B. Multiply
    C. Subtract
    D. Add

67. Which statement about your metabolism is FALSE?

    A.   More total calories are expended during rest (Basal Metabolic Rate) than exercise.

    B.   "Fasting" (not eating for long periods of time) speeds up your metabolism.

    C.   Exercise stimulates your metabolism.

    D.   Adjustments in metabolism are slow and take place over long periods of time.

68. Why might children in prekindergarten and kindergarten have problems understanding how the Earth is represented in globes and flat representations?

    A.   They might not be developmentally ready to understand symbolic representations.

    B.   They might pay more attention to the colors and features of globes and maps than the concepts being taught.

    C.   They might not be interested in maps and globes.

    D.   They might have problems recognizing the Earth's features presented on the 12-inch globe representation.

69. Which of the following words can be used as a good example for homonyms?

    A.   to – tube

    B.   club – club

    C.   to – toe

    D.   to – two

Use the information in this scenario to answer the next two questions.

Scenario: Corals are invertebrates that generally live in a symbiotic relationship with algae. Some of them build reefs, others do not. Most of them filter water to obtain nutrients for survival.

70. Based on this description, corals belong to which of the following kingdoms?

    A.   Monera

    B.   Animal

    C.   Plant

    D.   Fungi

71. The term *symbiotic* in this case means that corals

    A.   are parasites attached to algae.

    B.   share the same environment with algae.

    C.   exchange services with other organisms.

    D.   are living organisms.

72. Newspapers and magazines have traditionally been considered what type of media?

    A.   Electric media

    B.   Visual media

    C.   Print media

    D.   Electronic media

Use the following figure to answer the question that follows. Assume that point *C* is the center of the circle. Angles *xyz* and *xCz* intercept minor arc *xz*. The measure of angle *xyz* is 40°.

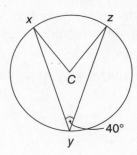

73. What is the measure of major arc *xyz*?

    A.   140°

    B.   280°

    C.   160°

    D.   320°

74. Which statement best describes an example of the Language Experience Approach?

    A.   The teacher records a student's story saying each word aloud while writing it down.

    B.   The students participate in writing down a shared experience by taking turns writing.

C. Students read a story orally while the teacher helps as needed with decoding.

D. The teacher models writing while orally thinking aloud about her own experiences.

75. Mrs. Cameron plans to buy carpeting for her living room floor. The room is a rectangle measuring 14 feet by 20 feet. She wants no carpet seams on her floor even if that means that some carpeting will go to waste. The carpeting she wants comes in 16-foot-wide rolls. What is the minimum amount of carpeting that will have to be wasted if Mrs. Cameron insists upon her no-seams requirement?

A. 40 ft^2

B. 60 ft^2

C. 80 ft^2

D. 100 ft^2

76. Why are Indian tribes from the Central and Great Plains of Texas better known than their counterparts from the Coastal Plains?

A. They had a more advanced civilization.

B. They were sedentary and built better ceremonial sites and permanent structures.

C. They domesticated the horse, which made them better hunters and warriors.

D. They had an abundance of food sources and were stronger.

77. Two coins are tossed at the same time. What is the probability that only one head is obtained in each of the tosses?

A. 0.25

B. 0.75

C. 0.5

D. 0.1

78. Identify the steps that best describe the writing process.

   A. Develop an outline of the intended writing project, complete an initial draft, and edit for content.

   B. Complete an initial draft, revise for the accuracy of the content, and publish.

   C. Brainstorm for ideas, develop an outline, complete an initial draft, edit, and publish.

   D. Write an initial draft, share it with peers, review it for grammaticality, and publish.

79. A card is drawn from a deck of cards. What is the probability that the card is a queen or a black four?

   A. $\dfrac{6}{52}$

   B. $\dfrac{8}{52}$

   C. $\dfrac{25}{52}$

   D. $\dfrac{12}{52}$

80. In a group of people, there are 18 blondes, 17 brunettes, and 5 redheads. What is the probability of selecting a redhead from the group?

   A. $\dfrac{1}{10}$

   B. $\dfrac{1}{8}$

   C. $\dfrac{1}{12}$

   D. $\dfrac{1}{7}$

Answer the two questions that follow based on the scenario below.

Scenario: Mr. James has seven students in his class who are having difficulties pronouncing English words containing the letters *sh* and *ch*. To support these students he organizes small-group instruction to address their specific needs. He introduces pronunciation and vocabulary concepts through a chart. The chart is color-coded to guide students in the pronunciation of phonemes (he uses blue for the /sh/, green for /ch/, brown for /k/. Every week he adds new words to the chart until he is satisfied that students have mastered the grapheme-phoneme correspondence. The chart for this week is shown below:

1. sh—/sh/ blue	2. ch—/ch/ green	3. ch—/k/ brown	4. ch—/sh/ green	5. s—/sh/ blue	6. t—/sh/ blue
shower	church	chronology	chef	sure	caution
short	chart	chemistry	chevron	sugar	contribution
shell	choice	chrome	chevalier	mission	communication

81. Based on the information provided in the chart, what is the primary reason for the confusion that ELLs experience with these two phonemes?

    A. They cannot distinguish the difference between the two phonemes.

    B. They cannot pronounce either of the two phonemes.

    C. They might not be interested in learning these differences.

    D. The grapheme-phoneme correspondence is inconsistent.

82. What might be the advantages of using the chart to teach pronunciation?

    A. The chart provides examples of the graphophonemic consistency of English.

    B. The students become aware of the words that follow grapheme-phoneme correspondence and those that do not.

    C. The chart can be used to teach the intonation pattern of the language.

    D. Children get exposed to vocabulary words and develop graphophonemic awareness.

83. What is the approximate volume of the following cylinder?

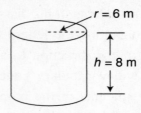

A. 904 m³

B. 301 m³

C. 151 m³

D. 452 m³

84. Mr. Rovira guides five-year-old children in the recitation of the following utterance: "Round the rugged rock the ragged rascal ran." Children have fun with this activity and try to say it without errors. What literary technique is he using?

A. Alliteration

B. Tongue twister

C. Nursery rhyme

D. Memorization drills

85. Which of the following sets of numbers is not an integer followed by its square?

A. −8, 64

B. 8, 64

C. 6, 32

D. −9, 81

86. Which of the following is equivalent to $17(64 + 8^2) - 4^3$?

A. $64(17 + 82) - 46$

B. 64×34

C. 64×33

D. $17(128) - 12$

87. Jamie rolls a pair of dice hoping to get an odd number. What is the probability that the sum of the dice will show an odd number?

    A. 0.625

    B. 0.75

    C. 0.25

    D. 0.5

88. The Sumerians, Akkadians, Babylonians, and Assyrians were some of the civilizations that flourished in Mesopotamia—the land between the rivers. What rivers are being alluded to in this statement?

    A. Nile and Amazon

    B. Tigris and Euphrates

    C. Nile and Indus

    D. Volga and Danube

89. Identify the statement that best describes the connection between reading and writing.

    A. The development of reading and writing skills is sequential.

    B. The development of reading and writing skills are interrelated and developed concurrently.

    C. The development of reading and writing skills is controlled by the structure of the language.

    D. The development of reading and writing skills is controlled by the age of exposure to the language and the type of strategies used to teach them.

90. Charts, tables, and graphs are commonly used in language arts to

    A. summarize information.

    B. entertain the audience.

    C. present detailed explanations of a topic covered in class.

    D. contradict information presented orally.

91. Identify the modern-day country that encompasses most of the territory of ancient Mesopotamia.

    A. Iran

    B. Pakistan

    C. Kuwait

    D. Iraq

92. George placed a metal spoon on an open flame and the spoon became so hot that it burned his hands. What scientific principle represents this type of energy transfer?

    A. Radiation

    B. Conduction

    C. Convection

    D. Kinetics

93. After devouring its prey, a crocodile opens its mouth to allow a bird to remove and eat the pieces of meat wedged between the teeth. Once the pieces of meat are removed, the bird flies away. What kind of relationship does this scenario create?

    A. Commensalism

    B. Parasitism

    C. Predator-prey

    D. Symbiotic

94. Mr. Ojeda supports his students' learning of writing by reading aloud examples of stories in which the author's uniqueness is portrayed and projected. This models which writing trait BEST for students?

    A. Organization

    B. Voice

    C. Sentence fluency

    D. Conventions

95. The U.S. Constitution was designed so that no single branch of the government—executive, judicial, or legislative—could exert full control over the other two. This unique feature of the Constitution is known as

    A.   judicial review.

    B.   the pocket veto.

    C.   checks and balances.

    D.   habeas corpus.

96. The main purpose of an interactive/dialogue journal is to provide children with opportunities to

    A.   practice speaking and writing skills.

    B.   communicate freely in a written form.

    C.   receive corrective feedback from peers.

    D.   practice listening, speaking, reading, and writing.

97. Stacy went to the store to purchase a loaf of bread. She originally thought she had only $9.55 in nickels in her purse. She then discovered she had 10 extra nickels in her pocket. How many nickels did she originally have in her purse?

    A.   161

    B.   173

    C.   192

    D.   191

98. Use the information below to answer the question that follows.

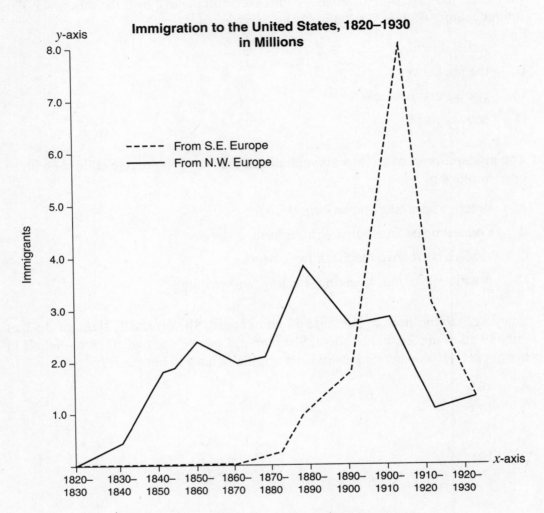

Immigration to the United States, 1820–1930 in Millions

y-axis

Immigrants

- - - - From S.E. Europe
——— From N.W. Europe

x-axis

1820–
1830 1830–
1840 1840–
1850 1850–
1860 1860–
1870 1870–
1880 1880–
1890 1890–
1900 1900–
1910 1910–
1920 1920–
1930

Source: Immigration and Naturalization Service of the U.S. Department of Justice

According to the information in the line graph, in which decade was immigration from each of Northwestern Europe and Southwestern Europe approximately 2.8 million?

A.   1871–1880

B.   1891–1900

C.   1901–1910

D.   1921–1930

99. What are Venn diagrams commonly used for in reading instruction?

    A.   Compare similarities and differences between two stories.

    B.   Identify the parts of a story.

    C.   Identify key attributes of a given concept.

    D.   Guide children to identify the main idea and supporting details.

100. A rubric to rate the writing skills of children in first grade should not place heavy emphasis on the mastery of spelling because

    A.   the use of phonemic and invented spelling is part of specific stages of writing development in children.

    B.   the use of standard spelling is not important in the development of compositions.

    C.   spelling addresses visual memory and should not be given great value.

    D.   the development of standard spelling requires students to use structural and phonics rules effectively.

101. An example of a prime number is

    A.   9

    B.   682

    C.   49

    D.   67

102. The most advanced pre-Columbian civilizations of Mesoamerica were the

    A.   Aztecs and Incas.

    B.   Maya and Aztecs.

    C.   Toltecs and Pueblos.

    D.   Olmecs and Iroquois.

103. A compass rose is a design printed on a chart to

    A.   show the orientation of a map of Earth.

    B.   show the distance between two places in the world.

    C.   represent features such as elevations and divisions.

    D.   show the distance between two corresponding points.

104. Students who develop an understanding of the key components of a story (i.e., the setting, characters, and the resolution) have mastered understanding through the use of

    A.   semantic clues.

    B.   comprehension monitoring.

    C.   story grammar.

    D.   shared reading.

105. Vinegar is composed of two substances—acetic acid (a colorless liquid) and water. This combination of substances is an example of a

    A.   compound.

    B.   mixture.

    C.   chemical.

    D.   substance.

106. What is the main purpose of the Federal Reserve System?

    A.   To promote fiscal stability and provide stimulus money to balance the economy

    B.   To promote economic growth

    C.   To create inflation and deflation

    D.   To keep the banking industry strong enough to ensure a supply of currency

107. Vocabulary development is a key predictor of success in reading in the content areas for all students, but especially for children new to the English language. Identify the best strategy to introduce vocabulary development for ELLs from diverse cultural and linguistic backgrounds.

    A.   Teach content vocabulary through direct, concrete experience as opposed to definitions.

    B.   Identify key vocabulary words in the content area and provide children with a translation of each word.

    C.   Teach content vocabulary in a comparative fashion, contrasting the meaning of vocabulary words in the various languages represented in class.

    D.   De-emphasize the importance of lexicon, introduce the words in context, and guide children to derive the meaning using context clues.

108. The main purpose for teaching sight words is to promote instant recognition of characters and words. Instant recognition of words can improve students'

    A.   reading fluency.

    B.   decoding skills.

    C.   reading comprehension.

    D.   writing skills.

109. The key function of the food chain in the ecosystem is to

    A.   control the number of animals.

    B.   preserve the types of plants in the habitat.

    C.   maintain a balance among organisms.

    D.   maintain a balance between fungi and dead matter.

110. Introducing the multiple versions of stories like *Cinderella* can help students understand how a theme can be developed from different points of views. Moreover, this kind of literature can help students in the development of

    A.   critical reading.

    B.   literal recall.

    C.   repairing understanding.

    D.   retelling checklist.

111. There are 16 more apples than oranges in a basket of 62 apples and oranges. How many oranges are in the basket?

   A.   23
   B.   39
   C.   32
   D.   30

112. How is knowledge of a student's instructional reading level useful when planning reading instruction?

   A.   It can help match the student to the right text for guided reading.
   B.   It can be used to form groups that last all year long.
   C.   It can be used to plan instruction for all subject areas.
   D.   The teacher can read a class set of novels with the entire class.

113. Identify the set of words representing the concept of antonyms.

   A.   small—smaller
   B.   small—large
   C.   bear—bare
   D.   small—little

114. Marcus can separate a word into its individual phonemes and put it back together to recreate the original word. However, he has problems separating words into syllables and identifying the syllable with the primary stress. Based on this scenario, Marcus needs additional support with

   A.   phonological awareness.
   B.   phonemic awareness.
   C.   syllabication.
   D.   word stress.

115. Traditionally, matter has been classified into three states, which are

   A.   rock, soil, and minerals.
   B.   ice, snow, and water.
   C.   liquid, gas, and solid.
   D.   nickel, lava, and magma.

116. As part of the celebration of Martin Luther King Day, fifth graders are getting ready to implement readers' theater on a book about the Civil Rights Movement. In preparation for the presentation, the teacher guides the students through several activities. Which of the preparation activities is **less likely** to help them get ready to implement readers' theater?

    A.   Working in groups to develop the characters in the story

    B.   Modifying the story so that they can all play a part in the actual performance

    C.   Rehearsing the parts that each student is supposed to read

    D.   Watching a video version of the story

117. Living things are classified into five groups: monera, protista, fungi, plants, and animals. Some of these groups are unicellular, while the others are made up of multiple cells; however, there is only one group that has prokaryotic cells. What kingdom contains prokaryotic cells?

    A.   Monera

    B.   Protista

    C.   Fungi

    D.   Plants

118. What is the main function of Earth's atmosphere?

    A.   Protect and preserve life

    B.   Prevent the contamination of Earth

    C.   Create a vacuum between Earth's crust and its mantle

    D.   Recycle water and gases

119. In an introductory unit about force and motion, Ms. Martínez brought to her fourth-grade class the following items: scissors, pliers, a hammer, tongs, and a miniature see-saw. These items are ideal to teach and demonstrate how _____ work.

    A.   complex machines

    B.   simple machines

    C.   household items

    D.   real-life objects

Use the numbers below to answer the question that follows.

7,823   5,963   6,002   755

120. If the numbers above are each rounded to the hundreds place and then added together, what will the sum be?

A.   20,400

B.   21,000

C.   20,600

D.   20,000

Constructed-Response Questions

Directions for the Open-Response Questions

Prepare a written response for each constructed-response assignment. Read each assignment carefully before you begin to write. Think about how you will organize what you plan to write.

Criteria for Scoring Your Response

Each response will be evaluated based on the following criteria:

- **PURPOSE:** The answer will be evaluated based on the extent to which the response fulfills the purpose of the assignment.

- **APPLICATION OF CONTENT KNOWLEDGE AND SKILLS:** The answer will be evaluated based on the extent to which the response accurately and effectively applies content knowledge and skills.

- **SUPPORT:** The answer will be evaluated based on the extent to which the response includes appropriate, specific supporting evidence of content knowledge and skills.

Each response is rated on a three-point scale. The three score points of the score scale correspond to varying degrees of performance that are related to the above criteria.

Score Description

3

The "3" response reflects thorough understanding of relevant content knowledge and skills.

- The response fully achieves the purpose of the assignment.
- The response demonstrates an accurate and effective application of relevant content knowledge and skills.
- The response provides appropriate, specific supporting evidence of relevant content knowledge and skills.

2

The "2" response reflects general understanding of relevant content knowledge and skills.

- The response largely achieves the purpose of the assignment.
- The response demonstrates a generally accurate, generally effective application of relevant content knowledge and skills.
- The response provides some appropriate and general supporting evidence of relevant content knowledge and skills.

1

The "1" response reflects limited or no understanding of relevant content knowledge and skills.

- The response partially achieves or fails to achieve the purpose of the assignment.
- The response demonstrates limited, inaccurate, and/or ineffective application of relevant content knowledge and skills.
- The response provides limited or no appropriate, specific supporting evidence of relevant content knowledge and skills.

0

The examinee has either not responded or responded off-topic, or the response is illegible.

Constructed-Response Question 1 (Math):

Use the information below to complete the task that follows.

Errors have been made in the problem below.

Problem: $4 + \left(\dfrac{1}{4} + \dfrac{1}{2} \right) \times 10 - 4 = n$

Step 1: $4 + \dfrac{3}{4} \times 10 - 4 = n$

Step 2: $4\dfrac{3}{4} \times 10 - 4 = n$

Step 3: $4\dfrac{3}{4} \times 6 = n$

Step 4: $\dfrac{48}{4} \times 6 = n$

Step 5: $72 = n$

- Analyze the problem-solving process above.

- Describe the conceptual or procedural error that was made in the attempted solution; and solve the problem correctly. Show your work.

Constructed-Response Question 2 (Social Studies)

- It is important to understand the early Native American cultures in North America. It is necessary to demonstrate knowledge of their interactions with the early European explorers.

- Describe the interactions of the Native Americans with the early European explorers. In your discussion, analyze the impact, both short and long term, of European contact on the Native Americans.

Constructed-Response Question 3 (Science)

Use the information below to complete the assignment that follows:

If you were to weigh yourself on a scale on earth and then could take that same scale to the moon and weigh yourself there, your weight on the moon would be 1/6 your earth weight. So, if you weighed 120 pounds on earth, you would weigh only about 20 pounds on the moon.

- Describe a scientific principle or phenomenon relevant to the situation described above; and

- Using the principle or phenomenon you have identified, provide a scientific explanation for the weight difference.

Constructed-Response Question 4 (Language Arts)

Ms. Suzanne Smith is a classroom kindergarten teacher. One of the children in her classroom is having difficulties with phonemic awareness. The child comes from a limited background with few books in the home. No one has read to the child or encouraged experiences with print.

- What is phonemic awareness?

- What types of phonemic awareness strategies can Ms. Smith use to help the child? Give three examples of strategies.

ANSWER KEY – MATHEMATICS PRACTICE TEST 1

Question number	Answer	Field	Objective
1	B	Social Studies	Objective 0009
2	C	Social Studies	Objective 0009
3	D	Social Studies	Objective 0010
4	B	Social Studies	Objective 0010
5	B	Social Studies	Objective 0011
6	A	Social Studies	Objective 0011
7	C	Reading and English Language Arts	Objective 0007
8	C	Reading and English Language Arts	Objective 0003
9	C	Reading and English Language Arts	Objective 0003
10	A	Reading and English Language Arts	Objective 0002
11	B	Reading and English Language Arts	Objective 0002
12	A	Reading and English Language Arts	Objective 0004
13	B	Reading and English Language Arts	Objective 0004
14	A	Reading and English Language Arts	Objective 0005
15	B	Reading and English Language Arts	Objective 0005
16	B	Reading and English Language Arts	Objective 0006
17	C	Reading and English Language Arts	Objective 0006
18	A	Math	Objective 0017

Question number	Answer	Field	Objective
19	A	Math	Objective 0014
20	A	Math	Objective 0015
21	B	Math	Objective 0015
22	B	Health, Physical Education, and the Arts	Objective 0024
23	D	Health, Physical Education, and the Arts	Objective 0024
24	A	Health, Physical Education, and the Arts	Objective 0024
25	B	Health, Physical Education, and the Arts	Objective 0022
26	A	Health, Physical Education, and the Arts	Objective 0023
27	B	Health, Physical Education, and the Arts	Objective 0023
28	D	Health, Physical Education, and the Arts	Objective 0023
29	B	Health, Physical Education, and the Arts	Objective 0023
30	B	Science	Objective 0020
31	A	Science	Objective 0019
32	B	Science	Objective 0021
33	C	Science	Objective 0019
34	A	Science	Objective 0019
35	B	Reading and English Language Arts	Objective 0002
36	D	Reading and English Language Arts	Objective 0001
37	B	Reading and English Language Arts	Objective 0002
38	C	Math	Objective 0014

Question number	Answer	Field	Objective
39	D	Math	Objective 0014
40	B	Math	Objective 0015
41	B	Health, Physical Education, and the Arts	Objective 0022
42	C	Social Studies	Objective 0010
43	B	Social Studies	Objective 0010
44	A	Social Studies	Objective 0009
45	B	Science	Objective 0018
46	B	Science	Objective 0021
47	D	Science	Objective 0021
48	C	Reading and English Language Arts	Objective 0004
49	D	Reading and English Language Arts	Objective 0001
50	B	Science	Objective 0019
51	C	Health, Physical Education, and the Arts	Objective 0024
52	B	Health, Physical Education, and the Arts	Objective 0024
53	C	Health, Physical Education, and the Arts	Objective 0023
54	C	Social Studies	Objective 0009
55	B	Social Studies	Objective 0010
56	A	Math	Objective 0016
57	B	Math	Objective 0015
58	C	Reading and English Language Arts	Objective 0001

Question number	Answer	Field	Objective
59	A	Health, Physical Education, and the Arts	Objective 0024
60	D	Health, Physical Education, and the Arts	Objective 0023
61	D	Science	Objective 0019
62	D	Reading and English Language Arts	Objective 0001
63	D	Reading and English Language Arts	Objective 0004
64	B	Math	Objective 0014
65	A	Social Studies	Objective 0012
66	B	Math	Objective 0014
67	B	Health, Physical Education, and the Arts	Objective 0022
68	A	Social Studies	Objective 0010
69	B	Reading and English Language Arts	Objective 0003
70	B	Science	Objective 0021
71	C	Science	Objective 0021
72	C	Reading and English Language Arts	Objective 0008
73	B	Math	Objective 0017
74	A	Reading and English Language Arts	Objective 0001
75	A	Math	Objective 0015
76	C	Social Studies	Objective 0009
77	C	Math	Objective 0016
78	C	Reading and English Language Arts	Objective 0006

Question number	Answer	Field	Objective
79	A	Math	Objective 0013
80	B	Math	Objective 0013
81	D	Reading and English Language Arts	Objective 0002
82	B	Reading and English Language Arts	Objective 0002
83	A	Math	Objective 0015
84	A	Reading and English Language Arts	Objective 0001
85	C	Math	Objective 0014
86	C	Math	Objective 0014
87	D	Math	Objective 0016
88	B	Social Studies	Objective 0009
89	B	Reading and English Language Arts	Objective 0001
90	D	Reading and English Language Arts	Objective 0005
91	D	Social Studies	Objective 0010
92	B	Science	Objective 0020
93	D	Science	Objective 0021
94	B	Reading and English Language Arts	Objective 0006
95	C	Social Studies	Objective 0011
96	B	Reading and English Language Arts	Objective 0006
97	D	Math	Objective 0013
98	B	Math	Objective 0017

Question number	Answer	Field	Objective
99	A	Reading and English Language Arts	Objective 0005
100	A	Reading and English Language Arts	Objective 0006
101	D	Math	Objective 0014
102	B	Social Studies	Objective 0009
103	A	Social Studies	Objective 0010
104	C	Reading and English Language Arts	Objective 0005
105	B	Science	Objective 0020
106	D	Social Studies	Objective 0012
107	A	Reading and English Language Arts	Objective 0003
108	A	Reading and English Language Arts	Objective 0004
109	C	Science	Objective 0021
110	A	Reading and English Language Arts	Objective 0005
111	A	Math	Objective 0013
112	A	Reading and English Language Arts	Objective 0004
113	B	Reading and English Language Arts	Objective 0003
114	A	Reading and English Language Arts	Objective 0001
115	C	Science	Objective 0020
116	D	Reading and English Language Arts	Objective 0003

Question number	Answer	Field	Objective
117	A	Science	Objective 0021
118	A	Science	Objective 0019
119	B	Science	Objective 0020
120	C	Math	Objective 0014

Practice Test 1 Progress Chart

**Reading and English Language Arts
Objective 0001** ___/8

36	49	58	62	74	84	89	114

**Reading and English Language Arts
Objective 0002** ___/6

10	11	35	37	81	82

**Reading and English Language Arts
Objective 0003** ___/6

8	9	69	107	113	116

**Reading and English Language Arts
Objective 0004** ___/6

12	13	48	63	108	112

**Reading and English Language Arts
Objective 0005** ___/6

14	15	90	99	104	110

Reading and English Language Arts
Objective 0006 ___/6

10 11 35 37 81 82

Reading and English Language Arts
Objective 0007 ___/1

7

Reading and English Language Arts
Objective 0008 ___/1

72

Social Studies
Objective 0009 ___/7

1 2 44 54 76 88 102

Social Studies
Objective 0010 ___/8

43 3 4 42 55 68 91 103

Social Studies
Objective 0011 ___/3

5 6 95

Social Studies
Objective 0012 ___/2

65 106

Mathematics
Objective 0013 ___/4

79 80 97 111

**Mathematics
Objective 0014**

___/9

19	38	39	64	66	85	86

101	120

**Mathematics
Objective 0015**

___/7

20	21	40	57	73	75	83

**Mathematics
Objective 0016**

___/3

56	77	87

**Mathematics
Objective 0017**

___/2

18	98

**Science
Objective 0018**

___/1

45

**Science
Objective 0019**

___/6

31	33	34	50	61	118

**Science
Objective 0020**

___/5

30	92	105	115	119

Science
Objective 0021   ___/8

32	46	47	70	71	93	109	117

Health, Physical Education and Art Ed.
Objective 0022   ___/3

25	41	67

Health, Physical Education and Art Ed.
Objective 0023   ___/6

26	27	28	29	53	60

Health, Physical Education and Art Ed.
Objective 0024   ___/6

22	23	24	51	52	59

Practice Test 1 Detailed Explanations

1.   **B**

Francisco Pizarro conquered the Incas of Peru, and Hernán Cortés conquered the Aztecs of Mexico. Choice A is incorrect because the Maya had virtually disappeared before the arrival of the Spaniards to America. Choice C is incorrect because these Mesoamerican groups, the Toltec and Olmec, disappeared before the Spanish colonization. Choice D is incorrect because the Tainos were from the Caribbean, an area that was under Spanish control before the intervention of Cortés and Pizarro. Additionally, the word *Quechua* refers to the language spoken by the Incas and other groups in the Andes Mountains. **Objective 0009**

2.   **C**

The Spaniards established St. Augustine, the first permanent European colony in North America, in 1565 near what today is Jacksonville, Florida. Subsequent to this, the English made an attempt to establish a colony off the coast of North Carolina—Roanoke. Choice A is incorrect because Virginia, Massachusetts, and all the American colonies were established in the seventeenth century. Choice B is incorrect because New Mexico was established a few years later, in 1598, to become the first European colony west of the Mississippi. The first mission in Texas was established more than one hundred years later, in 1682. Choice D is incorrect because the Dutch did not begin bringing families to the area of New York and New Jersey until 1624. **Objective 0009**

3.   **D**

The Earth, a sphere, has 365 degrees, and its rotation around its axis takes 24 hours. This rotation creates day and night. The correct choice is 15 degrees, which is calculated by dividing 365 degrees by 24 hours of day/night. Choices A, B, and C are incorrect based on the previous explanation. **Objective 0010**

4.   **B**

With the exception of peak K2, the top 10 mountain peaks are all part of the Himalayas Range. Choice A is incorrect, because, despite the fact that the Andes Range contains several high mountains, none of them ranks within the top 50 in the world. Choice C is incorrect because only three of the top 20 mountains in the world are part of the Karakoram Range. Choice D is incorrect because only one mountain from the Kunlun Range ranks within the first 25. **Objective 0010**

5.   **B**

The U.S. Constitution provides for two senators to represent each of the 50 states, for a total of 100. Territories are not represented in the U.S. Senate. Choices A and C are incorrect based on the previous explanation. Choice D is incorrect because it represents the current number of members of the U.S. House of Representatives. **Objective 0011**

6.   **A**

The number of members of the House of Representatives is adjusted to reflect a proportion of the total U.S. population; thus, every time there is a census, the number can change. Choices B, C, and D are incorrect because population changes do not affect the composition of the Senate, Supreme Court, or the Executive Branch. **Objective 0011**

7.   **C**

The sentence contains a noun (Mary), a transtive verb (gave), an indirect object (me), and a direct object (dollar). The key clue to answering this question correctly is found within the type of verb used in the sentence—a transitive verb. Transitive verbs by definition can take objects. To determine if the sentence contains a direct object or an indirect object, we ask the following two questions: Mary gave what?—the answer is the direct object—a dollar. The second question is, Mary gave it to whom?—the answer is *me*—the indirect object. Choices A and B are incorrect because both contain intransitive verbs. Choice D is incorrect because it does not contain an indirect object. **Objective 0007**

8.   **C**

Idiomatic expressions rely on culture referents and connotative, or implied, meanings. That is why ELLs experience difficulties understanding them. Choice A is incorrect because idioms are regarded not as academic English expressions but as a part of social language. Choice B is incorrect because denotative language refers to the literal meaning of the words, and obviously idioms have implied meaning. Choice D is incorrect because idioms do not necessarily incorporate direct (metaphors) or indirect comparisons (similes). **Objective 0003**

9.   **C**

The words presented in this activity show the importance of word stress and how it can alter the meaning and the syntactic classification of words. Choice A is incorrect because the words mentioned are typical of the type taught as sight words. Choice B is incorrect because written accents are not traditionally used to teach English pronunciation. However, teachers of ELLs often use accent marks to help students identify the primary stress in words. Choice D is incorrect because both sets of words are spelled identically. The activity presented emphasizes the importance of word stress to differentiate word meaning. **Objective 0003**

10. **A**

The use of onset and rime is used to compensate for the phoneme–grapheme inconsistency of English. Through the use of rime, children can learn to recognize and spell multiple words. Choice B is incorrect because the use of onset and rime can contribute to the ability to recognize words, but it does not constitute the main reason for their use. Choice C is incorrect because traditionally, onset and rime is not used to deal with polysyllabic words. Choice D is incorrect because prefixes generally represent morphemes, while the onsets generally do not. Prefixes and suffixes are generally introduced using structural analysis. **Objective 0002**

11. **B**

Teachers generally introduce the letters that can help the most in decoding written language. The first set of letters occurs more frequently in written text than the second set. Choice A is incorrect because there is no evidence to suggest that children might be more inclined to prefer one set of letters over the other. Choice C is incorrect because only the phoneme /m/ is a nasal sound. Choice D is incorrect because there is no evidence to suggest that the sounds of the graphemes x and q can create language interference. **Objective 0002**

12. **A**

By guiding children to notice the title, major headings, and pictorial clues, they can make predictions about the story. Approaching the story content in this way can increase a child's interest in reading because they want to corroborate their predictions with the actual content of what they read. Choices B, C, and D are incorrect because they describe activities typical of the post-reading stage, not the pre-reading stage. **Objective 0004**

13. **B**

Silent reading is designed primarily to improve vocabulary development and reading comprehension. It can also improve reading fluency, but reading fluency is best promoted through reading orally; thus, choice A is not the best answer. Choices C and D are incorrect because the primary goal of SSR is not to guide children to conduct word analysis or to practice decoding skills. These skills obviously happen during the reading process as a by-product of SSR. **Objective 0004**

14. **A**

Since students cannot write effectively in kindergarten, drawing becomes an alternate means to express their understanding of the story. Choices B and C are incorrect because children at this level of literacy development cannot write well. Choice D is also incorrect because children in kindergarten might not have the cognitive maturity to develop a detailed analysis of the story line. They are generally able to present the gist of the story and identify meaningful events. **Objective 0005**

15. **B**

Reciprocal teaching engages the teacher and students in a dialogue designed to guide children in reading comprehension (e.g., summarizing the content, generating questions, clarifying, and predicting). Choice A is incorrect because reciprocal teaching is not a technique to promote reading fluency. Choices C and D are incorrect because the primary goal of reciprocal teaching is not related to cooperative learning per se or the development of oral communication. **Objective 0005**

16. **B**

Students begin using writing for meaningful communication when they want to get information from teachers and peers. Choice A is incorrect because journal writing was not designed as a classroom management activity. Choice C is incorrect because error correction is not generally encouraged in journal writing. Teachers and more advanced students provide input through modeling. Choice D is incorrect because learning personal information about teachers and peers is not the primary goal of journal writing. **Objective 0006**

17. **C**

The connectors are guided to compare and contrast ideas and to identify the preference of the author. Choices A, B, and D are incorrect because the connectors presented do not call for opinions, sequencing, or results. **Objective 0006**

18. **A**

The correct answer is A . The combined percent of respondents who rated the mayor as Excellent (25%) or Very Good (35%) is 60%, which represents 1440 residents. We can find the total number of respondents by dividing 1440 by 60%. First convert the percentage to a decimal (.60). Then divide the known quantity (1,440) by the percentage (0.60). Therefore, $1,440 \div 0.60 = 2,400$. **Objective 0014**

19. **A**

The traditional whole number division algorithm (method) is helpful when dividing decimals longhand. The work can be set up like this:

$$0.05\overline{)6.2}$$

Dividing (while temporarily ignoring the zeros and decimal points) gives

$$
\begin{array}{r}
124 \\
0.05\overline{)6.20} \\
5 \\
\hline
12 \\
10 \\
\hline
20 \\
20 \\
\hline
0
\end{array}
$$

Next, you count the number of digits to the right of the decimal point in the divisor (two). **Two**, then, is the number of places that you shift the "inside" decimal point to the right, and then "up" into the answer:

$$
\begin{array}{r}
124 \\
0.05\overline{)\,6.2}
\end{array}
\qquad \longrightarrow \qquad
\begin{array}{r}
124 \\
0.05\overline{)\,6.20}
\end{array}
$$

Because the answer is a whole number, the decimal point does not have to be shown. **Objective 0014**

20. **A**

The area of any rectangle is equal to the measure of its length times the measure of its width (or, to say it differently, the measure of its base times the measure of its height). A right triangle can be seen as half of a rectangle (sliced diagonally). Choice A represents, in effect, a rectangle's area cut in half (i.e., divided by 2). Based on this explanation, choices B, C, and D are incorrect. **Objective 0015**

21. **B**

First, it is helpful to view the shaded area as the area of the square minus the area of the circle. With that in mind, you simply need to find the area of each simple figure, and then subtract one from the other. You know that the radius of the circle is 6 units in length. That tells you that the diameter of the circle is 12 units. Because the circle is inscribed in the square (meaning that the circle fits inside of the square touching in as many places as possible), you see that the sides of the square are each 12 units in length. Knowing that, you compute that the area of the square is 144 square units (12 × 12). Using the formula for finding the area of a circle (πr^2), and using 3.14 for π, you get approximately 113 square units. (3.14 × 6 × 6). Then, you subtract 113 (the area of the circle) from 144 (the area of the square) for the answer of 31. Based on the explanation given, choices A, C, and D are incorrect. **Objective 0015**

22. **B**

Red, yellow, and blue are the primary colors. Their respective complements are green, purple, and orange. Based on this explanation, choices A, C, and D are incorrect. **Objective 0024**

23. **D**

The flying buttress was a device invented specifically to support the high vaults of Gothic churches. Flying buttresses, pointed arches, and stained-glass windows appear together only on Gothic style buildings, most of which were built between 1150 and 1500. Choice A is incorrect because buildings of the Romanesque period (c. 1050–1150) usually employ wall buttresses and rounded arches, with only a few having pointed arches. Choices B and C are also incorrect because Byzantine and Renaissance buildings are often characterized by domes and rounded arches. **Objective 0024**

24. **A**

Rhythm instruments like the tambourine, triangle, and sticks are commonly used to allow children opportunities to explore musical sounds. Choices B, C, and D are instruments traditionally taught in middle school. **Objective 0024**

25. **B**

Heat exhaustion is not as severe as heat stroke. Getting the child to a shaded area and providing him/her with water should take care of the problem. Choice A is incorrect; heat exhaustion does not require CPR. Choice C is the appropriate action for a heat stroke victim. Choice D is incorrect because pouring ice water on a hot body can do more harm than good. **Objective 0022**

26. **A**

Gross motor-visual skills involve movement of the body's large muscles as visual information is processed. A ball is always used to perfect these skills. In some cases a bat or racquet will also aid in developing these skills. Choices B, C, and D are incorrect because they address motor skills, but fail to include a visual component in the activity. **Objective 0023**

27. **B**

Cardiovascular exercise for a minimum of 20 minutes per session, as part of an exercise program, will have positive physical effects when combined with a proper nutritional diet. Choice C (45 minutes) is an effective time period when performing slower-paced activities like weightlifting. Choice B (20 minutes) is the correct time for an aerobic workout. Choice D (5 minutes) is more appropriate for a warm-up or stretching exercise. **Objective 0023**

28. **D**

Games involving physical activity are the best way to exercise children in kindergarten and first grade. Choice A is incorrect because, traditionally, jogging might be inappropriate for children at this early age. Choices B and C are incorrect because contact sports and sports that require endurance are not developmentally appropriate for kindergarten and first grade students. **Objective 0023**

29. **B**

The sit-and-reach test measures the flexibility of the child. Choices A, C, and D are incorrect because they measure muscular strength and endurance. **Objective 0023**

30. **B**

Density is the amount of mass that is contained per unit of volume of a given substance. A combination of the density and the weight (pull of gravity) of an object determines whether it will sink or float. Choice A is incorrect because mass is a measurement of the amount of matter something contains, and mass by itself does not fully explain why the objects sink or float. Choice C is incorrect because it does not provide a specific scientific explanation of the experiment. Choice D is incorrect because weight by itself does not fully explain the forces acting on the objects. **Objective 0020**

31. **A**

The heat from the sun changes water into water vapor, which rises to the atmosphere until it reaches cool air. Upon contact with cool air, it changes into small droplets of water, forming clouds. Once the clouds are saturated, precipitation occurs. We say that the system redistributes the water because large amounts of the liquid resulting from the process comes from the ocean and other bodies of water. Rain will fall miles away from the source from which it originated. Choice B is not accurate since the function of the system is not necessarily cleaning the environment; however, pollutants might be washed away as a result of rain. Choice C provides a plausible answer; however, it does not address the main question. Choice D is incorrect because it describes the evaporation system but does not address condensation. **Objective 0019**

32. **B**

Organisms develop new features to cope with needs and demands of the environment. For example, predatory animals might develop stronger legs to run faster in order to catch prey. Potential prey, in turn, might develop stronger claws to dig holes for escaping from predators. Choice A is incorrect because "intelligent creation" refers to the creation of the universe by a supreme being—God. Choice C is incorrect because it describes primarily physical changes that organisms go through in the process of maturation. For example, frogs go through a series of metamorphoses before reaching maturity. Choice D is incorrect because there is no direct connection between developing new physical features and reproduction. **Objective 0021**

33. **C**

The movement of rotation around the sun constitutes a year, and the closer the planet is to the Sun, the shorter the year. Based on this, only Mercury and Venus have a year shorter than that of the Earth. **Objective 0019**

34. **A**

Cumulus clouds are formed during sunny summer days. Choices B and C are incorrect because cumulonimbus clouds cover the sky during cloudy and rainy days. Choice D is incorrect because nimbostratus clouds indicate the possibility of snow. **Objective 0019**

35. **B**

The word *thought* is a long word, even though it is monosyllabic. It has three phonemes. The word contains two consonant diagraphs, *th* and *ght*, and a vowel digraph, *ou*, representing one sound each for a total of three sounds. Choices A, C, and D are incorrect based on the previous explanation. **Objective 0002**

36. **D**

Emergent readers will make use of various strategies for understanding print and make meaningful use of texts. They begin to develop the awareness of the story's structures. They will also use illustrations to understand what they are reading and use visual imagery to represent their stories. Although some emergent readers may begin to use self-correction, it is typically not a characteristic of emergent readers D. **Objective 0001**

37. **B**

The analysis of the structure of the words for decoding and comprehension is definitely part of structural analysis. Choice A is incorrect because context goes beyond individual words. Choice C is incorrect because pictorial clues describe any kind of visual information, like pictures and charts. Choice D is incorrect because syntactic clues use whole sentences and determine meaning based on the position of words within sentences. **Objective 0002**

38. **C**

When subtraction involves any negative numbers, a good rule to use is, "Don't subtract the second number. Instead, add its opposite." Using that rule, the original expression, $(-36) - 11$ becomes $(-36) + -11$. To be "in debt" by 36, then to be further "in debt" by 11, puts one "in debt" by 47, shown as -47. **Objective 0014**

39. **D**

The order of operations must be obeyed here. Remembering the saying, "Please Excuse My Dear Aunt Sally," (PEMDAS) allows us to remember the order in which mathematical operations must be carried out, **P**arentheses **E**xponent **M**ultiply **D**ivide **A**dd **S**ubtract. Following this one will multiply 6 by 2 to obtain 12. Then, one will divide 3 by 3 obtaining 1. Finally, one will add the two results together to obtain $12 + 1 = 13$. **Objective 0014**

40. **B**

An easy way to solve this problem is to use basic algebra. Knowing that there are 16 oz. in a pound and that there are 2,000 lbs. in a ton helps ease the difficulty of the problem. We want to find out the number of cans x it will take to obtain a ton. Therefore, we have $\frac{14}{16}x = 2000$. If both sides of the equation are multiplied by 16 and then we divide both sides by 14, we will obtain the approximate number of cans it will take to obtain one ton. $x = \frac{16 \times 2000}{14} = \frac{32000}{14} \approx 2,285.7$. We see that many of the answers are close to this value. When we round this number, we obtain 2,286. **Objective 0015**

41. **B**

The only answer that is not risky behavior for causing illness and disease is (B) keeping the body hydrated by drinking water. All other answers put the body at risk for illness and/or disease. **Objective 0022**

42. **C**

The Earth is divided into 24 zones based on the meridians of longitude, which are determined using the rotation of the Earth and its exposure to sunlight. This rotation creates day and night, and consequently the concept of time. Choice A is incorrect because the International Date Line is only one of 24 meridians of the Earth. Choice B is incorrect because the term revolution describes the movement of the Earth around the sun, which affects the seasons but not necessarily the time zones. Choice D is incorrect because the parallels of latitude do not affect the time zones. **Objective 0010**

43. **B**

Iraq is a Muslim nation with multiple ethnic groups within its borders. The largest groups are the Arabs, consisting of Shiite and Sunni Muslims. The Kurds are the largest minority group. Choice A is incorrect. The multiple groups living in Iraq speak Arabic, Kurdish, Turkish, Assyrian, and other languages. Choice C is incorrect because Iraq is located in the Middle Eastern part of Asia. Choice D is incorrect because Pakistan is a Muslim country from the region, but there is no political association between the two nations. **Objective 0010**

44. **A**

The Mayflower Compact was drawn up and signed by the Pilgrims aboard the *Mayflower*. They pledged to consult one another to make decisions and to act by the will of the majority. It is one of the earliest agreements to establish a political body and to give that political body the power to act for the good of the colony. Choices B, C, and D are incorrect because these were aspects of colonial life but not the purpose of the Mayflower Compact. **Objective 0009**

45. **B**

Using high-interest activities like observing live animals and plants in an aquarium, students can be guided to use scientific inquiry and problem-solving skills. Choices A and C are incorrect because both describe non-scientific objectives. Choice D presents a generic statement that fails to address the main scientific objective. **Objective 0018**

46. **B**

   A healthy aquatic system should have sufficient space and conditions to support life. Aquarium A has a large number of animals for a small 25-gallon aquarium. Over-population can pollute the environment and affect the balance of the ecosystem. The size of the aquarium (A), the number of plants (C), and the number of fish (D) contribute to the success of the habitat, but individually, they cannot justify the students' decision. **Objective 0021**

47. **D**

   Fish of the same kind have a better chance of reproducing themselves. Aquarium B contains fish of the same kind, while aquarium A has different varieties. Choices A, B, and C present elements that can affect the overall habitat, but they do not provide key information about the chances of successful breeding. **Objective 0021**

48. **C**

   Pointing to the words as they are read is designed to establish the connection between speech and print. However, after the skill has been mastered, it is discontinued so students can engage in fluent reading. Choices A and B are incorrect because they offer non-substantial reasons for the strategy change. Choice D is incorrect because the practice of pointing to the words as they are being read is not archaic; it is indeed an effective practice for beginning readers. **Objective 0004**

49. **D**

   Students who are becoming literate are not yet writing conventionally. However, Choices A, B, and C all represent features and characteristics of emergent writers. As young writers grasp the concept of the alphabetic principle and are able to better map speech onto print in conventional ways, their spelling will become closer approximations to conventional spelling. **Objective 0001**

50. **B**

   The movement of the plates causes intense seismological activity near the faults, resulting in earthquakes. Choices A and C have some merit because thermal activity can have some implications, but these choices do not provide specific answers to the question. Choice D is totally incorrect; there is no known connection between the rotation of the Earth and earthquakes. **Objective 0019**

51.　**C**

　　Two-year-old children are primarily concerned with sensory experiences in their earliest art activities. Choice A is incorrect because children do not begin to self-express in their artwork until around age five years. Choice B is incorrect because children do not begin to use personal symbols in their artwork until around age four years. Choice D is incorrect because children do not begin to repeat themes or be concerned with photographic realism until the middle years of elementary school. **Objective 0024**

52.　**B**

　　The rhythm is typically called the melodic rhythm or word rhythm found in the song. The beginning of *Happy Birthday* ("Happy birthday to you") has the same word rhythm as "Oh, say can you see." Choice A is incorrect because the word rhythm "My country 'tis of thee" is not the same as "Happy Birthday to you." Choice C is incorrect because the word rhythm "Take me out to the ball game" is not the same as "Happy Birthday to you." Choice D is also incorrect because "Oh beautiful for spacious skies" is not the same as "Happy Birthday to you." **Objective 0024**

53.　**C**

　　The ADA requires school districts to place special education children in the least restrictive educational environment; thus, an orthopedic handicapped student would be placed in mainstream classrooms. Students are required to receive physical education using appropriate accommodations to allow their successful participation. Choice A is incorrect because only in extreme cases are special education children excluded from participating in the school curriculum. Choice B is partially correct, but it fails to mention the need to make accommodations for successful participation in physical education activities. Choice D is incorrect because it adopts an extreme position not applicable to limited mobility. **Objective 0023**

54.　**C**

　　The Virginia House of Burgesses was the first legislature established in the English colonies. It was established in 1619 and became the first form of government in the colony. Choice A is incorrect because the U.S. government did not exist during this time (1619). Choice B is incorrect because England regulated trading with the colonies. Choice D is incorrect because, there was no official entity in the colony to regulate the establishment of religions. **Objective 0009**

55. **B**

A globe is a scale model of the Earth shaped like a sphere. Because a globe is the same shape as the Earth, it shows sizes and shapes more accurately than a Mercator projection map (a flat representation of the Earth). Choice A is incorrect because a compass rose is a design used to show orientation and not a representation of the Earth. Choice C is incorrect because a map scale is used to show the distance between two places in the world. Choice D is incorrect because thematic maps are not used to show the size and shape of the Earth. **Objective 0010**

56. **A**

There are equal numbers of blue and red marbles in each bag. For a single bag on a single draw, the probability of pulling a red or a blue marble is equal to $\frac{4}{8}$, or $\frac{1}{2}$. Selecting a marble from one bag does not affect the probability of selecting a specific marble from the other bag; therefore, these events are said to be independent. When dealing with the probability of independent events, one may multiply the probabilities together to obtain the overall probability. In this case, we know the probability of selecting a blue marble is $\frac{1}{2}$ for the first bag and it is also $\frac{1}{2}$ for the second bag. Therefore, the overall probability of the independent events is $\frac{1}{4}$. **Objective 0016**

57. **B**

If you can fold a two-dimensional figure so that one side exactly matches or folds onto the other side, the fold line is a line of symmetry. The figure in the problem is a non-square rectangle meaning two of the sides are longer than the other two. Because of this, the shape only has two lines of symmetry. Folding the object from one corner to its opposite corner would not result in a fold where the sides were on top of each other. **Objective 0015**

58. **C**

Reading a story and asking a child to retell it promotes interest in writing. When the teacher writes down the dictated story, the child can see the connection of oral and written work. Choices A and B are incorrect because the children at the emerging stage don't have sufficient command of written language to correct their own writing or write a composition based on prompts. Choice D is incorrect because reading for 30 minutes a day without any kind of explicit or implicit writing support might not be effective for children at the emerging stage for writing. **Objective 0001**

59. **A**

    The Orff approach uses both unpitched rhythm instruments (e.g., wood blocks, triangles, etc.) and melodic or barred instruments (e.g., xylophones, metallophones, and glockenspiels). The Kodály Method (B) is incorrect because the primary goal is to teach music literacy and singing is the vehicle to achieve this goal. Mariachi (C) is a group of musicians that play violins, trumpets, a Spanish guitar, and a guitarrón. Tejano music (D) features the accordion, and the Tejano orchestra has been influenced by Mexican, Cuban, German, and Czech brass bands. **Objective 0024**

60. **D**

    Fun games involving physical activity are the best way to exercise children in kindergarten. Choice A is incorrect because, traditionally, jogging for fitness might be inappropriate for children at this early age. Choices B and C are incorrect because contact sports and activities that require skill and/or endurance are not developmentally appropriate for kindergarten or first-grade students. **Objective 0023**

61. **D**

    The teacher can discuss the theory of continental drift, which gave rise to the current theory of plate tectonics. According to this theory, the crust of the Earth is broken down into several floating tectonic plates, which move and change locations. Choice A is incorrect because it describes how organisms evolve throughout history. It also alludes to the work of Charles Darwin. Choice B is incorrect because it refers to the religious belief that the universe was created by a supreme being. Choice C describes the process by which organisms living on one continent manage to migrate to other continents or to other regions within a continent. **Objective 0019**

62. **D**

    Onsets represent the first phoneme of a syllable or a monosyllabic word like the words presented in Choice D. Rimes follow the onset and are linked to the concept of word families. The rime *ank* can be used to create multiple words, like *blank, tank, rank,* and *flank.* Choices A and C are generally used to represent verb tenses and cannot be considered the typical rime or word family. Choice B is incorrect because the two words do not represent onset and rimes. Instead, the example of *very–berry* represents a minimal pair—two words that differ in only one phoneme. **Objective 0001**

63. **D**

Semantic, structural, and visual cuing systems are all used by newly fluent readers to aid in their comprehension of texts. They also make use of graphophonemic cuing systems. These are used to self-monitor what they are reading as well as to begin to correct their errors without much support. **Objective 0004**

64. **B**

One of the basic properties of addition is that it can be carried out in any order. Therefore, since addition is the only operation that is performed in this exercise, one knows the correct answer is the associate property of addition. **Objective 0014**

65. **C**

Reducing the production of oil while keeping the same demand for the product creates an imbalance between supply and demand. This imbalance results in a price increase. Choice A is incorrect. Choice B is incorrect because the statement does not explain the economic principle required in the question. Generally speaking, war increases the demand and prices of many things, not only the price of fossil fuels. Choice B just presents a true statement—the American economy depends on foreign oil. Choice D presents an opinion that fails to address the true question. **Objective 0012**

66. **B**

Using the acronym PEMDAS as a mnemonic device to remember the order of operations, it allows us to see that the first operation required in the problems is multiplication. That is, the acronym calls for the following order: parentheses, exponents, multiplication, division, addition, and subtraction. However, since the problem does not contain parentheses or exponents, the first operation required in the problem is multiplication. **Objective 0014**

67. **B**

The only false statement about metabolism is choice B, fasting speeds up your metabolism. Fasting does not speed up metabolism; it shuts metabolism down in order to conserve energy due to little or no calories getting into the body. Choice A is true because your basal metabolism (basal metabolic rate) is constantly burning calories and converting energy. Choice C is true because physical activity always stimulates metabolic function. Choice D is true in that metabolism slowly adjusts to the demands placed on the body over long periods of time. **Objective 0022**

68. **A**

Maps use symbolic representation, and children at that age rely mostly on concrete experiences for learning. The abstraction typical of maps' legends and other symbolic representations might not be developmentally appropriate for this age group. Choice B is a plausible statement but not the best answer. Children initially will be inclined to use the globe as toys and pay attention to colors, but eventually they will understand its function through classroom instruction. Choice C is incorrect because it presents an opinion not supported in the scenario. Choice D is probably a true statement: Children will have problems conceptualizing how the Earth can be represented in a small 12-inch globe, but this choice is not the best answer because it addresses only one component of the question—globe representation. **Objective 0010**

69. **B**

Homonyms are words that have the same spelling and pronunciation, but have different meanings. The only pair of words that is a true homonym is Choice B. In this case, the word *club* can refer to a night club or a wooden stick. Choices A and C are incorrect because they represent two different words. Choice D represents an example of homophones, words that are pronounced in the same way, have different meanings, and are spelled differently. **Objective 0003**

70. **B**

Corals are invertebrates that fall under the animal kingdom. These small organisms can reproduce themselves sexually or asexually. Choice A is incorrect because unlike corals, the kingdom Monera is made up of unicellular organisms with very rudimentary cellular organization. Choices C and D are incorrect because corals are described in the question as invertebrates, a classification used exclusively for members of the animal kingdom. **Objective 0021**

71. **C**

Corals live in a symbiotic relationship with algae because both exchange nutrients or other kinds of services in order for both to survive. Choice A is incorrect because corals are not parasites living off algae. Instead, parasites and corals provide support services to each other for their mutual survival. Choices B and D might be true statements, but they do not define the term *symbiosis*. **Objective 0021**

72. **C**

Newspapers and magazines have been considered print media. Choice B is incorrect because images are often used to complement texts being displayed in such mediums. Choice A is incorrect because there is no such a thing as "electric" media; the correct term is "electronic" media. **Objective 0008**

73. **B**

Angle *xyz* is an inscribed angle (its vertex is on the circle). Angle *xCz* is a central angle (its vertex is at the circle's center). When two such angles intercept (or "cut off") the same arc of the circle, a specific size relationship exists between the two angles. The measure of the central angle will always be double the measure of the inscribed angle. In this case, that means that the measure of angle *xCz* must be 80°. Thus, minor arc *xz* also measures 80°. Every circle (considered as an arc) measures 360°. This means major arc *xyz* measures 280° (360 – 80). The explanation shows that Choices A, C and D are incorrect. **Objective 0015**

74. **A**

In the Language Experience Approach (LEA), the teacher is dictating the ideas and thoughts of the students. As the students share ideas, the teacher writes them down, thus connecting speech to print and also modeling how oral language is related to writing. Choice B is incorrect because in this approach, it is the teacher who "has the pen" and does the modeled writing as students contribute ideas. Choice C is incorrect because the focus is not on oral reading primarily; the emphasis is on both reading and writing for beginning readers with LEA. Choice D is incorrect because it focuses on the teacher's own ideas, whereas LEA focuses on the teacher dictating the ideas of the student or students. **Objective 0001**

75. **A**

Since Mrs. Cameron does not want any seams in her carpet, the carpet must be 20 ft long (at least) to cover the entire space. Since the room is only 14 ft wide and the carpet is 16 ft wide, there will be 2 ft of wasted carpet for the entire length of the room (20 ft). Therefore, the amount of carpet that is wasted is $20 \times 2 = 40$ ft^2 of carpet. **Objective 0015**

76. **C**

The Apache and the Comanche domesticated the horse and became skillful hunters and warriors. These skills allowed them to fight the whites for many years for control of the Central and Great Plains of Texas. Choice A is incorrect because the tribes from the plains were nomads and did not develop an advanced civilization. Choice B is incorrect because both the Comanche and the Apache were nomads and did not leave permanent constructions. Choice D is incorrect because the tribes from the area had to hunt for survival and they had to move continuously to find adequate food supplies. **Objective 0009**

77. **C**

Since tossing two separate coins does not effect the outcome of the other coin, we know that the probability of getting a head on either coin is 1/2. The probability of the outcome is then 2/4 or 0.5. **Objective 0016**

78. **C**

Brainstorming for ideas and developing an outline of the writing project are paramount for process writing. Choices A, B, and D are incorrect because they do not contain brainstorming as the initial component of the process. **Objective 0006**

79. **A**

In a normal deck of cards there are 52 total cards. Of the 52 cards, there are four suits and 13 cards per suit. Therefore, there are four queens in the deck. Additionally, of the four suits, two are black and two are red. So, there are two black fours giving a grand total of six cards of 52 that meet the criteria. **Objective 0013**

80. **B**

There is a total of 40 individuals in the group. Of the 40 people in the group, 5 are redheads. This gives a ratio of 5/40, which may be simplified to 1/8. **Objective 0013**

81. **D**

A visual analysis of columns 4, 5, and 6 shows that the phoneme /sh/ can be represented by at least four different graphemes—*ch, s, ss,* and *t*—in words like *chef, sure, mission,* and *caution*. The grapheme *ch* is also inconsistent. Column 3 shows that the grapheme *ch* represents the sound /k/. This inconsistency affects the ability of ELLs to separate the two phonemes. Choices A, B, and C are incorrect because the scenario does not provide evidence to suggest that ELLs cannot establish a difference or pronounce the two phonemes, or that they might not be interested in learning the difference between the two. **Objective 0002**

82. **B**

The chart provides examples of words that follow grapheme-phoneme correspondence. It also provides examples of words that use different graphemes to represent the sounds. This chart provides students with tangible information to help them deal with graphophonemic inconsistencies. Choice A is incorrect because this particular chart places more emphasis on graphophonemic inconsistencies than on consistencies. Choice C is incorrect because the chart presents words in isolation; thus, it cannot present information about the intonation pattern used in sentences or larger units. Choice D is a plausible answer, but it does not capture the true intent of the activity. The chart is designed to deal with specific, inconsistent sounds only. **Objective 0002**

83. **A**

   The formula for the volume of a cylinder is $V = \pi r^2 h$. Knowing the radius is 6 m and the height is 8 m gives an approximate value of 904 m^3 for the volume of the cylinder ($V \approx 3.14 \times 6^2 \times 8 = 3.14 \times 36 \times 8 \approx 904$). **Objective 0015**

84. **A**

   Alliteration is a technique to emphasize the connection between the consonant and the sound that it represents. In this particular case, the tongue twister is used to emphasize the sound of the /r/. Choice B is incorrect because the technique goes beyond the use of a tongue twister. Tongue twisters are examples of alliteration, and they emphasize pronunciation and fluency. Choice C is incorrect because the utterance does not represent an example of traditional nursery rhymes. Nursery rhymes are short poems, stories, or songs written to entertain children. **Objective 0001**

85. **C**

   An integer number is a whole number that is either positive or negative. Remembering that a negative times a negative gives a positive means that any of the answers could be possible and we cannot rule any out by process of elimination. Knowing that 8 times 8 gives 64 means both Choices A and B are true. Similarly, –9 times –9 results in 81 (D) meaning 81 is true. However, 6 times 6 gives 36, not 32. This means that Choice C is not a true statement and is the solution to the problem. **Objective 0014**

86. **C**

   In this problem it is necessary to perform the order of operations as well as look at equivalent representations of numbers. Since there are no exponents in any of the solutions, it may be beneficial to carry this out within the problem before proceeding further. Doing so results in $17(64 + 64) - 64$. This may also be written as $17 \times 64 \times 2 - 64$. Since 64 appears in the first multiplication sequence as well as being a subtrahend, it may be factored to produce $64(17 \times 2 - 1) = 64(34 - 1) = 64 \times 33$. **Objective 0014**

87. **D**

   Knowing that with a pair of dice there are 36 possible outcomes allows us to view all of the possible outcomes. Of the possible outcomes, half are odd and half are even. **Objective 0016**

88. **B**

   The convergence of the Tigris and the Euphrates created a fertile region where some of the greatest civilizations of the world emerged. This part of the world has been called the Fertile Crescent, and it is one of the areas called the cradle of civilization. Choice A is incorrect because the Nile gave birth to the Egyptian civilization, and the Amazon River is located in South America, far away from Mesopotamia. Choice C is incorrect because the Indus River is located in modern-day India. Choice D is incorrect because the Volga and Danube rivers are located in Europe. **Objective 0009**

89. **B**

   All language skills are interrelated, including reading and writing. Given appropriate instruction, the skills of reading and writing can be introduced and acquired concurrently. Current research does not support the idea that children learn language skills in a sequential manner (A). Based on the explanation given, Choices C and D are incorrect. **Objective 0001**

90. **D**

   Charts, tables, and graphs can be used to present, summarize, and/or complement the message being conveyed. These are not designed to provide detailed explanations (C) of topics covered in class. Regardless of their use, students must be aware that their use should never be intended to entertain (B) or contradict (D) any of their information. **Objective 0005**

91. **D**

   The country of Iraq is located in the region known as Mesopotamia. Choice A is incorrect because the country of Iran is located east of the Tigris River. Choice B is incorrect because Pakistan is located further southeast of these rivers. Choice C is also incorrect because the State of Kuwait is located southwest of the area and south of Iraq. **Objective 0010**

92. **B**

Conduction is a form of heat transfer. The metal of the spoon serves as a conductor of the heat emanating from the open flame. Choice A is too generic because radiation describes different kinds of energy produced naturally by the sun and artificially by microwaves and cellular phones. Choice C is incorrect because it does not describe the type of transfer of energy presented in the scenario. However, convection is also a form of heat transfer carried through movement of matter. For example, the heating of water in a pan creates movement of the liquid from the bottom to the top, forcing cold water down to the bottom of the pan, where it is heated. Kinetics (D) is a term used to describe movement, not energy transfer. **Objective 0020**

93. **D**

Both animals, the crocodile and the bird, benefit from this relationship. The bird gets food and at the same time cleans the teeth of the crocodile. Choice A is incorrect because the term *commensalism* describes a relationship in which only one organism benefit, from the interaction, while the second organism is not affected by the interaction. Choice B is incorrect because in a parasitism relationship, only one organism benefits from the interaction. The term predator-prey (C) relationship does not describe the interaction between the bird and the crocodile. **Objective 0021**

94. **B**

The teaching of the writing trait of "voice" can be taught through sharing examples, such as through reading aloud stories by authors who portray and exemplify strong voice in their unique style of writing. Teachers can ask their students what characteristics best exemplify this author's voice across multiple texts. Choice A focuses less on voice and more on the ways in which the writing is structured. Choices C and D focus more on syntax, grammar, and punctuation and less on voice, although they are related features to how authors construct voice. **Objective 0006**

95. **C**

The U.S. Constitution set up a system so that each branch has the power to control or regulate the power of the other two. Choice A is incorrect because judicial review addresses only the power of the judicial branch. Judicial review is the power to review legislation enacted by Congress and signed by the president. If the legislation is unconstitutional, it can be invalidated. Choice B is incorrect because it addresses the power of the president to veto or refuse to sign legislation approved by Congress. Choice D is incorrect because *habeas corpus* is one of the civil rights that guarantees people the right to a quick trial by jury. **Objective 0011**

96. **B**

The use of interactive journals allows children opportunities to communicate in meaningful and real-life situations. Choices A and D are incorrect because listening and speaking abilities are not emphasized in interactive journals. Choice C is incorrect because corrective feedback is not encouraged in communication activities. Teachers can provide indirect corrective feedback through modeling. **Objective 0006**

97. **D**

This problem provides unnecessary information to solve the problem. The fact that Stacy discovers 10 extra nickels in her pocket is inconsequential to the solution of the problem. Since a nickel is $0.05 and she had $9.55 in nickels in her purse, divide $9.55 by $0.05 to obtain the number of nickels she had in her purse. **Objective 0013**

98. **B**

According to the data displayed in the line graph, immigration from both Northwestern and Southeastern Europe were virtually equal during the decade of 1891–1900. First find the tic point on the y-axis that represents 2.8 million immigrants and follow the x-axis to the intersecting point. The fact that the question infers that the numbers were equal should confirm for you that you have found the correct intersecting point at the decade beginning in 1891, the points where the dotted line and the solid line meet. **Objective 0015**

99. **A**

Venn diagrams can be used for multiple purposes in education, but in language arts it is commonly used to compare similarities, differences, and common elements between two stories. Traditionally, Venn diagrams are not used to identify the parts of the story (B), nor to identify the main idea of a story (D). Semantic mappings (C), not Venn diagrams, are commonly used to identify key attributes of a given concept. **Objective 0005**

100. **A**

Children go through predictable stages of spelling development. During the initial stages, children invent words and use phonics skills as a foundation for spelling, which often results in nonstandard spelling. Choices B and C are incorrect because spelling might not be the most important element in writing, but it is definitely important for effective writing. Choice D is incorrect because it does not address the question. It just indicates that spelling requires phonics and structural rules, but it does not say why a rubric should not place heavy emphasis on spelling. **Objective 0006**

101. **D**

A prime number is a number whose only factors are 1 and itself. Even numbers greater than 2 can always be factored by 2, eliminating Choice B. Choice A can be factored as 3 times 3 and Choice C can be factored as 7 times 7. Therefore, Choice D must be the right answer as it only has factors of 1 and 67. **Objective 0014**

102. **B**

The Maya and the Aztecs occupied the area of Central America and Southern Mexico called Mesoamerica. Both groups were accomplished builders, astronomers, and mathematicians. Choice A is incorrect because the Inca civilization was not a Mesoamerican group. They developed an advanced civilization in South America, in present-day Peru and Ecuador. Choice C is incorrect because only the Toltecs were from Mesoamerica; the Pueblo Indians were from present-day New Mexico in North America. Choice D is incorrect because only the Olmecs were a Mesoamerican group. The Iroquois civilizations developed in North America. **Objective 0009**

103. **A**

A compass rose is a design printed on a chart or map for reference. It shows the orientation of a map on Earth and shows the four cardinal directions (north, south, east, and west). A compass rose may also show in-between directions such as northeast or northwest. Choice B is incorrect because a map scale shows the distance between two places in the world. Choice C is incorrect because features such as elevations and divisions are represented by different colors. Choice D is incorrect because the ratio of the distance between two points on the earth and the distance between the two corresponding points on the map is represented by a scale and not by a compass rose. **Objective 0010**

104. **C**

Story grammar focuses on the key elements in a story. By being able to recollect these key features common to many narrative stories, students can develop their understanding of commonalities across texts as well as their understanding of the specific story they are reading. Choice A is incorrect because it focuses mainly on meanings at the sentence or word level rather than across the entire text. Choice B is incorrect because it is a specific cognitive strategy the learner uses while reading any text. Shared reading (D) is a way to read a text together and is not specific to analyzing features of a text. **Objective 0005**

105. **B**

A mixture is a physical combination of two or more substances that retain their own chemical properties; i.e., the mixture can be separated into the original substances—acetic acid and water. Choice A is incorrect because in a compound the substances are chemically combined, and in the case of vinegar the substances are only mixed physically. Choices C and D are incorrect because they lack the specificity required of the answer. **Objective 0020**

106. **D**

The main purpose of the Federal Reserve System (FRS) is to keep the banking industry strong enough to ensure a supply of currency. When the banking industry is strong and there is an adequate supply of currency, fiscal stability and economic growth are more likely to occur. However, the direct role of the FRS is not to provide stimulus money to balance the economy (A), promote economic growth (B), nor create inflation and deflation (C) in the country. Policies adopted by the FRS can lead to a healthy economy—or a weak economy resulting in inflation or deflation. **Objective 0012**

107. **A**

The best way to teach vocabulary to ELLs is to present the word together with a visual or concrete representation—a word concept. The introduction of word concepts can avoid any possible cultural conflict with similar concepts in the students' cultures. Choice B is incorrect because translation can teach the word but fail to teach the concept that the word represents. Choice C is incorrect because it would be very difficult to teach every single word in a contrasting fashion. Plus, most ESL classes contain speakers of various languages, which makes this activity impractical. Choice D is incorrect because with ELLs, we cannot deemphasize the role of vocabulary development. Using context alone to obtain meaning will not work for children new to the English language. **Objective 0003**

108. **A**

When children don't have to struggle to decode words, reading fluency is facilitated. Choice B is incorrect because, by definition, no decoding is necessary when the reader recognizes the word instantly. Choice C is incorrect because comprehension goes beyond the instant recognition of words. Readers have to analyze the schema of the writing and evaluate other elements to achieve reading comprehension. Instant recognition of words can improve spelling skills; however, it does not necessarily improve the writing process (D). **Objective 0004**

109. **C**

An ecosystem needs to have a balance among organisms to ensure the ability of the system to support life. Choices A, B, and D are incorrect because they merely represent examples of how the system maintains a balance. **Objective 0021**

110. **A**

Comparing and contrasting variations of a fairly tale, like *Cinderella*, can foster higher-order thinking skills and critical reading. Students will have to analyze the new story to determine how it related to the traditional version, and how the theme is treated. Choices B, C, and D are not focusing specifically on such higher-level reading as it relates to comparing and contrasting across multiple texts. **Objective 0005**

111. **A**

This problem is easily solved by using some basic algebraic reasoning. Since we are interested in determining the number of oranges that are in the basket, we will set this as a variable called o. The number of apples, a, and the number of oranges, o, sum to a total of 62. We also know that there are 16 more apples than oranges ($a = o + 16$). This gives $o + (o + 16) = 2o + 16 = 62$. Solving for o yields 23 oranges in the basket. **Objective 0013**

112. **A**

Instructional reading levels are texts that a student can read with at least 90-94% accuracy. Students should be matched with text that has a readability level that is best suited for their instructional level for supported instruction such as in guided reading. Choice B is incorrect because teachers should use grouping for instruction in a more flexible fashion. Choice C is incorrect because the student may have differing levels of ability in other subject areas. Choice D is incorrect because it does not provide an example of more individualized reading instruction. Additionally, whole-class reading does not take into account each student's reading level. **Objective 0004**

113. **B**

Antonyms are words that indicate "opposites." The only pair that does so is Choice B, small—large. The set of words in Choice A, *small* and the comparative, *smaller*, represent two different words. The words in Choice C, bear—bare, represent an example of homophones—words with the same pronunciation but with different spelling or meaning. (D) represents an example of synonyms, words with equivalent meaning. **Objective 0003**

114. **A**

   The child is having problems with word stress and syllabication, and both terms are part of phonological awareness. Choice B is incorrect because the child is not having problems with phonemic awareness. He has mastered the ability to separate phonemes and blend them back to recreate the word. Choices C and D are incorrect because neither of them individually can explain the needs of the child. The reality is that the child needs support in both components; thus, Choices C or D individually cannot be the correct answer. **Objective 0001**

115. **C**

   Matter can change from liquid to solid to gas in a cyclical fashion. Choice A is incorrect because all three represent examples of solid matter. Choice B is incorrect because it presents only examples of the states and fails to address the stages represented. Choice D is incorrect because it presents just examples of solid and liquid matter. **Objective 0020**

116. **D**

   Readers' theater is a student-centered activity. They read the story, summarize it, work in groups, develop the characters and story line, and implement the activity. While watching a video version of the story (D) can help students get into the characters of the story, this activity is not required to implement readers' theater. Thus, options Choices A, B, and C are typically used as part of the preparation to implement reader's theater. **Objective 0003**

117. **A**

   The kingdom Monera is composed of unicellular organisms and primitive cells called prokaryotes. (B), (C), and (D) are incorrect because all three have more sophisticated cellular systems called eukaryotes. **Objective 0021**

118. **A**

   The main function of the atmosphere is to serve as a buffer between space and the Earth's crust. This buffer provides the ideal conditions to protect and preserve life on Earth. Choices B and D present two functions that can be linked to the atmosphere, recycling water and gases; however, they fail to highlight the real function of the atmosphere. Choice C is completely incorrect; the atmosphere is above the crust, not beneath it. **Objective 0019**

119. **B**

   All the items listed are classified as simple machines. Based on this answer, Choice A is incorrect. Choices C and D describe in general fashion the types of items brought to class, not the purpose of bringing them to class—to demonstrate the concept of simple machine. **Objective 0020**

120. **C**

   When rounded to the hundreds place, the numbers given in the problem become 7,800; 6,000; 6,000; and 800. These numbers added together equal 20,600. **Objective 0014**

Sample Answer for Constructed Response 1 (Math):

   The procedural error made here is the incorrect application of the order of operations. The order of operations is Parentheses, Exponents, then Multiplication and Division before Addition and Subtraction. In Step 1, the order of operations was followed by performing the addition in the parentheses first. In Step 2, an error is made when 4 and ¾ are added. Multiplication should have been performed before addition. The errors continued in Step 3 when subtraction was performed prior to multiplication. In Step 4, an error is made when stacked $4\frac{3}{4}$ is incorrectlly written as $\frac{48}{4}$. Using the correct order of operations, the problem should be solved as follows:

$$\text{Problem:} \quad 4 + \left(\frac{1}{4} + \frac{1}{2}\right) \times 10 - 4 = n$$

$$\text{Step 1:} \quad 4 + \frac{3}{4} \times 10 - 4 = n$$

$$\text{Step 2:} \quad 4 + 7\frac{1}{2} - 4 = n$$

$$\text{Step 3:} \quad 11\frac{1}{2} - 4 = n$$

$$\text{Step 4:} \quad 7\frac{1}{2} = n$$

Sample Answer for Constructed Response 2 (Social Studies)

   Native Americans and early European explorers interacted with each other and both groups had a profound effect on each other. Native Americans are often called "Indians," a name given by Christopher Columbus, because he thought he had sailed to the Orient rather than discovered the New World. This name has affected the way we think about the first Americans. Rather than viewing them as natives of this land, we have called them "Indians" and treated them as if they were the strangers.

According to Davis (1998), there were several stages of interactions between these native peoples and the Europeans. The first stage involved an exchange of plant and animal life between old and new worlds. Geographic isolation had come to an end. The Native Americans introduced crops to the Europeans, such as potatoes, beans, squash, and maize. These crops had a great nutritional impact on the Europeans. The Europeans introduced wheat, rice, bananas, sugar, and white grapes and these were soon grown across the new country. Domesticated animals were brought by coloniz-ers and these animals had an impact upon the tribal lifestyles. The grazing animals, however, were responsible for destroying large acres of cropland. The animals were also utilized for transport and clothing.

One cannot underestimate the impact of these early Europeans on the new world, both before and after the arrival of the English and French. "The Columbian Exchange" was one of the devastating effects of the relationship between the Native Americans and the Europeans. The native people had little immunity to European dis-ease. Diseases, such as measles, influenza, diphtheria, tuberculosis, smallpox, and the common cold swept throughout the New World in epidemic proportions.

The second stage of relations between the Europeans and the native peoples involved trade and cultural interchange. The settlers and the Native Americans lived side by side. The first colonists relied on the help of local tribes for survival. The Indian Squanto showed the Puritans in New England how to fertilize the land and plant corn. This is celebrated today with Thanksgiving. In Virginia, the Powhatan Confederacy helped the colony to succeed. Pocahontas was an important mediator between the Indians and the English. Trade during this time included many goods. European goods included tools, meads, clothes, cloth, blankets, guns, and alcohol. These were exchanged for Native expertise, land and hunting skills. Missionaries brought Christianity to Indians.

The trade and cultural interchange was devastating to the natives. There was a disruption of the natural ecological balance as more game was hunted. Also, the tra-ditional ways of living were devastated.

The last phase of relations of European and Indian contact involved friction and warfare. The colonies wanted to expand and the Native Americans slowly retreated as the white settlements extended westward. Indian lands were removed as the settlers wanted more and more of them. One of the most shameful events in the history of the United States was the "Trail of Tears." Native Americans from the east were moved to reservations in Oklahoma, with the removal beginning in 1838.

The long-term affects involved the destruction of the Native American way of life and removal from their homelands. Native Americans were placed on reservations where they were required to live.

The early European explorers encountered a land inhabited by natives with their own culture and way of life. The interactions of the two groups resulted in profound and devastating effects on the Native Americans. They lost their land, their cultural identity, and, for many, their lives as they were moved to reservations and forced to live there. The United States is a different place today, inhabited by descendents of Europeans, many of whom have little knowledge of these early natives.

Sample Answer for Constructed Response 3 (Science):

The scientific phenomenon relevant to this situation is gravity. Gravity is the force that causes two objects in the universe to be drawn to one another.

Gravity holds us down on the earth's surface. Weight, the measurement of the force on an object, is caused by gravity trying to pull the object down. The force of gravity is greater when the objects are larger. The moon is much smaller than the earth. As a result, the force of gravity on the moon is only about one sixth as strong as gravity on earth. Since the force of gravity on the moon is not as strong, you weigh less.

Sample Answer for Constructed Response 4 (Language Arts):

Phonemic awareness is a subcategory of phonological awareness. It is the ability to notice, think about, and work with the individual sounds in spoken language. Before children can formally learn to read printed language they must first become aware of how the sounds in words work—that words are made up of speech sounds, or phonemes. (National Institute for Literacy, 2001)

An example of how beginning readers show they are phonemically aware is by combining or blending the separate sounds of a word to say the word ("/d/ /o/ /g/ - *dog*."). Phonemic awareness tasks used for assessment and instructional purposes include: rhyming, phoneme identification, phoneme blending, phoneme substitution, phoneme addition, phoneme deletion, and phoneme segmentation. Phonemic awareness is not phonics. Phonemic awareness is an auditory skill that enables students to identify and orally manipulate the sounds of language.

The National Reading Panel (April 2000), reported research that showed that teaching children to manipulate phonemes in words was highly effective and emphasized the necessity for phonemic awareness training as a part of the comprehensive reading program for early learners.

Children develop phonemic awareness by singing songs, chanting rhymes, and listening to parents and teachers read books read aloud. Teachers also teach lessons to help students understand that their speech is composed of sounds. Big books are valuable tools for interactive reading, which assists children in developing phonemic awareness.

Practice Test 2

GACE Early Childhood Education

This test is also on CD-ROM in our special interactive TestWare® for the GACE Early Childhood Education Test. It is highly recommended that you first take this exam on computer. You will then have the additional study features and benefits of enforced timed conditions and instantaneous, accurate scoring. See page 7 for instructions on how to get the most out of our GACE Early Childhood Education book and software.

ANSWER SHEET
PRACTICE TEST 2

1 ___	25 ___	45 ___	73 ___	97 ___
2 ___	26 ___	50 ___	74 ___	98 ___
3 ___	27 ___	51 ___	75 ___	99 ___
4 ___	28 ___	52 ___	76 ___	100 ___
5 ___	29 ___	53 ___	77 ___	101 ___
6 ___	30 ___	54 ___	78 ___	102 ___
7 ___	31 ___	55 ___	79 ___	103 ___
8 ___	32 ___	56 ___	80 ___	104 ___
9 ___	33 ___	57 ___	81 ___	105 ___
10 ___	34 ___	58 ___	82 ___	106 ___
11 ___	35 ___	59 ___	83 ___	107 ___
12 ___	36 ___	60 ___	84 ___	108 ___
13 ___	37 ___	61 ___	85 ___	109 ___
14 ___	38 ___	62 ___	86 ___	100 ___
15 ___	39 ___	63 ___	87 ___	111 ___
16 ___	40 ___	64 ___	88 ___	112 ___
17 ___	41 ___	65 ___	89 ___	113 ___
18 ___	42 ___	66 ___	90 ___	114 ___
19 ___	43 ___	67 ___	91 ___	115 ___
20 ___	44 ___	68 ___	92 ___	116 ___
21 ___	45 ___	69 ___	93 ___	117 ___
22 ___	46 ___	70 ___	94 ___	118 ___
23 ___	47 ___	71 ___	95 ___	119 ___
24 ___	48 ___	72 ___	96 ___	120 ___

PRACTICE TEST 2

1. During the first reading of the shared book experience, the teacher reads the whole story in an enthusiastic and dramatic manner. The main purpose of this activity is

    A. to make the content understood by children so they can enjoy it and corroborate their earlier predictions about it.

    B. to introduce decoding skills and the main idea.

    C. to introduce unknown vocabulary and decoding skills to the children.

    D. to review the parts of the book, check for comprehension, and practice the use of contextual clues.

2. The word "predestined" is composed of

    A. one inflectional morpheme and one derivational morpheme.

    B. one derivational morpheme, the root of the word, and two inflectional morphemes.

    C. two inflectional morphemes and the root of the word.

    D. one derivational morpheme, the root, and one inflectional morpheme.

3. Mr. Chapman is a third-grade teacher who is working at a school that is implementing a balanced reading program. He will use all of the following reading strategies in his classroom EXCEPT

    A. reading to students (read-aloud).

    B. implementing shared reading, guided reading, and reading workshops.

    C. having students engage in independent reading.

    D. having students independently decode words in reading and writing.

4. Vocabulary development is a key predictor of success in reading. Identify a strategy that parents can use with preschool children to promote vocabulary development in a fun and relaxed environment.

    A.   Use flash cards and concrete objects to introduce vocabulary words.

    B.   Play a game in which the parent and the child teach each other a new word every day.

    C.   Play games in which children have to name antonyms and synonyms.

    D.   Ask children to memorize a list of vocabulary words every day.

5. Which of the following sets of symptoms best describes heat stroke?

    A.   Cool, moist, pale skin

    B.   Red, hot, dry skin, unconsciousness

    C.   Nausea and dizziness

    D.   Headache and excessive sweating

6. The process by which physical movements develop and become specialized for motor performance depends primarily upon

    A.   socioeconomic status.

    B.   natural talent.

    C.   daily practice.

    D.   a supportive environment.

7. Which of the following is a locomotor skill?

    A.   Bending

    B.   Catching

    C.   Throwing

    D.   Hopping

8. In music, the words "up" and "down" are usually associated with

    A. fast and slow.

    B. loud and soft.

    C. high and low.

    D. strong and gentle.

9. Identify the strategies that lead the child from the stage of *learning to read* to the stage of *reading to learn*.

    A. Expose children to different kinds of literature and vocabulary words specific to the content areas.

    B. Introduce children to different kinds of texts, and teach how to scan to locate and retrieve information.

    C. Allow students to read without interruptions for at least 20 minutes a day.

    D. Introduce the concepts of connotation and denotation in words and phrases.

10. There are two categories of maps—reference maps and thematic maps. An atlas is an example of

    A. a reference map.

    B. a thematic map.

    C. a physical map.

    D. a population map.

11. Which is not a critical step to follow when solving a mathematics problem?

    A. Understanding the problem

    B. Choosing a strategy and/or making a plan

    C. Checking your answer

    D. Thinking critically about the solution

12. Valerie has a bathtub that she needs to fill with water. To fill the tub, she first needs to fill a bucket with water and then dump this into the bathtub. If the bucket is a cylinder with a radius of 6 inches and a height of 12 inches, how many buckets will it take to fill the 5 × 3 × 3 foot tub?

    A. 50 buckets

    B. 48 buckets

    C. 57 buckets

    D. 62 buckets

13. The English colonies were established in three regions—the New England Colonies, the Middle Colonies, and the Southern Colonies. The economy of the Southern Colonies was based on

    A. farming, shipping, fishing, and trading.

    B. farming and very small industries such as fishing, lumber, and crafts.

    C. trading.

    D. crops of tobacco, rice, indigo, and cotton.

14. What percentage of a daily diet should be composed of carbohydrates?

    A. 5–10%

    B. 15–25%

    C. 35–50%

    D. 70–90%

15. The Declaration of Independence consists of a preamble or introduction followed by three main parts. The first part stresses natural unalienable rights and liberties that belong to all people from birth. The second part consists of a list of specific grievances and injustices committed by Britain. What does the third part announce?

    A. The creation of the United States of America

    B. The right to worship

    C. The right to vote

    D. The right to congregate and freedom of speech

16. The New England Colonies consisted of

    A. Virginia, North Carolina, South Carolina, and Georgia.

    B. Massachusetts, Connecticut, Rhode Island, and New Hampshire.

    C. New York, New Jersey, Delaware, Maryland, and Pennsylvania.

    D. North Carolina, Rhode Island, Delaware, and Maryland.

17. What might be the benefit of activating background knowledge (schema) of the students prior to reading about a given topic?

    A. Students become more interested and motivated to learn more about the topic.

    B. Students can make connections to the story and develop a better understanding of the content.

    C. Students can visualize the imagery of the story as they read it.

    D. Students develop fluency and increase the speed of reading while reading the text together.

18. Cesar Chávez and Dolores Huerta were two of the most important Mexican-American leaders of the civil rights movement. They fought for

    A. better educational opportunities for language minority groups.

    B. more employment opportunities for ethnic and racial minority groups in the U.S.

    C. better working conditions and fair compensation for agricultural workers.

    D. the development of more worker unions for Mexican Americans.

19. Dan is an eight-year-old whose vocabulary has significantly improved over the past two months. He is beginning to use relative pronoun clauses when speaking. Dan's teacher has discovered that he still struggles when using subordinate clauses. Which of the following sentences would be an example of a correct use of a subordinate clause?

    A. I like the cars, but I dislike motorcycles.

    B. He wants to sleep until late in the morning.

C.   If you want me to go, I will need to start getting ready now.

D.   My mom and my dad are real Texans.

20. The alphabetic principle has been described as the ability to

A.   create letters in print and say words out loud.

B.   connect letters with sounds and create words based on such associations.

C.   connect letters and sounds to pronounce words by syllables.

D.   connect sounds with those spoken by others.

21. Daniele is a third grader having problems identifying prefixes and suffixes in the words she reads and writes. When asked to identify the free morpheme of the word *predetermined,* she identified the segment *mine* as the answer. Based on the scenario, what might be the rationale for her answer?

A.   She is confused with suffixes and prefixes.

B.   She did not understand that the segment *mine* is not a free morpheme in that context.

C.   She does not understand the concept of free morpheme.

D.   She did not understand that free morphemes constitute the main component of the word.

22. **Use the numbers below to answer the question that follows.**

     10, 9, 3, 1, 2, 8, 4, 3, 9, 10, 5, 7, 6, 6, 2, 8, 9, 4, 1, 10, 5, 8, 4, 6, 2, 1, 9, 7

What is the mode of the data set?

A.   9

B.   3

C.   5

D.   6

23. What is the median of the data set in question 22?

A.   6

B.   7

C.   6.5

D.   7.5

24. What strategy can be used to assess reading comprehension for students who are not proficient readers?

    A. Drawing inferences

    B. Graphic organizers

    C. Written reflections

    D. Oral retelling of the story

25. Advanced organizers and graphic representations are commonly used in social studies. What is the advantage of using these strategies to teach content?

    A. They make content accessible to all children.

    B. They make learning more interesting.

    C. They can be used to teach other content areas.

    D. They can be used to teach high-order thinking skills.

26. The main value of using real-life situations to teach problem-solving skills involving mathematics is that the children in grades K–6 can see

    A. the connection between the school curriculum and mathematics.

    B. the value of mathematics in solving daily situations.

    C. that mathematics is an important part of the Georgia curriculum.

    D. that the use of learning centers has a specific value in life.

27. Some of the advantages of using a think-aloud, while reading to students, are that teachers can model comprehension strategies like making inferences, synthesizing information, and visualization. What is another type of comprehension strategy that teachers might model to help students develop reading comprehension skills?

    A. Readers' theater

    B. Confirming predictions

    C. Segmenting multisyllabic words

    D. Structural analysis

28. When teaching the grapheme-phoneme correspondence in English, teachers must

    A. make the activity interesting to all students.

    B. monitor the children so they do not pronounce the letters with a foreign accent.

    C. create an atmosphere of cooperation among students from diverse ethnic and linguistic backgrounds.

    D. control the inconsistency of the grapheme-phoneme correspondence of English by presenting consistent sounds first.

29. You and your family go out to dinner one night. At the end of the meal you receive a bill for the meal. The total bill, before tax, is $78.60. Assuming tax for the meal is 5%, what would you need to do first in order to find out the amount of tax you need to pay?

    A. Multiply the total by 5

    B. Multiply the total by 0.05

    C. Divide by 5

    D. Divide by 0.05

30. Latitude and longitude lines are used to locate points on a map. What is the term that best describes this type of geometric figure?

    A. A grid system

    B. A compass rose

    C. A legend

    D. A globe

31. What is a bound morpheme?

    A. A morpheme that occurs in isolation.

    B. A morpheme that occurs in isolation but is sometimes attached to a root word.

    C. A morpheme that occurs in isolation but can never be attached to a root word.

    D. A morpheme that cannot occur in isolation and, therefore, is attached to a root word or another morpheme.

32. The world region of North America consists of

    A. the United States and Mexico.

    B. the United States and Canada.

    C. the United States.

    D. Canada, the United States, and Mexico.

33. Many important battles were fought during the American Revolution. Which of the following revolutionary battles was fought in Georgia?

    A. The Battle of Gettysburg

    B. The Battle of Yorktown

    C. The Battle of Lexington

    D. The Battle of Kettle Creek

34. **Read the statement below; then answer the question that follows.**

    Three times one-half of a number less eighty percent

    Which of the following is an expression that represents this statement?

    A. $3 \times \dfrac{4}{2} - 0.8$

    B. $3 \times \dfrac{x}{2} - \dfrac{8}{100}$

    C. $3 \times \dfrac{x}{2} - 0.8$

    D. $3 \times \dfrac{x}{2} - 80$

35. Identify the statement that BEST describes sight words.

    A. Sight words are prevalent in environmental print.

    B. Sight words occur frequently in print.

    C. Children decode sight words using semantic and structural clues.

    D. Children have difficulty spelling sight words.

36. The first 10 amendments to the U.S. Constitution are known as the

    A. separation of church and state.

    B. Bill of Rights.

    C. Right to Privacy.

    D. Right to Due Process.

37. What is one of the key challenges that children in upper elementary school experience when moving from the stage of "learning to read" to "reading to learn?"

    A.   Use graphic organizers effectively to learn and to present information

    B.   Understand the organizational patterns of the text to read more efficiently

    C.   Develop an understanding of academic English

    D.   Predict the content of the writing efficiently

38. Ms. Pompa uses DRTA (Directed Reading-Thinking Activity) regularly during her guided reading groups. What is the main purpose of this instructional activity?

    A.   To interpret the text according to one's own background knowledge

    B.   To pose questions to students related to the themes in the text

    C.   To confirm or correct predictions as one reads

    D.   To synthesize information in order to better retell the story

39. What song has the same melody as *Twinkle, Twinkle Little Star*?

    A.   Are you Sleeping?

    B.   Skip to my Lou

    C.   Polly Put the Kettle On

    D.   Alphabet Song

40. Alliteration is a technique frequently used to begin developing students' reading skills as it aims to strengthen students' phonological and phonemic awareness. Which sentence is an example of alliteration?

    A.   Maria bought a muffin for my mom.

    B.   Maria baked a large muffin for my mom.

    C.   Maria made muffins for Mom.

    D.   Maria baked a muffin in a large oven.

41. This term describes the exchange or transmission of cultural information and lifestyles from people around the world.

    A. Diversity

    B. Ethnicity

    C. Culture

    D. Cultural diffusion

42. Identify the number of phonemes in the word *through*.

    A. Seven

    B. Two

    C. Four

    D. Three

43. The 118 elements of the periodic table represent the anatomical composition of

    A. matter.

    B. liquid.

    C. solid.

    D. gases.

44. Many of the leaders responsible for the writing of the Constitution were familiar with the best thinkers of the Enlightenment movement. Due to this influence, one of the key components of the Constitution was the protection of the

    A. religious beliefs of people in the new nation.

    B. natural rights of the individual and limiting the power of the government.

    C. power of the central government and the unification of the nation.

    D. rights to fair trading.

45. Which of the following attitudes are essential to scientific inquiry?

    A. Self-assurance, argumentative, curiosity, and enthusiasm

    B. Doubting, assertive, honesty, creative, and somber

    C. Restrained, reflective, tenacious, and temperate

    D. Curiosity, skepticism, honesty, and openness

46. Ms. Thomas introduces new vocabulary words within the context of a sentence and through the use of visuals. Once children understand the concept linked to the word, she repeats individual words, pausing after each syllable. Once children can separate the word into syllables, she guides them to separate syllables into individual phonemes. What skills is Ms. Thomas introducing with the last two activities?

   A. The intonation pattern of the language

   B. Phonological awareness

   C. Vocabulary development

   D. Pronunciation drills

47. Joe can place a maximum of 5 apples in a sack. If he needs to put 32 apples in sacks, how many sacks will he need?

   A. 7

   B. 6.4

   C. 5

   D. 8

Use the following scenario to answer question 48 below.

Scenario: Mr. Van Jones brought a small peach tree with peaches to school to explain the process of photosynthesis. He indicated that the tree takes energy from the sun and converts it into chemical energy. Part of the chemical energy produced is used for its survival and growth. The excess energy is stored in the leaves and in the fruits produced. To close the lesson, he gave students pieces of peaches and guided them to discuss how the process of photosynthesis supports life on Earth.

48. Based on this scenario, what is the main topic of the lesson?

   A. Energy transformation

   B. Survival of the fittest

   C. The importance of conservation and adoption of green practices

   D. The importance of peach trees for survival

49. The basic states of matter are

    A.   liquid, plasma, and solid.

    B.   gas, liquid, and solid.

    C.   liquid, water, ice, and gas.

    D.   plasma, liquid, solid, and gas.

50. When it is winter in North America, it is because

    A.   the Earth is farther away from the sun in its orbit.

    B.   the North Pole is tilted toward the sun.

    C.   the Earth is tilted on its axis with the North Pole tilted away.

    D.   Earth's moon is blocking the sun.

51. Mr. Martínez is going to be introducing the Dolch words to his first-grade students. Before showing the list of words to his students, Mr. Martínez explains that these words are the most frequently used words in English. Which of the following words SHOULD NOT be included in the list that Mr. Martínez is going to show to his students?

    A.   a

    B.   had

    C.   but

    D.   awesome

52. What is the correct expansion of $(a + b)3$?

    A. $a^3 + b^3$

    B. $a^3 + 3a^2b + 3ab^2 + b^3$

    C. $a^3 + 6a^3b^3 + b^3$

    D. $3a^2 + 3b$

53. In the past, mercury was commonly used in household thermometers. Why was this substance ideal for thermometers?

    A.   It is easily accessible and available in most countries.

    B.   The substance expands when heated.

    C.   It is a highly-volatile and flexible substance.

    D.   It is the only substance approved by the U.S. Department of Energy.

54. Which of these sets of numbers represents a true statement?

    A. $5 < 7$

    B. $10 > 11$

    C. $9 \leq 8$

    D. $3 \geq 5$

55. When people think about radiation, they conceptualize the arms of mass destruction like the atomic bombs used in Hiroshima and Nagasaki during World War II. However, radiation is currently being used for peaceful purposes in nuclear medicine and in household items like

    A. refrigerators.

    B. radios.

    C. gas stoves.

    D. microwaves.

56. Why is the lowest average temperature in New York City higher than the lowest average temperature of Lincoln, Nebraska, when these cities are at approximately the same latitude?

    A. New York City is farther south resulting in warmer temperatures.

    B. New York City is surrounded by water, which moderates the temperature.

    C. New York City is full of industries that warm the atmosphere.

    D. New York City is near the Appalachian Mountains, which trap sunlight and heat.

57. The invention of cell phones has revolutionized the communications industry. However, it has also become a health concern because these electronic devices

    A. distract people and cause automobile accidents.

    B. emit radiation that may cause cancer.

    C. make children easy targets for sexual predators.

    D. affect the growth of the traditional phone industry.

58. Petroleum products come from nonrenewable fossil fuels. These types of energy sources are nonrenewable because they come from

    A. the melting of rocks and other minerals.

    B. decayed remains of animal and plants.

    C. the bones and flesh from prehistoric lizards.

    D. the residue produced from volcanic activity.

59. The development of fatty tissue and hibernation typical of bears is a system _____ for survival.

    A. of adaptation

    B. to avoid competition with other predators

    C. to keep a healthy balance in the ecosystem

    D. to prevent the migration of bears to residential areas

60. What is an algorithm?

    A. A computer program used to evaluate students

    B. A system of discovering students' abilities

    C. A step-by-step procedure for evaluating students

    D. A step-by-step procedure for solving problems

61. Which of the following are objects in our solar system?

    A. Asteroids, planets, moons, and comets

    B. Planets, asteroids, moons, and black holes

    C. Planets, meteoroids, asteroids, and black holes

    D. Asteroids, milky way, quasars, and comets

62. Mr. Michel provides guiding questions to guide Tamara's writing. A couple of the questions are "What evidence do you need to prove your thesis to skeptics?" and "What would you say to convince them?" Based on this information, what type of writing is Tamara developing?

    A. Narrative writing

    B. Expository writing

    C. Descriptive writing

    D. Persuasive writing

63. What is another way to write $4 \times 4 \times 4$?

    A. 64

    B. 34

    C. 4×3

    D. 12

64. The scientific concept that best explains the formation of mountains and mountain ranges on Earth is

    A. the movement of underground water.

    B. the movement of tectonic plates.

    C. erosion.

    D. the effect of the moon and the resulting waves of the oceans.

65. Which strategy would LESS LIKELY support students' understanding of writing for different audiences?

    A. Having a group of students role play a given audience and asking them to react to a piece of writing

    B. In a persuasive writing, guiding students to revise the writing based on possible arguments from the intended audience

    C. Identifying the audience prior to beginning writing

    D. Telling students they will be writing narrative text

66. Ms. Pérez is planning a lesson that she can implement to increase her students' understanding of viewing and representing. She decides that one of the key issues for her students is to be able to identify how the visual materials they will be using must directly respond to the audience and their needs. As part of the lesson, she intends to have students work on this as a group project. Which of the following group project ideas would be a good choice for her students to select?

A. Students can discuss their own travel experiences and bring pictures from home to make a chart.

B. Students can search the Internet for clip art.

C. Students can create a video directly responding to issues raised by a reporter in a newspaper article and share their response on YouTube.

D. Students can select an illustration from a book they are reading and act it out in class.

67. Knowledge of the two words used to create compound words can help students in the interpretation of the compound word. However, there are examples of compound words in which the meaning of the two components does not contribute to, and often interferes with, the interpretation of the new word. Identify the set of compound words that fall into this category.

A. Doghouse, autograph, and boathouse

B. Greenhouse, White House, and mouthwash

C. Butterfly, nightmare, and brainstorm

D. Hotdog, birdhouse, and underground

68. Which type of writing focuses mainly on composition of information text that is primarily intended to inform the reader about a topic or subject while explaining and clarifying ideas?

A. Narrative writing

B. Expository writing

C. Descriptive writing

D. Persuasive writing

69. Identify the instructional activity for viewing and representing for first-grade students that also involves higher-order thinking.

    A.   Sketching an image of what a character might be thinking or feeling during a story

    B.   Developing a PowerPoint presentation with embedded clip art

    C.   Creating a video response to a story

    D.   Designing a newsletter related to a social studies unit

70. In a two-week period (including weekends and holidays), Max spent $71.47 on lunch. About how much money did Max spend on his daily lunch?

    A. $5.00

    B. $4.50

    C. $5.50

    D. $4.75

71. Select the answer that contains the correct sequence of Kodály rhythm syllables for this song line, *Twinkle, Twinkle Little Star*.

    A.   Ta Ta Ta Ta Ti ti Ta

    B.   Ta ti Ti ti Ta Ta Ti

    C.   Ti ti Ti ti Ti ti Ta

    D.   Ti ti Ta Ta Ta Ta Ti

72. Mr. Lee models using writing conventions as he writes using an electronic projection system. He says things like, "I use quotation marks here to indicate that I am quoting someone directly. Here's how I write the quotation marks and punctuation surrounding the words someone actually says." The main reason Mr. Lee talks out loud while writing is to

    A.   show prewriting strategies.

    B.   demonstrate the use of conventional grammar, spelling, capitalization, and punctuation.

    C.   address a topic or write to a prompt creatively and independently.

    D.   organize writing to include a beginning, middle, and end.

73. A teacher notices multiple bruising marks on a child. The teacher should

    A. ask the child about their home life for more information.

    B. do nothing.

    C. talk with the parents about child abuse.

    D. report the evidence immediately.

74. Mr. Lawrence reads a story to his kindergarten students in a very pleasant and natural tone of voice. Later, he uses a series of connected pictures representing events in the story. In addition to helping children understand the story, what other element is he teaching?

    A. The teacher is introducing the sound-symbol correspondence of the story.

    B. The teacher is filling the experiential gaps to be sure students can understand the story.

    C. The teacher is introducing sequencing and the story structure.

    D. The teacher is using developmentally appropriate practices since children at this stage cannot read on their own.

75. Volcano eruptions can cause other natural physical events like earthquakes, avalanches, mudslides, and

    A. human death.

    B. tsunamis.

    C. hurricanes.

    D. tornados

76. The civil rights movement sought equality for African Americans. Even after the Thirteenth, Fourteenth, and Fifteenth Amendments were added to the Constitution, blacks were denied full civil rights. Discrimination existed throughout the nation. Jim Crow laws were enforced in the

    A. South.

    B. North.

    C. East.

    D. West.

77. Marcos is a five-year-old student in the process of first language acquisition. He often produces statements like: This lollipop is the *bestest* Mom. Based on this speech sample, this child is

   A.   applying language rules.

   B.   experiencing language interference.

   C.   applying the concepts from L1 to L2.

   D.   imitating the speech sample of cartoons on television.

78. The Andes mountain range and the Amazon River are two of the key physical features in

   A.   North America.

   B.   Central America.

   C.   South America.

   D.   Central and South America.

79. Inactivity can increase the risk factor of contracting which of the following diseases or conditions?

   A.   heart disease

   B.   anemia

   C.   sleep apnea

   D.   psoriasis

80. Ms. Fuentes frequently leads students in choral reading to promote reading fluency. She also takes declarative statements from the story and asks students to change them to questions or exclamations. Students have fun generating these changes. What is the main purpose of the latter activity?

   A.   To emphasize listening and speaking skills

   B.   To teach the intonation pattern of the language

   C.   To teach singing and music skills

   D.   To make the class more enjoyable

81. Ms. Becerra uses a strategy with her sixth graders to help students monitor their own comprehension as they read independently. She instructs students to stop and check if they understand the main ideas in the story before moving on to the next section. This type of comprehension practice fosters which of the following?

    A.   Metacognition
    B.   Fluency
    C.   Decoding
    D.   Vocabulary

82. The movement of planets around the Sun creates what is known as a calendar year. Based on this information and the relative location of the planets in reference to the Sun, what is the planet with the shortest year?

    A.   Jupiter
    B.   Earth
    C.   Venus
    D.   Mercury

83. Volcanoes are formed with the motion of the tectonic plates. When the plates collapse, the motion creates cracks in the crust of the Earth, which eventually causes an eruption to release the excess heat, gases, and melted rocks and minerals from the center of the planet. The best indicator of the severity of the volcanic explosion is

    A.   the amount of magma inside the Earth.
    B.   the amount of lava available within the tectonic plates.
    C.   the amount of gas in the magma.
    D.   the number of faults in the area.

84. Steve is told that milk must remain at 50°F so it will not spoil and that a turkey must be cooked at 375°F for 2 hours. What is the difference in temperature of the milk and the turkey (while it is cooking)?

    A.   315°F
    B.   335°F
    C.   320°F
    D.   325°F

85. When plants take solar energy from the sun and transform it to usable energy, we say that energy was transformed to

    A.   chemical energy.

    B.   oxygen.

    C.   chlorophyll.

    D.   carbon dioxide.

86. What is the scientific explanation of the popular saying "once in a blue moon"?

    A.   An extra full moon period that occurs every two or three years.

    B.   A stage of the moon that precedes a lunar eclipse.

    C.   An idiomatic expression not directly linked to the stages of the moon.

    D.   An idiomatic expression implying that people are blue or sad.

87. This symbol represents the official declaration of patriotism in the United States.

    A.   United States of America National Flag

    B.   Liberty Bell

    C.   Pledge of Allegiance

    D.   Statue of Liberty

88. Which civil rights group challenged the laws of segregation with the *Brown v. Board of Education of Topeka* Supreme Court case?

    A.   The Civil Rights Organization

    B.   The National Association for the Advancement of Colored People

    C.   The Civil Rights Leadership Organization

    D.   The Southern Christian Leadership Conference

89. By ages four and five, children are generally able to stack cups in a pyramid, dribble a small ball, and tap their foot to a rhythm. They also begin dressing themselves using buttons and zippers. These kinds of activities represent an example of

    A.   gross motor skills.

    B.   required curriculum components in school.

    C.   fine motor skills.

    D.   a transition point from early childhood to adulthood.

90. Solve for x in the following problem. Express the answer as a mixed number.

    $$1.6 - \frac{3}{8} = x$$

    A. $1\frac{9}{49}$

    B. $1\frac{2}{25}$

    C. $1\frac{23}{100}$

    D. $1\frac{9}{40}$

91. An isosceles triangle is a polygon with two equal sides. What else does this imply?

    A. It is equilateral.

    B. Its angles sum to greater than 180°.

    C. It is also scalene.

    D. It has two equal angles.

92. A world region is an area identified based on

    A. topographical features.

    B. cultural features, political boundaries, and natural resources.

    C. political features.

    D. sharing similar, unifying cultural or physical characteristics.

93. The Fourteenth Amendment declared that all persons born in the U.S. were citizens and that all citizens were entitled to equal rights, and that their rights were protected by due process. A group of people living in the U.S. was not included. Which group was excluded from the equal rights provisions?

    A. Blacks

    B. Women

    C. Children

    D. Native Americans

94. Geographers have divided the world into ten regions: North America, Central and South America, Europe, Central Eurasia, the Middle East, North Africa, Sub-Saharan Africa, South Asia, East Asia, and Australasia. These divisions are based on

    A.   location and the presence of body of waters.

    B.   language.

    C.   climate.

    D.   physical and cultural similarities.

95. Which of the following best describes a lesson plan for elementary physical education students who need additional development and practice with a locomotor skill?

    A.   Introduction to traveling pathways such as straight, curved, or zigzag

    B.   Activities such as aerobics and circuit training

    C.   Refining flexibility, strength, and muscular endurance

    D.   Spotting during gymnastics and using nonskid footwear

96. Dr. Martin Luther King Jr. founded the Southern Christian Leadership Conference (SCLC) with other African-American leaders. His famous *I Have a Dream* speech took place during the march in Washington in support of the Civil Rights Act of 1964. This speech

    A.   motivated a riot.

    B.   prompted the creation of the Montgomery Improvement Association.

    C.   resulted in the lost of supporters.

    D.   gained more supporters for the cause.

97. Which of the following would be the best set of units to use when measuring a football field?

    A.   Centimeters

    B.   Inches

    C.   Meters

    D.   Miles

98. A second-grade student began writing a composition about his friend in the following way: (1) George is my friend. (2) Mary is my best friend. (3) Rachel are my friends too. What type of support does this child need to write a more cohesive and standard writing sample?

   A. Spelling and agreement instruction

   B. Use of active and passive voices

   C. Agreement and sentence connectors

   D. Use of appropriate capitalization and punctuation

99. The system most affected by aerobic activity is the

   A. muscular system.

   B. digestive system.

   C. cardiovascular system.

   D. skeletal system.

100. President John F. Kennedy proposed new civil rights laws as well as programs to help the millions of Americans living in poverty. After Kennedy's assassination in Dallas in 1963, President Lyndon B. Johnson urged Congress to pass the laws. As a result of the leadership of these two men, which piece of legislation was passed?

   A. The Civil Rights Act

   B. The Equal Education Act

   C. The Fair Employment Act

   D. The Desegregation Act

101. What are minimal pairs used to teach and assess?

   A. Morphology

   B. Phonology

   C. Syntax

   D. Lexicon

102. The ice cap of the North Pole is melting at an alarming rate. The melting of the ice cap is an example of a

    A.   chemical change.

    B.   physical change.

    C.   chemical reaction.

    D.   natural yearly process.

103. How many faces does a cube have?

    A.   7

    B.   6

    C.   5

    D.   4

104. Dan and Stacy live on a farm where they are no longer allowed to let their cattle roam free. They need to add a fence around their land which has a shape like the figure below. How many feet of fence do they need to buy in order to fence in all of their land?

223 ft

467 ft

    A.   103,341 ft

    B.   104,141 ft

    C.   1,380 ft

    D.   1,280 ft

105. Warm- and cold-blooded animals need heat to survive; however, only warm-blooded animals produce heat. Cold-blooded animals obtain heat from

    A.   the food that they eat.

    B.   the sun.

    C.   the moon.

    D.   the water that they drink.

106. What is the formula for the relationship between the number of faces, vertices, and edges of a cube?

   A. $F + E = V + 2$
   B. $E + V = F + 2$
   C. $F + V = E - 2$
   D. $F + V = E + 2$

107. While teaching a basketball unit to an elementary school class, the best way to develop skills would be to

   A. give a written test to assess students' knowledge of strategy.
   B. use smaller balls and lower the baskets.
   C. teach the foul shot before the jump shot.
   D. play full court, five-on-five games.

108. The principles of art describe

   A. the guidelines that artists follow to create art and to deliver their intended message.
   B. the individual components that combine to create artwork.
   C. the ideas, emotions, and experiences that can be communicated through art.
   D. the sequence of artistic concepts that are presented in kindergarten through grade 6.

109. What is one of the key advantages of using integrated thematic instruction?

   A. The four literacy skills—listening, speaking, reading, and writing—are introduced sequentially.
   B. It is used to introduce and practice basic computation skills.
   C. It eliminates the artificial boundaries created through traditional course scheduling.
   D. It allows for the teaching of the content areas using the inductive method.

Read the word problem below; then answer the question that follows.

Eric arranged loaves of bread on 5 shelves in the bakery. He put 1 loaf on the top shelf, 4 loaves on the second shelf, and 7 loaves on the third shelf. If he continues this pattern, how many loaves did Eric put on the 5th shelf?

110. Which of the following is the best strategy to use to solve the problem above?

   A.   Estimate.

   B.   Draw a diagram.

   C.   Guess and check.

   D.   Look for a pattern.

111. Students in the emergent stage of reading development

   A.   should be discouraged from "pretend reading" since it is merely an indication of having heard the book read many times.

   B.   should refrain from picture reading to avoid dependence on the illustrations for gaining meaning.

   C.   should use environmental print to make connections between written language and the things they represent.

   D.   should focus on reading fluency.

112. All of the following are characteristics of phonological awareness EXCEPT

   A.   the ability to distinguish between units of sound in a spoken word

   B.   the ability to substitute onsets and rimes.

   C.   the ability to identify syllables in a spoken word.

   D.   the ability to match the sounds in a spoken word to the corresponding symbols.

113. Phonemic awareness includes the ability to do all of the following EXCEPT

   A.   identify the letters that match the sounds in a spoken word.

   B.   identify a word after removing a sound.

   C.   segment words into sounds and to blend separate sounds into words.

   D.   determine whether or not spoken words rhyme.

114. Phonemic awareness includes two aspects:

   A.   the knowledge that spoken words are made up of individual sounds and the ability to point to the letters that make the sounds.

   B.   the knowledge that spoken words are made up of individual sounds and the ability to write the corresponding letters.

   C.   the knowledge that spoken words are made up of individual sounds and the ability to say the letters that make the sounds.

   D.   the knowledge that spoken words are made up of individual sounds and the ability to manipulate spoken sounds.

115. Strategies for promoting students' phonological and phonemic awareness include all of the following EXCEPT

   A.   identifying and making oral rhymes.

   B.   identifying onsets and rimes in one-syllable written words.

   C.   clapping the syllables of a word.

   D.   identifying and manipulating individual phonemes in spoken words.

116. In the word *bright*, the rime is made up of the letter:

   A.   br

   B.   ght

   C.   ight

   D.   bri

117. Which letters in the word below have a line of symmetry?

PEAR

    A.   A and R

    B.   P and R

    C.   E and A

    D.   A only

118. Grant has a rectangular piece of construction paper. If he folds the piece of paper along the dotted line, what kind of triangle will he form?

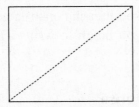

    A.   an equilateral triangle

    B.   a scalene triangle

    C.   an isosceles triangle

    D.   a right triangle

119. Kathleen is making cookies using chocolate chips, raisins, and marshmallows. She uses 10 fewer marshmallows than chocolate chips and twice as many chocolate chips as raisins. If she uses 50 raisins in her cookies, how many marshmallows will she use?

    A.   50

    B.   100

    C.   40

    D.   90

120. Which of the following shows the prime factorization for the number 36?

    A. $2 \times 2 \times 3 \times 3$

    B. $4 \times 3 \times 3$

    C. $2 \times 2 \times 9$

    D. 6×6

Constructed-Response Questions:

Directions for the Constructed- Response Questions:

Prepare a written response for each constructed-response assignment. Read each assignment carefully before you begin to write. Think about how you will organize what you plan to write.

Criteria For Scoring Your Response

Each response will be evaluated based on the following criteria:

- **PURPOSE:** The answer will be evaluated based on the extent to which the response fulfills the purpose of the assignment.

- **APPLICATION OF CONTENT KNOWLEDGE AND SKILLS:** The answer will be evaluated based on the extent to which the response accurately and effectively applies content knowledge and skills.

- **SUPPORT:** The answer will be evaluated based on the extent to which the response includes appropriate, specific supporting evidence of content knowledge and skills.

Each response is rated on a three-point scale. The three score points of the score scale correspond to varying degrees of performance that are related to the above criteria.

Score Description

3

The "3" response reflects thorough understanding of relevant content knowledge and skills.

- The response fully achieves the purpose of the assignment.

- The response demonstrates an accurate and effective application of relevant content knowledge and skills.

- The response provides appropriate, specific supporting evidence of relevant content knowledge and skills.

2

The "2" response reflects general understanding of relevant content knowledge and skills

- The response largely achieves the purpose of the assignment.

- The response demonstrates a generally accurate, generally effective application of relevant content knowledge and skills.

- The response provides some appropriate and general supporting evidence of relevant content knowledge and skills.

1

The "1" response reflects limited or no understanding of relevant content knowledge and skills.

- The response partially achieves or fails to achieve the purpose of the assignment.

- The response demonstrates limited, inaccurate, and/or ineffective application of relevant content knowledge and skills.

- The response provides limited or no appropriate, specific supporting evidence of relevant content knowledge and skills.

0

The examinee has either not responded or responded off-topic, or the response is illegible.

Constructed-Response Question 1 (Math—Objective 0013)

Use the information below to complete the task that follows.

Below is a problem given to a student to solve and his solution which shows his work. His work contains an error.

The poster below lists the prices of supplies at the school store.

> **School Supplies**
>
> Pencil....................................$0.30
> Pen..$0.75
> Notebook..............................$1.55
> Ruler.....................................$1.30

a. Piper had $3.00 to spend. She bought one ruler and one notebook. How much money did she have left after her purchase? Show your work.

$1.30　　　　$3.00
+ $1.55　　　− $2.85
$2.85　　　　$ .25

- Analyze the problem-solving process above using appropriate terminology.

- Describe the conceptual or procedural error that was made in the attempted solution; and explain the mathematical concept involved.

Constructed Response 2 (Reading and English Language Arts—Objective 0004)

Use the information below to complete the exercise that follows.

Mrs. Whalen, a fifth-grade teacher, is assessing Demetrius, a new student to the school, for reading fluency and comprehension. She has him read the following passage . . .

> My name is Jake. That's my first name, obviously. I can't tell you my last name. It would be too dangerous. The controllers are everywhere. Everywhere. And if they knew my full name, they could find me and my friends, and then . . . well, let's just say I don't want them to find me. What they do to people who resist them is too horrible to think about.
>
> I won't even tell you where I live. You'll just have to trust me that it is a real place, a real town. It may even be your town.
>
> I'm writing this all down so that more people will learn the truth. Maybe then, somehow, the human race can survive until the Algonites return and rescue us, as they promised they would.
>
> Maybe.
>
> My life used to be normal. Normal, that is, until one Friday night at the mall. I was there with Marco, my best friend. We were playing video games and hanging out at this cool store that sells comic books and stuff. The usual.

Demetrius has trouble pronouncing nearly every word longer than two syllables: "obviously," "controllers," and "Algonites," for example. He also needs help in pronouncing the word "resist." He reads with some expression and fairly quickly, except for the words he stumbles over. When questioned about the content of the passage, he answers as follows:

Mrs. Whalen:	Can you tell me something about what you were just reading?
Demetrius:	There's a guy who likes video games. I think his name is Jake.
Mrs. Whalen:	What can you tell me about Jake?
Demetrius:	Well, he's scared. He's in trouble.
Mrs. Whalen:	How do you know he's in trouble?

Demetrius:	He can't give out his last name.
Mrs. Whalen:	Do you have any idea what he's afraid of?
Demetrius:	Not really—they're An-guh- . . .
Mrs. Whalen:	The Algonites?
Demetrius:	Yeah, them. I guess they're after the whole world.

Based on your knowledge of reading comprehension, write a response that:

- identifies two comprehension needs demonstrated by this student;

- provides evidence for the needs you identify;

- suggests two different instructional strategies to address the needs you identify; and

- explains why these strategies might be effective.

Constructed Response 3 (Science—Objective 0019)

Use the information below to complete the assignment that follows:

- Fourth grade students are learning to observe, measure, predict, and communicate weather data.

- Describe three tools the students could use to measure or predict the weather.

- Describe a relevant scientific concept relating to earth's processes.

Constructed Response 4 (Social Studies—Objective 0009)

Analyze the major events that led to the War of Independence.

The main reasons for the War of Independence were economic in nature. England, as well as other European nations, had established the mercantilism system to exploit the colonies. This system had three main principles:

1. The wealth of the nation is measured in terms of commodities accrued, especially gold and silver.

2. Economic activities can increase the power and control of the national government.

3. The colonies existed for the benefit of the mother country.

ANSWER KEY – PRACTICE TEST 2

Question Number	Answer	Field	Objective
1	A	Reading and English Language Arts	Objective 0005
2	D	Reading and English Language Arts	Objective 0002
3	D	Reading and English Language Arts	Objective 0005
4	A	Reading and English Language Arts	Objective 0003
5	B	Health, Physical Education and the Arts	Objective 0022
6	C	Health, Physical Education and the Arts	Objective 0023
7	D	Health, Physical Education and the Arts	Objective 0023
8	C	Health, Physical Education and the Arts	Objective 0024
9	B	Reading and English Language Arts	Objective 0005
10	A	Social Studies	Objective 0010
11	D	Math	Objective 0013
12	C	Math	Objective 0015
13	D	Social Studies	Objective 0009
14	C	Health, Physical Education and the Arts	Objective 0022
15	A	Social Studies	Objective 0009
16	B	Social Studies	Objective 0009

Question Number	Answer	Field	Objective
17	B	Reading and English Language Arts	Objective 0004
18	C	Social Studies	Objective 0009
19	C	Reading and English Language Arts	Objective 0007
20	B	Reading and English Language Arts	Objective 0001
21	B	Reading and English Language Arts	Objective 0002
22	A	Math	Objective 0017
23	A	Math	Objective 0017
24	D	Reading and English Language Arts	Objective 0005
25	A	Social Studies	Objective 0012
26	B	Math	Objective 0013
27	B	Reading and English Language Arts	Objective 0004
28	D	Reading and English Language Arts	Objective 0002
29	B	Math	Objective 0014
30	A	Social Studies	Objective 0010
31	D	Reading and English Language Arts	Objective 0002
32	D	Social Studies	Objective 0010
33	D	Social Studies	Objective 0009
34	C	Math	Objective 0016
35	B	Reading and English Language Arts	Objective 0003
36	B	Social Studies	Objective 0011

Question Number	Answer	Field	Objective
37	B	Reading and English Language Arts	Objective 0005
38	C	Reading and English Language Arts	Objective 0004
39	D	Health, Physical Education and the Arts	Objective 0024
40	C	Reading and English Language Arts	Objective 0001
41	D	Social Studies	Objective 0009
42	D	Reading and English Language Arts	Objective 0002
43	A	Science	Objective 0020
44	B	Science	Objective 0009
45	D	Science	Objective 0018
46	B	Reading and English Language Arts	Objective 0001
47	A	Math	Objective 0014
48	A	Science	Objective 0020
49	D	Science	Objective 0020
50	C	Science	Objective 0013
51	D	Reading and English Language Arts	Objective 0003
52	B	Math	Objective 0014
53	B	Science	Objective 0020
54	A	Math	Objective 0014
55	D	Science	Objective 0020
56	B	Social Studies	Objective 0010

Question Number	Answer	Field	Objective
57	B	Health, Physical Education and the Arts	Objective 0022
58	B	Science	Objective 0019
59	A	Science	Objective 0021
60	D	Math	Objective 0013
61	A	Science	Objective 0019
62	D	Reading and English Language Arts	Objective 0006
63	A	Math	Objective 0014
64	B	Science	Objective 0019
65	D	Reading and English Language Arts	Objective 0006
66	C	Reading and English Language Arts	Objective 0008
67	C	Reading and English Language Arts	Objective 0003
68	B	Reading and English Language Arts	Objective 0006
69	A	Reading and English Language Arts	Objective 0005
70	A	Math	Objective 0014
71	C	Reading and English Language Arts	Objective 0024
72	B	Reading and English Language Arts	Objective 0007
73	D	Health, Physical Education and the Arts	Objective 0022
74	C	Reading and English Language Arts	Objective 0005

Question Number	Answer	Field	Objective
75	B	Science	Objective 0019
76	A	Social Studies	Objective 0009
77	A	Reading and English Language Arts	Objective 0007
78	D	Social Studies	Objective 0010
79	A	Health, Physical Education and the Arts	Objective 0022
80	B	Reading and English Language Arts	Objective 0004
81	A	Reading and English Language Arts	Objective 0004
82	D	Science	Objective 0019
83	C	Science	Objective 0019
84	D	Math	Objective 0014
85	A	Science	Objective 0020
86	A	Science	Objective 0019
87	C	Social Studies	Objective 0011
88	B	Social Studies	Objective 0011
89	C	Health, Physical Education and the Arts	Objective 0023
90	D	Math	Objective 0014
91	D	Math	Objective 0015
92	D	Social Studies	Objective 0010
93	D	Social Studies	Objective 0011
94	D	Social Studies	Objective 0010
95	A	Health, Physical Education and the Arts	Objective 0023
96	D	Social Studies	Objective 0009

Question Number	Answer	Field	Objective
97	C	Math	Objective 0015
98	C	Reading and English Language Arts	Objective 0007
99	C	Health, Physical Education and the Arts	Objective 0023
100	A	Social Studies	Objective 0011
101	B	Reading and English Language Arts	Objective 0001
102	B	Science	Objective 0020
103	B	Math	Objective 0015
104	C	Math	Objective 0015
105	B	Science	Objective 0021
106	D	Math	Objective 0015
107	B	Health, Physical Education and the Arts	Objective 0023
108	A	Reading and English Language Arts	Objective 0024
109	C	Reading and English Language Arts	Objective 0008
110	D	Math	Objective 0013
111	C	Reading and English Language Arts	Objective 0001
112	D	Reading and English Language Arts	Objective 0001
113	A	Reading and English Language Arts	Objective 0001
114	D	Reading and English Language Arts	Objective 0001

Question Number	Answer	Field	Objective
115	B	Reading and English Language Arts	Objective 0001
116	C	Reading and English Language Arts	Objective 0001
117	C	Reading and English Language Arts	Objective 0001
118	D	Math	Objective 0015
119	D	Math	Objective 0013
120	A	Math	Objective 0014

Practice Test 2 Progress Chart

Reading and English Language Arts   __/11
Objective 0001

20	40	46	110	111	112	113	114

115	116	117					

Reading and English Language Arts   __/5
Objective 0002

2	21	28	31	42

Reading and English Language Arts   __/4
Objective 0003

4	35	51	67

Reading and English Language Arts   __/5
Objective 0004

17	27	38	80	81

**Reading and English Language Arts
Objective 0005**   __/7

1	3	9	24	37	69	74

**Reading and English Language Arts
Objective 0006**   __/3

62	65	68

**Reading and English Language Arts
Objective 0007**   __/4

19	72	77	98

**Reading and English Language Arts
Objective 0008**   __/2

66	109

**Social Studies
Objective 0009**   __/9

76	13	15	16	18	33	41	44	96

**Social Studies
Objective 0010**   __/7

10	30	32	56	78	92	94

**Social Studies
Objective 0011**   __/5

36	87	88	93	100

**Social Studies
Objective 0012**   __/1

25

**Mathematics
Objective 0013**

11	60	110	119	50	26

**Mathematics
Objective 0014**

29	47	52	54	63	70	84	90	120

**Mathematics
Objective 0015**

12	91	97	103	104	106	118

**Mathematics
Objective 0016**

34

**Mathematics
Objective 0017**

22	23

**Science
Objective 0018**

45

**Science
Objective 0019**

58	61	64	75	82	83	86

**Science
Objective 0020**

43	48	49	53	55	85	102

Science
Objective 0021   __/2

59	105

Health, Physical Education and Art Ed.
Objective 0022   __/5

5	14	57	73	79

Health, Physical Education and Art Ed.
Objective 0023   __/6

6	7	89	95	99	107

Health, Physical Education and Art Ed.
Objective 0024   __/4

8	39	71	108

Practice Test 2 Detailed Explanations

1. **A**

    The first reading is designed to communicate the content of the story; by doing so, children will determine if their predictions were accurate. Choice B is incorrect because activities involving decoding strategies that determine the main idea are usually addressed after the initial activity. Choices C and D are incorrect because the parts of the book and the vocabulary of the story are usually introduced prior to reading the story. **Objective 0005**

2. **D**

    The word *predestined* contains three morpheme-units of meaning. The first morpheme is a derivational morpheme—*pre*, the second is the root word—*destin*(y), and the third is the inflectional ending—*ed*. **Objective 0002**

3. **D**

    A balanced reading program is one in which the teaching of reading requires solid skill instruction, including several techniques for decoding unknown words. However, having students decode words on their own is not considered to be the cornerstone of such a program. Therefore Choices A, B, and C are all strategies that will be implemented in this program. **Objective 0005**

4. **A**

    The use of flash cards with pictures representing concepts and concrete objects can definitely be effective in teaching vocabulary to preschool children. Choice B is incorrect because parents can teach a word every day to the child, but the child might not be able to participate effectively because preschoolers generally do not have the vocabulary development to teach parents new words. Choice C is also incorrect because preschoolers might not have the necessary vocabulary development to participate in a game dealing with antonyms and synonyms. Choice D is incorrect because the practice of memorizing vocabulary is quite boring and ineffective for children of all ages. **Objective 0003**

5. **B**

    Heat stroke is best recognized and described by red, hot, dry skin due to lack of hydration—a condition not allowing the body to cool itself efficiently. Unconsciousness is another sign of heat stroke in extreme situations. Choice A does not include the typical signs of heat stroke—rather heat exhaustion—which is not as severe. Choices C and D may accompany heat stroke but are not by themselves primary indicators of the problem. **Objective 0022**

6. **C**

Repetition and practice of a movement pattern is the fastest way to master a physical skill no matter the age level. Choice A has no relevance to skill acquisition. Choices B and D could in part attribute to skill development, although not to the same level of guided repetition and practice. **Objective 0023**

7. **D**

Locomotor activities describe the types of movement that children use to move from one place to the other. In this case, hopping is the only choice that accomplishes this goal. Choice A is incorrect because bending is not a locomotor activity, but rather a non-locomotor activity. Choices B and C are also incorrect because they are manipulative skills requiring interaction with equipment or objects. **Objective 0023**

8. **C**

Pitch describes how high (up) and low (down) sounds are produced. Choice A is incorrect because it describes characteristics of rhythm. Choice B is incorrect because it describes characteristics of dynamics. Choice D is incorrect because it describes characteristics of weight. **Objective 0024**

9. **B**

The main purpose of *reading to learn* is to obtain content information efficiently and effectively. One way to accomplish this task is to make students aware of the format used in the content areas and to guide them to retrieve the information by reading for the main idea or scanning for information. Choice A is incorrect because it addresses only one component of the process—vocabulary development. Choice C is incorrect because it does not address the issue of the complexity of expository writing. Choice D is incorrect because it addresses only the issue of vocabulary development—connotation and denotation. **Objective 0005**

10. **A**

Reference maps show the locations of places, and boundaries of countries, states, counties, and towns. Atlases or road maps are examples of reference maps. Choice B is incorrect because thematic maps show a particular topic such as population density, distribution of world religions, or physical, social, economic, political, agricultural, or economic features. Choice C is incorrect because a physical map is a thematic map that shows the topography of the land including land features and elevations. Choice D is incorrect because population maps are thematic maps that are used to show where people live in a particular region. **Objective 0010**

11. **D**

In order to solve a problem, we must understand it, choose a strategy and/or make a plan, carry out the plan, and check our answer. The only answer that is not a critical component of the process is Choice D. **Objective 0013**

12. **C**

This problem requires critical thinking and some basic knowledge of math. Solving for the volume of the bathtub one obtains 45 ft³ and the volume of the bucket is

$$\pi \times 0.5^2 \times 1 \approx 0.7854 \text{ ft}^3$$

To find how many buckets of water it will take to fill the tub, we must divide 45 by 0.7854. This gives approximately 57 buckets. **Objective 0015**

13. **D**

The economy of the Southern Colonies was based on the crops of tobacco, rice, indigo, and cotton. Plantations produced agricultural crops in large scale and exploited workers as well as the environment. Choice A is incorrect because it was the economy of the Middle Colonies that was based on farming, shipping, fishing, and trading. Choice B is incorrect because it was the economy of the New England colonies that was based on farming and very small industries such as fishing, lumber, and crafts. Choice C is incorrect because trading was a part of the Middle Colonies economy. **Objective 0019**

14. **C**

Complex carbohydrates should constitute at least half of the calories consumed for the healthy diet of an active person (a little less for an inactive person). Carbohydrates are the primary and most efficient source of energy for the body. Based on this, choices A, B, and D are incorrect. **Objective 0022**

15. **A**

The Declaration of Independence pronounced the colonies free and independent states. It consists of a preamble or introduction followed by three main parts. The third part announces the creation of the new country. Choices B, C, and D are incorrect because these choices stress rights that are not explicitly stated in the Declaration of Independence. The unalienable rights, stated in the first part of the Declaration of Independence, are life, liberty, and the pursuit of happiness. **Objective 0009**

16. **B**

The New England Colonies consisted of Massachusetts, Connecticut, Rhode Island, and New Hampshire. Choice A is incorrect because Virginia, North Carolina, South Carolina, and Georgia formed the Southern Colonies. Choice C is incorrect because New York, New Jersey, Delaware, Maryland, and Pennsylvania formed the Middle Colonies. Choice D is incorrect because this answer represents a combination of some of the Southern Colonies and some of the Middle Colonies. **Objective 0009**

17. **B**

Activating schema, or background knowledge related to a topic, helps students to make connections between new information and what they already know. Teachers can help students to activate the correct schema as a pre-reading strategy so that students can better understand new ideas and terminology. While motivation is important (A), it does not activate their schema of the topic. Choices C and D are related comprehension strategies; however, they are not the primary reason for a teacher to activate prior knowledge in students. **Objective 0004**

18. **C**

Cesar Chávez and Dolores Huerta founded the United Farm Workers union (UFW). The UFW fought for better working conditions and fair compensation for agricultural workers. Choice A is incorrect because, while this was an important issue at the time it was not the focus of the United Farm Workers union. Choice B is incorrect because this was not the focus of their work. Choice D is incorrect because the development of more workers' unions was not their intent. **Objective 0009**

19. **C**

Technically, a subordinate clause is a dependent clause that must be attached to a main clause to complete the intended meaning. Choice A contains a relative clause that provides additional information. Choices A, B, and D do not use subordinate clauses. **Objective 0007**

20. **B**

The alphabetic principle has been described as the ability to connect letters with sounds and to create words based on these associations. The only option that

377

completely captures these two components is choice B. Therefore, choices A, C, and D are incorrect. C describes the process to identify and create syllables—syllabication. **Objective 0001**

21. **B**

The word *mine* is a free morpheme when used in isolation; however, it is not a free morpheme in the word *predetermined* (B). There is no evidence to suggest that the student is having problems with suffixes or prefixes A. Since she recognized that the segment *mine* can be classified as a free morpheme in certain conditions, there is no evidence to suggest that she does not understand the concept of free morphemes (C and D). **Objective 0002**

22. **A**

The mode is the number that occurs most often in a number sequence. If we place the numbers in order, we can see that the number 9 occurs 4 times while all other numbers occur fewer than 4 times. **Objective 0017**

23. **A**

The median is the middle number when the numbers are lined up from the greatest to the least. If this is done, one can see that since there are 28 total numbers, there is no clear "middle number." The middle number falls between the fourteenth and fifteenth numbers which happen to be 6 and 6, respectively. Therefore, the two numbers are averaged, obtaining the median of 6. **Objective 0017**

24. **D**

Oral retelling is a good strategy to use when having emergent and beginning readers recall the main elements of the story. It allows students opportunities to recall key events and details of the story, even before they become fluent readers. Choices A, B, and C describe informal assessment techniques used with students who are already reading and writing at the intermediate and advanced levels. **Objective 0005**

25. **A**

Information in social studies can be presented in graphic form through the use of graphs and charts. This makes the content accessible to all children, including ELLs. Choices B, C, and D describe possible ways to use advanced organizers and graphic representations, but individually these options do not fully explain their value. **Objective 0012**

26. **B**

Children can see that knowledge of mathematics has a functional value in their lives. Choices A and C are incorrect because most children generally cannot make a connection between the content studied and the mathematics curriculum. Choice D is incorrect because children in K–6 generally cannot make extrapolations between activities in the learning centers and their intrinsic value in life. **Objective 001**

27. **B**

Confirming predictions is one of the most common ways to engage students in reading, focus their reading, and help them read with comprehension. By thinking aloud a teacher can explicitly model the procedures used when reading a text. Reader's theater (A) is a technique designed for the purpose of building fluency through repeated reading, while choices C and D focus primarily on decoding words or word meanings. **Objective 0004**

28. **D**

Teachers have to present the consistent sounds of English first to develop self-confidence among children. Once children master those initial grapheme-phoneme correspondences, they can attempt more challenging components. Choice A is incorrect because it deals with a generic well-accepted practice, but it does not address the question. Choice B is incorrect because the alphabetic principle does not specifically deal with the issue of the development of foreign accents. Choice C is incorrect because it fails to address the question. It is always important to create an atmosphere of collaboration among students, but this statement does not address the linguistic nature of the question. **Objective 0002**

29. **B**

Since a percentage represents a part of 100, a tax of 5% is equal to a decimal value of $\dfrac{5}{100} = 0.05$.

To find out how much tax is added to a bill of $78.60, we must multiply this total by the percentage of tax. **Objective 0014**

30. **A**

A grid system is a network of horizontal and vertical lines used to locate points on a map or a chart by means of coordinates. This grid shows the location of places. Latitude and longitude lines form divisions in this grid system. These divisions consist of geometrical coordinates used in designating the location of places on the surface of the earth in a globe or map. The lines measure distances in degrees. Based on this explanation Choices B, C, and D are incorrect. **Objective 0010**

31. **D**

The word *bound* in this type of morpheme should immediately indicate that this type of morpheme cannot occur in isolation; that is, it is bound to "something else." In this case, a bound morpheme must always be attached to a root word or another morpheme. This explanation makes A, B and C incorrect. **Objective 0002**

32. **D**

The world region of North America consists of Canada, the United States, and Mexico. Choice A is incorrect because it is missing Canada. Choice B is incorrect because it is missing Mexico. Choice C is incorrect because it is missing Canada and Mexico. **Objective 0010**

33. **D**

Not far from Washington, Georgia, in today's Wilkes county, Colonel Elijah Clarke defeated more than 800 British troops at the Battle of Kettle Creek. Choice A, the Battle of Gettysburg is incorrect because that battle was fought in the Civil War, and not in Georgia. Both choices B and C were battles fought in the American Revolution, but not in Georgia. **Objective 0009**

34. **C**

The statement "three times one-half of a number less eighty percent" implies that we do not know the actual number. Therefore, it must be represented by a variable. This fact eliminates choice A. Knowing that 80% is equivalent to $\frac{80}{100}$, or 0.8 eliminates choices B and D. Therefore, the only choice that is left happens to be choice C.

Objective 0016

35. **B**

Sight words occur frequently in writing, and often the best way to teach them is by instant recognition. Choice A is not correct because environmental print does not necessarily contain sight words. Street signs and store names can have long and very unique names that cannot be taught as sight words. Choice C is incorrect because sight words are taught to be recognized instantly, without analyzing their structural or semantic representation. Choice D is incorrect because most sight words are short and easy to spell. Because they occur so frequently in reading, spelling is facilitated. **Objective 0003**

36. **B**

    Civil rights are the legal and political rights of the people who live in a particular country. In the United States, the Constitution and the Bill of Rights guarantee civil rights to American citizens and residents. The first 10 amendments to the U.S. Constitution are known as the Bill of Rights. Choices A, C, and D are incorrect because these name certain rights included in the Bill of Rights and fail to address the question. **Objective 0011**

37. **B**

    When reading informational text, students have to analyze the type of text structure and organizational pattern used in the writing. The faster they learn to decipher the structure, the faster they will be able to retrieve information and read with greater efficiency. Using graphic organizers (A) and developing academic English (C) are important but secondary strategies that children need to master to move to the stage of "reading to learn." Predicting the content (D) is an effective strategy for narrative text, but it loses its effectiveness with expository writing. **Objective 0005**

38. **C**

    The main purpose of DRTA is to enable students to make ongoing predictions and confirmations of those predictions while reading a text. The teacher models this during a read-aloud or shared reading and instructs students to do the same as they read. Choices A, B, and D focus on activities that will enhance and develop students' comprehension; however, they are not centrally related to the specific instructional focus of DRTA. **Objective 0004**

39. **D**

    Melody is the "tune" or singable part of a song. The *Alphabet Song* has the same "tune" as *Twinkle, Twinkle Little Star*. As a matter of fact, *Baa, Baa Black Sheep* also employs the same melody. Choices A, B, and C have different "tunes" than *Twinkle, Twinkle Little Star*. **Objective 0024**

40. **C**

    Alliterations are created when words in a sentence or poem begin with the same phoneme. The option that best represents this concept is choice C. Four of the five words in option C begin with the phoneme /m/. The rest of the options do not consistently use the same phonemes at the beginning of the words. **Objective 0001**

41. **D**

The term *cultural diffusion* describes the exchange or transmission of cultural information and lifestyles from people around the world. *Diversity* describes differences among people around the world (A). *Ethnicity* (B) is a term used to describe people based on historical and cultural background, including religion, language, and other features. *Culture* (C) is a term to describe the learned and common behavior of a group. **Objective 0009**

42. **D**

The word contains seven graphemes (letters), but only three phonemes (sounds). Based on this explanation, the rest of the options are eliminated. **Objective 0002**

43. **A**

The periodic table represents the 118 elements that constitute matter. Liquid (B), solid (C), and gases (D) are forms or states of matter. **Objective 0020**

44. **B**

The ideas of the Enlightenment quickly reached the British colonies. Many of the leaders responsible for the writing of the Constitution were familiar with the leading thinkers of the movement, and framed the Constitution protecting the natural rights of the individual and limiting the power of the government. Choice A is incorrect because it addresses only one aspect of the natural rights of the individual. Choice C is incorrect because the purpose of the Constitution was actually to limit the power of the government and not to protect it. Choice D is incorrect because it does not represent the ideals of the Age of Reason. **Objective 0009**

45. **D**

The attitudes most important to scientific inquiry include curiosity, honesty, openness, and skepticism. Curiosity fuels investigation, and honesty compels reliable and accurate inquiry, as well as the accurate reporting of findings. Openness is the foundation of new discoveries and, therefore, an important attitude for scientists; and yet skepticism allows the scientist to question findings and look at them from different vantage points. While the some of the attitudes represented in options A, B, and C would be important, none of the groupings in total is essential to the process of scientific inquiry. **Objective 0018**

46. **B**

Separating syllables into individual phonemes calls for syllabication and phoneme segmentation. Both concepts are part of phonological awareness. Choice A is incorrect because sentence analysis is not the primary concern in the scenario. The intonation pattern describes the rhythm and pitch used in phrases and sentences. Choice C is incorrect because in the latter activity, the issue is the phonological analysis of words. Vocabulary development was emphasized in the first part of the scenario only. Choice D is incorrect because the scenario does not address pronunciation at all. **Objective 0001**

47. **A**

To find out how many sacks are required, we can divide the amount of apples that Joe has by the number that fit in a sack. The result of the division is 6.4. So, it could be assumed from this that choices C and D are not correct. However, choice B is also incorrect because it is not physically possible to obtain 0.4 of a bag. Therefore, one should round up to 7. **Objective 0014**

48. **A**

The survival of the fittest (B) or the conservation efforts (C) are not addressed in the scenario. Choice D is a very simplistic answer, and it does not address the main purpose of the lesson. **Objective 0020**

49. **D**

The traditional states of matter found in the Earth are liquid, solid, and gas. In space, the most common form of mass is plasma. Plasma cannot be identified as a solid, liquid, or gas; thus, this new classification was created to describe it. **Objective 0020**

50. **C**

The Earth's $23\frac{1}{2}$-degree tilt causes the seasons, and in winter in the Northern Hemisphere, the Earth is tilted away from the sun along its north pole. **Objective 0013**

51. **D**

The introduction of sight words can expedite students' decoding skills and it can also help develop fluency among early readers. From the options presented, the only word that is not in the Dolch's list is choice D, *awesome*. **Objective 0003**

52. **B**

Using the F.O.I.L. method, we know that there should be more than two terms in the resulting expansion. Therefore, we may eliminate selections A and D. After expansion, we realize that choice B is correct. **Objective 0014**

53. **B**

Mercury is one substance that reacts to heat, which facilitates its measuring. Mercury is available throughout the world (A), but that is not the main reason why the substance is used in thermometers. (The U.S. stopped mining it in the 1990s.) Mercury is not a volatile substance (C). Choice D is highly irrelevant. In the past, the U.S. Department of Energy did not regulate the use of mercury, but it has regulated it since 2008. **Objective 0020**

54. **A**

The *less than* symbol resembles an "alligator mouth" opening and moving away from the smaller number. "It is also helpful to notice that the smaller end in the sign will always point to the smaller number ($5 < 7$). Choice A is the correct answer because it correctly states that: 5 is less than 7. Choice B is incorrect because it incorrectly states that the number 10 is greater than 11. Choices C and D are eliminated because both contain an extra line representing the concept of "equal to"; thus, the symbol in choice C incorrectly states that "9 is less than or equal to 8" and choice D states than "3 is greater than or equal to 5." **Objective 0014**

55. **D**

Microwaves use a form of radiation to cook meals. Refrigerators and gas stoves do not use radiation to function. Radios use electromagnetic waves to transmit sound. **Objective 0020**

56. **B**

Water cools down and heats up more slowly than any substance on Earth. Therefore, in the winter the average low temperature would be warmer in New York City—a coastal city, than it would be in Nebraska. The warm water (warmed from summer's sun and heat) keeps the air over the water warm and moving toward the city for a longer period of time than the air inland. **Objective 0010**

57. **B**

Cell phones emit a type of radiation that some studies suggest may slightly increase risks for certain types of brain tumors. Current research suggests that heavy, long-term cell phone usage may be linked to infertility among men. Choices A and C are incorrect because they present non-medical effects attributed to cell phone usage. **Objective 0022**

58. **B**

Fossil fuels like natural gas, coal, and oil come from the remains of living matter, and by definition, they are nonrenewable resources. **Objective 0019**

59. **A**

Bears add fatty tissue to their body in preparation for hibernation during the winter months. Hibernation is a survival mechanism and a system of adaption to avoid starvation during the winter months. It is highly improbable that hibernation is done to avoid competition with other animals (B), to maintain a healthy ecosystem (C), or to prevent the movement of animals to residential areas (D). **Objective 0021**

60. **D**

An algorithm is a step-by-step procedure for solving problems. Although algorithms are often implemented using computers and can be used to evaluate students (A), this does not give the fundamental property of an algorithm. Choices B and C are not appropriate answers for the definition of an algorithm, although they may be true. Therefore, choice D is the correct answer. **Objective 0013**

61. **A**

Asteroids, planets, moons, and comets are all objects in the solar system. Black holes and quasars are theorized objects in distant galaxies, and the Milky Way is the name of our own cluster of stars or galaxy in which the solar system (sun, planets, dwarf planets, comets, asteroids, and meteoroids) reside. **Objective 0019**

62. **D**

In trying to convince the reader of something, posing a question relating to reasons why the argument might be convincing will help the writer to see the reader's point of view. In narrative writing, expository writing, and descriptive writing, the need to convince may be present; however, it is more essential in the very nature of persuasive writing. **Objective 0006**

63. **A**

Recalling that exponential notation is used when numbers are multiplied by themselves numerous times, we may try to simplify the expression. Choice B is not correct because this implies 3 is multiplied by itself 4 times. Choices C and D are the same answer in different representations, but both are incorrect. Since 4 is multiplied by itself 3 times in this problem, we know it should be A. **Objective 0004**

64. **B**

When the tectonic plates collapse, they can create mountains and mountain ranges. The movement of underground water (A) does not have an effect on the formation of the mountains. Erosion (C) refers to the movement of sediment from one location to the other; however, this movement cannot account for the formation of mountains. The effect of the moon on tides (D) does not have a direct effect on the formation of mountains. **Objective 0019**

65. **D**

Telling the students the mode of writing is likely not sufficient to support students' understanding of writing for an audience (D). Revising a piece of writing based on feedback provided from the audience (B), and asking students to role play and react to it can guide children to adjust the writing (A). Choice C helps students internalize that a specific audience will be reading their paper and that they need to develop the writing accordingly. **Objective 0006**

66. **C**

While students implementing all of these project ideas may need to use visual materials to complement their message, students considering implementing choices A, B, and D would actually not be involved in selecting these for a specific audience, as is the case in choice C. Moreover, none of these three options provides specific information to identify the audience, thus they will not be the best options. **Objective 0008**

67. **C**

The words *butterfly*, *nightmare*, and *brainstorm* may confuse students because they do not provide a reliable point of view to comprehend their meaning. Choices A, B, and D are incorrect because they contain information to help children in the comprehension process. Words like *doghouse*, *underground*, and *mouthwash* provide clear indications of the intended meaning. **Objective 0003**

68. **B**

Informative writing is also known as expository writing. The purpose of expository writing is to explain and clarify ideas. Choice A focuses on text that is more "storylike" and is often told from a first-person or third-person perspective about an account or series of events. Choice C is more often associated with narrative text, poetry, and advertising than informational text per se. Choice D primarily aims to convince the reader of something and provides arguments and counterarguments instead of mainly writing for the purpose of informing. **Objective 0006**

69. **A**

Sketching a character is developmentally appropriate for students in first grade for viewing and representing and involves creating a visual depiction of a character that can then be discussed. Choices B, C, and D are more appropriate activities for students in grades 3–6. **Objective 0005**

70. **A**

There are many ways to approach this problem. One way is to realize that there are 14 days in a two-week period. Then, take the amount of money Max spent on lunch ($71.47) and divide this by 14. However, this may result in a messy solution when all we need is an approximation. Instead, try to find a number that, when multiplied by 14, gets you pretty close to the total Max spent. In this case, if $5 is selected, this will approximate an expense of $70 over the two-week period. **Objective 0014**

71. **C**

The question addresses the basic understanding of the Kodály rhythm syllables. The two syllables included in this example are *ta*, which would be notated as a quarter note on the staff, and *ti*, which would be notated as an eighth note on the staff. If a person were to keep the beat and sing the song *Twinkle, Twinkle Little Star*, it should be apparent that the answer is choice C. Choices A and B begin with the wrong note (*ta*), and choice D ends with the wrong note (*ti*). **Objective 0024**

72. **B**

Mr. Lee is modeling conventional use of punctuation. By thinking aloud he is making his own knowledge about conventions explicit and thereby scaffolding the understanding of his students. The students know they will also be expected to use the same conventions in their own writing. Choices A, C, and, D focus less on mechanical conventions and writing and focus more on the writing and composing process itself in terms of selecting ideas and organizing them into a coherent piece of writing. **Objective 0007**

73. **D**

If a teacher notices abuse or neglect of a child, he/she should calmly and immediately report it to the proper authorities at the school (i.e., principal or assistant principal). Although choices A and C may appear to be natural for humanistic educators, it is not a good course of action for a variety of reasons. One, the teacher is not trained in the field(s) of counseling or psychology. Two, the teacher will not be as familiar or knowledgeable with the leadership policies and procedures regarding abuse as the principal. Or, three, the teacher no longer remains anonymous and/or protected by the school district in case of legal issues. Choice B is not an option as the teacher has a legal responsibility to advocate for (act on behalf of) the child and to report the case to the appropriate authorities. **Objective 0022**

74. **C**

The use of pictures to represent events in the story can be used to represent the sequencing of events in the story. It can also be used to introduce visually the parts of the story, i.e., characters, setting, plot, climax, and resolution. A is incorrect because the teacher is not connecting directly the pictures with the written text and the appropriate pronunciation. Teachers can fill in the background knowledge of the students through visuals (B); however, this activity is usually done as a pre-reading activity. Since the visuals were used as a post-reading activity, we can believe that filling the gaps was not the primary purpose of the activity. The teacher is definitely using developmentally appropriate practices (D), but the real intent of the activity goes beyond that. **Objective 0005**

75. **B**

Volcanoes, especially those underwater, can cause tsunamis or tidal waves. Volcanoes can indeed cause death (A); however, it is not an automatic occurrence. Volcanic eruptions happen continuously without human casualties. Moreover, early evacuation can prevent human casualties. The development of hurricanes (C) and tornados (D) is not linked to volcanic activity. **Objective 0019**

76. **A**

Jim Crow laws enforced strict separation in the South. Segregation rules restricted blacks to separate facilities in public places such as theaters, restaurants, buses, restrooms, and schools. Choices B, C, and D are incorrect because in other parts of the country this separation was not law. **Objective 0009**

77. **A**

When children overgeneralize like in the example—*bestest*—they are in reality applying grammar rules which indicate that they have passed the stage of mere repetition, and they are beginning to decipher the grammar of the language. This overgeneralization is typical of English native speakers acquiring a language, and does not show any kind of interference from a language. This statement eliminates choices B and C. Choice D is incorrect but it can be confusing because cartoons such as "Rugrats" often use this kind of overgeneralization to mimic the speech of children; however, the continuous overgeneralization typical of children cannot be attributed to cartoons on television. **Objective 0007**

78. **D**

The Andes and the Amazon River are geographical barriers that separate the many ethnic groups in Central and South America. **Objective 0010**

79. **A**

Sedentary lifestyle behavior is a primary risk factor for heart disease as well as other preventable diseases. Choices B, C, and D are not directly caused by inactivity. **Objective 0022**

80. **B**

When children change declarative sentences to questions or exclamations, they have to change the intonation pattern of the language. Choice A is incorrect because sentence transformations are not designed to teach listening skills. Choice C is incorrect because there is no connection between the linguistic transformation requested and teaching singing and music. Conducting sentence transformation can be an enjoyable activity; however, making the class more enjoyable is just a derivative of the process. Therefore, Choice D is incorrect. **Objective 0004**

81. **A**

Metacognition encompasses being aware and self-regulating one's own thinking as comprehension takes place. Self-monitoring, or stopping to self-assess and check one's own understanding is most related to metacognition. Choices B, C, and D focus on reading skills that are important to comprehension; however, they are not directly related to self-monitoring. **Objective 0004**

82. **D**

The year is calculated based on the time needed for the planet to go around the sun (revolution), and the distance from the Sun determines the length of the year. Since Mercury is the closes planet to the Sun, it takes shorter time to complete the revolution. **Objective 0019**

83. **C**

The amount of gas determines how violent the eruption can be. When the accumulation of gas reaches its peak, violent explosions can occur. The amount of magma inside the Earth (A) is a contributing factor, but not the primary factor. Choice B is incorrect because technically, there is no lava inside the Earth. The term *lava* is used to describe when the magma reaches the surface and becomes solid creating volcanic rocks. The number of faults in the area (D) can contribute to eruptions, but it cannot explain why some eruptions are more violent than others. **Objective 0019**

84. **D**

In this problem we are not concerned with negative or positive results because we are only asked about the relative difference between the two temperatures. So, the difference between 375° and 50° is 325°. **Objective 0014**

85. **A**

Plants take energy from sunlight and convert it to produce chemical energy. Through the process of cellular respiration, this type of energy in converted into ATP—the type of fuel used by living things. As part of the process of photosynthesis, plants take carbon dioxide (B) from the environment and convert it into oxygen (D). Thus, these two elements are part of the process, not the final product. Plants contain a pigment called chlorophyll (C), which also plays a role but does not constitute the product of photosynthesis. **Objective 0020**

86. **A**

A full moon occurs 12 months a year. Because the year contains about eleven extra days, these days accumulate in such a way that every two or three years, we have an extra full moon a year. This extra full moon is called a blue moon. Choice B is incorrect because a blue moon does not necessarily precede a lunar eclipse. Choices C and D are incorrect because they do not provide a scientific explanation for the saying. In choice C, the idiomatic expression makes reference to a strange rare event in general. Choice D incorrectly links this expression to another idiomatic expression that links the color blue with sadness. **Objective 0019**

87. **C**

   The Pledge of Allegiance is a declaration of patriotism. It was first published in 1892 in *The Youth's Companion*, and was believed to be written by the magazine's editor, Francis Bellamy. The original purpose was for the pledge to be used by school-children in activities to celebrate the 400th anniversary of the discovery of America. The Pledge was widely used in morning school routines for many years and received official recognition by Congress on 1942. In 1954 the phrase "under God" was added with a law to indicate the proper behavior when reciting the pledge, which includes standing straight, removing hats or any other headgear, and placing the right hand over the heart. Choices A, B, and D are incorrect because while they are all American patriotic national symbols, choice C is an actual declaration of patriotism. Therefore, choice C is a better answer. **Objective 0011**

88. **B**

   In the wake of World War II, civil rights issues came to the forefront. In *Brown v. Board of Education of Topeka* (1954), Thurgood Marshall, a lawyer for the National Association for the Advancement of Colored People, challenged the doctrine of "separate but equal." The Court stated that separate educational facilities were unequal. In 1955, the court ordered states to integrate "with all deliberate speed." So choice B is the correct answer. There is no organization named The Civil Rights Organization, choice A or an organization called the The Civil Rights Leadership Organization, choice C. So, neither of those choices is correct. The Southern Christian Leadership Conference, choice D, is famous as the organization founded by Reverend Martin Luther King, Jr., but was not responsible for bringing the suit against the Board of Education of Topeka, Kansas. **Objective 0011**

89. **C**

   Stacking cups, dribbling a small ball, and tapping their foot to the rhythm, as well as dressing themselves require children to master fine motor skills. Based on this explanation, choice A is incorrect because gross motor skills include the use of large muscle groups in the body to perform big movements like running. Choice B is a plausible answer but it is too generic in nature and does not address the question. Choice D also is incorrect because all of the skills outlined in the question should be achievable long before any transition into adulthood. **Objective 0014**

90. **D**

   This problem can be solved by converting the decimal to a fraction, or the fraction to a decimal and then subtracting. If the decimal is converted to a fraction, 1.6

becomes $1\dfrac{6}{10}$. In order to subtract, we should now get a common denominator. The lowest common denominator between 8 and 5 is 40. Therefore, the problem becomes $1\dfrac{24}{40} - \dfrac{15}{40} = \dfrac{19}{140}$. **Objective 0015**

91. **D**

In any triangle, the sum of the angles must equal 180°. If a triangle has two equal sides, the triangle cannot be scalene. The lines associated with the equal sides will intersect the third side at the same angle. Therefore, the only answer that can be determined to be true from the information is choice D. **Objective 0010**

92. **D**

A world region is an area of the world that shares similar, unifying cultural or physical characteristics that are different from those of surrounding areas. Choice A is incorrect because topographical characteristics like elevation, rivers, and mountains are part of the unifying elements of a world region but not the only ones. Choices B and C present partial descriptions of a region, but fail to capture all the elements linked to the concept of a region. **Objective 0011**

93. **D**

The Fourteenth Amendment declared that all persons born in the U.S. were citizens, that all citizens were entitled to equal rights, and that their rights were protected by due process. The amendment, however, excludes Native Americans. Choices A and B are incorrect because while blacks and women did not enjoy the benefits of full equal rights, such as voting rights, until later on; the amendment did not specifically exclude them. Choice C is incorrect because the rights of children were not mentioned in the amendment. **Objective 0010**

94. **D**

These divisions are based on physical and cultural similarities. Choices A, B, and C are partial answers, but individually they do not constitute an appropriate answer. **Objective 0023**

95. **A**

Locomotor skills are general movement skills done through space (i.e., skipping, running, jumping, etc.). To increase the challenge when practicing these skills, a physical education teacher would instruct learners to perform them via different directions, levels, and pathways. Choices B, C, and D have nothing to do with performing locomotor movements. **Objective 0009**

96. **D**

Dr. Martin Luther King Jr.'s famous *I Have a Dream* speech took place during the march in Washington in support of the Civil Rights Act of 1964. The eloquent speech and orderly demonstration gained more supporters for the cause. He was assassinated in 1968 in Memphis, Tennessee, but his work resulted in the Civil Rights Act in 1964. Choice A is incorrect because the speech did not prompt a riot. Choice B is incorrect because the Montgomery Improvement Association was formed after Rosa Parks refused to give up her seat on a bus in 1955. Choice C is incorrect because the speech did not result in a loss of supporters. **Objective 0015**

97. **C**

While all of these units will accurately express the length of the football field, centimeters and inches would not be a convenient scale to use, as the resolution of the measurement would be too great, resulting in an extremely large number (or a long time to measure). Miles is another inconvenient method to measure a football field, as a mile is much larger than a single football field. **Objective 0007**

98. **C**

The three sentences can be combined with appropriate connectors to avoid repetitions. In this particular case, the conjunctions can be used to create compound sentences. Sentence 3 shows faulty agreement, which suggests that the child can also benefit from this kind of instructional support. Choices A and B are incorrect because the writing sample does not show problems with spelling or the use of active and passive voices. Choice D is incorrect because the writing sample does not show problems with capitalization and punctuation. **Objective 0011**

99. **C**

Although A and D are largely necessary for aerobic kinds of activity, it is the cardiovascular system that works the hardest to support and sustain the energy and oxygen necessary for continuous activity (via blood circulation). Choice B is not directly relevant to aerobic activity. **Objective 0023**

100. **A**

The Civil Rights Act of 1964 prohibited segregation in all public facilities and discrimination in education and employment. President John F. Kennedy had proposed new civil rights laws as well as programs to help the millions of Americans living in poverty. After his assassination in Dallas in 1963, President Lyndon B. Johnson urged Congress to pass the Civil Rights Act in honor of Kennedy, persuading the majority of Democrats and some Republicans. Choices B, C, and D are incorrect because these were important aspects of the Act but not the name of the Act. **Objective 0020**

101. **B**

In minimal pairs, students are required to identify whether two sets of words are different or the same based on the phoneme sequence contained in each word. For example, the words *vine* and *fine* are different because they differ in at least one phoneme, i.e., the /v/ and /f/. Choice A is incorrect because morphology is not taken into account when comparing the two words. Choice C is incorrect because there is no connection between minimal pairs and syntax. Choice D is incorrect because lexicon deals with vocabulary development, and minimal pairs attempt to test whether children can understand how phonemes change the meaning of the words. **Objective 0015**

102. **B**

The melting of the ice caps represents a physical change. It changes from solid to liquid, and it can revert to solid again. There are no chemical changes (A) or chemical reactions (C) when the ice turns into liquid, because the chemical composition of the liquid (water) remains unchanged. Ice melting occurs every summer, but the rate of melting of the last decade has surpassed previous years; thus, we cannot say that it is a natural yearly process (D). **Objective 0015**

103. **B**

Remembering that a face is a plain region of a geometric body, one can determine that since there are six sides to a cube, there are also six faces. **Objective 0021**

104. **C**

This problem deals with finding the perimeter of the rectangle. Since the two short legs of the fence have the same length and the two long legs have the same length, we know $P = 2l + 2w$. This gives us a value of $2 \cdot 223 + 2 \cdot 467 = 1380$ ft. **Objective 0015**

105. **B**

Cold-blooded animals, like snakes and turtles, get their heat from solar energy. **Objective 00**

106. D

Recall that the Face (F) of a cube is a plain region of a geometric body, the Edge (E) is a line segment where two faces of a three-dimensional figure meet, and a Vertex (V) is the union of two segments or the point of intersection of two sides of a polygon. Knowing this we can see that for a cube there are 6 faces, 8 vertices, and 12 edges. Substituting these numbers into the appropriate spot in each formula allows us to determine choice D as the only correct answer. **Objective 0024**

107. B

Developmentally speaking, children in elementary school do not have the strength or the ability to play with official basketball equipment (i.e., basketballs and baskets). Therefore, the only way to give a basketball lesson would be to modify the types of balls used (i.e., lighter and smaller) and lower the baskets so the students can be successful with the game. Choice A does not apply because few children at that level understand the strategy of the game. Choice C is partly correct in that you would teach the foul shot before the jump shot for developmental progression reasons, although not enough information is given that the shots have been modified for elementary students. Choice D is incorrect for the same reasons as above. **Objective 0008**

108. A

Artists use the principles of art to create and communicate through their artwork. Choice B is incorrect because it describes the *elements of art*, as opposed to the principles of art. Choice C is incorrect because subjects are communicated through art. Choice D is incorrect because there are several different artistic concepts presented in the standards for kindergarten through grade 6. **Objective 0015**

109. C

Integrated thematic units are organized around a common theme. Thus, the lesson can contain basic mathematics objectives in conjunction with science and social studies concepts. Choice A is incorrect because thematic instruction does not require the introduction of literacy skills in a sequential fashion. Choice B is too limited in scope; it addresses only one of the possible topics that can be covered in thematic instruction. Choice D is also too limited in scope, because thematic instruction can be delivered in both ways—inductively (from the specific to the general) or deductively (general to specific). **Objective 0013**

110. **D**

      This problem involves a number pattern. With each shelf, the number of loaves increases by three. Therefore, the best way to solve the problem is to determine the pattern and use it to find the number of loaves on the 5th shelf. **Objective 0001**

111. **C**

      This question deals with reading development. Children in the emergent stage of reading development should use environmental print to make connections between written language and the things they represent. The correct answer is C. **Objective 0001**

112. **D**

      This question relates to phonological awareness. Sound/symbol relationship is phonics, a word identification skill. The correct answer is D. **Objective 0001**

113. **A**

      This question relates to phonemic awareness. Phonemic awareness focuses on speech sounds in our language. Sound/symbol relationship is phonics, a word identification skill. The correct answer is A. **Objective 0001**

114. **D**

      This question relates to the components of phonemic awareness. Phonemic awareness has 2 aspects: the knowledge that spoken words are made up of individual sounds and the ability to manipulate spoken sounds. **Objective 0001**

115. **B**

      This question relates to teaching phonemic awareness. Phonemic awareness focuses on speech sounds in our oral language. It does not focus on matching speech sounds with written symbols. **Objective 0001**

116. **C**

      In one-syllable words, the rime is the vowel and any consonant sounds that follow it. In the word *bright*, the rime is made up of the letters *–ight*. The correct answer is C. **Objective 0001**

117. C

The letter E has a horizontal line of symmetry. The letter A has a vertical line of symmetry. The correct answer is C. **Objective 0001**

118. D

If the paper is folded along the dotted line, a triangle with one right angle will be formed. The answer is D. **Objective 0015**

119. D

If Kathleen uses 50 raisins in her cookies, she would use 100 chocolate chips. Ten fewer marshmallows would be 90 marshmallows. The answer is D. **Objective 0013**

120. A

To find the prime factorization of a number, we must break the number down into its prime components. Prime numbers are divisible only by 1 and that number. The answer is A. **Objective 0014**

Sample Answer for Constructed Response 1:

Solution: This problem involves two steps. First, the student needed to find out how much money was spent. Second, the student needed to subtract that sum from the original amount of $3.00 to determine what was left over. The first step involves addition with no regrouping. The second step involves subtraction with borrowing. In addition, students must also be able to identify the information needed from the table and record it accurately during problem solving.

The student correctly recorded the prices of the two items from the list, $1.30 and $1.55, and added them together, for a total of $2.85. This simple addition problem involved no regrouping. The student also correctly set up the subtraction problem for the second step, showing $3.00 as the original sum and $2.85 as the amount to subtract to find the difference. However, an error was made in the subtraction process. The student correctly borrowed from the tens place in order to subtract five from ten in the ones place. The student also correctly borrowed from the hundreds place, making the "3" a "2." However, when borrowing from the tens place, the number of tens remaining should have been nine. Eight subtracted from nine would be 1, which would result in the correct answer of $0.15.

Sample Answer for Constructed Response 2:

For Demetrius to read this text at an independent level, he needs better word identification skills and better acquaintance with the passage's genre.

If he does not know the meaning of the word "obviously," he not only misses a clue about Jake's personality, but he also goes into decoding mode, which prevents him from enjoying the text and from making connections between the text and other experiences.

Although Demetrius has two major word identification problems—decoding words phonologically and simply not having a sufficient vocabulary to read this passage—the inability I will concentrate on here is the insufficient vocabulary. Two of the words Demetrius had trouble with—"obviously" and "resist"—should be in a fifth grader's vocabulary, and they both follow somewhat unusual phonological models.

Even with better skills in this area, however, Demetrius will still have trouble with comprehension. This passage appears to be from a science fiction book, and he definitely seems unfamiliar with the genre. Thus, his first response to Mrs. Whalen's question concerning what the passage is about is Jake's affinity for video games, which may be the only thing Demetrius grasps well about the passage. When asked what else he knows about Jake, he concentrates on Jake's trouble rather than the trouble for the human race, probably because Demetrius is more accustomed to reading books in which individuals are in trouble of their own (or maybe he's just used to being "in trouble" himself).

Both strategies that Mrs. Whalen should try could be done on either an individual basis just with Demetrius or on a class-wide (or small-group) basis, depending on how many other readers in the class are at Demetrius's level. The first strategy, to increase his vocabulary, is to work with the student(s) to analyze new and unfamiliar words in all their reading. Assuming Demetrius will be worked with on an individual basis, he should read a book that is at his current instructional level (that is he can read it independently). He should make word lists of the words that he is unfamiliar with. He should define them and try to think of (or find) other words that have similar phonemes. For instance, his words and their phonemic analogies in this passage might be "obviously ↔ previously" and "resist ↔ insist." He may need help finding meanings or analogies, so Mrs. Whalen should have occasional short conferences with him to assess whether the word lists and their analogies are useful or even possible. This strategy will theoretically increase the number of words he knows and his ability to decipher unfamiliar words as well.

A second strategy is one that Mrs. Whalen would probably want to do with the whole class, and that would be to introduce the science fiction genre. Surely many students in the class will be acquainted with science fiction at least through movies and television shows, and they will be able to list a number of standard science fiction plots. Mrs. Whalen should diagram some of these plots on a board or overhead so that students will know what to expect as they read science fiction—for example, that big matters such as human survival are often at stake.

Demetrius already shows that he can make connections between what he reads and his own life, but his connections are flawed because he relies too much on his own life and too little on the text. By learning better word-recognition strategies and by recognizing conventions of the genre he is reading, he can raise his comprehension to a higher level.

Sample Answer for Constructed Response 3:

Three tools that students could use to measure or predict the weather include a thermometer, which is used to measure air temperature, an anemometer, which is used to measure wind speed, and a wind vane, which is used to determine the direction of the wind.

A relevant scientific concept relating to earth's processes is the water cycle. Students need to understand the water cycle in order to recognize why we have precipitation. The water cycle is the continuous movement of water on, above, and below the earth's surface. The sun heats water in the oceans. Some the water evaporates into the air. The vapor rises into the air, where it cools and condenses into clouds. As air currents move clouds around the earth, the air particles collide, grow, and fall out of the sky as precipitation.

Sample Answer for Constructed Response 4:

England used the system of mercantilism quite effectively in the thirteen colonies, but after more than a century of British rule, the colonies were primed for independence, and war with England became inevitable.

Another reason for the rebellion was the cost of the French and Indian War. This war emptied the British coffers, and the British Crown needed a quick way to recover financially. The taxation that followed the French and Indian War was unbearable for the colonies. The colonies responded with civil disobedience and by boycotting the government of King George. There was civil disobedience and the British sent troops to Boston, where the groups clashed and several colonists were killed. This was called the Boston Massacre. Another boycott was the Boston Tea Party. The colonists dumped tea in the Boston harbor to protest against taxation. All of these events and the repression that followed led to the American War of Independence.

Index

A

Adjectives, 48
Adverbs, 48
Affixes, 22
Africa, 85, 91
   art history of, 221
African Americans
   slavery, 73–74
   slave trade, 68
Algebraic expressions, 145–146
Amendments to Constitution, 113
American Revolution, 68–69
Americas
   early civilization in, 66
Ancient times, 85
   art during, 217
Anticipation guides, 39
Antonyms, 26
Apostrophe, 52
Art concepts
   dance, 235–243
   drama, 231–235
   elements of art, 212–213
   evaluating works of art, 221–222
   historical periods of art, 217–220
   identifying characteristics of style in
      art, 216–220
   integration of art into content areas,
      221
   music education, 222–231
   in other cultures, 220–221
   principles of art, 213–215
   visual art activities for K-5,
      215–216
   visual arts, 211–212
Articles of Confederation, 71

Arts. *See* Art concepts; Health,
   Physical Education, and the Arts
Associative Law, 134–135
Autobiographies, 40

B

Baroque style, 218
Bill of Rights, 112
Biographies, 40
Black Death, 87
Bourbon Triumvirate, 63
Buddhism
   in China, 84, 220
   in India, 84
Bush, George, W, 79–80
Bush, George H. W., 78–79
Byzantine Empire, 83

C

Calvin, John, 88
Camp David Accords, 78
Capitalization, 50
Carter, Jimmy, 64, 78
Castro, Fidel, 76
Catholicism
   Reformation and, 88–89
Charlemagne, 86
Children's literature, 39–41
China
   art history of, 220
   Buddhism and, 84
   Confucius and, 84
Chinese Exclusion Act, 74
Circulatory system, 191
Civil Rights Act, 64, 76–77

Civil War, 72–73
Classical Age, 82
   art during, 217
Cold War, 76
Commas, 50–52
Common nouns, 47
Commutative Law, 134
Compare-and-contrast chart, 38
Compound words, 23
Comprehension, reading
   fluency and, 30–31
   levels of, 31–34
   for literary and informational text,
      35–41
   strategies for, 33–35
Confucius, 84
Congress, 102–104
Congruence, 142–143
Conjunction, 48
Constitution, U.S., 69–70
   Amendments to, 112–113
   Bill of Rights, 112
Contemporary realistic fiction, 40
Context clues, 28
Contractions, 23
Coordinate system, 143
Crusades, 87
Cuban Missile Crisis, 76

D

Dance education
   beauty and aesthetics of, 238
   body as medium, 241
   in classroom and across curriculum,
      242–243
   as creative pursuit, 241

cultural values of, 236
dance content, 242
elements of, 235–236
folk dances from around the world, 238–239
gender roles and, 237
as performing art, 239–241
religion and, 236–237
roles of dance, 236
as social activity, 238
social dances of Western cultures, 239
Data analysis
in mathematics, 146–149
in science, 167–168
Decimal calculations, 137
Declaration of Independence, 106–107
Developmental stages of writing, 41–42
Dictionaries, 28–29
Digestive system, 191
Direct measurement, 138–139
Disease prevention, 196–197
Distributive Law, 135
Drafting, 44
Drama education
activities for, 232–234
benefits of, 234–235
elements of drama, 231–232

E

Earth
composition of, 171–172
processes of, 172–173
Earth Science concepts, 169–173
Economics, 109–114
basic concepts of, 110–111
business, bank and government functions in, 113
consumer and producer interactions, 112
Federal Reserve Bank, 111, 113
free enterprise, 111–112
macroeconomics, 113
references for, 114–115
research strategies for, 114

responsible financial decisions, 113–114
structure of U.S. economy, 111–112
Editing, 45–46
Egypt, 81
Eisenhower, Dwight D., 75
Electricity, 176
End marks, 50
Energy, 175–178
Enlightenment, 67–68, 89
Environmental interactions, 180–181
Equivalent forms, 130–131
Estimation, 138
Europe
Medieval times, 85–87
Evaluative level of comprehension, 33
Executive Branch, 104–105
Expository text structures, 36–37

F

Fables, 39
Federal Reserve Bank, 111, 113
First Great Awakening, 67
Fluency, reading, 29–35
Folktales, 39
Food pyramid, 195–196
Fossils, 173
Fraction calculation, 137
Francem 69, 75, 85, 86–87
Freedmen, 63
Free enterprise, 111–112

G

GACE Early Childhood Education test
administration of test, 6–7
objectives for, 4–5
purpose, 2–3
receiving scores, 6
registration fee for, 7
retaking test, 6
scoring of test, 3
study tips for, 7–10
test sessions, 2
test sessions for, 2
test-taking tips for, 10–14
types of questions on, 10

when to take, 7
Genghis Khan, 83
Geographic concepts, 94–100
human-environmental interaction, 95
interaction of physical systems and human systems, 96–98
location, 95
major physical and human-constructed features, 96
map knowledge, 98–99
movement and connection, 95
place, 94
regions, patterns, and processes, 95–96
research strategies for, 99–100
Geometric concepts, 142–143
Geometric figures, 140–142
Georgia history, 61–64
Georgia Professional Standards Commission, 6
Glorious Revolution, 67–68
Government and civics, 100–109
Congress, 102–104
Declaration of Independence, 106–107
Executive Branch, 104–105
function of government, 100
Judicial Branch, 105
Legislative branch, 102–104
President, 104–105
research strategies for, 109
rights and responsibilities of citizenship, 108–109
roles and interrelationships of national, state and local government, 101–102
U. S. Constitution, 106–108
U.S. government as republic, 101
Graffiti, 220
Grammar, usage and mechanics, 47–52
adjectives and adverbs, 48
apostrophe, 52
capitalization, 50
commas, 50–52
end marks, 50
nouns and pronouns, 47–48

prepositions, 48
punctuation, 50–52
quotation marks, 51–52
sentence structure and types, 49–50
verbs, 48–49
Grant, Ulysses S., 73
Graphic cues, 31
Graphic organizers, 38–39
Graphs
  data analysis, 146–149
Great Awakening, 67
Great Depression, 75
Greece
  Classical Age, 82
  Rome, 82–83

H

Haiku, 41
Harmonic instruments, 228
Harmony, 224
Health, Physical Education, and the
  Arts, 189–244
  art concepts
    dance, 235–243
    drama, 231–235
    elements of art, 212–213
    evaluating works of art, 221–222
    historical periods of art,
      217–220
    identifying characteristics of
      style in art, 216–220
    integration of art into content
      areas, 221
    music education, 222–231
    in other cultures, 220–221
    principles of art`, 213–215
    visual art activities for K-5,
      215–216
    visual arts, 211–212
  health and safety
    disease prevention, 196–197
    healthy interpersonal
      relationships, 197–198
    human body systems, 190–192
    human growth and development,
      192–194
    nutrition and exercise, 194–196

stress management, 198–199
substance use and abuse,
  199–200
objectives for, 5, 189–190
physical education
  adaptive physical education, 210
  benefits of active lifestyle,
    203–204
  development of motor skills,
    204–206
  managing instruction, 208–210
  National Standards for Physical
    Education, 201–202
  principles of, 201–203
  promoting physical fitness,
    206–208
  references, 243–244
Hebrews
  Palestine and, 82
Hellenistic period, 217
Heredity, 179–180
Historical fiction, 40
History
  of Georgia, 61–64
  of United States, 65–80
  of world, 80–91
Hitler, Adolf, 75
Holy Roman Empire, 86–87
Homographic homophones, 27
Homographs, 27
Homonyms, 26
Homophones, 27
House of Representatives, 102–104
Human body systems, 190–192
Human-environmental interaction, 95
Human growth and development,
  192–194

I

Identity Properties, 136
Immigration, 74
Immune system, 191–192
Inca, 85
India
  Buddhism and, 84
Indian Removal Act, 72
Indirect measurement, 138–139

Industrialism, 74
Industrial Revolution, 90–91
Inflectional endings, 22
Informational text, 36–37, 40
Informational writing, 43
Instruments in music education, 228
Interpretive level of comprehension, 32
Intolerable Acts, 68
Islam
  Islamic civilization in Middle Ages,
    83

J

Jamestown, 66
Japan
  feudalism, 83–84
Jefferson, Thomas, 105
Judicial Branch, 105

K

Kennedy, John F., 64, 76
King, Martin Luther, Jr., 64, 76, 77
K-W-L chart, 38

L

Lee, Robert E., 73
Legends, 40
Legislative branch, 102–104
Life cycles, 179–180
Life Science concepts, 178–181
Light, 176
Limericks, 40
Listening skills, 54–55
Literal level of comprehension, 32
Literary text structures, 36–39
Location, 95
Locke, John, 89
Locomotor skills, 205
Luther, Martin, 88
Lyric, 40

M

Macroeconomics, 113
Magna Carta, 87

Manifest destiny, 72
Manipulative skills, 206
Map knowledge, 98–99
Marx, Karl, 91
Marxism, 91
Mathematical arguments, 123–125
Mathematical communication, 125–126
Mathematical connections, 126–128
Mathematics, 119–159
    algebraic expressions, 145–146
    Algebra skills, 143–146
    Associative Law, 134–135
    Commutative Law, 134
    coordinate system, 143
    data analysis, 146–149
    Distributive Law, 135
    equivalent forms, 130–131
    estimation, 138
    geometric concepts, 142–143
    geometric figures, 140–142
    Identity Properties, 136
    mathematical arguments, 123–125
    mathematical communication, 125–126
    mathematical connections, 126–128
    measurement, 138–140
    number sense, 128–129
    objectives for, 5, 115–116, 119–120
    order of operations, 131–133
    patterns, 144–145
    place value, 129–130
    practice test, 151–159
    problem-solving strategies, 120–123
    properties, 134–136
    references, 159
    test-taking tips, 149–151
    whole number, decimal, fraction
        calculations, 137
Matter, properties of, 174–175
Measurement, 138–140
Mechanical energy, 177–178
Mechanics
    capitalization, 50
    commas, 50–52
    end marks, 50
    quotation marks, 51–52
Melodic instruments, 228
Melody, 223–224

Mesolithic Period, 81
Mesopotamia, 81
Meter, 223
Middle Ages, 83–87
    art during, 217–218
    Black Death, 87
    Crusades, 87
    Germanic state, 85–86
    Holy Roman Empire, 86–87
    Late Middle Ages, 87–89
    literature, art and scholarship, 87–88
    Magna Carta, 87
    Reformation, 88–89
Modern fantasy, 40
Mohammed, 83
Moore, Thomas, 91
Motor skills, 204–206
Movement and connection, 95
Multiple meaning words, 26
Music education, 222–231
    content areas and, 229
    elements of music, 223–226
    evaluating musical performance,
        229–231
    instruments in, 228
    music in classroom, 226
    terminology for, 222–223
    vocal performance, 226–227
Myths, 39

N

Narrative, 40
National Standards for Physical
    Education, 201–202
Native Americans
    art history of, 221
    Columbian Exchange, 92
    early interactions with early
        explorers, 92–93
    Indian Removal Act and, 72
    Trail of Tears, 72
Neolithic Period, 81
Nervous system, 192
New Conservatism, 78
New Deal, 75
Nineteenth-century art, 218–219
Nixon, Richard, 77

Nonlocomotor skills, 205–206
Nouns, 47–48
Number sense, 128–129
Nutrition, 194–196

O

Order of operations, 131–133
Obama, Barack, 80

P

Paleolithic Period, 80–81
Palestine, 82
Parks, Rosa, 76
Patterns, 144–145
Pearl Harbor, 75
Personal writing, 43
Persuasive writing, 44
Phonemic awareness, 19–21
Phonics, 21–24
Phonological awareness, 19–21
Photorealism, 220
Physical education
    adaptive physical education, 210
    benefits of active lifestyle, 203–204
    development of motor skills,
        204–206
    managing instruction, 208–210
    National Standards for Physical
        Education, 201–202
    principles of, 201–203
    promoting physical fitness, 206–208
Physical Science concepts, 174–178
Pitch, 223
Place, 94
Place value, 129–130
Poetry, 36, 44
Predicate, 49
Prefixes, 22
Prehistory, 80–81
    art during, 217
Prepositions, 48
President of United States, 104–105
Previewing strategy, 38
Prewriting, 44
Print knowledge, 18–19
Prior knowledge, 30–31

Problem-solving strategies, 120–123
Progressive Era, 63, 74
Pronouns, 48
Proper nouns, 47
Properties, mathematical, 134–136
Publishing, 46
Punctuation, 50–52

Q

Question-answer relationships, 33–34
Quotation marks, 51–52

R

Reading and English Language Arts
    children's literature, 39–41
    comprehension strategies for literary
      and informational text, 35–41
    developmental stages of writing,
      41–42
    evaluative level of comprehension, 33
    genres of writing, 42–44
    grammar, usage and mechanics,
      47–52
    interpretive level of comprehension,
      32
    literal level of comprehension, 32
    literary text structures, 36–39
    objectives for, 4, 15–16
    phonemic awareness, 19–21
    phonics, 21–24
    phonological awareness, 19–21
    print knowledge, 18–19
    reading and writing development,
      17–18
    reading fluency and comprehension,
      29–35
    reading stages, 17–18
    references for, 56–57
    speaking, listening and viewing
      skills, 52–56
    vocabulary knowledge and skill,
      25–29
    word identification, 24–25
    writing for various purposes, 41–47
    writing process, 44–47
Reagan, Ronald, 78

Reciprocal questioning, 33
Reconstruction Era, 73–74
Reformation, 88–89
Renaissance
    art during, 218
Research skills, 46–47
Respiratory system, 191
Response journal, 38
Revision, 44–45
Rhythm, 223
Rhythmic instruments, 228
Roman Empire, 83
Rome, 82–83
Roosevelt, Franklin D., 75

S

Scholasticism, 87
Science, 161–188
    classification and needs of living
      things, 178–179
    composition of Earth, 171–172
    data analysis, 167–168
    Earth processes, 172–173
    Earth Science concepts, 169–173
    electricity, 176
    energy, 175–178
    environmental interactions, 180–181
    fossils, 173
    heredity and life cycles, 179–180
    Life Science concepts, 178–181
    light, 176
    matter, properties of, 174–175
    mechanical energy, 177–178
    objectives for, 5, 157–158, 161–162
    Physical Science concepts, 174–178
    practice test, 184–188
    references, 188
    scientific connections, 169
    scientific inquiry principles,
      164–165
    scientific knowledge and values,
      162–164
    solar system and universe, 170–171
    sound, 176
    test-taking tips, 182–183
    unifying concepts of, 165–167
Scientific connections, 169

Scientific inquiry, 164–165
Scientific knowledge, 162–164
Scientific Revolution, 89
Semantic feature analysis, 37
Senate, 102–104
Sentence structure, 49–50
Similarity, 142–143
Skeletal system, 192
Sketch-to-sketch, 37
Skimming strategy, 38
Slavery
    Civil War and, 72–73
Slave trade, 66
Smith, John, 66
Socialism, 91
Social realism, 220
Social Studies, 59–115
    chronological relationships among
      historical events, 91
    economics, 109–114
    geography concepts, 94–100
    Georgia history, 61–64
    government and civics, 100–109
    historical inquiry skills, 93–94
    implications of events, 93
    objectives for, 4, 59–60
    references, 114–115
    United States history, 65–80, 92–93
    world history, 80–91
Solar system, 170–171
Sound, 176
Soviet Union, 75–76, 78
Speaking, 52–54
Spelling, developmental stages of, 42
Spelling patterns, 23–24
Stamp Act, 68
Stories, 36, 43
Story mapping activities, 37
Stress management, 198–199
Structural analysis, 22
Study tips
    basic tips for, 8–9
    how to study efficiently, 9
    study schedule for, 9
    when to start studying, 7
Subject, 49
Substance use and abuse, 199–200
Suffixes, 22

Sugar Act, 68
Syllabication, 23–24
Symmetry, 142–143
Synonyms, 26

T

Tempo, 222
Test-taking tips
    day of test, 11–13
    general tips, 10–11
    for mathematics portion, 149–151
    for science portion, 182–183
    during test, 13–14
Thesaurus, 28–29
Thirty Years' War, 89
Timbre, 226
Tone, 222
Traditional literature, 39–40
Trail of Tears, 72

U

United States history, 65–80
    American Revolution, 68–69
    Articles of Confederation, 69–70
    Bush, George, H. W., 78–79
    Bush, George, W, 79–80
    Carter and, 78
    colonization, 66
    Constitution, 70–71
    Enlightenment, 67–68
    explorers and settlements, 66
    first Americans, 65–66
    Great Awakening, 67
    Great Depression and New Deal, 75
    immigration, 74

Industrialism, World War I and
    Progressive Era, 74
    Kennedy's "New Frontier," Vietnam
    and social unrest, 76–77
    manifest destiny and westward
    expansion, 72
    Native Americans and Indian
    Removal Act, 72
    Native Americans' interactions with
    early explorers, 92–93
    New Conservatism, 78
    postwar, civil rights, Cold War,
    75–76
    Reconstruction era, 73–74
    slavery and Civil War, 72–73
    Slave trade, 66
    War of 1812, 71
    Watergate, 77–78
    World War II, 75
Universe, 170–171

V

Verbs, 48–49
Vietnam War, 77
Visual arts, 211–212
Vocabulary knowledge and skill, 25–29
Vocal performance, 226–227
Vowel patterns, 23–24

W

War of 1812, 71
Washington, George, 68–69
Watergate, 77–78
Westward expansion, 72
Whole number calculations, 137

Wilson, Woodrow, 74
Word identification, 24–25
World history, 80–91
    ancient times, 81–83
    French Revolution, 89–90
    Industrial Revolution, 90–91
    Late Middle Ages, 87–89
    Middle Ages, 83–87
    Napoleon, 90
    prehistory, 80–81
    Reformation, 88–89
    Scientific Revolution, 89
    Socialism, 91
World War I, 74
World War II, 75
Writing
    developmental stages of, 41–42
    drafting, 44
    editing, 45–46
    genres of, 42–44
    grammar, usage and mechanics,
    47–52
    informational, 43
    personal, 43
    persuasive, 44
    poetry, 44
    prewriting, 44
    process of, 44–47
    publishing, 46
    research skills and technology,
    46–47
    revision, 44–45
    spelling, stages of, 42
    stages of, 17–18
    stories, 43
    for various purposes, 41–47

REA's Test Preps

The Best in Test Preparation

- REA "Test Preps" are **far more** comprehensive than any other test preparation series
- Each book contains full-length practice tests based on the most recent exams
- **Every** type of question likely to be given on the exams is included
- Answers are accompanied by **full** and **detailed** explanations

REA publishes hundreds of test prep books. Some of our titles include:

Advanced Placement Exams (APs)
Art History
Biology
Calculus AB & BC
Chemistry
Economics
English Language & Composition
English Literature & Composition
European History
French Language
Government & Politics
Latin
Physics B & C
Psychology
Spanish Language
Statistics
United States History
World History

College-Level Examination Program (CLEP)
Analyzing and Interpreting Literature
College Algebra
Freshman College Composition
General Examinations
History of the United States I
History of the United States II
Introduction to Educational Psychology
Human Growth and Development
Introductory Psychology
Introductory Sociology
Principles of Management
Principles of Marketing
Spanish
Western Civilization I
Western Civilization II

SAT Subject Tests
Biology E/M
Chemistry
French
German
Literature
Mathematics Level 1, 2
Physics
Spanish
United States History

Graduate Record Exams (GREs)
Biology
Chemistry
Computer Science
General
Literature in English
Mathematics
Physics
Psychology

ACT - ACT Assessment
ASVAB - Armed Services Vocational Aptitude Battery
CBEST - California Basic Educational Skills Test
CDL - Commercial Driver License Exam
CLAST - College Level Academic Skills Test
COOP, HSPT & TACHS - Catholic High School Admission Tests
FE (EIT) - Fundamentals of Engineering Exams
FTCE - Florida Teacher Certification Examinations

GED
GMAT - Graduate Management Admission Test
LSAT - Law School Admission Test
MAT - Miller Analogies Test
MCAT - Medical College Admission Test
MTEL - Massachusetts Tests for Educator Licensure
NJ HSPA - New Jersey High School Proficiency Assessment
NYSTCE - New York State Teacher Certification Examinations
PRAXIS PLT - Principles of Learning & Teaching Tests
PRAXIS PPST - Pre-Professional Skills Tests
PSAT/NMSQT
SAT
TExES - Texas Examinations of Educator Standards
THEA - Texas Higher Education Assessment
TOEFL - Test of English as a Foreign Language
USMLE Steps 1,2,3 - U.S. Medical Licensing Exams

For information about any of REA's books, visit www.rea.com

Research & Education Association
61 Ethel Road W., Piscataway, NJ 08854
Phone: (732) 819-8880

Installing REA's TestWare®

SYSTEM REQUIREMENTS

Pentium 75 MHz (300 MHz recommended) or a higher or compatible processor; Microsoft Windows XP or later; 64 MB available RAM; Internet Explorer 5.5 or higher.

INSTALLATION

1. Insert the GACE Early Childhood CD-ROM into the CD-ROM drive.

2. If the installation doesn't begin automatically, from the Start Menu choose the RUN command. When the RUN dialog box appears, type d:\setup (where d is the letter of your CD-ROM drive) at the prompt and click OK.

3. The installation process will begin. A dialog box proposing the directory "C:\Program Files\ REA\GACE_EC\" will appear. If the name and location are suitable, click OK. If you wish to specify a different name or location, type it in and click OK.

4. Start the GACE Early Childhood TestWare® application by double-clicking on the icon.

GACE Early Childhood TestWare® is **EASY** to **LEARN AND USE**. To achieve maximum benefits, we recommend that you take a few minutes to go through the on-screen tutorial on your computer. The "screen buttons" are also explained here to familiarize you with the program.

SSD ACCOMMODATIONS FOR STUDENTS WITH DISABILITIES

Many students qualify for extra time to take the GACE Early Childhood exam, and our TestWare® can be adapted to accommodate your time extension. This allows you to practice under the same extended-time accommodations that you will receive on the actual test day. To customize your TestWare® to suit the most common extensions, visit our website at www.rea.com/ssd.

TECHNICAL SUPPORT

REA's TestWare® is backed by customer and technical support. For questions about **installation or operation of your software**, contact us at:

> **Research & Education Association**
> **Phone: (732) 819-8880 (9 a.m. to 5 p.m. ET, Monday–Friday)**
> **Fax: (732) 819-8808**
> **Website: *www.rea.com***
> **E-mail: info@rea.com**

Note to Windows Users: In order for the TestWare® to function properly, please install and run the application under the same computer administrator-level user account. Installing the TestWare® as one user and running it as another could cause file-access path conflicts.